School Reform Proposals:
The Research Evidence

A Volume in the Research in Educational Productivity Series
Herbert J. Walberg, Series Editor

School Reform Proposals:
The Research Evidence

Edited by

Alex Molnar

Arizona State University

INFORMATION AGE
PUBLISHING

80 Mason Street • Greenwich, Connecticut 06830 • www.infoagepub.com

Library of Congress Cataloging-in-Publication Data

School reform proposals : the research evidence / edited by Alex Molnar.

   p. cm. – (Research in educational productivity)
  ISBN 1-931576-59-9 – ISBN 1-931576-58-0 (pbk.)
  1. School improvement programs–United States. I. Molnar, Alex. II.
Series.
  LB2822.82 .S3715 2002
  371.2'00973–dc21

                    2002003165

ISBN: 1-931576-58-0 (paper); 1-931576-59-9 (cloth)

Printed in the United States of America

*In memory of John Thompson
and his dedication to public education*

CONTENTS

Acknowledgments   *ix*

Foreword   *xi*

Introduction
  Alex Molnar   *xiii*

1. Early Childhood Education
   W. Steven Barnett   *1*

2. Class-Size Reduction in Grades K–3
   Jeremy D. Finn   *27*

3. Small Schools
   Craig Howley   *49*

4. Time for School: Its Duration and Allocation
   Gene V Glass   *79*

5. Grouping Students for Instruction
   Gene V Glass   *95*

6. Parental and Family Involvement in Education
   Douglas B. Downey   *113*

7. Public Schools and their Communities
   Catherine Lugg   *135*

8. Teacher Characteristics
   Gene V Glass   *155*

9. Converging Findings on Classroom Instruction
   Barak Rosenshine   *175*

10. Teacher Unions and Student Achievement
   Robert M. Carini   *197*

11. Value-Added Assessment of Teachers: The Empirical Evidence
   Haggai Kupermintz   *217*

12. Professional Development
   Ulrich C. Reitzug   *235*

13. Charter Schools, Vouchers, and EMOs
   Gerald W. Bracey   *259*

Contributors   *281*

ACKNOWLEDGMENTS

I never met John Thompson. Yet this book would not have been possible without him. John, a researcher with the Ohio Education Association, convinced colleagues in Pennsylvania and New Jersey that their respective education associations should collectively sponsor leading scholars to conduct a series of literature reviews on important education reform topics.

The idea was deceptively simple. Find the most talented academics and have them write comprehensive reviews of the literature in their areas of expertise. The outcome was sure to help teachers and parents improve their schools and assist policymakers and the public formulate enlightened education policy.

Realizing John Thompson's vision was not so simple. His colleagues had to convince their associations that to play a significant constructive role in education reform they must have access to the best knowledge available even if, on occasion, what was learned might be at odds with organization policy. To their credit, each of the state teacher unions involved in this project decided that solid information was more important than organizational politics. Each wanted to learn better how to connect research evidence to school improvement.

It was at this point that I entered the picture. Mary Ann Jandoli of the New Jersey Education Association and Dave Wazeter of the Pennsylvania State Education Association had, over the years, heard me give impassioned speeches about the need for teacher unions to formulate substantive proposals for school improvement. They knew John Thompson's idea would be dear to my heart. When they asked if I would organize the literature review project through the Education Policy Studies Laboratory at Arizona State University, I agreed with two conditions: That I alone would select the experts who wrote the literature reviews and that no one from the teacher unions would have any role in approving the content of the manuscripts. In other words the literature reviews were to be approached in an academically rigorous way with complete editorial control in the hands of the authors.

There are many reasons concrete examples of academic work informing professional practice are few and far between. For one thing it is a lot of work. It requires that practitioners and academics each step outside of their familiar patterns of behavior. For another, the reward structure for academics very often points them away from practice. And, of course, academic writing often tends to be dry and the implications proffered maddeningly tentative from the perspective of practitioners and policy makers. People who work in schools or who serve on schools boards or in state legislatures are asked to make decisions every day using the imperfect information available to them. It is most often not possible for them to conclude, as academics frequently must, that such and such "merits further study" and leave the matter at that.

Thus John Thompson's simple idea required risk-taking behavior on the part of several teacher unions, academics with both the expertise and the willingness to write for practitioners and policymakers, and an editorial process that insured that the work done had academic integrity and would be usable by practitioners and policy makers.

The contributors to this volume put in an enormous amount of time not just to write their literature reviews but also to revise them and refine them until each was plainly written and clearly formulated with a lay audience in mind. It was essential to the success of this effort that after reading a literature review, readers would know what could be said with assurance, what was not known, and what policy implications could be derived from the research being reviewed.

Erik Gunn, an experienced journalist, raised thoughtful questions and made countless editorial suggestions. Erik aided in polishing the prose, clarifying the format, and producing a consistent editorial voice for each review. Dave Wazeter served as the near perfect manuscript reader, knowledgeable about research and alert to the perspective of practitioners. His informed and persistent questions helped keep us on target and enhanced the quality of the final draft. At the Education Policy Studies Laboratory Glen Wilson and John Hutchison pitched in with close readings of the final manuscript for errors in the copy and inconsistencies in the bibliographical style. Without their hard work, under considerable time pressure, it's hard to tell when this project might finally have been put to bed.

School Reform Proposals: The Research Evidence will, I think, make an important contribution to the formulation of sound education policy. I hope that it also serves as model for future practitioner-academic collaborations. The credit for the success of this project goes to many people, only some of whom have been mentioned here by name. All of us, however, owe a debt to John Thompson for getting the ball rolling.

—Alex Molnar
Tempe, Arizona

FOREWORD

The present volume *School Reform Proposals: The Research Evidence* is the second in the Series Research in Educational Productivity. It follows the first volume *Improving Educational Productivity* (2001) edited by David Monk, Margaret Wang, and myself.

The series features original studies and syntheses of research on educational effectiveness and efficiency. The term effectiveness means here the promotion of educational outcomes particularly achievement but also including favorable attitudes toward learning, the propensity for further study, adult earnings, and other consequences of schooling that are less often studied. Efficiency concerns how to promote effectiveness at minimal priced and unpriced costs. Indicators of priced costs such as per-student spending on schools are obviously important, but equally important are such usually unpriced costs of student and teacher time, the difficulties of choosing and implementing programs, and parental time investments in their children.

The series concerns educational conditions, policies, and practices. Educational conditions, though perhaps often less intentional and focused on learning than policies and practices, are, nonetheless, greatly influential. They are not restricted to schooling alone since typical students spend only about 8 percent of the hours in the first 18 years of life in school, and home conditions have powerful effects on their learning particularly in the years before children enter school. Media and peer groups also influence student learning and it is desirable to estimate the influences of all such possible learning determinants.

The term policies refers to the possible learning influences of federal, state, district, and school rules and regulations. They typically do not affect students directly but influence educational conditions and practices that more directly affect students. They include policies of judicial, legislative, and executive branches of government as well as such groups such as business, school boards, and professional organizations.

The term practices refers to the more direct or proximal, influences of teachers, parents, and others on children's learning. Usually intentional with respect to learning, practices concern what professional procedures within schools. Most obvious is teaching, but administration, organization, curriculum, and related factors may also require consideration.

The first volume in the series provides economic policy perspectives on raising productivity. The present volume provides research syntheses of research on conditions, policies, and practices. The contributions are explained in the editor's introduction. As series editor, I thank editor of this book Alex Molnar and the contributors who were supported in their efforts by the National Education Association.

—Herbert J. Walberg
Series Editor

INTRODUCTION AND EXECUTIVE SUMMARY

Alex Molnar
Arizona State University

For nearly two decades numerous prominent critics have pronounced American public education broken. The debate over the state of the nation's public schools has been joined by business leaders, teachers unions, and think tanks from all points on the political spectrum. The chorus of criticism has produced a curious disconnect between Americans' perception of their local schools and their assessment of the nation's schools as a whole. Of more than 1,100 respondents to a new Phi Delta Kappa/Gallup poll, for instance, just over half told surveyors that they would give the nation's schools a grade of "C," even though an identical number—51%—gave their own local schools A's and B's.[1]

The contention that the public education system has failed in turn has prompted a wide variety of reform proposals. Some, such as educational vouchers, would radically reorganize the system's governance. Others, such as universal early childhood education, may demand equal or even greater changes in the educational system's design and structure, while retaining the central feature of the system that has served public education for more than a century: the common school. Still other reform proposals are far more measured in their scope. Amid the welter of ideas put forth it is often far from clear how to best improve what is not working well without subverting the many successes of American public education.

In the last decade especially, reforms have tended to be justified as necessary to improve the academic achievement of children living in poverty. Moreover, the widespread and intense scrutiny of public school performance has increased the pressure on legislatures to act quickly, even as it has made it more important than ever for them to carefully weigh the benefits and costs of competing reform proposals. Unfortunately, the research evidence available to policy makers is often non-existent, incomplete, or appears to be contradictory. School reform is, therefore, frequently debated in an environment that is long on emotion and short on hard data. Furthermore, the data supporting proposals to reform public education varies enormously in its quality. It ranges from carefully conducted and rigorously reviewed research to ideologically oriented commentary. Often there are few indicators for policy makers to distinguish one from the other.

In order to clarify what we know about effective public schools, the Education Policy Studies Laboratory (EPSL) at Arizona State University invited a group of distinguished education scholars to review the research on a series of education reform topics.

The following literature reviews are the result. Some reviews focus on specific proposals that are proffered for making public schools more effective. Others examine core components or practices in our public schools in order to evaluate the impact of those components and practices on student achievement. In each case, the reviewers examined the research on the topic at hand with a particular eye toward its findings with regard to student achievement, especially that of children living in poverty.

INSTITUTIONS, PEOPLE, AND MONEY

These 13 reviews can be grouped into three broad clusters. The first group examines schools as institutions and their structures. It includes reports on the efficacy of early education programs; the movements to reduce class size and to create smaller schools; alternatives in structuring the school day and year; variations in how students may be grouped; and the role that schools have played in the past and might play in the future in their larger communities and in involving parents in their children's education.

The second group of reviews focuses on the teachers who deliver public education. They examine research on teacher characteristics and instructional behaviors; the role of teacher unions as obstacles or assets to educational improvement; proposals to quantify the value that teachers add to the educational process and thereby assess teacher performance; and on the effectiveness of current approaches to professional development of teachers, and how those approaches might be improved.

The final review is a comprehensive look at various proposals to supplant all or part of the traditional public education system with institutions from outside that system. Those include vouchers that citizens might use to gain entry to private schools instead of their local public schools; charter schools, which present themselves as alternatives to public schools that have been released from some of the requirements and regulations under which public schools operate; and proposals to contract the management of public schools out to private, for-profit companies.

THE VARYING QUALITY OF RESEARCH

It should be no surprise to the informed reader that, from one topic to the next, the quality of available research varies greatly. Some topics, such as class-size reduction, have been the subject of rigorous and well-controlled experiments that have undergone the intense scrutiny of peer review and stood up to the test. Other topics, such as private school vouchers, have produced much in the way of strong opinions but very little well-founded research to support the conclusions drawn by their staunchest advocates.

Notwithstanding such limitations, each review represents the best information available to us on the topic at hand. Each presents evidence for the effectiveness—or the ineffectiveness—of certain reform proposals. Several include calls for additional research where our knowledge is too scanty to draw well-reasoned conclusions. And where the reviewers are able to uncover reforms that do work, they have presented evidence as well for how we can make each reform as effective as possible.

Many of these reviews point to reforms that can be achieved with only modest investments, or indeed simply a reallocation of additional resources. Others offer a warning worth heeding about proposals that seem certain to waste funds. For the most promising reforms, however, a common theme emerges: Money does matter. The reforms that offer the greatest promise, reforms supported by solid scientific research, cannot be advanced merely by working smarter. They require a deeper investment than we are currently making in the nation's school systems.

SPENDING: ESSENTIAL, BUT NOT SUFFICIENT

Yet, as one review after another suggests, simply spending more money is not sufficient, and is no guarantee of success. Rather, any enrichment of resources must be husbanded carefully and spent thoughtfully, with due consideration given to what works and what doesn't in the pursuit of each reform strategy.

There is good news, here, however: the research evidence strongly identifies those investments that promise the highest return. There is more good news as well. Support for committing additional resources, when that commitment is made thoughtfully and with a sound basis in action, may run deeper than many might assume. Fully 65% of Americans polled for the *Washington Post* and ABC News in the spring of 2000 advocated increased federal spending on schools.[2] Two-thirds of those responding to a 1998 Gallup Poll for Phi Delta Kappa said they would be willing to pay more in taxes to improve the quality of the nation's inner-city schools.[3] The most recent Gallup/Phi Delta Kappa poll shows support for reforming the existing public education system increasing and interest in radical reforms such as vouchers fading. Seventy-one percent of respondents, for example, said they favored public school reforms over measures, such as private school vouchers, that would seek to supplant the public schools.[4]

Taken together, the chapters that follow constitute a comprehensive resource guide on the state of education reform and research into reform. Among the many reforms examined are those that have demonstrated their effectiveness beyond all reasonable doubt. Others, although they may have won widespread attention and praise, have already demonstrated through research to be at best far more limited than their promoters have warranted, or at worst, completely ineffectual. Still others have not lived up to claims made on their behalf, and require much more research before they can be considered worthy of endorsement.

These reports, then, offer to policy-makers and citizens a road map for making public schools more effective, and to scholars an agenda for further research. It is our hope that they will sort out for all of us a clearer understanding of what works, and what we still need to know.

REFERENCES

1.   Phi Delta Kappa/Gallup Poll, 23 May–6 June 2001, <http://www.pdkintl.org/kappan/k0109gal.htm>.
2.   Washington Post/ABC News poll, 30 March–2 April 2000, <http://www.pollingreport.com/educatio.htm>.
3.   Phi Delta Kappa/Gallup poll, 5 June–23 June 1998, <http://www.pollingreport.com/educatio.htm>.
4.   *Op. Cit.*, Phi Delta Kappa/Gallup Poll, 23 May–6 June 2001.

CHAPTER 1

EARLY CHILDHOOD EDUCATION

W. Steven Barnett
Rutgers University Center for Early Education

SUMMARY OF RESEARCH FINDINGS

Pre-kindergarten education for disadvantaged children can greatly increase their cognitive abilities, leading to long-term increases in achievement and school success. Although general cognitive abilities as measured by IQ may only temporarily increase, persistent increases can be produced in the specific abilities measured by standardized achievement tests in reading and math. In addition, programs can have positive effects on children's long-term social and emotional development, reducing crime and delinquency. To reap all of their potential benefits, pre-kindergarten programs for disadvantaged children must be intensive, high in quality, and emphasize both cognitive and social development.

RECOMMENDATIONS

- Class sizes and child-teacher ratios must be kept low.
- Teachers must be highly qualified, with at least a bachelor's degree and with specialized training in early education, and must be paid well.
- Curricula must be intellectually rich and sufficiently broad to address children's developmental needs in all domains.

1

- Programs must have an infrastructure adequate to support best practices, professional development, and ongoing evaluation and accountability.
- Programs must engage in an active partnership with parents and accommodate their needs, including their needs for child care.
- Programs should start no later than age three.
- Resources should be focused primarily on disadvantaged children.
- The existing array of public school, Head Start, and private programs all can be used, but both standards and resources must be substantially increased to produce the desired results.

A number of long-term social and economic trends have contributed to increasing interest in the education of children under five over the past several decades.[1] Before 1960, the education of young children was regarded as primarily a matter of parenting in the home. Since that time the percentage of young children cared for by someone other than a parent has risen steadily. Today, most young children in the United States spend much of their day away from their parents, and most attend a center-based program prior to kindergarten. Attendance at a center-based program is becoming the norm at ages three and four. In 1999, center-based program participation was 70% at age four and 45% at age three.[2]

The center-based programs attended by children at ages three and four go by a variety of names—child care, preschool, day care, and nursery school. They provide different numbers of hours, from a couple of hours one or two days per week to 10 hours per day 250 days per year. They also operate under a variety of auspices—churches, independent non-profits, for-profits, public schools, and Head Start. Parents regard virtually all of these programs as educational regardless of the nomenclature used to describe the program, the hours of operation, or the auspices under which they operate.[3] Participation rates increase with income and parental education, despite greater government support for programs targeting children in low-income families. Children under three are much less likely to attend center-based programs, and parents seem to view infant and toddler care as of less educational consequence.[4]

As non-parental education of young children becomes the norm, the extent to which such programs affect children's learning and development has become a vital question for families and governments. Inequalities in early care and education may be responsible for much of the inequality in later educational outcomes in the United States.[5] Moreover, there are concerns that parents may be unaware of the potential for their decisions about early care and education to have either adverse or positive impacts on their children's development. Some have raised hopes that public support for early education might provide a means for improving the productivity of our educational system and reducing educational and social inequalities.[6]

This report seeks to clarify the potential benefits and possible adverse effects of early care and education, with particular emphasis on the effects for children disadvantaged by social and economic circumstances. In addition, it seeks to summarize what is known about the extent to which variations in child characteristics, program characteristics, and the social environment alter the magnitude of the educational benefits from early education. Key issues in the review are the nature and duration of program effects. Often there is no dispute about whether programs have immediate or short-term effects on children, but there are disputes about the meaning or importance of the observed effects and whether they persist or result in other long-term effects that are more consequential.[7]

EARLY CHILDHOOD EDUCATION RESEARCH

Short-Term Studies

A great deal of research has been conducted on the immediate and short-term effects of early education and child care. Much of this research is found in two largely separate but related sets of literature: one on child care and the other on educational interventions. Traditionally, these two bodies of research have focused on different questions and had different theoretical and methodological orientations. In recent years, there has been some convergence, but differences remain.

Early Intervention Program Studies
In many cases, but not all, the educational interventions have been half-day or school-day programs that operate over a school year. Some have been home-based programs seeking to improve parent-child interactions in ways that are hypothesized to contribute to improvements in child development. A few home-based programs have provided educational services directly to the child. Some programs have delivered both center-based and home-based services and some have worked fairly extensively with both parents and children. Virtually all center-based programs have made efforts to involve parents in some way. These programs typically target children who are expected to have greater difficulty with school and high rates of grade repetition, special education, and other problems.

Children have been identified for intervention based on social and economic factors that are taken as indicators of risk of school failure, or based on individual assessments of developmental delay or disability. Poverty is the most frequently used criterion for disadvantage or risk, but other factors that might be employed include low levels of parental education or IQ, poor health or nutrition, poor housing, maternal depression, and family and neighborhood violence.[8] Targeting based on socioeconomic disadvantage and based on developmental delay are clearly different conceptually. As socioeconomic disadvantage can lead to developmental delay, however, there is some overlap.

The early intervention literature has focused on looking for positive effects on children's development, most often looking at cognitive development, but assessing effects in other domains as well. There are hundreds of studies of immediate and short-term effects, and their findings have been conveniently summarized in both quantitative meta-analyses and traditional literature reviews.[9] Across these studies, the average initial effect on cognitive abilities is about 0.50 standard deviations, 7 or 8 points on an IQ test. Average effects on such socio-emotional outcomes as self-esteem, self-efficacy, motivation, and social behavior also were positive, though somewhat smaller, 0.25 to 0.40 standard deviations. No evidence of consistent negative effects appears in these studies. A strength of this literature is that similar results are found across studies employing a wide variety of research designs, including randomized trials and single-subject designs in which the "treatment" was experimentally manipulated. Effects are similar in size for disadvantaged populations and for children with disabilities or developmental delays.

Recent years have produced important advances in research as randomized trials, sometimes on a quite large scale, have been employed to examine the effects of specific approaches to early educational intervention at specific ages. The findings of these studies add substantially to the knowledge provided by the studies summarized in previous reviews of the literature. In particular, these randomized trials have tested the effects of home visitation and other approaches that focus on parents and the improvement of parenting as means to improve the development of young children. These include models emphasizing case management to coordinate and increase the use of existing services for children beginning in the first year of life. Randomized trials may be especially important for studies of these types of programs; unmeasured differences among parents might play a large role in who chooses to enroll in such programs, leading to substantial biases when researchers attempt to estimate program effects simply by comparing program families and children to others who did not choose to enroll.

Results of these studies indicate that home visit programs frequently fail to influence parenting or to improve children's cognitive development. Two randomized trials have been conducted in California on Parents as Teachers (PAT).[10] Both found small and inconsistent effects on parenting knowledge, attitudes, and behavior and no effects on child development. A randomized trial of the Home Instruction Program for Preschool Youngsters (HIPPY) serving children ages four and five found significant effects on cognitive development for one cohort, but not another, and found no explanation for the inconsistent findings.[11]

The Carolina Approach to Responsive Education (CARE) study randomly assigned children to three conditions: full-day, year-round educational child care and home visits for parent education, parent education alone, and control.[12] Treatment began shortly after birth and continued to age five. The home-visit group of children had no better outcomes than the no-treatment controls. A randomized trial of home visits in Head Start similarly found no effects of home visits on home environment or child development.[13]

A test of Levenstein's Verbal Interaction Program (VIP) in Bermuda failed to find positive effects, replicating the results of Levenstein's own earlier experimental results, but contradicting findings from quasi-experimental studies.[14] One potential explanation for lack of consistent effects comes from a randomized trial that varied frequency of visitation and found that three visits per week were necessary to produce significant cognitive benefits.[15] Most programs have provided home visits much less frequently.[16]

Several studies of attempts to provide comprehensive services in "two generation" models also have produced disappointing results. A multi-site randomized trial of the Comprehensive Child Development Program (CCDP) found that CCDP substantially increased maternal participation in parenting education, mental health services, and their own schooling while producing modest increases in children's participation in health services and early care and education over the first five years of life.[17] At age two, small effects were found on some parent behaviors and child development (2 points on the Bayley Scales of Mental Development, an effect size of 0.10 standard deviations[18]). No meaningful effects were found at the age five follow-up, however.[19] Similarly, studies of the Avance family support program, Child and Family Resource Program, and New Chance all failed to find significant effects on child development.[20] Research on Even Start found small effects, at best, on child development.[21] The recent large-scale multi-site randomized trial of Early Head Start found very small effects on child development and parent outcomes at age two, replicating the early findings of the CCDP study with 2 points on the Bayley and 0.10 effect sizes generally.[22]

The results of research on home visitation and two-generation approaches that do not provide substantial direct services to children in centers strongly suggest two conclusions. First, attempts to influence child development indirectly through parents are relatively weak. Second, the size of the effect on child development varies with the amount, in frequency and in duration, of intervention provided. These conclusions are consistent with conclusions from earlier reviews of the literature.[23] A fairly intensive level of direct service may be required to consistently produce effects on child development of the average size observed in the literature generally.

A few seeming exceptions in the literature suggest that further research is warranted on the circumstances under which parent-directed programs might be highly effective.[24] Recent studies, however, also document the high costs of parent-focused programs, which are so substantial that even programs that demonstrate positive effects are unlikely to be deemed cost-effective.[25]

Although the evidence presented above is not encouraging regarding the effects of home visitation on children's cognitive development, there is evidence that some home visitation programs can improve the lives and development of young children in other ways. Over 20 years, David Olds and colleagues have found that a program in which nurses conducted home visits to economically disadvantaged new mothers produced significant positive effects: reducing the number and improving the timing of pregnancies and births after the first child, and reducing children's need for health care for injuries or ingestions.[26]

The Infant Health and Development Program (IHDP) study was a multi-site randomized trial to investigate the effects of weekly home visits starting just after birth, with the addition of full-day educational child care from ages one to three for low-birth weight children.[27] The IHDP substantially increased IQ (by more than 0.50 standard deviations) and decreased parent-reported problem behaviors through age three. Effects were found to be larger for children with less educated mothers and for children with heavier birth weights.[28] At the age five and age eight follow-ups, significant effects were no longer found for the total sample. Significant (though reduced) effects, however, were found for the heavier birth weight stratum on IQ at ages five and eight and on mathematics achievement at age eight. No differences in treatment effects were found for any of the parental education subgroups.[29]

Why effects for the total group in the IHDP study disappeared is not clear. It is possible that lower-birth weight children in the control group had access to additional services—such as early intervention services or preschool special education programs—before the age of three and between the ages of three and five, which could lead to the disappearance of differential findings. Conversely, the lighter birth weight stratum might have greater incidence of neurological damage that limited the effectiveness of the program. Some researchers have disputed the follow-up findings of effects for the heavier birth weight group.[30] It is worth noting, however, that the birth weight strata were defined prior to the analysis, differential effects for the two birth weight strata were found at three different points over five years, and plausible explanations have been offered.

Child Care Studies

Research on child care has tended to study the effects of typical programs on the general population, though some studies have focused on children in low-income families, with an emphasis on social and emotional development. In particular, child care researchers have been concerned with the potential for separation from the mother to harm social and emotional development. More recently, the field has broadened its attention to cognitive development and the potential for positive effects, just as educational research has increased its concerns with social and emotional development and potential negative effects. Most child care studies have relied on statistical analysis of natural variation rather than experiments or even quasi-experiments with specific "treatments." Over time, child care research has evolved from asking about the average effects of care to asking how the effects of care vary depending on interactions among the characteristics of care, children and families.[31]

Although programs for young children under a wide variety of names provide both care and educational experiences, child care is distinguished from preschool education by having as a primary goal enabling parents to work or pursue other activities. Child care centers are open for the hours parents work—typically 10 hours a day, 5 days a week—and children often attend more than 30 hours per week. Of course, child care centers are not the only providers of child care—family day care homes, nannies, and others, including relatives and neighbors, provide care outside or inside the child's home. However, the focus here is on child care centers and their influences on learning and development.

Looking across many studies, child care for young children, especially care for infants and toddlers, appears to produce small negative effects in the short term on child-mother attachment and on social behavior, particularly aggression.[32] The effects on aggression may be contemporaneous or at entry to school. Although there is much agreement about these findings, some researchers have questioned the conceptualization and measurement of attachment, and it is essential to recognize that the social behaviors of the vast majority of children in care are in the normal range.[33] In addition, there is no evidence that negative effects on social behavior persist past the first few years of school or result in other later problems.[34] Some studies have failed to find negative effects on aggression and have found positive effects on other social behaviors.[35]

Recently, new evidence on the short-term effects of child care on social behavior has come from the NICHD study of early child care, which had a sample of over 1,300 children across 10 sites.[36] Media reports based on a conference paper indicated that new findings contradicted previous work and the views of most "experts" that child care was not harmful for children's social and emotional development.[37] In fact, the NICHD results reveal nothing new. Child care (of all types, including father care) for 30 hours or more per week was associated with more reported behavior problems at age two, but not at age three, and then again at ages four and five. At age five, children who received child care for 30 or more hours per week during the first four years of life had higher rates of reported problem behavior than those who had attended less than 10 hours per week. However, as in other studies, the effects were small. Behavior problems for children with 30 or more hours of care were not more common than would be expected for the general population. In addition, the negative effects on problem behavior were somewhat reduced for higher quality child care.[38]

Child care also has been found to produce modest positive effects (effect sizes in the neighborhood of 0.10–0.15) on cognitive and language development.[39] Some studies find that effects are larger for children who enter care earlier.[40] Some studies find larger effects for children from economically and educationally disadvantaged families. In addition, some studies have found that there may even be small negative effects of child care (in the first three years) for children from homes offering the richest environments.[41] There is an implication that the difference between the resources provided to the child through parental and non-parental care is the active factor. This is consistent with evidence that the magnitude of effects increases with the quality of child care as well as evidence on the effects of parental education and other home resources.[42]

Recent large-scale longitudinal studies provide additional evidence regarding the effects of child care on the development of language and cognitive abilities. The NICHD study of early child care found associations between quality and child's language and cognitive development throughout the first three years of life.[43] At age four, higher child care quality was associated with greater language abilities and better short-term memory and attention. Child care centers were associated with better language and cognitive test scores at age four than other forms of care. In addition to associations with observed quality, it was found that children enrolled in child care centers meeting a greater number of professional guidelines for child-staff ratio, group size, teacher training, and teacher education had higher cognitive and language ability, and higher school readiness. All of these associations were modest in size, controlling for family background and home environment.[44] Variations in effects with family background have not been found consistently.[45]

A follow-up of the Cost, Quality, and Outcomes study investigated the effects of child care classroom quality on over 800 children in four states from ages four through eight, statistically controlling for family background.[46] This study found that children who attended higher quality child care classrooms had higher scores on the Peabody Picture Vocabulary Test-Revised (PPVT-R) and on achievement tests for pre-reading and math abilities at age four. The PPVT-R is a test of receptive language, but it often is used as a "quick" IQ test. Continued follow-up found significant effects on PPVT-R scores through kindergarten, but effects declined as children moved toward age eight (controlling for quality of later schooling). Effects on math scores persisted through age eight. Depending upon the specifics of the analysis, effects on pre-reading and math achievement are found for children with less well-educated mothers, but not for children with highly educated mothers.[47]

Long-Term Effects

Reviews that simply summarize the results of studies of early care and education have found that cognitive effects frequently decline over time and are negligible several years after children leave the programs.[48] This pattern has led some to conclude that even intensive preschool programs produce no lasting effects on cognitive development. In this view, initial effects are either artificial (children learn to answer test questions better, but are not really smarter) or do not lead to long-term gains in cognitive ability. Others have called attention to differences among programs and concluded that large-scale public programs for children in poverty produce no meaningful improvements in cognitive abilities, while more intensive, small-scale (and impractical) programs may produce small gains in cognitive development. For example, Herrnstein and Murray conclude: "Head Start, the largest program, does not improve cognitive functioning. More intensive, hence more costly, preschool programs may raise intelligence, but both the size and the reality of the improvements are in dispute."[49] They and others contend that to the extent more intensive programs have substantive long-term benefits these are more likely due to socialization than to effects on cognitive abilities.[50]

Barnett challenged this view through a review of the literature with a specific focus on the long-term effects of programs on achievement and school success, selecting studies for inclusion if they met four criteria: (1) children entered the program as preschoolers (in Head Start this could include some five-year-olds prior to the availability of kindergarten); (2) the program served economically disadvantaged children; (3) at least one measure of achievement or school success was collected at or beyond age eight (Grade 3); and, (4) the research design identified treatment and no-treatment groups from program records.[51] The requirement for follow-up through third grade allowed sufficient time to observe the fade-out in effects that is widely believed to occur.[52]

Thirty-seven studies were found that met these criteria, a larger number of long-term studies than had been included in previous research reviews and syntheses. All are studies of educational interventions, although five of the model programs provided services through full-day child care. The studies can be divided into two categories: one for small-scale research models, the other for large-scale public programs. In 15 studies, researchers developed model programs to study the effects of controlled treatments. In 22 other studies, researchers investigated the effects of on-going, large-scale public programs: 10 studied Head Start programs, eight examined public school programs, and four studied a mix of Head Start and public school programs.[53]

Model Program Studies

The model program studies varied in entrance age, duration, services provided, and historical context (1962 to 1980). In later years, significant percentages of the comparison groups are likely to have attended a preschool or child care program, leading to underestimation of program effects. All focused on highly disadvantaged populations. The average level of mother's education was under 12 years in all studies, and under 10 years in five studies. The majority of children were African-American in every study except for one, in which they were Hispanic. From program descriptions of teacher qualifications, class size, student-teacher ratio, and other information, it is apparent that model programs were much more resource-intensive, and therefore more expensive, than typical public programs for young children. Two studies limited their samples in additional ways that could have affected their results. The Perry Preschool study selected children based on low IQ scores, and its sample had substantially lower IQ's at age three than children in other studies.[54] The Milwaukee study selected children whose mothers had IQ's below 75.[55]

Seven of the model program studies were randomized trials. Two stand out because they began with sample sizes larger than 30 in each group, and had low attrition throughout follow-up: the Abecedarian and Perry Preschool studies.[56] The others suffered from extremely small initial samples or serious attrition. The remaining eight model program studies constructed comparison groups, and it is possible that the groups differ in ways that may have biased the comparisons either for or against the program. When randomized trials are not used, it is difficult to distinguish program effects from the effects of pre-existing differences (which may be unmeasured) between children and families in the preschool group and the comparison group, a problem sometimes referred to as "selection bias."

Large-Scale Public School Programs

The 22 large-scale public program studies generally represent public preschool programs targeting children in poverty. Most programs served children part-day for one school year at age four. Four programs served children from age three. In nearly all of the studies children moved on to regular public elementary schools. In the Child Parent Center (CPC) studies, intervention continued through third grade, and the effects of the preschool and school-age programs have been estimated separately. All of the large-scale public program studies used quasi-experimental designs. In most studies, comparison groups were identified later, and there are no pre-program measures of children's cognitive abilities to verify that the two groups began with the same abilities. Many studies employ family background measures to assess comparability and adjust for initial group differences, but the family background measures tend to be crude, increasing the risk that unmeasured differences between groups bias the results.

Study Findings

IQ.   All of the model program studies found positive initial effects on IQ. In most cases IQ effects were sustained at least until school entry. Estimated effects for 12 model program studies with IQ data at age five ranged from 4 to 11 IQ points (effect sizes of 0.25 to 0.75), with the exception of two studies, one quasi-experimental reporting no effect and one randomized trial of a highly intensive program reporting an estimated effect of 25 points. None of the large-scale program studies provided IQ test data, but a few administered the PPVT; these reported no significant effects on the PPVT after school entry. In all but two studies, the effects on IQ clearly are transitory.

Randomized trials of two model programs (the Milwaukee and Abecedarian interventions) that provided full-day intensive interventions over the first five years of life provide evidence that such programs may produce very long-term, possibly permanent, increases in IQ. The long-term effect is about 5 IQ points, which is substantially smaller than the initial effects of the programs. Their findings contrast sharply with the apparent failure of later, less intensive interventions to produce lasting IQ gains. This suggests that very early intensive interventions may have more fundamental or general effects on the cognitive development of children in poverty.

The IQ findings of both studies have been discounted by scholars advocating the importance of heredity as an explanation for the low cognitive abilities of children in poverty.[57] Even the strongest claims for heredity leave sufficient room for the estimated effects, however. Moreover, their arguments that the study results are questionable because IQ effects appear early (in the Abecedarian study) or are inconsistent with insignificant effect estimates for school outcomes (Milwaukee) do not hold up to scrutiny. The Abecedarian study finds persistent IQ effects after controlling for maternal IQ and infant home environment, presumably sources of pre-existing differences in IQ between groups.[58] Estimated effect sizes for special education, grade repetition, and academic achievement are large in the Milwaukee study. With the limited statistical power provided by a very small sample size, it is inappropriate to construe lack of statistical significance as evidence that IQ effects occurred without effects on academic success.[59]

Achievement.   In contrast to the IQ findings, results regarding long-term effects on achievement varied considerably across studies. Five of 11 model program studies with achievement data found statistically significant positive effects on achievement test scores beyond Grade 3. Evidence of achievement effects was strongest in the seven randomized trials, as all found statistically significant effects on achievement at some point. The two randomized trials with low attrition rates, the Abecedarian and Perry Preschool studies, found effects on test scores persisting into high school. Nine studies of large-scale programs never found statistically significant effects or lost statistical significance by Grade 3. Twelve studies of large-scale programs found significant positive effects on achievement at least through Grade 3.

Much of the variation in findings regarding long-term effects on achievement across programs can be explained by differences in research methods and procedures. Detailed analyses indicate that in many studies the apparent fade-out in effects on achievement can be attributed to flawed research methods, which bias estimated effects toward zero, and high rates of attrition, which decrease statistical power over time. Reliance on achievement test data from schools' routine testing programs is a major source of potential problems. As testing typically is conducted by grade level for children in regular education, studies systematically lose the more poorly performing students from year to year as the cumulative percentage of children retained in grade, placed in special education, or otherwise omitted from testing grows. Program and comparison group children with valid test scores become more similar over time (essentially equated on grade level), gradually hiding the true differences between the groups.[60]

School Progress and Placement.   School progress and placement were primarily measured by the percentage of children repeating grades, given special education services, and graduating from high school. Cumulative school records data on these outcomes are not subject to the attrition bias introduced by the use of school test data. Estimated effects on school progress and placement are uniformly positive and overwhelmingly statistically significant. The evidence regarding high school graduation is highly consistent as well. All six studies (including model, Head Start, and public school programs) produced large estimates of effects on the graduation rate, although only in the four with larger sample sizes were these statistically significant.

Estimated effects on grade repetition and special education placements can be combined across studies to estimate average effects across studies and compare the effects of model and large-scale programs. Model programs were associated with 20 percentage point lower rates of special education placement and 15 percentage point lower rates of grade repetition. The comparable figures for large-scale public programs are 5 percentage points and 8 percentage points, which are significantly less than the model program estimates in both cases.[61]

Social Development.   Most long-term studies of educational interventions for disadvantaged children have emphasized research on cognitive and academic outcomes. However, most studies that assessed effects on social behavior have found positive effects (though a few have found no significant effects), and no study reported elevated aggression beyond Grade 1.[62] Five studies of educational interventions that investigated long-term effects on social behavior found positive effects on classroom behavior, social adjustment, and crime and delinquency reports.[63] This includes two of the three studies that found elevated aggression associated with full-time child care that began in infancy.[64] The third found no long-term effect on crime and delinquency, but rates were low for both groups.[65]

New Long-Term Research

Recent research on the long-term effects of Child Parent Centers (CPC) in Chicago provides an extremely valuable addition to knowledge regarding early education for disadvantaged children.[66] This longitudinal study with a sample of over 1,500 children estimated the effects of a Title I funded half-day preschool and extended elementary program from ages three to nine operated by the Chicago public schools. Separate estimates are provided for the preschool and elementary components and effects are estimated through age 21. Controlling for family economic disadvantage, CPC preschool participants had significantly lower rates of special education placement, grade retention, juvenile arrest, and arrest for a violent offense. They also had significantly higher achievement test scores in reading and math through age 15 and a higher rate of high school completion. Effect sizes are in the 0.20 to 0.50 range, perhaps on the high side for large-scale programs generally. Effects are somewhat larger for children in the highest poverty neighborhoods.

In addition, the CPC study data were used to estimate structural models to investigate the chain of effects from preschool program to long-term outcomes. These analyses support the view that early education's long-term effects on achievement and school success primarily result from initial effects on cognitive abilities. These results replicate findings of structural equation modeling with the much smaller Perry Preschool data set, and the estimated chain of effects is remarkably similar to that for the Perry Preschool program.[67]

Costs and Benefits

While skeptics of making early education more broadly available through public funds frequently cite cost as the basis of their objections, some research has shown that quantifiable benefits result that can make a high quality early education program cost-effective when properly accounted for. Barnett has estimated the costs of benefits of a high quality early education program based on the findings of the Perry Preschool study.[68] The cost savings to society from avoiding crime and delinquency contribute a great deal to benefits. However, there also are important economic benefits from reducing the direct costs of educational failure and from increasing adult economic success by preventing educational failure. These benefits are not hypothetical, but are based on demonstrated increases in earnings and employment and decreases in reliance on public assistance. His estimates reveal a high rate of return, comparable or better than one could expect to earn from investing in the stock market. Even after discounting to calculate present value (a financial technique for making present costs and future benefits comparable), the estimated benefits are roughly ten times the costs.[69] It is important to note that this includes none of the economic benefits that a full-day, year-round program might generate by enabling parents to work more or participate in education and training. Barnett's results have been confirmed by a recent Rand report[70] that scrutinized his estimates and by similar estimates finding that the benefits of the Chicago Child Parent Centers far exceeded costs.[71]

Program Design and Effectiveness

From the evidence reviewed so far, it should be clear that some programs are more effective than others. Educational interventions for disadvantaged children, including Head Start and public school programs, have larger estimated effects than child care programs. This is true whether child care program effects are estimated for the general population or for disadvantaged children. Model programs have larger estimated effects than Head Start and public school programs. However, some caution is required in drawing conclusions because programs vary with respect to the disadvantage of the children served and their social, political, and economic contexts, as well as in their design.

Nevertheless, it seems clear that a dose-response is observed with respect to quality, or intensity of resources provided. Studies of the effects of child care quality find that higher quality is associated with greater effects, and the quality of child care generally is lower than the quality of large-scale public programs, which in turn are of lower educational quality than model programs.[72] Child care programs typically produce smaller effects even with disadvantaged children, compared with Head Start and public school programs. Studies that compare model programs with large-scale public programs (including child care) serving the same population find model programs to be more effective, confirming the cross-study inference.[73]

Additional guidance regarding program design can be gleaned from analyses of the model programs, cross-study comparisons of programs and their outcomes, research on variations in the quality and effects of child care programs, and research on the effectiveness of elementary school education. Conclusions drawn from all of these sources are remarkably consistent. More highly educated, better prepared, and better compensated teachers are more effective.[74] Smaller class sizes and better teacher-student ratios result in better teaching, more individual attention, and larger cognitive gains that improve achievement and school success, especially for disadvantaged students.[75] Other characteristics of programs that have generated the largest achievement and other gains for disadvantaged children include: a strong focus on language, strengthening children's cognitive abilities generally, interactions that prepare children for the discourse patterns and other demands of school without pushing down the elementary school curriculum, individualized support for learning, regular opportunities for teachers to reflect with highly knowledgeable leaders or others, and collaborative relationships with parents to support the child's learning and development.[76]

Research provides less guidance than policy makers and administrators might like regarding two key aspects of program design that have significant implications for cost: age of start and hours per year (length of day and days per year). Highly intensive programs beginning earlier have had larger effects than those in which children start later, but the optimal entry age is unclear as each additional year adds to cost. Two longitudinal studies indicate that programs beginning at age three produce substantial long-term benefits for disadvantaged children and that the benefits substantially exceed the costs.[77] Even intensive programs beginning at age four might bring significantly fewer disadvantaged children up to the thresholds of learning and development required for early school success. With respect to length of day and number of days per year, the research on the relative lack of progress for disadvantaged elementary school children during the summer is suggestive, and many parents may choose not to send their children to programs that do not address their needs for child care.[78] In addition, benefits from effects on parental employment associated with child care should be incorporated into any assessment of costs and benefits.

SUMMARY AND RECOMMENDATIONS

Pre-kindergarten education for disadvantaged children can greatly increase their cognitive abilities, leading to long-term increases in achievement and school success. Although general cognitive abilities as measured by IQ may only temporarily increase, persistent increases can be produced in the specific abilities measured by standardized achievement tests in reading and math. In addition, programs can have positive effects on children's long-term social and emotional development, reducing crime and delinquency. To reap all of their potential benefits, pre-kindergarten programs for disadvantaged children must be intensive, high in quality, and emphasize both cognitive and social development.

Pre-kindergarten programs for disadvantaged children are among the most strongly evidence-based of those approaches to improving academic achievement and educational attainment that have been tested. However, they will produce the desired results only if implemented in accord with the principles for effective programs that emerged in this review. These include:

- Class sizes and child-teacher ratios must be kept low. The research literature suggests that the best practice is probably a class size of 15 with a teacher and an aide.
- Teachers must be highly qualified, with at least a bachelor's degree and with specialized training in early education, and must be paid well.
- Curricula must be intellectually rich and sufficiently broad to address children's developmental needs in all domains.
- Programs must have an infrastructure adequate to support best practices, professional development, and ongoing evaluation and accountability.
- Programs must engage in an active partnership with parents and accommodate their needs, including their needs for child care.
- Programs should start no later than age three. Beginning prior to age three might produce substantially better results, but only if a highly intensive center-based program is provided up to school entry.
- Resources should be focused primarily on disadvantaged children, recognizing that income is not the only risk factor for poor achievement and that the poverty line is an arbitrary cut-off for educational purposes. Universal pre-kindergarten programs can target resources on disadvantaged children by providing them with smaller classes, better teachers, more hours, and a sliding fee scale so that higher-income families share the cost.
- The existing array of public school, Head Start, and private programs all can be used, but both standards and resources must be substan-

tially increased to produce the desired results. There are many advantages to such a strategy, but the time and costs of increasing quality to the necessary level should not be underestimated.

The way that educational costs are conventionally calculated, the foregoing recommendations will be seen as expensive. However, they are not as expensive as the costs of failing to implement them: poor achievement, high rates of school failure and special education, low productivity, and high crime and delinquency. Also, because disadvantaged children are highly concentrated geographically, these costs contribute to problems of segregation, urban decay, and suburban sprawl that add to the costs of current policy.[79] From this perspective, it is difficult to see how society can afford not to implement high-quality pre-kindergarten education for disadvantaged children.

NOTES

1. W. S. Barnett and S. S. Boocock, *Early Care and Education for Children in Poverty: Promises, Programs, and Long-Term Results* (Albany, NY: SUNY Press, 1998).

2. D. J. Yarosz and W. S. Barnett, *Early Care and Education Program Participation: 1991–1999* (New Brunswick, NJ: Center for Early Education Research, Rutgers University, 2001).

3. J. West, E. Hausken, and M. Collins, *Profile of Preschool Children's Child Care and Early Education Program Participation* (Washington, DC: US Department of Education, National Center for Educational Statistics, 1993).

4. Yarosz and Barnett.

5. D. R. Entwisle , K. L Alexander, and L. S. Olson, "Summer Learning and Home Environment" in *A Notion at Risk: Preserving Public Education as an Engine for Social Mobility*, ed. R. Kahlenberg (Twentieth Century Foundation/Twentieth Century Fund, Inc., 2000), 9–30.

6. Ibid.

    Barnett and Boocock.

    S. L. Ramey and C. T. Ramey, "Early Educational Intervention with Disadvantaged Children- To What Effect?" *Applied and Preventative Psychology 1* (1992): 131–140.

7. L. Jacobson, "Study Says More Time in Child Care Connected to Bad Behavior," *Education Week on the Web*, 25 April 2001, <www.edweek.org>.

    R. Haskins, "Beyond Metaphor: The Efficacy of Early Childhood Education," *American Psychologist* 44 (1989): 274–282.

    R. J. Herrnstein and C. Murray, *The Bell Curve: Intelligence and Class Structure in American Life* (New York, NY: Free Press, 1994).

    M. Woodhead, "When Psychology Informs Public Policy: The Case of Early-Childhood Intervention," *American Psychologist* 43, no. 6 (1988): 443–454.

E. Zigler and J. Freedman, "Early Experience, Malleability, and Head Start," in *The Malleability of Children*, eds. J.J. Gallagher and C.T. Ramey (Baltimore, MD: Brookes, 1987), 85–96.

S. L. Ramey and C. T. Ramey.

8. S. L. Ramey and C. T. Ramey.

B. Bowman, M. S. Donovan, and S. Burns, *Eager to Learn: Educating Our Preschoolers* (Washington, DC: National Academy Press, 2001).

9. R. H. McKey et al., *The Impact of Head Start on Children, Families, and Communities* (Washington, DC: Head Start Evaluation Synthesis and Utilization Project, 1985).

K. White and G. Casto, "An Integrative Review of Early Intervention Efficacy Studies with At-Risk Children: Implications for the Handicapped," *Analysis and Intervention in Developmental Disabilities* 5 (1985): 7–31.

C. T Ramey, D. M. Bryant, and T. M. Suarez, "Preschool Compensatory Education and the Modifiability of Intelligence: A Critical Review." in *Current Topics in Human Intelligence*, ed. D. Detterman (Norwood, NJ: Ablex, 1985), 247–296.

The Effectiveness of Early Intervention for At-Risk and Handicapped Children, eds. M. J. Guralnick and F. C. Bennett (New York, NY: Academy Press, 1987).

S. L. Ramey and C. T. Ramey.

M. J. Guralnick, "Second Generation Research on the Effectiveness of Early Intervention," *Early Education and Development* 4, no. 4 (1993): 366–378.

J. P. Shonkoff and P. Hauser-Cram, "Early Intervention for Disabled Infants and Their Families: A Quantitative Analysis," *Pediatrics* 80 (1987): 650–658.

Handbook of Early Childhood Intervention, eds. J. P. Shonkoff and S. J.Meisels (Cambridge, UK: Cambridge University Press, 2000).

10. M. M. Wagner, and S. L. Clayton, "The Parents as Teachers Program: Results from Two Demonstrations," *Future of Children* 9, no. 1 (1999): 91–116.

11. A. J. L. Baker, C. S. Piotrkowski, and J. Brooks-Gunn, "The Home Instruction Program for Preschool Youngsters (HIPPY)," *Future of Children* 9, no. 1 (1999): 116–133.

12. B. H. Wasik et al., "A Longitudinal Study of Two Early-Intervention Strategies: Project CARE," *Child Development* 61 (1990): 1682–1696.

13. G. Boutte, *The Effects of Home Intervention on Rural Children's Home Environments, Academic Self- Esteem, and Achievement Scores* (Ann Arbor, MI: UMI Dissertation Services, 1992).

14. S. Scarr and K. McCartney, "Far from Home: An Experimental Evaluation of the Mother-Child Home Program in Bermuda," *Child Development* 59 (1988): 531–543.

P. Levenstein, J. O'Hara, and J. Madden, "The Mother-Child Home Program of the Verbal Interaction Project," in *As the Twig is Bent...Lasting Effects of Preschool Programs*, ed. Consortium for Longitudinal Studies (Hillsdale, NJ: Erlbaum, 1983), 237–263.

15. C. Powell and S. Grantham-McGregor, "Home Visiting of Varying Frequency and Child Development," *Pediatrics* 84 (1989): 157–164.

16. D. S. Gomby, P. L. Culross, and R. E. Behrman, "Home Visiting: Recent Program Evaluations—Analysis and Recommendations," *Future of Children* 9, no.1 (1999): 4–26.

17. R. G. St.Pierre, and J. I. Layzer, "Using Home Visits for Multiple Purposes: The Comprehensive Child Development Program," *Future of Children* 9, no.1 (1999): 134–151.

18. N. Bayley, *The Bayley Scales of Infant Development—II*, (San Antonio: Psychological Corporation, 1993).

19. R.G. St. Pierre et al., *National Impact Evaluation of the Comprehensive Child Development Program* (Cambridge, MA: Abt. Associates, Inc., 1997).

20. R. G. St. Pierre, J. I. Layzer, and H. V. Barnes, "Regenerating Two-Generation Programs," in *Early Care and Education for Children in Poverty: Promises, Programs, and Long-Term Results*, eds. W.S. Barnett and S.S. Boocock (Albany, NY: SUNY Press, 1998), 99–121.

21. Ibid.

22. J. M. Love et al., *Early Head Start Research-Building Their Futures: How Earl Head Start Programs Are Enhancing the Lives of Infants and Toddlers in Low-Income Families* (Princeton, NJ: Mathematica Policy Research, Inc., 2001).

23. G. Casto and A. Lewis, "Parent Involvement in Infant and Preschool Programs," *Journal of the Division of Early Childhood* 9 (1984): 49–56.

     D. M. Bryant and C. T. Ramey, "Prevention Oriented Infant Education Programs," *Journal of Children in Contemporary Society* 7 (1987): 17–35.

24. C. Kagitcibasi, "Parent Education and Child Development." in *Early Child Development: Investing in our Children's Future*, ed. M. E. Young (Amsterdam, Netherlands: Elsevier Science B.V., 1997), 243–272.

     W. S. Barnett, C. M. Escobar, and M. T. Ravsten, "Parent and Clinic Early Intervention for Children with Language Handicaps: A Cost-Effectiveness Analysis," *Journal of the Division for Early Childhood* 12, no. 4 (1988): 290–298.

     C. van Tuijl, P. P. M. Leseman, and J. Rispens, "Efficacy of an Intensive Home-Based Educational Intervention Programme for 4- to 6-Year Old Ethnic Minority Children in the Netherlands," *International Journal of Behavioral Development* 25, no. 2 (2001): 148–159.

25. St. Pierre, Layzer, and Barnes.

26. D. L. Olds et al., "Prenatal and Infancy Home Visitation by Nurses: Recent Findings," *Future of Children* 9, no. 1 (1999): 44–66.

27. C. T. Ramey et al., "Infant Health and Development Program for Low Birth Weight, Premature Infants: Program Elements, Family Participation, and Child Intelligence," *Pediatrics* 89 (1992): 454–465.

     The Infant Health and Development Program, "Enhancing the Outcomes of Low-birth-weight, Premature Infants," *Journal of the American Medical Association* 263 (1990): 3035–3042.

     J. Brooks-Gunn et al., "Early Intervention in Low-Birth-Weight Premature Infants," *Journal of the American Medical Association* 272, no. 16 (1994): 1257–1262.

28. C. M. McCarton et al., "Results at Age 8 Years of Early Intervention for Low-Birth-Weight Premature Infants: The Infant Health and Development Program," *Journal of the American Medical Association* 277, no.2 (1997): 126–132.

     Ramey, et al.

29. McCarton, et al.

30. A. Baumeister, and V. Bachrach, "A Critical Analysis of the Infant Health and Development Program," *Intelligence* 23 (1996): 79–104.

31.   S. Scarr and M. Eisenberg, "Child Care Research: Issues, Perspectives, and Results," *Annual Reviews Psychology* 44 (1993): 613–644.

32.   M. E. Lamb, K. J. Sternberg, and R. Ketterlinus, "Child Care in the United States." in *Child Care in Context*, eds. M.E. Lamb, K. Sternberg, C.P. Hwang, and A. G. Broberg (Hillside, NJ: Erlbaum, 1992).

Scarr and Eisenberg.

J. Belsky, "The 'Effects' of Infant Day Care Reconsidered," *Early Childhood Research Quarterly* 3 (1988): 235–272.

R. Haskins, "Public Aggression Among Children with Varying Day Care Experience," *Child Development* 57 (1985): 692–703.

33.   Scarr and Eisenberg.

M. R. Burchinal, "Child Care Experiences and Developmental Outcomes," *The Annals of the American Academy of Political and Social Science: The Silent Crisis in U.S. Child Care* 563 (1999): 73–97.

34.   Scarr and Eisenberg.

M. Prodroidis et al., "Aggression and Noncompliance Among Center-Based Care, Family Day Care and Home Care," *International Journal of Behavioral Development* 18 (1995): 43–62.

K. McCartney and S. Rosenthal, "Maternal Employment Should be Studied Within Social Ecologies," *Journal of Marriage and the Family* 53 (1991): 1103–1107.

Burchinal.

F. A. Campbell, et al., "Early Childhood Programs and Success in Schools: The Abecedarian Study," in *Early Care and Education for Children in Poverty: Promises, Programs, and Long-Term Results*, eds. W. S. Barnett and S. S. Boocock (Albany, NY: State University of New York Press, 1998).

S. H. Clarke, and F. A. Campbell, "Can Intervention Early Prevent Crime Later? The Abecedarian Project Compared with Other Programs," *Early Childhood Research Quarterly* 13, no. 2 (1998) 319–343.

35.   C. Howes et al., "Attachment and Child Care: Relationships with Mother and Care Giver," *Early Childhood Research Quarterly* 3 (1988): 403–416.

A. I. H. Borge and E. C. Melhuish, "A Longitudinal Study of Childhood Behaviour Problems, Maternal Employment and Day Care in a Norweigian Community," *International Journal of Behavioural Development* 18 (1995): 23–42.

Scarr and Eisenberg.

36.   R. Peth-Pierce, *The NICHD Study of Early Child Care* (Washington, DC: U.S. Department of Health and Human Services, 1998), NIH pub. no. 98-4318.

37.   B. M. Caldwell, "Déjà vu All Over Again: A Researcher Explains the NICHD Study," *Young Children* 56, no. 4 (2001): 58–59.

NICHD Early Child Care Research Network, "Early child care and children's development prior to school entry," Paper presented at the Biennial Meeting of the Society for Research in Child Development, Minneapolis, MN, April 2001.

NICHD Early Child Care Research Network, "Further explorations of the detected effects of quantity of early child care on socioemotional development," Paper presented at the Biennial Meeting of the Society for Research in Child Development, Minneapolis, MN, April, 2001

38.   Caldwell.

39.   Scarr and Eisenberg.

From Neurons to Neighborhoods: the Science of Early Childhood Development, eds. J. Shonkoff and D. Phillips (Washingont, DC: National Academy Press, 2000). Burchinal.

S. L. Hofferth, "Child Care in the First Three Years of Life and Preschoolers' Language and Behavior." Paper presented at the Society for Research in Child Development-Biennial Meeting, Alberquerque, NM, April 1999.

40.   B. E. Andersson, "Effects of Public Day Care- A Longitudinal Study," *Child Development* 60 (1989): 857–866.

T. Field, "Quality Infant Day Care and Grade School Behavior and Performance," *Child Development* 62 (1991): 863–870.

41.   S. Desai, P. L. Chase-Lansdale, and R. T. Michael, "Mother or Market? Effects of Maternal Employment on the Intellectual Ability of Four-Year-Old Children," *Demography* 26 (1989): 545–561.

N. Baydar and J. Brooks-Gunn, "Effects of Maternal Employment and Child-Care Arrangements on Preschoolers' Cognitive and Behavioral Outcomes: Evidence from the Children of the National Longitudinal Survey of Youth. Special Section Data Analyses on Developmental Psychology," *Developmental Psychology* 27 (1991): 932–945.

42.   Burchinal.

43.   Peth-Pierce.

44.   NICHD Early Child Care Research Network, "Early child care and children's development prior to school entry." Paper presented at the Biennial Meeting of the Society for Research in Child Development, Minneapolis, MN, April 2001.

NICHD Early Child Care Research Network, "Further explorations of the detected effects of quantity of early child care on socioemotional development." Paper presented at the Biennial Meeting of the Society for Research in Child Development, Minneapolis, MN, April, 2001.

45.   Burchinal.

46.   E. S. Peisner-Feinberg et al., *The Children of the Cost, Quality, and Outcomes Study Go To School* (Chapel Hill, NC: The University of North Carolina, Frank Porter Graham Child Development Center, 1999).

E. S. Peisner-Feinberg and M.R. Burchinal, "Relations Between Preschool Children's Child Care Experiences and Concurrent Development: The Cost, Quality, and Outcomes Study," *Merill-Palmer Quarterly* 43, no. 3 (1997): 451–477.

47.   E. S. Peisner-Feinberg et al.

Burchinal.

48.   K. White and G. Casto, "An Integrative Review of Early Intervention Efficacy Studies with At-Risk Children: Implications for the Handicapped," *Analysis and Intervention in Developmental Disabilities* 5 (1985): 7–31.

R. H. McKey et al., *The Impact of Head Start on Children, Families and Communities. Final Report of the Head Start Evaluation, Synthesis, and Utilization Project* (Washington, DC: U.S. Department of Health and Human Services, 1985).

C. T. Ramey, D.M. Bryant and T.M. Suarez, "Preschool Compensatory Education and the Modifiability of Intelligence: A Critical Review." in *Current Topics in Human Intelligence*, ed. D. Detterman (Norwood, NJ: Ablex, 1986), 247–296.

M. Woodhead, "When Psychology Informs Public Policy: The Case of Early Childhood Intervention," *American Psychologist*, 43 (1988): 443–454.

R. Haskins, "Beyond Metaphor: The Efficacy of Early Childhood Education," *American Psychologist* 44 (1989): 274–282.

C. Locurto, "Beyond IQ in Preschool Programs?" *Intelligence* 15 (1991): 295–312.

H. H. Spitz, *The Raising of Intelligence: A Selected History of Attempts to Raise Retarded Intelligence* (Hillsdale, NJ: Erlbaum, 1986).

H. H. Spitz, "Commentary on Locurto's 'Beyond IQ in Preschool Programs?'" *Intelligence* 15 (1991): 327–333.

49. Herrnstein and Murray.

50. Herrnstein and Murray.

Woodhead.

51. W. S. Barnett, "Preschool Education for Economically Disadvantaged Children: Effects on Reading Achievement and Related Outcomes," in *Handbook of Early Literacy Research*, eds. S. B. Neuman and D. K. Dickinson (New York, NY: Guilford Press, 2001), 421–443.

52. B. M. Caldwell, "Sustaining Intervention Effects: Putting Malleability to the Test," in *The Malleability of Children*, eds. J. J. Gallagher and C. T. Ramey (Baltimore, MD: Brookes, 1987), 115–126.

Haskins.

Burchinal.

53. Barnett.

54. L. J. Schweinhart et al., *Significant Benefits: The High/ Scope Perry Preschool Study Through Age 27*, [Monographs of the High/Scope Educational Research Foundation No. 10] (Ypsilanti, MI: High/Scope Press, 1993)

55. H. L. Garber, *The Milwaukee Project: Prevention of Mental Retardation in Children at Risk* (Washington, DC: American Association on Mental Retardation, 1988).

56. Schweinhart et al.

F. A.Campbell and C. T. Ramey, "Cognitive and School Outcomes for High-Risk African-American Students at Middle Adolescence: Positive Effects of Early Intervention," *American Educational Journal* 32, no. 4 (1995): 743–772.

57. Spitz.

Herrnstein and Murray.

Locurto.

58. Campbell and Ramey.

Carolina Abecedarian Project, *Early Learning, Later Success: The Abecedarian Study* (Chapel Hill, NC: University of North Carolina, Frank Porter Graham Child Development Center, 1999).

59. Garber.

60. W.S. Barnett, "Long-Term Effects on Cognitive Development and School Success." in *Early Care and Education for Children in Poverty: Promises, Programs,*

and Long-Term Outcomes, eds. W. S. Barnett and S. S. Boocock (Buffalo, NY: State University of New York Press, 1998), 11–14.

A. McGill-Franzen and R. L. Allington, "Flunk 'em or Get Them Classified: The Contamination of Primary Grade Accountability Data," *Educational Researcher* 22, no. 1 (1993): 19–22.

61.   (t-test, p < .05, n = 20 and 24) Barnett.

62.   W. S.Barnett, "Long-Term Effects of Early Childhood Programs on Cognitive and School Outcomes," *The Future of Children* 4 (1995): 25–50.

H. Yoshikawa, "Prevention as Cumulative Protection: Effects of Early Family Support and Education on Chronic Delinquency and Its Risks," *Psychological Bulletin* 115 (1994): 27–54.

63.   D. Johnson and T. Walker, "A Follow-up Evaluation of the Houston Parent Child Development Center: School Performance," *Journal of Early Intervention* 15, no. 3 (1991) 226–236.

R. J. Lally, P. Mangione, and A. S. Honig, "The Syracuse University Family Development Research Program: Long-Range Impact on an Early Intervention with Low-Income Children and Their Families," *Parent Education As Early Intervention: Emerging Directions in Theory, Research and Practice* (Norwood, NJ: Ablex Publishers, 1988), 79–104.

Schweinhart et al.

V. Seitz and N. H. Apfel, "Parent-Focused Intervention: Diffusion Effects on Siblings," *Child Development* 56 (1994): 376–391.

A. J. Reynolds, *Success in Early Intervention: The Chicago Child-Parent Centers* (Lincoln, NE: University of Nebraska Press, 2000).

64.   Lally, Mangione, and Honig.

Seitz and Apfel.

65.   Clarke and Campbell.

66.   Reynolds.

A. J. Reynolds et al., "Long-Term Effects of an Early Childhood Intervention on Educational Achievement and Juvenile Arrest: A 15-Year Follow-Up of Low-Income Children in Public Schools," *JAMA* 285 (2001): 2339–2346.

J. A. Temple, A. J. Reynolds, and W. T. Miedel, "Can Early Childhood Intervention Prevent High School Dropout? Evidence from the Chicago Child-Parent Centers," *Urban Education* 35 (2001): 31–56.

A. J. Reynolds, W. T. Miedel, and E. A. Mann, "Innovation in Early Intervention for Children in Families with Low Incomes: Lessons from the Chicago Child-Parent Centers," *Young Children* 55 (2000): 84–88.

"Educational Success in High-Risk Settings: Contributions of the Chicago Longitudinal Study," ed. A. J. Reynolds, *Journal of School Psychology* (Special issue), Vol. 37, No. 4, 1999

67.   Reynolds.

68.   W. S. Barnett, "Benefit-cost Analysis of Preschool Education: Findings from a 25-year Follow-up," *American Journal of Orthopsychiatry* 63, no. 4 (1993): 500–508.

69.   Ibid.

70.   L. Karoly et al., *Investing In Our Children: What We Know And Don't Know About The Costs And Benefits Of Early Childhood Intervention* (Santa Monica, CA: RAND, 1998).

71.   Reynolds.

72.   Burchinal.

N. Zill et al., *Head Start Program Performances Measures: Second Progress Report* (Washington, DC: Research, Demonstration and Evaluation Branch and Head Start Bureau, Administration on Children, Youth and Families, U.s. Department of Health and Human Services, 1998).

W. S. Barnett et al., *Fragile Lives, Shattered Dreams: A Report on Implementation of Preschool Education in New Jersey's Abbott Districts* (New Brunswick, NJ: The Center for Early Education Research, Rutgers, The State University of New Jersey, 2001).

73.   M. Burchinal, M. Lee, and C. Ramey, "Type of Day-Care and Intellectual Development in Disadvantaged Children," *Child Development* 60 (1989): 128–137.

V. Van de Reit and M. B. Resnick, *Learning to Learn: An Effective Model for Early Childhood Education.* Gainesville (FL: University of Florida Press, 1973).

74.   E. A. Hanushek, "Teacher Characteristics and Gains in Student Achievement: Estimation Using Micro Data," *American Economic Review* 60, no. 2 (1971): 280–288.

R. J. Murnane and B. Phillips, "What Do Effective Teachers of Inner-City Children Have in Common?" *Social Science Research* 10 (1981): 83–100.

R. F. Ferguson, "Can Schools Narrow the Black-White Test Score Gap?" in *The Black-White Test Score Gap*, eds. C. Jencks and M. Phillips (Washington, DC: Brookings Institute Press, 1998), 318–374.

A. Clarke-Stewart and L.Gruber, *Children at Home and in Day Care* (Hillsdale, NJ: Lawrence Erlbaurn Associates, 1994).

C. Howes and M. Olenick, "Child Care and Family Influences on Toddlers' Compliance," *Child Development,* 57 (1986): 202–216.

M. Whitebook, C. Howes, and D. Phillips, *Who Cares? Child Care Teachers and the Quality of Care in America-Final Report of the National Child Care Staffing Study* (Oakland, CA: Child Care Employee Project, 1989).

C. Howes, D. Phillips, and M. Whitebook, "Thresholds of Quality: Implications for the Social Development of Children in Center-Based Child Care," *Child Development* 63 (1992): 449–460.

J. Arnett, "Caregivers in Day Care Centers: Does Training Matter?" *Journal of Applied Developmental Psychology* 10 (1989): 541–522.

C. Howes, "Children's Experiences in Center-Based Child Care as a Function of Teacher Background and Adult-Child Ratio," *Merrill-Palmer Quarterly* 43, no. 3 (1997): 404–425.

L. Dunn, "Proximal and Distal Features of Day Care Quality and Children's Development," *Early Childhood Research Quarterly* 8, no. 2 (1993): 167–192.

B.Tizard, J. Philps, and I. Plewis, "Play in Preschool Centers, II: Effects on Play of the Child's Social Class and of the Educational Orientation of the Center," *Journal of Child Psychology and Psychiatry* 17 (1976): 265–274.

M. Whitebook, D. Phillips, and C. Howes, *National Child Care Staffing Study Revisited: Four Years in the Life of Center-Based Child Care* (Oakland, CA: Child Care Employee Project, 1993).

L. Phillipsen, M. Burchinal, C. Howes, and D. Cryer, "The Prediction of Process Quality from Structural Features of Child Care," *Early Childhood Research Quarterly* 12 (1997): 281–304.

S. Scarr, M. Eisenberg, and K. Deater-Deckerd, "Measurements of Quality in Child Care Centers," *Early Childhood Research Quarterly* 9, no 2 (1994): 131–152.

Eager to Learn: Educating our Preschoolers, eds. B. T. Bowman, M. S. Donovan, and M. S. Burns (Washington, DC: National Academy Press, 2001)

75.   Eds. Bowman, Donovan, and Burns.

H. McGurk, A. et al., *Staff-Child Ratios in Care and Education Services for Young Children* (London: HMSO, 1995).

J. I. Layzer, B. D. Goodson, and M. Moss, *Life in Preschool-Volume One of an Observational Study of Early Childhood Programs for Disadvantaged Four-Year-Olds: Final Report* (Cambridge, MA:Abt Associates, 1993).

Clarke-Stewart and Gruber.

Howes.

S. C. Kontos, C. Howes, and E. Galinsky, " Does Training Make a Difference to Quality in Family Child Care?" *Early Childhood Research Quarterly* 12 (1997): 351–372.

Howes, Phillips, and Whitebook.

A. B. Smith, "Quality Child Care and Joint Attention," *International Journal of Early Years Education* 7, no. 1 (1999): 85–98.

Phillipsen, Burchinal, Howes, and Cryer.

Dunn.

R. Ruopp, J. Travers, F. M. Glantz, and C. Coelen, "Children at the Center: Summary Findings and Their Implications," *Final Report of the National Day Care Study: Children at the Center, Vol. 1* (Cambridge, MA: Abt Associates, 1979).

C. M. Achilles, P. Harman, and P. Egelson, "Using Research Results on Class Size to Improve Pupil Achievement Outcomes," *Research in the Schools* 2, no. 2 (1995): 23–30.

A. Russell, *An Observational Study of the Effect of Staff-Child Ratios on Staff and Child Behavior in South Australian Kindergartens* (Adelaide: Flinders University, 1985).

Ferguson.

A. Krueger, *Experimental Estimates of Educational Production Functions* (Princeton, NJ: Princeton University, 1997).

H. Wenglinsky, "How Money Matters: The Effect of School District Spending on Academic Achievement," *Sociology of Education* 70, no. 3 (1997): 377–399.

F. Mosteller, "The Tennessee Study of Class Size in the Early School Grades," *The Future of Children*, 5, no. 2 (1995): 113–127.

J. Boyd-Zaharias and H. Pate-Bain, "The Continuing Impact of Elementary Small Classes." Paper presented at the annual meeting of the American Educational Research Association, New Orleans, LA, April 2000.

A. Krueger, "Experimental Estimates of Educational Production Functions," *Quarterly Journal of Economics* 114, no. 2 (1999): 497–532.

J. D. Finn, S. B. Gerber, C. M. Achilles and J. Boyd-Zaharias, "Short and Long-Term Effects of Small Classes." Paper prepared for conference on the economics of school reform, State University of New York, Buffalo, NY, May 1999.

76.   E. Frede, "Preschool program quality for children in poverty." in *Early Care and Education for Children in Poverty: Promises, Programs, and Long-Term Outcomes*, eds. W. S. Barnett and S. S. Boocock (Buffalo, NY: State University of New York Press, 1998), 77–98.

Reynolds.

Bowman, Donovan, and Burns.

77.   W. S. Barnett, *Lives in the Balance: Age 27 Benefit-Cost Analysis of the High/Scope Perry Preschool Program* (Ypsilanti, MI: High/Scope Press, 1996).

A. J. Reynolds et al., *Age 21 Cost-Benefit Analysis of the Title I Chicago Child-Parent Center Program* (Madison, WI: University of Wisconsin-Madison, 2001).

78.   W. S. Barnett, J. Tarr, and E. Frede, *Early Childhood Education Needs in Low Income Communities: Final Report of an Assessment of Young Children's Educational Needs and Community Capacity in New Jersey's Abbott Districts* (New Brunswick, NJ: Center for Early Education Research, Rutgers, The State University of New Jersey, 1999).

79.   E. Blakely, "Separate and Not Equal: America's Diversity Crisis." in *America's Demographic Tapestry: Baseline for the New Millennium*, eds. J.W. Hughes and J.J. Seneca (New Brunswick, NJ: Rutgers University Press, 1999), 187–202.

CHAPTER 2

CLASS-SIZE REDUCTION IN GRADES K–3

Jeremy D. Finn[1]
State University of New York at Buffalo

SUMMARY OF RESEARCH FINDINGS

Reducing class size in Grades K–3 has been found to have academic benefits in all subject areas, especially for children living in poverty. Studies published since the mid-1980s show that classroom behavior and test scores improve while students are in small classes. Further, the improvement persists through the middle school and high school years, even though students return to full-size classes. To reap the full range of benefits, it is important that pupils enter small classes in the early years (Grades K or 1) and continue in small classes for three or more years. Students who attend small classes are also more likely to take college-entrance examinations; this is especially true for minority students.

RECOMMENDATIONS

- Resources should be provided to schools and districts serving low-income pupils to restrict class sizes in the primary grades to no more than 18 pupils.
- To ensure that the research-documented benefits of small classes are realized, policies for implementing small classes should include the following provisions:

- Begin class-size reduction in K-1 and add additional grades in each subsequent year.
- Use the reduced-class model supported by the research: one teacher in a classroom with 18 or fewer pupils. Pupils assigned to small classes should represent a cross-section of students in the school, *not* just difficult-to-manage students.
- Plan for class-size reduction in advance, hiring fully qualified teachers. Additionally, some programs of professional support and development are likely to be helpful.
- Systems should be established to monitor class-size reduction initiatives continually and closely, providing feedback to administrators, policy makers, and parents about the successes of the program. Teachers should be afforded opportunities to discuss problems as they arise, and to have them addressed by the school administration.

The advantages of small classes have been touted by parents and educators throughout modern history. Only in recent years, however, has there been a significant impetus for reducing class sizes in American public schools. This is partially due to the fact that teachers, parents, policy makers, and the courts understand the importance of small classes for teaching and learning, that education has risen to the top of state and national agendas, and that high-quality research has demonstrated the academic and behavioral benefits of small classes, especially for children at risk. This report summarizes the current state of research on class-size reduction and its implications for educational policy—especially as it pertains to the academic performance of students at risk.

CLASS-SIZE REDUCTION RESEARCH

The impact of class size on educational outcomes is among the most researched areas in education. By the 1980s, more than 200 studies had appeared on the topic. Some early studies did not establish a connection between smaller class sizes and student achievement, but mainly attempted to weigh the value of small classes against larger classes. Others suffered from problems of methodology and data collection. Most acceptable studies, however, supported the importance of smaller classes in promoting student success. In a review of early studies, Educational Research Service[2] and Robinson[3] concluded that reducing class sizes in the primary grades to 22 or fewer students appeared to have a beneficial effect on reading and math scores, especially for economically disadvantaged pupils. Since that time, more sophisticated experiments have confirmed and extended this conclusion.

The first refined analysis to connect reduced class size to academic achievement was a 1978 meta-analysis by Glass and Smith of 77 earlier research studies.[4] This analysis found that not only did small classes improve the chances for academic achievement, but that small classes could also be used as a predictor of student success. Glass and Smith showed that "as class size increases, achievement decreases." Repeated studies have provided evidence of important relationships between the number of students in the classroom and the success of teaching and learning in the same classrooms. This research demonstrated that an appropriate class size was fewer than 20 students, and that the greatest benefits of small classes are obtained in the early grades.

Large Scale Studies

Based on this early work—particularly the findings of benefits to poor students and to young students—beginning in the mid-1980s some large-scale projects and an actual experiment in class size and student outcomes were started. Among them were Indiana's Prime Time; HB 72, which limited class sizes in Grades K–4 to 22 students in Texas; STAR and its related studies in Tennessee; Wisconsin's SAGE Project; and California's massive Class-Size Reduction (CSR) effort. Prime Time and STAR were particularly important because they provided the motivation for many districts, states, and the federal government to reduce class sizes on a large scale. Several overviews of the more recent class size research are available including a book by Achilles[5] and monographs by Finn[6] and by Ehrenberg, Brewer, Gamoran, and Willms.[7]

Prime Time in Indiana

Between 1981 and 1983, Indiana launched Project Prime Time as a statewide initiative. Prime Time began this reduction with first grade, but was not entirely a CSR initiative. In particular, it added teacher aides to classrooms to reduce the adult-to-child ratio—not truly resulting in small classes. Prime Time reported mixed results with some gains in student achievement on reading and math scores. Gains in reading were larger than those in math.[8] An important outcome of Prime Time was the demonstrated feasibility of large-scale efforts to change classroom organization in the pursuit of improved student learning.

Project STAR in Tennessee

From 1985–1989, the STAR (Student/Teacher Achievement Ratio) experiment was conducted in Tennessee. This large-scale (n=11,600) longitudinal study of class sizes provided the legislature and administrators with convincing data to support class-size reduction for students statewide. At each grade level K–3, a strictly controlled study was set up to examine whether small (13–17) classes made a difference in student accomplishments in the early years, when compared to regular (22–25) classes, or regular classes with a full-time teacher aide.[9]

Because of its magnitude and scientific rigor, the results of STAR carried more weight than the earlier studies. The most important findings are:

- In every grade level (K–3) students in small classes outperformed students in larger classes on every achievement test administered—in all subject areas and on both norm-referenced and criterion-referenced achievement tests.
- The benefits of small classes were greater for minority students and students attending inner-city schools than for white students or those in non-urban areas. In many cases, the advantages were *two to three times as great* for African-American students as for white students.
- New analyses of the STAR data have shown that both *starting early* (K or 1) and *continuous participation* (3 to 4 years) in small classes lead to the greatest benefits.[10]

Students who had participated in Project STAR in K–3 were followed after they returned to full-size classes in Grade 4. The most important long-term findings are:

- Pupils who attended small classes in K–3 performed significantly better in all academic subjects in all subsequent Grades, 4, 6, and 8.[11]
- The more years pupils spent in small classes in K–3, the longer the benefits lasted into later grades. For example, at the end of Grade 6, pupils who had attended small classes for one year had a 1.2-month advantage in reading over pupils who attended full-size classes. Pupils who had attended small classes for two years had a 2.8-month advantage. Three years in a small classes produced a 4.4-month advantage, and four years produced a 6-month advantage in reading.
- Pupils who attended small classes in K–3 were more likely to graduate from high school and more likely to take SAT/ACT college admissions tests. The impact on minority students was particularly strong, thus reducing by 60% the gap in SAT/ACT rates between black students and white students.[12]

Additional strength was added to the STAR results by secondary analysts at the University of London, The University of Chicago, and Princeton University who examined the STAR data using different statistical approaches.[13] All approaches yielded the same conclusions.

Other large-scale CSR efforts, described below, have confirmed the basic findings of STAR in other locations. Research using the STAR data continues today; researchers are examining the long-term effects of small classes on teen births[14] and on employment and schooling after high school.[15]

Besides the impact on academic achievement, Project STAR revealed that:

- Teacher morale is increased in small classes, a finding consistent with all prior research.
- Teachers of small classes spend more time on active teaching and less on classroom management, a finding substantiated in other research in addition to STAR.
- There are fewer disruptions in small classes and fewer discipline problems, a finding replicated in other studies.
- Students' engagement in learning activities is increased.[16]
- In-grade retentions are reduced.[17] Because retained students are disproportionately minority, male, and from low-income homes, the reduction in retentions also reduces the achievement gap in schooling.[18]

Project STAR found no achievement advantages associated with full-time teacher aides. In the most complete examination of this issue, researchers concluded that there were no differences in academic achievement "between ... students in teacher aide classes and students in regular classes on any test in any grade (K–3)."[19] The authors continue:

> In several instances, students in aide classes performed more poorly than students in non-aide classes... In terms of learning behavior, again no significant differences were found ... In several instances, behavior was marginally *poorer* among students in classes with aides.[20]

Also, the problems teachers encounter in teaching and in managing classes "are not reduced when a teaching assistant is present."[21]

STAR and the Black-White Achievement Gap. The disproportionate impact of small classes on minority students and students attending inner-city schools reduced the achievement gap between black and white students. For example, the black-white gap in pass rates on the first grade reading mastery test was 14.3% in full-size classes—that is, 14.3% more whites mastered the reading tests. In small classes, the gap was reduced to 4.1%. Both black students and white students gained significantly by being in small classes, but black students gained more.[22] Other research has examined the achievement gap in more detail and reached the same conclusions.[23] Bingham performed a comparative analysis examining white vs. minority differences and also concluded that smaller class sizes are an effective strategy in reducing the gap. According to Bingham, the smallest white-minority gap was associated with small classes beginning no later than in Grade 1 and lasting for a minimum of two years. The finding of a reduced black-white gap in college aspirations, indicated by students taking SAT/ACT tests, shows a positive impact on behavior in later grades as well.[24] The effect of small classes on the achievement gap has been confirmed in other class-size initiatives, particularly Wisconsin's Project SAGE, discussed below.

Critique of Project STAR.   Despite the exceptional research design used in STAR, some factors were beyond the control of the research team. In particular, students moved from one neighborhood to another and changed schools in the process. This led to some attrition from STAR schools over the four-year period and, in a small number of cases, students changing from one class type to another when they changed schools. Economist Eric Hanushek has suggested that these factors may have compromised STAR's findings, a criticism echoed by Witte[25] as well as by Ehrenberg et al.[26] These issues have been addressed by several data analysts. Krueger[27] undertook a thorough analysis of attrition in STAR. His work showed that neither of these factors produce "bias" in the study's main findings, that is, average differences in performance among the class types. Hedges and his colleagues[28] compared the Grade 3 performance of STAR participants who were still in the sample in Grades 4, 6, and 8 with that of participants who left the sample. Again, the difference between small-class and large-class students was the same for "stayers" and "leavers." Although attrition did result in a somewhat selective long-term sample, the basic findings of the experiment still hold.

Other Large-scale Class-size Initiatives

Project STAR provided the scientific support for the long-held belief of educators and parents that small classes in the early grades had many advantages. Because the impact was particularly strong for students at risk, STAR helped motivate many districts, states, and even the U.S. Department of Education to undertake further reduced class initiatives. By the year 2000, approximately 35 states had class-size legislation.

Wisconsin's Project SAGE, the Burke County project in North Carolina, the massive CSR program in California, and the federal initiative begun during the Clinton administration are among the CSR initiatives that were accompanied by formal evaluations. These programs were not intended to be controlled experiments: their foremost purpose was to provide an intervention—small classes—whose efficacy had already been demonstrated. Occasionally, critics lose sight of that purpose and comment on these programs' lack of tightly controlled research designs.[29] Despite this criticism, each of the programs was accompanied by an extensive evaluation and each produced results consistent with those of STAR.

The SAGE Program in Wisconsin

The Student Achievement Guarantee in Education (SAGE) program is a statewide effort to increase the academic achievement of children living in poverty by reducing the student-teacher ratio in kindergarten through Grade 3 to 15:1. The program began in 1996 and was targeted toward schools with a high proportion of students living in poverty. School districts in Wisconsin that had a least one school with 50% of children or more living below the poverty level were eligible to apply for participation in SAGE. Within these districts, any school with 30% of students or more below the poverty level was eligible to become a SAGE school. Funding was set at a maximum of $2,000 per low-income student enrolled in SAGE classrooms (K–3). During the 1996–7 school year, 30 schools in 21 school districts, including seven in Milwaukee, began the program in K-1. Grade 2 was added in these schools in 1997–98 and Grade 3 in 1998–99.

The program requires that participating schools implement four interventions: (a) reduce the pupil-teacher ratio within a classroom to 15 students per teacher, (b) establish "lighted schoolhouses" open from early in the morning until late in the evening, (c) develop "rigorous" curricula, and (d) create a system of staff development and professional accountability. While most class-size reductions were accomplished by assigning 15 or fewer students to a teacher within one classroom, some alternate configurations were also adopted. They included classrooms of approximately 30 students with two-teacher teams, shared space classrooms with two separate teaching spaces each with one teacher and about 15 students, and floating teacher classrooms where an additional teacher supports classes of about 30 students during reading and math instruction. The class-size reduction was an immediate intervention in the schools whereas the other SAGE provisions were implemented by schools with considerable variation and, at times, with considerable delays.[30]

To determine the impact of SAGE pupil-teacher reductions on student achievement, the SAGE evaluation uses a quasi-experimental, comparative change design. The quasi-experimental design was used because it was not possible to randomly assign students and teachers to classrooms and to keep classroom cohorts intact from year to year. The evaluation uses a control or comparison group of classrooms from districts participating in the SAGE program for the purpose of assessing the impact of SAGE class-size reductions. These comparison schools have normal class sizes, and, as group, resemble SAGE schools in family income, achievement in reading, K–3 enrollment, and racial composition.

The longitudinal evaluation of the SAGE program has produced substantial scientific data on the effects of small classes in Grades K–3. The positive impact of small classes on student achievement in SAGE classrooms, especially for minority students, has been a consistent finding for four years and has confirmed earlier findings from STAR. The greatest achievement gains were made in first grade with second- and third-grade students maintaining the gains. Perhaps of greater significance, SAGE has provided guidance for policy makers and administrators about how best to implement small classes at the district and local level through extensive non-experimental data collection such as principal and teacher questionnaires and classroom observations and teacher interviews.[31]

Like STAR, Project SAGE has not been without its critics. Some criticisms concern weaknesses in the project's experimental design and methods of analysis, for example, the lack of random assignment, student attrition, a ceiling effect on some of the tests.[32] These comments may not be germane because SAGE, although it included a formal evaluation component, was not intended to be a controlled experiment. More pertinent are the comments that the expansion of SAGE has met with a shortage of qualified teachers and classroom space, especially in the Milwaukee Public Schools. To deal with these problems at some schools, teachers have "doubled up," putting two teachers in one classroom with 30 students.[33] Team teaching presents both benefits and problems. Among the latter, teachers have to work well together and collaborate well in order for instruction to be optimal. Extensive advance planning is needed in order for this to occur, a principle also learned in California (below).

The Burke County Project in North Carolina

Studies of the effects of small classes in Burke County, North Carolina, reinforce SAGE and STAR findings, while addressing questions about financial and educational policy implications of CSR.[34] With the goal of improving education in relatively poor Burke County, a pilot program in 1991–1992 reduced class size to 18 in Grade 1 in four schools, and in Grades 2 and 3 in subsequent years. Pilot program results were highly positive. On the strength of these findings, the program was extended in 1995–1996 to all elementary schools, Grades 1–3, providing the same positive findings. By 2000, classes of about 17:1 were in all 17 schools with Grades 1–3. By comparing the CSR classes with the control classes, researchers reported higher rates of time on task for students and more emphasis on student interaction. The smaller classes significantly outperformed regular classes in math and reading at the end of Grades 1, 2, and 3, and later these same students continued to outperform the others after returning to regular classes in Grades 4 and 7. An important feature of the Burke County initiative was the ability of administrators to implement small class sizes with no increase of per-pupil expenditures for the district. This was accomplished through the careful reallocation of existing resources, especially the reassignment of qualified staff members who had not been teaching their own classes all day, to reduced size classes.

The California CSR Program

Class-size reduction began in California in 1996. Within a period of several months, new teachers were hired and placed in Grade K–3 classrooms across the state, reducing class sizes to 20 pupils or fewer. In three years of operation, this largest CSR initiative has resulted in 28,000 new teachers being deployed and virtually every classroom in Grades 1–2 being reduced in size. Since the program was implemented so quickly, very few large classes were available to serve as a comparison group for evaluators. The evaluation has focused on Grade 3, in which small but statistically significant achievement gains were reported in reading, language, and mathematics.[35] The benefits of small classes were in the range 0.05 to 0.10 standard deviations. Although these would be considered small effects, they replicate the results from project STAR for pupils who entered small classes in Grade 3; in STAR, the largest effects were obtained for students who entered small classes in earlier years (K or 1).

California's experience provided important insight into the types of planning needed before implementing a large-scale CSR initiative: The speed with which teachers were hired resulted in many teachers being placed in classrooms who had not even completed their formal teacher credentialing programs. As a result, in the first year of California's CSR program, the percentage of K–3 teachers who were not fully credentialed rose from 1.8% to 4%; this figure increased to 12.5% and 13.4% in subsequent years.[36] Had the program been implemented in phases, the drop in the preparation and experience levels of California's teachers could have been remedied.

Federal Initiatives

Begun in 1999–2000, the federal class-size reduction program provided funds to schools serving high-poverty populations. By the second year of operation the program supported CSR initiatives in 36 major urban school systems and increased its funding to $1.3 billion from $1.2 billion. School districts targeted their funds toward low-achieving schools and those identified as highest-need schools. Local school districts used 87% of the federal funds to hire new teachers. In its first-year report, *The Class-Size Reduction Program: Boosting Student Achievement in Schools Across the Nation,* the U. S. Department of Education highlighted the expected benefits of class-size reduction. Federal class-size reduction funds were aimed at helping to make classrooms more manageable so that teachers could focus on teaching and learning. Further, teachers were expected to report more enthusiasm for teaching and opportunities to address students' individual needs, accompanied by a boost in students' reading scores and overall achievement scores.[37]

The federal class-size reduction program permitted schools to implement several models of small classes, including some that were not small classes at all. The latter included large classes (e.g., 32–40 pupils) that were team-taught by two full-time teachers, and pairs or triplets of larger classes (e.g. 30 pupils) that shared a "rotating" teacher who would spend part of the day in each classroom. Both of these models reduce the *pupil-teacher ratio* (PTR) in classrooms but do not reduce the actual class size, that is, the actual number of pupils in the room who interact with the teacher full-time each day. STAR researchers have pointed out that the strong findings of reduced-class benefits do not apply to these settings.[38]

In its first year of operation, approximately 29,000 new teachers were hired under the federal CSR initiative. An evaluation contract was awarded to Abt Associates, a Boston firm. However, the ensuing calendar year saw a change in administrations in Washington. President Bush's education plan, "No Child Left Behind," targets federal class-size reduction money for elimination, apparently disregarding the research base that supports class-size reduction. Nevertheless, with or without support from the federal government, small classes have become standard practice in many states and districts across the country and are producing noticeable benefits to teachers and pupils.

Research, Policy, and Practice

The research on class size supports a number of practices that can be implemented to enhance students' academic performance. The benefits of small classes, especially for minority students and students from low-income homes, have been confirmed time and again. STAR and the studies to follow STAR have also drawn these conclusions:

Timing and Continuity of Class-Size Reduction
The most recent analyses of STAR data show that the greatest initial impact on student achievement is obtained when students enter reduced-size classes in kindergarten or Grade 1.[39] Pupils who attended small classes for at least three years had significant sustained benefits through Grade 8; the carry-over effects of fewer than three years were mixed. Several large CSR initiatives have started in Kindergarten or Grade 1 and expanded to Grades 2 and 3 in subsequent years. This is good policy, especially if the same students attend small classes for several years in a row.

What Does "Small Class" Mean?

Research on class size has been conducted according to high scientific standards; this cannot be said of any other educational intervention to improve pupil achievement. Project STAR has received praise from scientists and policy makers;[40] it has provided the starting point for several national conferences of researchers concerned with the need to base educational decisions (like medical decisions) on strong empirical evidence.[41]

The evidence provided by STAR, and by other CSR efforts that confirm STAR findings, are not relevant to other classroom arrangements. The results tell us little or nothing about programs that reduce pupil-teacher ratios without decreasing the number of students in the room. They tell us little or nothing about team-taught classrooms, about "push-in" or "pull-out" classrooms with a common teacher, or about part-time class-size reduction, for example, just for reading. The STAR results do tell us about one alternative reduced-ratio arrangement: a full-size class with a full-time teacher aide does not work.

Alternative class configurations such as team-taught classes or classes with support teachers for reading and math instruction need their own research to evaluate whether or not they offer viable options to increase student achievement. This research is important, especially given the shortage of space faced by many schools and districts. However, for schools to benefit from the strong findings about small classes, the accumulated body of research indicates that actual class sizes must be small: that is, fewer than 20 pupils for the entire school day.

Professional Support and Development for Teachers of Small Classes

Due to the short lead time in hiring teachers for California's CSR program, the quality of the entire state's teaching force declined. In other locations, difficulties in locating and placing qualified teachers in newly created classrooms has created a level of disorganization that required weeks or months to settle.[42] These dynamics can easily offset the benefits that small classes provide.

The experiences of districts across the country show that CSR initiatives benefit from careful advance planning. The most effective settings were those in which school administrators, parents, and community leaders were informed about the program and what it was expected to accomplish.[43] Several initiatives were hindered by the lack of lead time to find space for CSR classes or to identify teachers before the school year began.

Professional support and development activities for teachers have been useful as well. Research has demonstrated clearly that the academic benefits of small classes are obtained without programs of professional development. Project STAR demonstrated advantages with no intervention other than reduced classes (and teacher aides). Nonetheless:

- Many teachers being placed in elementary classrooms are new to teaching, new to the classroom, and new to their school setting. They have a critical need for help "getting started" and for targeted on-the-job training.
- Many veteran teachers are transferring from other kinds of settings to small classes. The instructional practices that may be ingrained from years of experience in these settings are often not current best practice.
- It may be possible to *enhance* the benefits of small classes by taking advantage of the opportunities the class size provides; good professional development can help make this happen.

The recent report, "The Professional Development and Support Needs of Beginning Teachers," discusses this issue in depth.[44] Particular classroom strategies and particular domains of professional support are identified in the report that are especially useful when implementing CSR programs.

The Need to Monitor CSR Programs Closely

In recent years, many districts have undertaken CSR programs, both with and without an accompanying evaluation. The absence of a systematic evaluation can create problems subsequently. It may not be necessary to document that academic achievement is improved by CSR in every site; the benefits have already been demonstrated scientifically. Follow-up evaluation is necessary, however, to make sure that smaller classes are implemented correctly and that problems are addressed quickly. Several evaluations, including one in Buffalo, New York, were able to identify implementation problems during the school year and to provide mid-course corrections. It is also important that basic information is available to administrators, parents, and legislators to demonstrate that the investment in small classes has been spent properly.

There is also a great deal yet to be learned about small classes and the opportunities they provide, as the SAGE, California, Burke County, and US Department of Education programs have demonstrated. A regular system for monitoring reduced-class programs, addressing problems that arise, and reporting progress to administrators and the public has been demonstrated to be an important ingredient of CSR initiatives. Several models have been forwarded to help districts monitor or conduct a formative evaluation of their CSR program.[45]

Questions that Remain

Many questions about small classes remain to be answered. For example:

- How small does a class have to be in order to reap the benefits demonstrated by STAR and other studies? Most CSR interventions are using "fewer than 20 pupils" as their guideline, but research has not established a specific threshold that must be met.
- What are the effects of small classes in later grades, for example, the middle school years or high school years? The early overviews of research on class size[46] reported mixed results based on a relatively small number of studies. Recent years have not seen an increased number of studies of class size in the upper grades. Several studies have been performed using a federal data set, the National Longitudinal Study of 1988. These have produced non-significant results[47] and mixed results,[48] respectively, for Grade 8. The complexity of the situation, with students moving from class to class for different subjects, has undoubtedly discouraged research in this arena.
- What are the effects of combining small classes with other interventions, especially those targeted to students at risk, such as full-day kindergarten, preschool programs, and remedial reading programs?
- What are the long-term effects of small classes on high school and post-secondary outcomes, for example, college attendance and employment? Researchers are currently studying these questions.

The broadest question not fully answered to date is, "*Why is it that small classes work as well as they do?*" Many studies of teachers' instructional strategies have compared teachers in small classes with teachers in full-size classes, but few if any systematic differences have been found.[49] It is clear that small classes make additional time available to teachers—time that would be spent on record keeping or classroom management in larger classes.[50] The time saved may be used to provide more active teaching to the class and, in theory, more individualized instruction. However, research has not shown consistently that students in small classes receive more individual attention or instruction directed to their specific needs.[51]

The strongest hypothesis about why small classes work concerns *students' classroom behavior.* Evidence is mounting that students in small classes are more engaged in learning activities and exhibit less disruptive behavior.[52] Educational and psychological theory explain why this may occur. For example, in a small class, each student is constantly on the firing line; he or she may be called on at any time to answer questions or complete assignments. Students cannot escape by sitting in back corners of the room or avoiding the teacher's attention. By the same token, teachers cannot ignore students that they might otherwise prefer not to attend to, for whatever reasons. Psychologists have forwarded the principle of "diffusion of responsibility" to explain why members of small groups tend to take more individual responsibility than do members of large groups—a principle supported by empirical research.[53] Further, if one's classmates are well behaved and engaged in the learning process, then this behavior will become the norm that others will follow. Research on the socializing effect of group norms is also extensive.[54]

Further research is needed to explain fully why small classes have behavioral and academic benefits. However, the evidence to date suggests that it is the very feature of *smallness* that has the greatest impact. If this principle is correct, then it is also clear that large classes with two teachers (reduced pupil-teacher ratio but not reduced class sizes) are less likely to yield the same benefits.

Controversy Over the Value of Reduced Class Size

Despite the appeal of small classes and despite the strong evidence of their value, the ideas have not gone unchallenged. In particular, economist Eric Hanushek has engaged in a vigorous campaign to convince policy makers and the public that small classes are not an efficient way to improve student performance. Few researchers take this position, but Mr. Hanushek has promulgated this view widely in the professional and public media. The view is consistent with his thesis of many years that fiscal resources spent on public education are not related to academic outcomes.

The conclusions are based on two sets of analyses, summarized in a monograph published by the University of Rochester, then Professor Hanushek's institution,[55] and in a document giving both sides of the argument produced by the Economic Policy Institute.[56] The first analysis is an examination of pupil-teacher ratios and academic performance for the entire country from 1970 to 1995. According to Hanushek, although the ratios declined regularly during that period, academic performance as indicated by the National Assessment of Educational Progress (NAEP) did not increase. The second analysis is a meta-analysis of the results of 277 econometric studies of the relationship between educational "inputs" (including class size) and academic achievement. According to Hanushek, these studies show no systematic relationship with class size.

Hanushek's position holds sway with some policy makers, and he has advised the current administration, which has marked reduced-class-size funds for elimination. A number of education researchers and other economists, not to mention most practitioners, dispute Hanushek's conclusions, however. Among the points that have been forwarded to rebut Hanushek's position are these:

All of the studies cited by Hanushek are studies of pupil-teacher ratios (PTRs), mainly computed at the district, state, or national level. Pupil-teacher ratios at these levels do not reveal the actual class sizes—that is, how many students are actually in classrooms. The PTR includes regular teachers, special education and Title-I teachers, teachers who don't have their own regular classrooms (for example, remedial teachers, language, music, or art teachers, or librarians), administrators, and other staff members as well.[57] Pupil-teacher ratios at these highly aggregated levels reveal little or nothing about the actual classroom conditions in which pupils are learning. In fact, it has been shown that large urban districts tend to have low pupil-teacher ratios because of the large numbers of Title I and remedial teachers, yet often have badly overcrowded classrooms.[58] This distinction is discussed in depth in Ehrenberg et al., who concluded "class size is not the same thing as the pupil/teacher ratio. Indeed, it is quite different."[59]

Hanushek's reviews do not include any of the studies of class size reviewed by either Glass and Smith or by Educational Research Service. He also does not include class-size studies such as Prime Time, Project STAR, or SAGE.

Project STAR, being a controlled scientific experiment, provides stronger evidence than is possible through "production function analysis," the technique used in all the studies cited by Hanushek. A randomized experiment such as STAR is the highest quality research design available; it is the method of choice used by the Food and Drug Administration, for example. This point is acknowledged by Hanushek in these two manuscripts and others. For this reason, Princeton economist Alan Krueger concluded: "The design of the STAR experiment clearly produces results that are more persuasive than [all] the rest of the literature on class size."[60]

Hanushek's conclusions are selected in order to show just one view of the data. For example, in order to show that NAEP scores did not increase in the period from 1970 to 1995, Hanushek focused on the reading performance of 17-year-olds, with no attention to the NAEP Grade 4 or Grade 8 results and no attention to topics that are taught explicitly to older students.

One extensive PTR study using NAEP data has been performed at Educational Testing Service.[61] The study involved a national sample of 10,000 fourth-grade students and 10,000 eighth-grade students. This study found significant gains in mathematics of reduced PTRs, with greater impact on fourth-grade students than on eighth-grade students. Also, the gains were larger for inner-city students than for any other group. This study is not included in the Hanushek review.

Hanushek's methods of analysis have also come under attack. Researchers at the University of Chicago noted that Hanushek's analyses did not take into account that some studies were more informative than others because they were based on larger samples.[62] They reanalyzed a portion of Hanushek's data using meta-analysis methods that weight studies according to the sample sizes, and found the opposite conclusion—that resources (including class size) *do* have an impact on academic achievement.

Economist Alan Krueger performed an even more complete reanalysis of Hanushek's studies.[63] First, Krueger noted that the 277 "studies" cited by Hanushek were in fact 59 studies from which 277 statistics ("effect sizes") were drawn. Some studies contributed far more to Hanushek's conclusions than others. (In fact, between them, two studies contributed 48 of the 277 effect sizes; as it happens, these two studies accounted for most of the negative findings reported by Hanushek.) Several other studies were misinterpreted or miscoded before being entered into Hanushek's analysis. Overlooking the latter issue, Krueger performed a complete reanalysis of Hanushek's studies, counting each of the 59 investigations just once. In additional analyses, he also took into account that some studies were of higher quality than others, and that some studies had more atypical samples than others. In all three analyses, Krueger's results were the reverse of Hanushek's. He concluded that resources in general, and pupil-teacher ratios in particular, are significantly related to academic performance in the direction consistent with Project STAR: lower ratios associated with higher performance.

SUMMARY AND RECOMMENDATIONS

Class-size reduction is sound education policy. It has been shown to be effective time and again, and no serious challenge has been made to the research findings that support those conclusions. Educators have long known this. No school improvement effort relies on larger rather than smaller classes. Indeed, programs targeted to students with academic problems (for example, special education or other remedial programs) are all based on small-class arrangements. Parents often place children in private schools at least in part because of small classes. Many interventions, such as home schooling, Reading Recovery, or Success for All, rely on the ultimate small class, one-on-one instruction.

Research has now documented the advantages of small classes, especially in the elementary grades and especially for students who attend small classes for two, three, or four consecutive years. The effects are especially pronounced for minority students and those attending school in large urban districts. As a result, the achievement gap is reduced, both in the years while pupils attend small classes and later on when they consider applying to college. Teachers, meanwhile, benefit as well. They spend less time on classroom management and clerical tasks, and have more time available to get to know each student better. Reduced-size classes provide the *opportunity* for improved instruction and for increased learning to take place.

The weight of this evidence supports the following recommendations for policy makers:

- Resources should be provided to schools and districts serving low-income pupils to restrict class sizes in the primary grades to no more than 18 pupils.
- To ensure that the research-documented benefits of small classes are realized, policies for implementing small classes should include the following provisions:
  1) Begin class-size reduction in K-1 and add additional grades in each subsequent year.
  2) Use the reduced-class model supported by the research: one teacher in a classroom with 18 or fewer pupils. Pupils assigned to small classes should represent a cross-section of students in the school, *not* just difficult-to-manage students.
  3) Plan for class-size reduction in advance, hiring fully-qualified teachers. Additionally, some programs of professional support and development are likely to be helpful.
- Systems should be established to monitor class-size reduction initiatives continually and closely, providing feedback to administrators, policy makers, and parents about the successes of the program. Teachers should be afforded opportunities to discuss problems as they arise, and to have them addressed by the school administration.

REFERENCES

1. Research assistance was provided by Anke Halbach, University of Wisconsin-Milwaukee.
2. Educational Research Service, *Class Size: A Summary of Research* (Arlington, VA: ERS, 1978).
3. G. E. Robinson, "Synthesis of Research on the Effects of Class Size," *Educational Leadership* 47, no. 7 (1990): 80–90.
4. G. V Glass and M. L. Smith, *Meta-Analysis of Research on the Relationship of Class Size and Achievement.* (San Francisco, CA: Far West Laboratory for Educational Research and Development, 1978).
5. C. M. Achilles, *Lets Put Kids First Finally: Getting Class Size Right.* (Thousand Oaks, CA: Corwin Press, 1999).
6. J. D. Finn, "Class Size and Students at Risk: What is Known? What is Next?" Washington, DC: US Department of Education, Office of Educational Research and Improvement, <http://www.ed.gov/pubs/ClassSize/title.html> (1998).

7.   R. G. Ehrenberg et al., "Class Size and Student Achievement," *Psychological Science in the Public Interest* 1, no. 1 (2001).

8.   D. J. Mueller, C. I. Chase, and J. D. Walden, "Effects of Reduced Class Sizes in Primary Classes," *Educational Leadership* 45, no. 7 (1998): 48–50.

       C. I. Chase, D. J. Mueller, and J. D. Walden, *PRIME TIME: Its Impact on Instruction and Achievement* (Indianapolis, IN: Indiana Department of Education, December 1986).

9.   E. Word et al., *Student/Teacher Achievement Ratio (STAR): Tennessee's K–3 Class Size Study* (Nashville, TN: Tennessee State Department of Education, 1990).

       J. D. Finn and C. M. Achilles, "Answers and Questions About Class Size: A Statewide Experiment," *American Educational Research Journal* 27 (1990): 557–577.

10.   J. D. Finn et al., "The Enduring Effects of Small Classes," *Teachers College Record* 103 (2001): 145–183.

11.   Finn et al.

12.   A. B. Krueger and D. M. Whitmore, *Would Smaller Classes Help Close the Black-White Achievement Gap?* Princeton University Industrial Relations Section Working Paper #451 <www.irs.princeton.edu/pubs/working_papers.html> (March 2001).

13.   H. Goldstein and P. Blatchford, "Class Size and Educational Achievement: A Review of Methodology with Particular Reference to Study Design," *British Educational Research Journal* 24 (1998): 255–268.

       B. Nye, L. V. Hedges, and S. Konstantopoulos, "The Effects of Small Classes on Academic Achievement: The Results of the Tennessee Class Size Experiment," *American Educational Research Journal* 37 (2000): 123–151.

       A. B. Krueger, "Experimental Estimates of Educational Production Functions," *Quarterly Journal of Economics* 114 (1999) 497–532.

14.   Krueger and Whitmore.

15.   J. Finn and J. Boyd-Zaharias, with support from the W. T. Grant Foundation, are conducting a three-year study of "Antecedents and Consequences of High-School Gateway Events," This study includes an examination of post-secondary outcomes.

16.   J. D. Finn et al., "Carry-over Effects of Small Classes," *Peabody Journal of Education* 67 (1989): 75–84.

17.   Word et al., *An Analysis of Grade Retention for Pupils in K–3.* (Ph.D. diss., University of North Carolina at Greensboro, 1993).

18.   C. M. Achilles, *Lets Put Kids First Finally: Getting Class Size Right.* Thousand Oaks (CA: Corwin Press, 1999).

       C. M. Achilles, J. D. Finn, and J. Boyd-Zaharias, *Small Classes Impact the Test-Score Achievement Gap Positively.* Paper presented at the annual meeting of the American Association of School Administrators, Orlando, FL, February 2001.

19.   J. D. Finn, S. B. Gerber, et al., "Teacher Aides: An Alternative to Small Classes?" in *How Small Classes Help Teachers Do Their Best*, eds. M. C. Wang and J. D. Finn (Philadelphia: Temple University Center for Research in Human Development and Education, and the U. S. Department of Education, 2000), 131–174.

20.   Ibid.

21.   Ibid., 165.

22.   Finn and Achilles.

23.   C. M. Achilles and J. D. Finn (October 2000). *Small classes reduce the achievement gap.* Paper presented at the annual meeting of the Council of the Great City Schools, Los Angeles.

      C. S. Bingham, *White-Minority Achievement Gap Reduction and Small Class Size: A Research and Literature Review* (Nashville, TN: Center of Excellence for Research and Policy of Basic Skills, 1993).

24.   Krueger and Whitmore.

25.   E. A. Hanushek, "Some Findings from an Independent Investigation of the Tennessee STAR Experiment and from Other Investigations of Class Size Effects," *Educational Evaluation and Policy Analysis* 21, no. 2 (1999): 143–164.

      J. F. Witte, "Reducing Class Size in Public Schools: Cost-benefit Issues and Implications," In S. W. M. Laine and J. G. Ward (Eds.), *Using What We Know: A Review of the Research on Implementing Class-Size Reduction Initiatives for State and Local Policymakers* (Oak Brook, IL: North Central Regional Educational Laboratory, 2000), 5–19.

26.   Ehrenberg et al.

27.   Krueger.

28.   Nye, Hedges, and Konstantopoulos.

29.   For example, Witte.

30.   A. Molnar, P. Smith, and J. Zahorik, *1998–99 Evaluation results of the student achievement guarantee in education (SAGE) program* (Milwaukee: University of Wisconsin, School of Education, 1999).

      A. Molnar et al., *1999–00 Evaluation results of the student achievement guarantee in education (SAGE) program* (Milwaukee: University of Wisconsin, School of Education, 2000).

31.   Molnar et al.

      A. Molnar, P. Smith, et al., "Wisconsin's Student Achievement Guarantee in Education (SAGE) Class-Size Reduction Program: Achievement Effects, Teaching and Classroom Implications," in *How Small Classes Help Teachers Do Their Best*, eds. M. C. Wang and J. D. Finn (Philadelphia: Temple University Center for Research in Human Development and Education, and the U. S. Department of Education, 2000), 227–277.

      A. Molnar, P. Smith, J. Zahorik, et al., "Evaluating the SAGE Program: A Pilot Program in Targeted Pupil-Teacher Reduction in Wisconsin," *Educational Evaluation and Policy Analysis* 21, no. 2 (1999): 165–177.

32.   Witte.

      T. Hruz, *The Costs and Benefits of Smaller Classes in Wisconsin: A Further Evaluation of the SAGE Program.* Milwaukee: Wisconsin Policy Research Institute <http://www.wpri.org> (2000).

33.   R. Legler, "Implementing a Class-Size Reduction Policy: Barriers and Opportunities," in *Using What We Know: A Review of the Research on Implementing Class-Size Reduction Initiatives for State and Local Policymakers*, eds. S. W. M. Laine and J. G. Ward (Oak Brook, IL: North Central Regional Educational Laboratory, 2000), 75–83.

34.   P. Egelson, P. Harman, and C. M. Achilles, *Does Class Size Make a Difference? Recent Findings from State and District Initiatives* (Greensboro, NC: Southeast Regional Vision for Education, 1996).

C. M. Achilles, P. Harman, and P. Egelson, "Using Research Results on Class Size to Improve Pupil Achievement," *Research in the Schools* 2, no. 2 (1995): 23–30.

35.   CSR Research Consortium, *Class Size Reduction in California: The 1998–1999 Evaluation Findings* (Sacramento, CA: California State Department of Education, 2000).

G. W. Bohrnstedt, B. M. Stecher, and E. W. Wiley, "The California Class Size Reduction Evaluation: Lessons Learned," in *How Small Classes Help Teachers Do Their Best*, eds. M. C. Wang and J. D. Finn (Philadelphia: Temple University Center for Research in Human Development and Education, and the U. S. Department of Education, 2000), 201–226.

36.   B. Stecher et al., "Class-size Reduction in California. A Story of Hope, Promise, and Unintended Consequences," *Phi Delta Kappan* 82 (2001): 670–674.

37.   Council of the Great City Schools (CGCS), *Reducing Class Size. A Smart Way to Improve America's Urban Schools* (Washington, DC: CGCS, October 2000).

U. S. Department of Education, *The Class-Size Reduction Program: Boosting Student Achievement in Schools Across the Nation—A First-Year Report* (Jessup, MD: Editorial Publications, U. S. Department of Education, 2000).

38.   J. D. Finn and C. M. Achilles, "Tennessee's Class Size Study: Findings, Implications, Misconceptions," *Educational Evaluation and Policy Analysis* 21 (1999): 97–109.

39.   Finn, Gerber, Achilles, and Boyd-Zaharias.

40.   F. Mosteller, "The Tennessee Study of Class Size in the Early School Grades," *The Future of Children* 5, no. 2 (1995): 113–127.

D. C. Orlich, "Brown v. Board of Education: Time for a Reassessment," *Phi Delta Kappan* 72 (1991): 631–632.

41.   For example, the meeting of the American Academy of Arts and Sciences held in Boston in 1999 and others sponsored by the U. S. Department of Education.

42.   J. D. Finn, S. B. Gerber, and G. M. Pannozzo, *Evaluation of the Class Size Reduction Initiative, Buffalo Public Schools 1999–2000* (Buffalo, NY: State University of New York at Buffalo, August 2000).

43.   C. G. Arroyo and M. Martinez, *Building a Communication/Dissemination Network to Support Class Size Reduction.* Paper presented at the National Invitational Conference on Taking Small Classes One Step Further, Washington, DC, 30 November–1 December 2000.

44.   G. M. Pannozzo and J. D. Finn, *Professional Development and Support Needs of Beginning Teachers.* Paper presented at the National Invitational Conference on Taking Small Classes One Step Further, Washington, DC, 30 November–1 December 2000.

45.   Finn, Gerber, and Pannozzo.

C. M. Achilles, J. D. Finn, and H. Pate-Bain, *Base School Restructuring Efforts on Long-Term Experimental Evidence.* Paper presented at the annual meeting of the American Educational Research Association, Seattle, WA, April 2001.

L. Bland, *Evaluation of the Reduced-Ratio Program Final Report* (Fairfax, VA: Fairfax County Public Schools, Office of Program Evaluation, 1997).

C. Howley-Rowe, "Thompson Elementary School: A Case Report," in *How Small Classes Help Teachers Do Their Best*, eds. M. C. Wang and J. D. Finn (Philadelphia: Temple University Center for Research in Human Development and Education, and the U. S. Department of Education, 2000), 349–364.

46. Educational Research Service; Robinson; Glass and Smith.

47. M. Elliott, "School Finance and Opportunities to Learn: Does Money Well Spent Enhance Students' Achievement?" *Sociology of Education* 71 (1998): 223–245.

48. M. Boozer and C. Rouse, *Intraschool variation in class size: Patterns and implications* (Princeton, NJ: Princeton University Industrial Relations Section, Working Paper #344, June 1995).

49. Finn and Achilles.

50. J. R. Betts and J. L. Shkolnik, "The Behavioral Effects of Variations in Class Size: The Case of Math Teachers," *Educational Evaluation and Policy Analysis* 21 (1999): 193–214.

     J. King Rice, "The Impact of Class Size on Instructional Strategies and the Use of Time in High School Mathematics and Science Courses," *Educational Evaluation and Policy Analysis* 21, no. 2 (1999): 215–230.

51. Stecher et. al, 2001, is one exception, although the data from California are only suggestive at best.

52. Achilles; Finn, Fulton, Zaharias, and Nye; CSR Research Consortium.

53. J. M. Darley and B. Latane, "Bystander Intervention in Emergencies: Diffusion of Responsibility," *Journal of Personality and Social Psychology* 10 (1968): 202–214.

54. J. M. Levine and R. L. Moreland, "Group Socialization: Theory and Research," eds. W. Stroebe and M. Hewstone (Eds.), in *The European Review of Social Psychology* 5 (1994): 305–336.

     T. Postmes and R. Spears, "Deindividuation and Antinormative Behavior: A Meta-Analysis," *Psychological Bulletin* 123 (1998): 238–259.

55. E. A. Hanushek, *The Evidence on Class Size* (Rochester, NY: University of Rochester, W. Allen Wallis Institute of Political Economy, 1998).

56. Economic Policy Institute (EPI), *The Class Size Policy Debate. Working Paper No. 121* (Washington, DC: EPI, October 2000).

57. Finn and Achilles.

     C. M. Achilles and J. D. Finn, *The Varieties of Small Classes and Their Outcomes.* Paper presented at the National Invitational Conference on Taking Small Classes One Step Further, Washington, DC, 30 November–1 December 2000.

58. K. H. Miles, "Freeing Resources for Improving Schools: A Case Study of Teacher Allocation in Boston Public Schools," *Educational Evaluation and Policy Analysis* 17 (1995): 476–493.

     M. Boozer and C. Rouse, *Intraschool Variation in Class Size. Patterns and Implications. Working Paper No. 344*, Washington, DC: National Bureau of Economic Research, Industrial Relations Section, 1995, ERIC, ED 385 935.

59. Ehrenberg, Brewer, Gamoran, and Willms, 1. (Oddly, after making that point emphatically, the authors include a 12-page review of research on pupil-teacher ratios in their report, which is titled "Class Size and Student Achievement.")

60. A. B. Krueger, "An Economist's View of Class Size Research," in *How Small Classes Help Teachers Do Their Best*, eds. M. C. Wang and J. D. Finn (Philadel-

phia: Temple University Center for Research in Human Development and Education, and the U. S. Department of Education, 2000), 101.

61.   H. Wenglinsky, *A Policy Information Memorandum: The Effect of Class Size on Achievement. What the Research Says* <www.ets.org/research/pic/memorandum.html> (19 June 2001).

H. Wenglinsky, *When Money Matters: How Educational Expenditures Improve Student Performance and How They Don't, A policy Information Perspective* (Princeton, NJ: Policy Information Center, Educational Testing Service, 1997).

62.   L. V. Hedges, R. D. Laine, and R. Greenwald, "Does Money Matter? A Meta-Analysis of Studies of the Effects of Differential School Inputs on Student Outcomes," *Educational Researcher* 23 (1994), 5–14.

R. D. Laine, R. Greenwald, and L. V. Hedges, "Money Does Matter: A Research Synthesis of a New Universe of Education Production Function Studies," in *Where Does the Money Go? Resource Allocation in Elementary and Secondary Schools*, eds. L. O. Pincus and J. L. Wattenbarger (Thousand Oaks, CA: Corwin Press, 1995), 44–70.

63.   Krueger; Economic Policy Institute.

CHAPTER 3

SMALL SCHOOLS

Craig Howley
ERIC Clearinghouse on Rural Education and Small Schools

SUMMARY OF RESEARCH FINDINGS

Research on school size points to several conclusions about the benefits of smaller schools. Smaller school size has been associated with higher achievement under certain conditions. Smaller schools promote substantially improved equity in achievement among all students, and smaller schools may be especially important for disadvantaged students. Many US schools are too large to serve students well, while smaller schools, especially in impoverished communities, are widely needed. The evidence favoring the benefits of small schools, however, cannot be generalized to so-called "Schools Within Schools," which to date lack a substantial research base supporting the belief that they provide benefits equivalent to smaller schools.

RECOMMENDATIONS

Policy makers should:

- Find ways to sustain existing small schools, especially in impoverished rural and urban communities.
- Acknowledge an upper limit for school size, acknowledgment that means many schools should be much smaller than the upper limit.
- Not design, build, or sustain mega-schools serving upwards of 500 to 2,000 students, depending on educational level and grade-span configuration.

- Design, build, and sustain much smaller schools in impoverished districts or districts with a mixed social-class composition. In very poor communities, design, build, and sustain the smallest schools.
- Not oversell smaller schools. Operating smaller schools in impoverished communities is good policy, but it is not a "magic bullet."
- Not believe that mega-schools serving affluent areas are necessarily excellent or even very good. Most accountability schemes obscure this fact because they do not generally take socio-economic status into account.
- Recognize that smaller schools in impoverished settings accomplish miracles even when their test scores are about average.

Even though the study of school effects has been a major sociological enterprise over the past two decades, empirical analyses tend to slight structural variables such as size.[1]

Matters have changed a bit since Morgan and Alwin made their observation in 1980, and, today, despite a surprisingly thin research literature, "small schools" is a concept in danger of becoming a slogan. Because slogans can impede thoughtfulness, a critical assessment of the concept is now timely.

What are "small schools"? What do different authorities mean by "small schools"? Is there a difference between "small schools" as set off by quotation marks, and schools that just happen to be small?[2] What influence does school size exert on student achievement? What do we know? What don't we know? What relationship does school size bear to the achievement of poor children? What are the points of contention? Given our inevitably limited knowledge, what are the implications for practice?

"Small schools," in short, is not so simple a topic as it might seem at first glance. This review aims to convey both the complexities and the practical applicability of research on small schools. In particular, it seeks to present the *most substantive empirical* work as the best chance for understanding this complex issue.[3]

SMALL SCHOOLS RESEARCH

Effusive praise of small schools is easily found in the education literature these days. One of the most frequently cited syntheses, for instance, portrays small schools as superior on virtually all measures of concern.[4] Warrants for the conclusions drawn in that synthesis come from sources— magazine articles, evaluations of single projects, first-person narratives, and empirical studies (that is, actual research)—of widely varying quality, and readers are provided with no assessment of that quality. Similar reports abound.[5]

In contrast with such syntheses, this one gives most weight to studies that exhibit larger sample sizes, peer-reviewed publication, and, for one set of studies, state-level replications. Evaluations, syntheses, and anecdotal reports are used in the present review to support discussion of the focal studies. This review also takes note of the substantial number of unknowns in the area of small-schools research, and of related methodological differences in the focal studies.

Defining Small Schools

The first challenge is to examine what we really mean by "small schools." The best empirical literature has focused its efforts simply on school size.

Small schools exist everywhere, as a feature of the variability of school size. Some states, however, maintain proportionally more small schools—sometimes far more—than do others, but no agreement prevails, even among small-schools advocates, about what defines a small school. Small in rural Vermont is apt to differ sharply from small in Queens, New York, and high schools in rural Vermont are considerably larger than they are in rural Montana. This variability indicates that school size, more than class size, is an issue that requires research designs sensitive to within-state variability.[6]

In general, one can think of high schools enrolling 400 or fewer and K–8 or K–6 elementary schools enrolling 200 or fewer (on the basis of a 2:1 ratio with high schools) as small. The related positions taken in state-level policies are very wide, and all of them lack solid justification from the research literature, which has not examined possible threshold effects of size.[7]

In cities and suburbs, "small schools" has recently become a *reform movement*.[8] Rural communities, however, struggle to *maintain* small schools in the face of states' attempts to close them on business principles based on cheap inputs.[9] These differing interpretations have practical significance because confounding *new, reformist* small schools with *extant, traditional* small schools obscures the salient structural issues that are the actual object of most research related to small schools.

Norms of Size

In contrast to many nations, the U.S. Constitution is silent about the human right to education and leaves the provisions for schooling to the discretion of the various states. The geography, history, economics, politics, and cultures of the states differ considerably, and, in consequence, school size varies substantially from state to state.

For instance, the percentage of 9–12 high schools enrolling 400 or fewer students (a small school by most definitions) ranges from 81% in Montana to 0% (none) in Hawaii, Rhode Island, and Vermont.[10] Hawaii is also the state with the largest percentage of 9–12 high schools enrolling 1,000 or more students (92%). Though there is a relationship between the rural nature of a state and the proportion of small schools it maintains, the relationship is not strong. In comparison with the urban states of California (where 78% of the state's high schools enroll 1,000 or more students), Florida (84%), Hawaii (92%), and Maryland (76%), such urbanized states as Illinois, New Jersey, and Massachusetts have only about 40% of high schools enrolling 1,000 or more students.[11] In the District of Columbia, just 22% of all 9–12 high schools enroll this many students, whereas 28% of DC high schools enroll 400 or fewer students. Thus, DC maintains proportionately more small high schools than Vermont.

There is an apparent relationship between school and district size as well. States that have retained small districts are somewhat less likely to have created large high schools, all else being equal. The data for Hawaii—which is administered as a single district—make sense in this light: as a single huge district, it operates almost all high schools with 1,000 or more students and none with 400 or fewer.

Small Versus Smaller

Although many observers of the school size issue long for a uniform definition of small and large schools,[12] *smaller* and *larger* are by far the more useful terms, since, as suggested above, school size varies so dramatically by state.[13] Look within states, rather than across states, for useful comparisons. Vermont and California, for instance, confront dramatically different circumstances, and their *de facto* approaches to school size differ accordingly. In making within-state comparisons, however, size rank (students per grade in rank order) needs to be viewed in consideration of grade-span configuration, educational level, and locale (rural, suburban, urban). A small elementary school in Vermont will not be the same size as one in California.

Enrollment Per Grade as School Size

Why should the number of students a school enrolls be of much concern? In fact, it turns out that school size is not best represented as total enrollment. Surprisingly, exactly the same total enrollment can describe schools of quite different size. This assertion is counterintuitive, but consider a 9–12 school with 800 students and a 9th grade academy enrolling 800 students. Are they really the same size? What about a 6–8 middle school with 800 students and a K–2 primary school with 800 students? It is easy to see that the 9th grade academy is really larger than a four-year high school with the same enrollment. Because it is both the expectation of the public and a professional norm that elementary schools are smaller than middle or high schools, the K–2 school is also "larger" than a middle school with the same enrollment. Thus in each case, the latter school is larger than the former, though total enrollment is the same in all four schools.

For this reason, for both research and real-world action, *enrollment per grade* is a better metric of size than total enrollment. With this measure it's easy to see that a ninth-grade academy with 1,500 students is really four times as large as a 9–12 high school with exactly the same total enrollment, just as a K–2 school enrolling 800 students is at least three times the size of a K–8 school enrolling 800 students.

If policy makers can better appreciate the role of grade span configuration in determining school size, they can avoid the misconception that merely reducing total enrollment in a school (by building new schools with narrower grade span configurations, a national trend) necessarily constitutes a reduction in school size. More likely, this trend is resulting in larger schools.[14] Reconfiguring the grade spans of schools is a time-honored tradition in American education used to make schools larger, but it could also be used to make schools smaller.[15] For instance, imagine a district with 1,200 students in separate buildings that house Grades K–2, 3–5, and 6–8. Each school houses 400 students, or 133 students per grade. If, however, the same buildings were used to house three K–8 schools, the reconfigured schools would actually be *smaller* (400/9 = 44 students per grade). Creating smaller schools, then, is probably easier than most educators and policy makers seem to realize.[16] One research team has found substantial achievement benefits for smaller schools in impoverished communities, using this definition of size.[17]

The Upper Limits of Size

The notion that some size might be absolutely too large for a school is a comparatively recent development. Most of the 20th century was required to make schools as large as they are, and the emerging popular consensus on small schools probably reflects a widely held perception that schools have grown too large.[18] Authoritative *opinions* now exist about the upper limits of school size. Various authorities have given "informed judgments" about absolute upper limits of school size. Predictably, the opinions differ significantly. Howley[19] has advised 1,000 as the absolute upper limit for high schools and 500 as the absolute upper limit for K–8 or K–6 elementary schools. Tom Sergiovanni, on the other hand, believes that no school should enroll more than 300 students.[20] Deborah Meier clearly agrees.[21] Lawton concluded that fiscal studies point to an upper limit of 500 for a K–8 elementary school.[22] The bases of these opinions vary. Howley and Lawton claim a basis in different research literatures (student achievement and finance, respectively). Sergiovanni and Meier base their opinions on long and thoughtful practice.

Official policy has, however, also addressed the issue. Florida recently adopted legislation setting 900 as the upper limit for new high schools, 700 for new middle schools, and 500 for new elementary schools.[23] Hawaii, with the largest high schools in the nation,[24] adopted, and then scuttled, upper-limit legislation.[25] In a 1999 speech to the American Institute of Architects, former Secretary of Education Richard Riley suggested 600 as the upper limit for any school.[26] The Education Commission of the States opined that 1,000 was the boundary between "large" and "too large."[27] Finally, representing professional organizations, the National Association of Secondary School Principals proposed 600 as the upper limit for high schools.[28] Once again, all of these limits reflect the previously noted general public expectation and the professional norm that elementary schools require a lower size limit than middle or high schools.

To set an upper limit is to advise against the construction of schools larger than the limit. As has already been explained, however (see note 7), just because a school's enrollment falls under that limit does not necessarily make it small. This is an issue of logic and language, not of research findings.

Many schools, though not all, should probably be substantially smaller than the upper limits. Additional information—aside from "authoritative opinion"—is clearly needed to make good judgments about locally appropriate size: the findings from research summarized shortly suggest how much smaller they should be, at least for the purpose of maximizing the academic achievement of impoverished students.

The School Within a School

Because of the prevalence of the school-within-a-school (SWAS) strategy for coping with the organizational challenges of mega-schools, it's worth reiterating the structural view of size adopted here. A structural view recognizes that a whole system is more than the sum of its parts; if a structure is broken apart, the advantages of the *structural* whole vanish. On this view, larger schools that adopt administrative simulations of smallness are *unlikely* to exhibit the benefits of structurally smaller size. In fact, research evidence of the effectiveness of SWAS is negligible.[29]

Educators tend to believe that a practice proven effective in one setting can be transferred to another. This belief is the assumption behind "what works" and "validated programs." When, however, the practice itself and the setting (smaller school size) are one and the same, the assumption seems more especially dubious than usual. Can one transfer a setting out of its setting? It seems illogical. Unfortunately, educators' faith that processes can be effectively abstracted from the real structures that house them has popularized SWAS as a "small schools option." In fact, separate schools housed under a single roof need to be truly autonomous. Otherwise, they will not be small schools, but just another grouping stratagem.

School Size and Student Achievement: The Extant Literature

Despite widespread interest in small schools, few large-scale studies or replications have addressed the issue.[30] Certainly, a huge professional literature does address school size, (largely a result of the 20th-century push to build larger schools), but a surprisingly small proportion of this literature constitutes the research base, and even fewer studies jointly address the issues of school size and poverty as a major contemporary concern.

The ERIC database now indexes approximately 2,750 items with the terms "small schools" or "school size." Among this very large number of resources, however, just 47 research reports have addressed the relationship of achievement, school size, and poverty in some fashion between 1966 and 2001. More surprising still, only 23 research reports—during the whole period from 1966 to 2001—define school size, socioeconomic status, and student achievement as a major focus of investigation.[31] Within this surprisingly small literature, the studies that are conceptually related to the Matthew Project[32] are the only ones that pursue the issue systematically in multiple replications.[33]

Surprise at the thinness of the research base should be tempered by the realization that, until very recently, researchers, practitioners, and policy makers alike generally assumed that smaller schools, in general, must be academically *inferior* to larger ones, especially at the secondary level. Given this legacy, the early part of the research literature related to academic achievement and school size aimed to demonstrate that there was no significant difference between the achievement of larger and smaller schools, once statistical controls for socioeconomic status (SES) were imposed.[34] The previous literature had not deployed such controls.

Subsequent investigations, building on the work of Noah Friedkin and Juan Necochea,[35] suggested that the interaction between size and socioeconomic status may explain the apparent absence of a significant difference at the school and district level. Another line of investigation focused not on school- or district-level test scores, but on *student-level* gains, and concluded that smaller high schools had an advantage, regardless of SES.[36]

Selecting the Best Research

Three bodies of research, contributed by three different teams of researchers, represent the best empirical work done to date examining the influence of school size on academic performance with particular attention to poverty or socioeconomic status. The work done by these teams includes prominent peer-reviewed publication, quantitative methodologies, large-scale research designs, and various replications and quasi-replications. Issues of theory, method, and ability to generalize persist within this group of studies, and it would be wrong to say that all the evidence points to a single set of clearly demarcated conclusions. Nonetheless, after presenting the evidence, the author offers a practical interpretation of the accumulated evidence for policy and administrative action.

The three bodies of work are those by:

1)   Herbert Walberg and colleagues;[37]
2)   Valerie Lee and colleagues;[38] and
3)   Craig Howley and colleagues.[39]

The studies highlighted here all used some form of achievement test scores, not grades or GPA, as dependent variables. They all used some form of regression analysis to estimate the influence of size on achievement. The Walberg and Howley teams' studies analyzed test scores at the school and district level at single points in time. Lee and colleagues used individual students' test scores, computed as gain scores (achievement change over time) rather than scores from a single point in time.[40]

Despite many similar qualities, then, these three bodies of work address somewhat different issues (school and district performance in the case of the Howley and Walberg teams, and growth in student learning in the case of the Lee team) and deploy different ways of looking at the issues (different regression models, national versus state data sets, and substantially different theoretical models and research questions).

School Size, Academic Achievement, and Socioeconomic Status

Circumstances influence student achievement complexly, of course, and simply comparing achievement levels in smaller versus larger schools will often show that smaller schools have *lower* achievement levels than larger schools, simply because smaller schools are often located in poorer communities in many (not all) states.

Dealing Responsively with SES

Valid comparison across schools and districts requires *at least* that the direct influence of poverty be accounted for in some legitimate fashion, since poverty (or SES) is one of the major influences on achievement;

ignoring its well-documented influence is a mistake even worse than pre-suming that nothing can mitigate its influence.[41] The three major lines of research assessed here adopted two methods of accounting for SES: *controlling* for it (the usual method in educational studies) and theorizing about its particular *interaction* with school size.

Herbert Walberg and colleagues were among the first to control for SES in significant studies of the relationship school size and district size to achievement.[42] These studies, in effect, removed the influence of SES, leveling the playing field. Lee and Smith's studies controlled for the influence of SES in the same fashion as the Walberg team, but in a more complex fashion.[43] For both teams, the relevant SES control variables are, in effect, additional (additive) terms in a linear equation.[44]

In contrast to the Walberg and Lee teams, the Howley team adopted a specific school- and district-size theory originated by Noah Friedkin and Juan Necochea,[45] which multiply size and SES. Friedkin and Necochea viewed the size of both schools and districts as a structural feature presenting opportunities and constraints in the realization of student achievement.[46] They postulate that schools and districts differ in their capacity to realize opportunities and to overcome restraints. If this is the case, the effects of size should vary rather than (as is assumed in other studies) remaining constant across settings. The key question is what feature of settings might make such variation regular and predictable, rather than chaotic and unpredictable. Friedkin and Necochea observed:

> Studies of the distribution of public funds ... suggest that the power of a system to extract resources from its environment, the wealth of the environment from which a system draws its resources, and the priority accorded to the delivery of high quality services all are associated with the SES of a system's client population.[47]

Hypothetically, then, affluent communities would be in a good position to maximize the opportunities and minimize the constraints of size, but the reverse would hypothetically be true in impoverished communities. In this model, the interaction is realized as a multiplicative term in the equation. SES, then, is an environmental condition hypothetically capable of regulating the effects of school and district size.

The Walberg Team

The small-schools-are-good line of evidence has been under development since the early 1980s, particularly by University of Chicago researcher Herbert Walberg in collaboration with various associates.[48] Others contributing significantly to this line of evidence include Mark Fetler.[49] Although Fetler is not part of the Walberg team, his important study on this issue is considered here because its findings favor smaller size generally rather than differentially, and his unit of analysis is the school rather than individual students.

Walberg's investigations included a variety of influential variables such as various SES measures, expenditures, class size, teacher characteristics, and various measures of school and district size.[50] With SES controlled, the Walberg team's studies have focused on the influence of school and district size, using data sets from New Jersey.

As reported by Fowler and Walberg,[51] the influence of district size was several times as great as school size.[52] The significance of this body of work, on the whole, is that it rigorously and consistently identified school and district size as negative influences on achievement. The research established the possibility that smaller schools and districts were academically, and not just socially, advantageous regardless of SES.

In a study focusing on dropout rates, but using achievement as an independent variable, Fetler, working with data on California high schools, reported findings similar to those of Walberg and colleagues.[53] School enrollment in his study was negatively correlated to achievement without any controls for SES.[54] After controlling for size and SES, Fetler sought to determine whether schools with better aggregate achievement also exhibited higher dropout rates, which would suggest that the higher achievement was the result of lower-achieving students dropping out. His analysis showed the opposite: With SES and size controlled, higher achievement was actually associated with a lower dropout rate. This finding suggests that equity and excellence not only can be realized simultaneously but also might actually reinforce one another.[55]

The Lee Team

Lee and colleagues' principal interest was school restructuring, and included school size as one feature of interest, rather than as the key focus of research.[56] Whereas the Walberg and Howley teams studied only public schools, the Lee team's key study[57] also included Catholic schools and elite private schools, with sector an additional control variable. This body of work is based exclusively on data from the National Center for Education Statistics' National Educational Longitudinal Study of 1988 (NELS:88), and the focal study analyzes the individual achievement gains of students over the course of their time in high school.

Lee and Smith formed eight high school size categories.[58] Compared with students attending high schools of 1,201–1,500 students, those in schools enrolling 601–900 students, and those enrolling 901–1,200 students showed higher achievement gains. Students in the 301–600 student category performed somewhat better in reading and somewhat worse in mathematics than those in high schools of 1,201–1,500 students. Students in high schools enrolling fewer than 300 students performed significantly worse, however.[59]

Improvements in the *equity of achievement gains*,[60] however, were robust in high schools attended by NELS:88 students in the three smallest size categories. In other words, disparities in achievement gains based on SES were smallest in those categories of school. The improvement in the equity of gains in reading achievement was stronger than improvement in the equity of gains in math achievement and was highest in the 301–600 category.[61]

Lee and Smith derived these recommendations for policy makers:

1) many high schools should be smaller than they are;
2) high schools can be too small;
3) ideal size does not vary by type of student enrolled (i.e., low-SES or minority); and
4) size is more important in some types of schools, because disadvantaged students suffer disproportionate achievement costs in very large or very small schools.[62]

Overall, Lee and Smith concluded that a one-size-fits-all ideal size (600–901) was the best equity and excellence compromise. The next section of this review will take exception to some of these findings and recommendations.

The Howley Team

The author and his colleagues extended the Friedkin-Necochea theory and investigations to a series of state-level replication studies.[63] Like the Lee team, this team was concerned with both achievement excellence and equity. The studies, along with the original Friedkin and Necochea study in California in 1988, show that in affluent settings, the influence of school size on the excellence of student achievement (at the school and district level as measured with state-mandated tests) is positive, but in impoverished settings, the influence is negative. In other words, larger sizes are academically beneficial in affluent communities, but they are harmful in impoverished communities, producing a *differential excellence effect*.[64] In addition, as with the Lee studies, achievement equity was substantially enhanced in smaller schools (schools in each state were divided by the median size). Importantly, these findings apply equally to district size.

The strength of the differential excellence effects, however, varied markedly from state to state. For instance, predominately rural Montana maintains many small schools. The state showed weaker differential excellence effects, and generally higher achievement equity across the board, than did other states. The smaller half of schools in the state exhibited lower socioeconomic status than the larger, somewhat more affluent, half of schools.

Despite that difference, achievement equity was so high in Montana that the smaller half of schools exhibited *higher* achievement levels than the larger, more affluent half. Even with a reduced correlation of poverty and achievement across the board, however, equity was greatest in the smaller schools and districts in the state. At some grade levels within the smaller half of schools, the relationship between poverty and achievement was not statistically significant.[65]

Evidence of the differential excellence effect of school size was strong in California, Georgia, Ohio, West Virginia, and Texas. The Alaska study,[66] unlike the others, used student-level data and a host of control variables relevant to students, schools, and communities. But even with such extensive controls in place, the interaction between SES and school size remained a statistically significant influence on individual-level achievement.

Bickel and Howley extended the Matthew Project investigations to a multi-level analysis using their Georgia data set, and examining schools within districts.[67] The single-level Georgia analyses had not found a differential excellence effect at the district level. The multi-level study, however, found influences interacting in a variety of ways. Poverty at the school level, for instance, interacted with the overall size of a district. A number of other such interactions between multiple influences also were found. The multi-level study also discovered a remarkable pattern to equity results among four groups of schools, created by dividing schools and districts at the medians of school and district size.[68] Achievement was *least* equitable in larger schools in larger districts (many of these "larger districts" were rural countywide districts) and *most* equitable in smaller schools in smaller districts (some of which operated in urban locales). Smaller schools in larger districts were the second most *equitable* configuration, and larger schools in smaller districts were the second most *inequitable* configuration. In general this study showed that school- and district-level variables interacted complexly to influence achievement excellence and equity.

Critiquing the Best Research

Three consensus implications seem to lurk in this body of work:

1) smaller school size is associated with higher achievement under some conditions;
2) smaller schools promote substantially improved achievement equity; and
3) smaller schools may be especially important for disadvantaged students.

Without a broader critique of the limitations and the sharp differences among the works cited, however, translating these vague implications directly into practice is unwise.

The Walberg studies seemed to suggest that smaller schools and districts were universally more efficient and effective, but the findings pertain almost exclusively to New Jersey and are hardly generalizable to other states or to the nation as a whole. The norms of school and district size are quite different from state to state.[69] It's quite possible that replications in contrasting states would yield substantially different results.

Nonetheless, the studies of the Walberg team were among the first to suggest the possibility that smallness might harbor an achievement advantage, a hypothesis that had not previously been taken very seriously by prominent researchers.[70] The Walberg team's district-level findings have been almost entirely ignored, as have those of the Howley team.[71]

Lee and Smith analyzed a national data set (NELS:88), rather than state data sets, largely because their research questions focused not on school size, but on national efforts to sponsor school restructuring. Use of a national data set to study school size specifically is problematic if the state-level variations in the norms of size are not accounted for. This critique, in the author's view, compromises the external validity of the focal study.[72] Policy makers must regard claims about "ideal high school size" as unproven in the context of actual practice in the various states.[73]

The Howley team's studies, like the Walberg team's, focused not on student-level achievement but on school and district performance on a variety of state-mandated tests. The problem with such analyses, however, is that school- and district-level scores exhibit less variability than do individual-level scores. A complete model would examine individual-level achievement within classroom, school, district, and state contexts of size. This insight links the notion of the scaling of the educational system,[74] which has hardly been studied at all.[75] Bickel and Howley (by examining schools within districts) and Lee and Smith (by examining individuals within schools), however, have made a beginning with two-level analyses.

In essence, the Walberg, Lee, and Howley teams studied different phenomena using different methods. The Walberg team's work was exploratory and conducted in one state; the Lee team modeled gains in student achievement, but ignored variability in state contexts and imputed a dubious "ideal" size; the Howley team replicated the California work of Friedkin and Necochea in six additional states, providing support for the original theory about school and district size. Nonetheless, student-level variability is absent from this team's work, which is more relevant to policy than to instructional manipulations themselves.

What Remains Unknown

Much more is unknown than is known about school size, despite the popularity of the issue in current writing for practitioners and in state and national legislation (e.g., the Feinstein amendment to the ESEA reauthorization). In particular the author believes that assertions about "ideal size" are misleading abstractions, and that the school-within-schools strategy of simulating smallness has emerged with no basis in research to suggest that it will produce the achievement advantages confirmed for extant smaller schools operating under certain circumstances.

Several of the key unknowns have hardly been addressed in the research literature at all. In the author's judgment, the following unknowns merit substantial attention from scholars of schooling (with student achievement the dependent variable):

- To what extent do the popular but unresearched administrative simulations of smaller size (i.e., houses, pods, "academies" or other such within-school grouping arrangements) realize achievement advantages (including improvements in achievement equity) comparable to those reported for *actually small* schools?
- To what extent does "ideal size," as asserted by Lee and Smith, vary by state and under what conditions (type of locale, educational level, grade span configuration)?
- Do minimum and maximum size thresholds actually exist (and under what conditions—state, type of locale, educational level, grade span configuration), beyond which larger or smaller size magnifies the negative effects of poverty?[76]
- What is the relationship of grade span configuration to student learning, given differing state policy contexts and the likely influence of community socioeconomic status?
- What are the simultaneous and interacting relationships of class size, school size, district size, and state context to the achievement level (particularly achievement gains) of individual students with respect to SES? What are the relationships of these interacting contexts to school-level achievement equity?

Many, many other unanswered questions exist. For instance, *why* is smaller school size (variously defined) associated with higher and more equitable levels of achievement for individuals, schools, and districts? Hypotheses abound, with most having to do with the care, attention, and respect enabled by smallness in the conduct of personal relations. Links between achievement level and equity and such possible influences have hardly been investigated at all, however.[77]

SUMMARY AND RECOMMENDATIONS[78]

It would be an educational tragedy for current and future generations if, after a decade or so of experimentation with "small schools," policy makers were to conclude that "small schools don't work." The danger is real, however, because in the name of "small schools" as a reform tactic, there has been a tendency to confound schools-within-schools, established in the name of "small schools" reform, but which have not been seriously studied, with the school size research reviewed here. As a reform product, "small schools" has almost nothing to do with the extant research base on school size, and lacks a pertinent research base of its own.[79]

"Small schools" will become another fad unless approached thoughtfully in the realms of practice and policy. Research can supply some, but not even most, of the necessary thoughtfulness. Because so many small schools continue to exist, however, small schools are not principally a reform project, so far as the research into school size goes. Some schools are smaller than others, and some smaller schools are awful places. On average, though, smaller schools come out ahead of larger schools, but under certain conditions and not always.

Major Conclusions

Three overarching implications seem warranted across all the works cited:

1) Many US schools are too large to serve students well.
2) Smaller schools are widely needed.
3) Smaller schools are particularly valuable in impoverished communities.

Common to many literature reviews on this topic,[80] such implications have been translated into practical decision-making principles for policy makers by the author:[81]

- **Find ways to sustain existing small schools,** especially in impoverished rural and urban communities.
- **Acknowledge an upper limit for school size** (even though not confirmed by research), acknowledgment that means many schools should be much smaller than the upper limit.
- **Don't design, build, or sustain mega-schools** (serving upwards of 500 to 2,000 students depending on educational level and grade-span configuration).[82] Schools this large provide no detectable advantage

to affluent students (the elite New England private high schools, for instance, enroll about 1,000 students in grades 9–12) and probably do academic harm to impoverished students.

- **Design, build, and sustain much smaller schools in impoverished districts** or districts with a mixed social-class composition. In very poor communities, design, build, and sustain the smallest schools.[83]
- **Don't oversell smaller schools.** Like other schools, smaller schools can be wonderful or awful, but, all else equal, their odds of being awful are reduced as compared to larger schools. Operating smaller schools in impoverished communities is good policy, but it is not a "magic bullet."
- **Do not believe that mega-schools serving affluent areas are necessarily excellent or even very good.** Most accountability schemes obscure this fact because they do not generally take SES into account. Graduates of such schools, however, can articulate the problems: cliques, careerism, anti-intellectualism, de facto tracking, and so forth.[84]
- **Recognize that smaller schools in impoverished settings accomplish miracles even when test their scores are about average.** Such schools exhibit a very real but almost entirely unacknowledged degree of excellence, compared to which the vaunted "excellence" of large, well-funded suburban schools is more properly understood as mediocrity.

Increasing the Number of Smaller Schools

Three efforts need to be engaged simultaneously—retaining existing small schools in impoverished communities (especially necessary in rural communities), establishing new autonomous small schools in impoverished communities (especially necessary in urban communities), and helping struggling small schools to thrive. *Small* in this instance means high schools enrolling approximately 400 or fewer students, and elementary schools enrolling approximately 200 or fewer students. Recommendations for policy makers include the following:[85]

1) Provide capital outlay mechanisms not based on big-school norms.
2) Put an absolute enrollment cap of between 600 and 1,000 students on the size of new high schools and between 300 and 500 on the size of new elementary schools.[86]
3) In impoverished locales establish, sustain, and improve schools that are substantially smaller than the absolute upper limits.
4) Revise curriculum policies to implement small-school (rather than big-school) principles.

5) Implement a statewide salary scale (which helps stabilize staffing, with stable staffing a foundation of school improvement).[87]

Superintendents, principals, and teachers work in particular communities and schools, and, with this fact in mind, the author has offered the following counsel:[88]

1) Become better informed about the recent literature on small schools.
2) Take communities' desires to retain or to re-establish smaller schools seriously, and not as a symptom of sentimentality or as a wild pipe dream.
3) Engineer the political will locally to support smaller schools, if the district currently operates mega-schools, or if it serves either mixed-social-composition or impoverished communities. Engineering this political will is a lengthy process, and waiting to discuss the issue when construction funds materialize is dangerously reactive. Obviously, stable leadership is required.
4) Develop community purposes for smaller schools; smaller schools are most sustainable when levels of community engagement are high.[89]
5) Work with other administrators and with policy makers to facilitate appropriate policy changes (see above).
6) Regard claims made about "schools-within-schools" with great skepticism. Research on the variety of SWAS options does not exist, and this review regards claims about achievement-related benefits for "pods," "houses," and *non-autonomous* "schools" as unwarranted.

Surely it makes sense to reorganize mega-schools in the attempt to foil the anonymity and impersonality of bureaucratically oriented high schools. It is, however, not necessary to justify this move with reference to the school size literature related to student achievement; to do so misuses the literature and, worse, misrepresents the facts.

The best way to capture the achievement benefits of smaller size is to establish new smaller schools and to sustain and to exert effort to improve the ones already in existence. Schools everywhere need not be small—unless by "small" one means a school enrolling fewer than 1,000 students, the benchmark used in the Feinstein amendment. One thousand students, however, is a large school. Nothing in the empirically based research literature on school size and achievement suggests that academic benefits of any sort accrue in schools larger than this, even in schools serving a very affluent clientele.

REFERENCES AND NOTES

1. D. Morgan and D. Alwin, "When Less is More: School Size and Social Partic-ipation," *Social Psychology Quarterly* 43 (1980): 241–252.

2. This discussion will use the phrase *small schools* without quotes to indicate the entire realm of interest in smaller-scale schooling, but with an emphasis on schools rather than classrooms or school districts, though these features will receive consideration as required to examine the related issues.

3. Large-scale studies that produce generalizable findings are privileged in this synthesis.

4. K. Cotton, *Affective and Social Benefits of Small-Scale Schooling* (Charleston, WV: ERIC Clearinghouse on Rural Education and Small Schools, 1996), ERIC, ED 401088.

5. See, for example:

    K. Irmsher, *School Size* (Eugene, OR: ERIC Clearinghouse on Educational Management, 1997), ERIC, ED 414615.

    M. Klonsky, *Small Schools: The Numbers Tell a Story. A Review of Research and Current Experiences* (Chicago: Small Schools Workshop, 1995), ERIC, ED 386517.

6. A recent study confirms the policy importance of conducting state-level analyses of the relationship between school size and student achievement. Based on an innovative methodology that combines information from the National Assessment of Educational Progress (NAEP), state reading assess-ments, and the Schools and Staffing Survey (SASS) in 20 states, Donald McLaughlin and Gili Drori estimate that the relationship between *class size* and their experimental achievement measure is almost exclusively a *national-level phenomenon* (since the various states regulate class size rather stringently, within-state variation in class size is much less than between-state variation). The situation is different, however, with respect to *school size*. See:

    D. McLaughlin and G. Drori, *School-Level Correlates of Academic Achievement: Student Assessment Scores in SASS Public Schools* (Washington, DC: U.S. Department of Education, 2000), ERIC.

    McLaughlin and Drori report that school size varies more within than between states (Table 7, p. 42). McLaughlin and Drori, using national level data, and controlling for SES, concluded that a modest *positive* relationship existed between school size and their experimental achievement measure at the secondary level, but not at the elementary or middle school level. This finding stands in sharp contrast to the findings summarized in this review. In fact, however, Table 12 (p. 48) demonstrates that state by state regression coefficients of the experimental achievement measure regressed on school size vary between –.44 and +.99, a finding that is seemingly consistent with the interaction hypothesis that SES regulates the influence of size on achievement (see subsequent consideration of this approach in the main discussion). Findings from this study are pointedly deemed "tentative" due to its emphasis on methodological innovation. Indeed, the study is most useful as a pioneering attempt to separate within and between state variabil-ity in school size, class size, school climate and other supposed correlates of achievement.

7.   An exception is V. Lee and J. Smith, "High School Size: Which Works Best and for Whom?" *Educational Evaluation and Policy Analysis* 19, no. 3 (1997), 205–227.

Threshold effects are substantial changes in results associated with relatively modest changes in circumstances or conditions. Much of the opinion literature suggests dramatic differences in outcomes for large versus small schools, but fails to justify lines that might divide small from large. That gap in the empirical literature is one reason that this review advises readers to consider size in relatively (smaller and larger) rather than categorically (small versus large).

Studies have used 300 or 400 as cut points for small 9–12 high school for some time. See:

J. Conant, *The American High School Today: A First Report to Citizens* (New York: McGraw-Hill, 1959).

Elementary schools (K–8 or K–6) in the U.S. enroll about half so many students as high schools, and, therefore, if 400 defines the upper limit of "small" for high schools, 200 is a reasonable cut point for elementary schools. Oakland's new "Autonomous Small Schools" policy defines as "small" those schools with enrollments up to the following numbers of students: K–5—250; K–8—400; K–12—500; 6–8—400; 6–12—500; 9–12—400. See:

Oakland Unified School District, *New Small Autonomous Schools District Policy*, May 2000 <http://www.ousd.k12.ca.us/news/New_Schools/Revised _NSA_%20Policy.htm>.

The recently adopted Feinstein amendment to the reauthorized ESEA, which supports construction of "smaller schools," defines as small schools with enrollments less than the following maxima: K–5—500; 6–8—750; 9–12—1,500. See:

U.S. Senate Approves Feinstein Amendment to Build Smaller Schools, 12 June 2001, <http://feinstein.senate.gove/releases01/school_size_esea.html>.

The Feinstein limits are two to five times higher than those proposed by most authorities. See:

C. Howley, *Research on Smaller Schools: What Education Leaders Need to Know to Make Better Decisions*, (Arlington, VA: Educational Research Service, 2001).

They also stand in sharp contrast to the Oakland (CA) limits, which are more consistent with positions held by most researchers and small-schools advocates. In the author's view the Feinstein limits represent defensible *absolute upper limits of (large) size* rather than cutpoints between small and "not small." See:

C. Howley, "Dumbing Down by Sizing Up," *School Administrator* 54, no. 9 (1997): 24-26,28,30.

In fact, a 9–12 high school enrolling 1,400 students would be a *large* school according to the school size researchers cited in this review. Again, these figures are offered to readers as multiple reference points; the work to be considered in this review does not focus on smallness per se but on school size. For the very wide state-by-state variations of high school size, see:

Small High Schools That Flourish: Rural Context, Case Studies, and Resources, eds. C. Howley and H. Harmon (Charleston, WV: AEL, Inc., 2000).

Finally, state capital outlay mechanisms reportedly have widely set enrollment floors beneath which state funding for new construction is unavailable. According to Barbara Lawrence, for instance, Alabama will not fund K–6 schools enrolling fewer than 140 students or 9–12 high schools enrolling fewer than 240. Kentucky will not support construction of schools enrolling fewer than 300 (elementary), 400 (middle), or 500 (high schools) students. Ohio will not fund construction of any school enrolling fewer than 350 students (any level). North Carolina claims that "ideal" sizes for schools are 300–400 (elementary), 300–600 (middle), and 400–800 (high school). Tennessee will not fund schools enrolling fewer than 100 (middle) and 300 (high school). Virginia recommends the following sizes: 500–600 (elementary), 800–1200 (middle), and 1200–1500 (high school). West Virginia requires 50 students per grade at the elementary level (i.e., 1–6 minimum enrollment of 300) and 150 students per grade at the high school level (9–12 enrollment minimum of 600 students). By contrast, Nebraska will not fund construction of high schools enrolling fewer than 25 students, and the North Dakota high school minimum is 35. See:

> B. Lawrence, "Facilities minimum # of students," 23 June 2001, <facilities@lists.ruraledu.org>.

None of the positions referenced in the Lawrence report are solidly warranted by research. *Lower* limits of size are without any research justification at all, though the positions in Nebraska and North Dakota are clearly consistent with much current thinking about smaller school size. The Feinstein definition ("small" defined as fewer than 1,500 students) substantially exceeds the *upper* limits of size recommended in all recent reports known to this author. The intent of the Feinstein amendment, readers should realize, appears to be to prevent construction of mega-schools. For that purpose, 1,500 students seems a reasonable dividing line between "large school" and "mega-school." If 1,500 is accepted as the line dividing small from large, however, the likely result is to be the proliferation of large schools masquerading as small schools. Educators should avoid this form of self-deception.

8.   *Small Schools, Big Imaginations: A Creative Look at Urban Public Schools*, eds. M. Fine and J. Somerville, J. (Chicago: Cross City Campaign for Urban School Reform, 1998), ERIC, ED 427127.

Klonsky.

D. Meier, *The Power of Their Ideas: Lessons for American from a Small School in Harlem* (Boston: Beacon Press, 1995).

P. Wasley et al., *Small Schools, Great Strides: A Study of New Small Schools in Chicago* (New York: Bank Street College of Education, 2000).

9.   Howley and Harmon.

Only a few studies have conducted before- and after-consolidation comparisons. The general finding is that the desired cost benefits are not likely to be realized. See:

> T. Schwinden and L. Brannon, *School Reorganization in Montana: A Time for Decision* (Helena, MT: Montana School Boards Association, 1993).

J. Streifel, G. Foldsey, and D. Holman, "The Financial Effects of Consolidation," *Journal of Research in Rural Education* 7, no. 2 (1991), 13–20.

R. Valencia, *School Closures and Policy Issues (Policy Paper No. 84-C3)* (Stanford, CA: Institute for Research on Educational Finance and Governance, 1984), ERIC, ED 323040.

Astute observers agree that promises of monetary savings are exaggerations and that consolidation's real purpose is to reallocate expenditures away from funds required to maintain smaller units and toward other purposes. See, for instance:

> E. Cubberley, *Rural Life and Education: A Study of the Rural-School Problem as a Phase of the Rural-Life Problem* (New York: Houghton-Mifflin, 1915), ERIC, ED 392559.

> R. Dunn, *The Rural Education Dichotomy: Disadvantaged Systems and School Strengths*, 2000, <http://www.ncrel.org/policy/pubs/html/dichot.htm>.

10.   Howley and Harmon.

11.   Ibid.

12.   S. Lawton, "School Size, Cost, and Quality," *School Business Affairs*, November 1999, 19–21.

13.   National averages obscure the real dimensions of practice locally. The smallest public K–6 school in the US (in Nebraska) enrolled four students in 1997–1998, whereas the largest 9–12 high school (in Florida) enrolled about 5,160. See:

> National Center for Education Statistics, *Common Core of Data (CCD): School Years 1993–94 through 1997–98* (Washington, DC: U.S. Department of Education, Office of Educational Research and Improvement., 2000), CD-ROM, NCES 2000-370.

14.   One reason that schools continue to grow larger is that the people who plan them misunderstand the issue of school size. The author has worked with school systems whose leadership teams have planned consolidated elementary-level schools with narrow grade-span configurations (e.g., K–4 or 3–6) projected to enroll (in rural areas) between 1,000 and 2,000 students. Elementary schools of this size are mega-schools like the center city high schools enrolling 2,000 to 4,000 students and thought to be far too large to serve students well.

15.   A small literature is emerging on the relationship of student achievement to grade span configuration. See, for example:

> R. Bickel, C. Howley, T. Williams, and C. Glascock, "Will the Real 'Texas Miracle in Education Please Stand Up? Grade Span Configuration, Achievement, and Expenditure Per Pupil," *Education Policy Analysis Archives*, ERIC, ED 447995.

> B. Franklin and C. Glascock, "The Relationship Between Grade Configuration And Student Performance In Rural Schools," *Journal of Research in Rural Education* 14, no. 3 (1998): 149–153.

> D. Wihry, T. Coladarci, and C. Meadow, "Grade span and eighth-grade academic achievement: Evidence from a predominantly rural state," *Journal of Research in rural Education* 8, no. 2 (1992): 58–70.

Wihry and colleagues found that 8th grade student achievement in Maine was highest in K–8 schools as opposed to middle schools or 7–12 high schools. Franklin and Glascock found that 6th and 7th grade students performed better in K–12 schools, and high school achievement did not differ significantly as compared to other schools. Bickel and colleagues concluded that small K–12 schools in Texas not only helped mitigate the negative relationship between SES and achievement but were cost effective.

16.   In other words, bricks-and-mortar is not quite the impediment to creating smaller schools that it is usually made out to be. What really gets in the way of reconfiguring grade spans in this way? The way professional educators think about child development is a likely culprit. Narrower grade span configurations supposedly cater better to the "developmental needs" primary, elementary, and secondary students. In the example, the three narrowly configured schools house all students in the district, and they may be located on a single campus. Creating three K–8 schools on a single campus violates professional norms about "developmentally appropriate education" that are themselves the outcome of long struggle. Creating three K–8 schools would also be viewed as a slap in the face to the communities whose K–8 schools were originally closed to make the single-campus, more "developmentally appropriate" schools. In short, ideology, more than bricks-and-mortar, may be at stake.

17.   R. Bickel and C. Howley, "The Influence of Scale on Student Performance: A Multi-Level Extension of the Matthew Principle," *Education Policy Analysis Archives* 8, no. 22 (2000), <http://seamonkey.ed.asu.edu/epaa/v8n22.html.>.

18.   Howley, 2001.

19.   Howley, 1997; Howley, 2001.

20.   T. Sergiovanni, "Organizations or Communities? Changing the Metaphor Changes the Theory," *Educational Administration Quarterly* 30, no. 2 (1994): 214–226.

21.   Meier.

22.   Lawton.

23.   Rural Trust, "Busing hearings in West Virginia: Citizens tell their tales," *Rural Policy Matters*, February 2000, <Available online: http://www.ruralchallenge-policy.org/rpm/rpm.html>.

24.   Howley and Harmon.

25.   M. Raywid, "How do we downsize our schools?" October 2000, <http://www.ael.org/eric/scaletrn.htm>.

26.   R. Riley, "Schools as centers of community," 13 October 1999, <http://www.ed.gov/Speeches/10-1999/991013.html>.

27.   M. Fulton, *The ABC's of Investing in Student Performance* (Denver, CO: Education Commission of the States, 1996).

28.   National Association of Secondary School Principals and the Carnegie Foundation, *Breaking ranks: Changing an American institution* (Reston, VA: Author, 1996), ERIC, ED 393205.

29.   M. Raywid, personal communication (June 2001).

      V. Lee with J. Smith, *Restructuring High Schools For Equity And Excellence* (New York: Teachers College Press, 2001).

      SWAS is one strategy used to humanize large schools. Schools thus "humanized" may be newly built—designed around houses, pods, or one or several separately run "schools within the school." Lee with Smith notes "our own field-based research in five [urban] high schools divided into schools-within-schools has suggested that social stratification is a definite possibility with this reform." (p. 143)

      As a strategy to simulate smallness in a newly constructed and intentionally large school (a not uncommon contemporary scenario in rural areas), the simultaneous deployment of the SWAS stratagem should be viewed as cynical because research evidence of the effectiveness of SWAS in simulating the achievement advantage of small size is *negligible*. Even evaluation evidence on SWAS is much thinner than the school size research evidence reported in this review. Small schools—each with its own faculty, principal, unique curriculum and co-curriculum, and fiscal autonomy—can, of course, be housed under a single roof. This arrangement, however, is *much less common* than SWAS arrangements that more resemble grouping arrangements than they resemble autonomous schools with evident organizational integrity—i.e., all those things that make a school a "school". See Meier, 1995, for a very thoughtful consideration.

30.   Lee and Smith, 217.

31.   See, for instance, Bickel and Howley; Franklin and Glascock; and Lee and Smith.

The poverty-related portion of the search strategy used was "poverty OR disadvantaged OR socioeconomic status OR socioeconomic influence." From 1966–2001 31 ERIC resources were classified with indexing terms noted as *major* topics (descriptors so indicated) of the documents and as also being "research reports." Of these 31, 9 were either not *focused* on these three issues or represented a conference paper subsequently published in the journal literature (and which should therefore be considered a duplicate entry for this assessment). Of the remaining 22, just 10 were also published as journal articles. The search was illustrative rather than definitive: it did not retrieve all of the focal studies discussed in this review.

32.   Building on prior findings in Alaska, California, and West Virginia, the Matthew Project was particularly concerned to investigate the possible contributions of small size to academic success in impoverished communities regardless of rural, suburban, or urban locale. The Matthew Project, with funding (1997–1999) from the Rural School and Community Trust, investigated the Friedkin and Necochea hypothesis of possible equity and excellence effects of school and district size in Georgia, Montana, Ohio, and Texas. The project title refers to a parable about stewardship in the gospel according to Matthew (13:12); "For whosoever hath, to him shall be given, and he shall have more abundance: but whosoever hath not, from him shall be taken away even that he hath."

33.   Bickel and Howley.

N. Friedkin and J. Necochea, "School System Size and Performance: A Contingency Perspective," *Educational Evaluation and Policy Analysis* 10, no. 3 (1988): 237–249.

C. Howley, "Compounding Disadvantage: The Effects of School and District Size on Student Achievement in West Virginia," *Journal of Research in Rural Education* 12, no. 1 (1996): 25–32.

C. Howley, "Sizing Up Schooling: A West Virginia Analysis and Critique," *Dissertation Abstracts International (A)* 57, no. 3 (1996): 940.

C. Howley and R. Bickel, *The Matthew Project: National Report* (Randolph, VT: Rural School and Community Trust Policy Program, 1999), ERIC, ED 433174.

G. Huang and C. Howley, "Mitigating Disadvantage: Effects of Small-Scale Schooling on Student Achievement in Alaska," *Journal of Research in Rural Education* 9, no. 3 (1993): 137–149.

34.   Howley, *Sizing Up Schooling*.

35.   Friedkin and Necochea.

36.   See, for instance, Lee and Smith.

Not considered here are the wide claims made about the *general superiority* of small versus large schools on a host of input (e.g., cost, curriculum, faculty characteristics), process (e.g., faculty cohesion, student alienation, truancy), and output (e.g., self-esteem, postsecondary enrollment rates, postsecondary success) measures. Readers interested to assess such claims should consult the works cited in:

> M. Raywid, *Current Literature on Small Schools* (Charleston, WV: ERIC Clearinghouse on Rural Education and Small Schools, 1999), ERIC, ED 425049.

Irmsher.

Cotton, *Affective and Social Benefits of Small-Scale Schooling*.

K. Cotton, *School Size, School Climate, and Student Performance* (Close-Up No. 20) (Portland, OR: Northwest Regional Educational Laboratory, 1996), ERIC, ED 397476.

In the author's view, qualitative or mixed-method accounts of the experience of small-scale schooling (Meier; Wasley et al.) are a more appropriate source of insight into such disparate issues as faculty collegiality or cohesion, student self-actualization, and leadership than large-scale studies can ever be.

37.   W. Fowler, "What Do We Know About School Size? What Should We Know?" paper presented at the annual meeting of the American Educational Research Association, San Francisco, April 1992, ERIC, ED 347675.

W. Fowler and H. Walberg, "School Size, Characteristics, And Outcomes," *Educational Evaluation and Policy Analysis* 13, no. 2 (1991): 189–202.

H. Walberg, "District Size and Student Learning," *Education and Urban Society* 21, no. 2 (1989): 154–163.

H. Walberg and W. Fowler, "Expenditure and Size Efficiencies of Public School Districts," *Educational Researcher* 16, no. 7 (1987): 5–13.

H. Walberg and H. Walberg, "Losing Local Control," *Educational Researcher* 23, no. 5 (1994): 19–26.

38.   V. Lee and S. Loeb, "School Size in Chicago Elementary Schools: Effects on Teachers' Attitudes and Students' Achievement," *American Educational Research Journal* 37, no. 1 (2000): 3–31.

V. Lee and J. Smith, "Effects of School Restructuring on the Achievement and Engagement of Middle-Grade Students," *Sociology of Education* 66, no. 3 (1993): 164–187.

V. Lee and J. Smith, "Effects of High School Restructuring and Size on Early Gains in Achievement and Engagement," *Sociology of Education* 68, no. 3 (1995): 241–270.

Lee with Smith.

39.   R. Bickel, *School Size, Socioeconomic Status, and Achievement: A Georgia Replication of Inequity in Education* (Randolph, VT: Rural Challenge Policy Program, 1999), ERIC, ED 433985.

R. Bickel, *School Size, Socioeconomic Status, and Achievement: A Texas Replication of Inequity in Education,* (Randolph, VT: Rural Challenge Policy Program, 1999), ERIC, ED 433986.

Bickel and Howley.

Bickel, Howley, Glascock and Williams.

C. Howley, *The Matthew Project: State Report for Montana* (Randolph, VT: Rural Challenge Policy Program, 1999), ERIC, ED 433173.

C. Howley, *The Matthew Project: State Report for Ohio* (Randolph, VT: Rural Challenge Policy Program, 1999), ERIC, ED 433175.

C. Howley, *Compounding Disadvantage.*

C. Howley, *Sizing up Schooling.*

Huang & Howley.

40.   Differences in the unit of analysis and the definition of the dependent variable (achievement level in the Howley and Walberg teams' work and achievement gain in the Lee team's) make direct comparison of study findings inappropriate.

41.   Nearly everyone can agree that mitigating the *negative* influence of *poverty* is a public good. But what about mitigating the negative influence of SES overall? The question is worth asking because the notion that the *positive* influence of *affluence* on academic achievement is also unfair strikes many people as too politically radical a position, suggesting, as it does, that the negative influence of poverty is related to the positive influence of affluence. The fear seems to be that reducing the influence of SES overall may repress the academic competence of students from affluent backgrounds (an effect known since at least the 17th century as "leveling"). But this is not necessarily so. In the context of this concern, Mark Fetler's study is very important, as it shows that reduced dropout rates (in his California data) are associated with higher levels of achievement. See:

> M. Fetler, "School Dropout Rates, Academic Performance, Size, and Poverty: Correlates of Educational Reform," *Educational Evaluation and Policy Analysis* 11, no. 2 (1989): 109-116.

One should speculate that learning is not a "zero-sum game" and that productive synergies in healthy schools and districts can indeed improve the intellectual lot of students quite broadly. The Lee and Howley teams, as well, show a link between excellence and equity.

42.   Fowler and Walberg; Walberg; Walberg and Fowler; Walberg and Walberg.

43.   Lee and Smith used a two-level hierarchical linear model (students nested within schools) with student gain scores the dependent variable. SES controls are in place for both levels of the analyses in Lee and Smith (1997), which, for the purpose of this review, is the most seminal article in the Lee team series.

44.   Regression analysis predicts one variable ("dependent variable") from an assortment of other variables ("independent variables"). The equations take this general form: $z = ax + by + c$, which should be familiar to readers from their days in high school algebra classes. The studies described are all based on some variation of this basic equation. For the purposes of this review, z could represent predicted achievement, x could represent SES, and y could represent school size (a, b, and c would be constants that describe the slope and intercept of the equation). The variables *x* and *y* are the "independent variables" that predict achievement, *z*, with known degrees of strength and accuracy.

45.   Friedkin and Necochea.

46.   Size-related opportunities, according to Friedkin and Necochea's theory, are (1) economies of scale, (2) market domination (a sort of monopoly influence over funders), (3) benefits of size when funding is awarded on a percentage basis, and (4) ability to improve operations (talent, expertise, facilities). Size-related constraints include (1) problems of coordination and control, (2) factionalism among line personnel, (3) increased free-riding (deflection of resources to irrelevant functions), (4) administrative bloat (deflection of resources to administration), and (5) special program bloat (deflection of resources away from the mass of students and toward exceptional students).

47.   Friedkin and Necochea, 240.

48.   See, for example, Fowler and Walberg; Walberg; Walberg and Fowler.

49.   Fetler.

50.   Walberg and Fowler; Fowler and Walberg.

51.   Fowler and Walberg.

52.   In bivariate analyses, district enrollment reported in Walberg and Fowler, correlated between −.24 (third grade) and −.56 (ninth grade) with achievement. The regression coefficients of school size in the focal studies (Walberg & Fowler, 1987; Fowler & Walberg, 1991) remained negative and were the most influential variables after SES. The *net* magnitude of *school* size, however, was not great.

Beta weights (standardized regression coefficients) for school size varied between about −.05 and −.10 in Fowler and Walberg . This means that for every increase of one-standard deviation in school size—approximately 520 students—the average test score of a school would decrease by 1/20th to 1/10th of a standard deviation; e.g., a decrease of 1% passing the then-mandated New Jersey high school proficiency test in reading, for each additional 520 students enrolled in a high school (Beta = −.05). In fact, the influence of the *number of schools in the district* (a measure of district size) in most of the equations exerted a much stronger influence than did school size, a fact which received no comment in the discussion section of this article. In the case of the percentage passing the reading test, for instance, the strength of this influence was equivalent to an average 35% decrease in percent passing for each additional 14 schools in the district. Now, readers should understand that New Jersey maintains over 600 districts, ranging from very small rural-suburban districts to extremely large inner-city districts. Outlier districts were not removed from the analysis in Walberg (1991) and this fact may partially account for the strong influence of this measure of district size.

53.   Fetler.

54.   (r = −0.24). This is a somewhat lower correlation than prevailed in New Jersey, but still stronger than in many states, where bivariate correlations generally hover near zero.

55.   Fetler's results also suggest a kind of mediating role for size, though the use of achievement as an independent rather than a dependent variable would tend to obscure such a relationship, if it existed. Hypothetically, his findings are related to the work of the Howley and Lee teams, in which equity and excellence are cultivated simultaneously in smaller schools.

56.   This entire body of work—Lee & Smith, 1993, 1995, 1997—is summarized in Lee with Smith, 2001.

57.   Lee and Smith, 1997.

58.   In 300-student increments: <300, 301–600, 601–900, 901–1200, 1201–1500 (the category to which relative effects were compared), 1501–1800, 1801–2100, and >2100. Lee and Smith, 1997

59.   Effect sizes were approximately as follows (301–600: –0.1 in mathematics, +0.2 in reading; 601–900: +1.6 in mathematics, +0.6 in reading; 901–1200: +0.6 in mathematics, +0.4 in reading). Negative effect sizes in all other categories (except 1201–1500, the reference category, with effect sizes equated to zero) ranged from about –.03 to about –1.8.

60.   This concept refers to the comparative strength of the relationship between SES and achievement. A strong relationship is inequitable, and a weak relationship is more equitable. A statistically non-significant relationship (reported for some analyses in this line of research) is equitable by definition.

61.   Effect size of 3.2

62.   Lee and Smith, 1997

63.   Alaska (Huang and Howley); Georgia (Bickel, *School Size...Georgia*; Bickel and Howley); Ohio (Howley, *Matthew Project...Ohio*); Montana (Howley, *Matthew Project...Montana*); Texas (Bickel, *School Size...Texas*; Bickel, Howley, Glascock & Williams); West Virginia (Howley, *Compounding Disadvantage* and *Sizing Up Schooling*)

      The model was Friedkin and Necochea. Friedkin and Necochea, however, did not investigate equity effects of size.

64.   This concept refers to differences in achievement level associated with the interaction of SES and size. This line of research found that the effect of size is not constant, but changeable, depending on SES.

65.   The Montana system enrolls about 12% American Indian students, and predominately Indian schools were included in the data set.

66.   Huang and Howley.

67.   Bickel and Howley.

68.   The four categories follow: (1) larger schools in larger districts, (2) smaller schools in larger districts, (3) larger schools in smaller districts, and (4) smaller schools in smaller districts.

69.   For example, Howley and Harmon.

70.   With a few exceptions. See

      L. Baird, "Big School, Small School: A Critical Examination of the Hypothesis," *Journal of Educational Psychology* 60, no. 4 (1969): 253–260.

      James Coleman's famous *Equality of Educational Opportunity Report* was, circa 1966, among the first to report an overall negative correlation of school size and achievement, about r = –.10. See:

      Howley, *Compounding Disadvantage.*

71.   C. Howley, *School District Size and School Performance* (Charleston, WV: AEL, Inc., 2000), ERIC, ED 448961.

72.   Lee and Smith.

73.   To achieve the "ideal" high school size, many states would have to implement massive consolidations that (as in the Montana case) are not feasible

on account of terrain or population density, or, in fact, community prefer-
ence. The very notion of an ideal size derives conceptually from an abstrac-
tion (the nation as a whole) that has little bearing on the social institutions
and circumstances that have actually determined school size. Given the
shortcoming of national data sets for approaching the issues of school and
district size, the author advises educators to look skeptically on one-size-fits-
all prescriptions. Such prescriptions in educational matters seem remarkably unresponsive to the variety of lifeways and purposes that characterize
U.S. society. For a full discussion as related to schooling, see:

> S. Arons, *A short route to chaos: Conscience, community, and the reconstitution of
> American schooling* (Amherst, MA: University of Massachusetts Press, 1997).

The cultural tenor of the current era (postmodern or information-age)
rejects one-best solutions in favor of multiple perspectives.

74.   J. Guthrie, "Organizational Scale and School Success," *Educational Evalua-
      tion and Policy Analysis* 1, no. 1 (1979): 17–27.

      R. Slater, "Education Scale," *Education and Urban Society* 21, no. 2 (1989):
      207–217.

75.   R. Jewell, "School and School District Size Relationships," *Education and
      Urban Society* 21, no. 2 (1989): 140–153.

76.   See Bickel and Howley.

77.   See Fowler; Huang and Howley; and Lee and Loeb for related discussions.

78.   This discussion, in particular, relies heavily on a similar section in Howley,
      *Research on Smaller Schools: What Education Leaders Need to Know to Make Better
      Decisions.*

79.   This is so partly because the state-to-state variation of what might be consid-
      ered a small school is very wide, a variation that the author regards as prop-
      erly responsive to the local circumstances prevailing within states.

80.   See, for example, Cotton, *Affective and Social Benefits...* and *School Size, School
      Climate...*; Howley; Irmsher; Raywid.

81.   See Howley, 1997, 2001.

82.   Again, readers are cautioned to recognize that a K–2 school enrolling 500
      students is a very large school indeed; in comparison, a K–8 school of 500 is
      one-third the size.

83.   See Lee & Smith, 1997, for a tempering view.

84.   C. Howley, A. Howley, and E. Pendarvis, *Anti-intellectualism and Talent Devel-
      opment in American Schooling* (New York: Teachers College Press, 1995).

85.   Howley, 1997, 2001; Howley and Harmon.

86.   The danger with upper limits is that they are confused with "optimal" or
      "ideal" size. The point of the Feinstein legislation is to encourage the con-
      struction of schools smaller than these maxima. Readers should note well
      that these upper limits accord with many interpreters' views of the absolute
      upper limit of school size, *which means that these upper limits describe large, not
      small, schools.* In practice, many administrators may be tempted to build
      schools as large as the upper limits given in the Feinstein amendment in
      order to maximize both size and resources. Administrators are largely
      responsible for the construction of large schools and districts (see Howley,
      1997, 2001).

87.   Most of the research about educator salaries concerns salary level, rather than between-district differences (inequities). Inequities are theoretically important because of their probable influence on a district's organizational capacity to sustain improvement efforts. A few studies treat the issue of between-district differences tangentially, and just one (Beaudin) considers the issue directly (ERIC searches conducted by the author in October, 2001). In a Connecticut study, Beaudin found that districts filled 20% of vacancies with "migrants" from other districts. The migrants were younger and less experienced than the 80% of within-district hires, and they received larger salary increases as a result of "migrating." Disadvantaged districts lost more migrants than did advantaged districts. In general, it seems, wealthier and larger districts pay higher salaries than poorer and smaller districts (a hypothesis confirmed by Ready & Hart in an Ohio study). The issue of statewide salary equity is vastly under-researched and merits substantially more attention from researchers and policy makers. In the meantime, the recommendation given is based on logic, the small extant research base, and the counsel of superintendents of small districts interviewed by Howley and Harmon.

See: Howley and Harmon.

K. Ready and M. Hart, "Pattern Bargaining in Education," *Education Economics* 1, no. 3 (1993): 259–266.

B. Beaudin, *Teacher Interdistrict Migration: A Comparison of Teacher, Position, and District Characteristics for the 1992 and 1997 Cohorts.* Paper presented at the annual meeting of the American Educational Research Association, San Diego, CA, April 1998, ERIC, ED 422616.

88.   Howley.

89.   Howley and Harmon.

CHAPTER 4

TIME FOR SCHOOL: ITS DURATION AND ALLOCATION

Gene V Glass
Arizona State University

RESEARCH FINDINGS

Small marginal increases (10–15%) in the time allocated to schooling show no appreciable gains in student achievement. Alternative calendars on which the typical 180 days of schooling are offered (e.g., year-round calendars) show no increased benefits for student learning over the traditional 9-months-on/3-months-off calendar. Summer programs for at-risk students are probably effective, though more research is needed.

RECOMMENDATIONS

- Small—10–15%—increases in the time allocated for schooling would be expensive and would not be expected to produce appreciable gains in academic achievement.
- Furthermore, changes in the calendar by which those 180 days are delivered are very unlikely to yield higher levels of pupil achievement. In terms of pupil achievement, it matters not at all whether those 180 days are interrupted by one long recess or four short ones.

- There is no reason *not* to expect—but little research to support—that three months summer school would result in the same rate of academic progress as any three months of the traditional academic calendar.
- Within reason, the productivity of the schools is not a matter of the time allocated to them as much as it is a matter of how they use the time they already have.

On average, America's children spend six hours each weekday and 180 days each year in school between the ages of 5 and 18. Roughly 25% of school districts have longer school years, and another 25% spend fewer than 175 days in school.[1] The questions addressed here have to do with the duration of schooling (allocated time) within the yearly school calendar, and the arrangement of that school time throughout the year. Would adding hours to the school day or days to the school year increase the amount that students learn? Would rearranging a fixed number of days schooling within the school year produce greater academic achievement? These are the central questions around which this review is organized. It is important to note that this report examines *allocated time*—the total amount of time students are in school. One commonly discussed and very visible aspect of school time will not be addressed in this review, namely, *engaged time* or *academic learning time* or *time-on-task*. Of the many hours children spend in school, the majority of them do not involve attention to learning the intended curriculum. Berliner estimated that American students are actively engaged in learning for less than 40% of the time they are in school.[2]

We are here dealing with the question of the potential effect on academic achievement of increasing the length of the school day, or increasing the number of days of schooling during a calendar year, or both. In addition, the research on alternative yearly calendars will be reviewed to see what advice it might have for increasing achievement. Other options not investigated here involve the assignment of homework as a means of increasing students' learning time (this area has been thoroughly investigated by Walberg, Paschal and Weinstein[3] and more recently by Cooper[4]), or the rearrangement of a fixed amount of allocated time within the school day or week, as in block scheduling (see, for example, Cobb and Baker,[5] Veal and Schreiber[6]).

SCHOOL TIME RESEARCH

Allocated Time and Achievement

Attention to allocated time as an important factor in accounting for differences in academic achievement received a huge boost in 1974 with the publication of research by Wiley and Harnischfeger.[7] These authors published the results of secondary analyses of the Equality of Educational Opportunity[8] dataset that seemed to indicate that the amount of schooling a student receives is a powerful determinant of the degree to which that student achieves academically. Wiley and Harnischfeger (hereafter W&H) based their analysis and conclusions on a group of sixth-grade students in 40 elementary schools in Detroit, Michigan. They quantified the amount of schooling present in a particular school by combining measures of "average daily attendance," "days in the school year," and "hours in the school day." When W&H related quantity of schooling to achievement holding constant a school's socio-economic status (as measured by "percent white," "average-items-in-the-home," and "average number of siblings"), they discovered what they regarded as an impressive effect of quantity of schooling on achievement. Indeed, W&H christened quantity of schooling (allocated time) a "potent path for policy."[9]

The Wiley and Harnischfeger findings did not go long unchallenged, even by researchers who were quite sympathetic with W&H's conclusions. Karweit[10] worried that the number of schools in W&H's secondary analysis of the Coleman data was small (40) and that the effect of quantity of schooling only appeared for a subset of schools in the central city of Detroit. Moreover, the attempt to equate schools operating under very different circumstances by performing statistical adjustments on only three background variables, imperfectly measured, could well have left unaccounted for variability in the achievement data that might have been improperly attributed to quantity of schooling by W&H. The best corrective for these problems would be to attempt to replicate the effect on different data sets, each with its unique strengths and limitations. Karweit set out to do just that. Using the same Coleman EEO data set, Karweit analyzed the effect of quantity of schooling on achievement for schools in the inner city of Philadelphia, Milwaukee, Washington D.C., Cleveland, and Baltimore. In none of these instances was the W&H effect of quantity of schooling found. Next, Karweit conducted similar analyses using data for all schools in the state of Maryland. In this analysis, school-level test scores on the Iowa Test of Basic Skills (vocabulary, reading comprehension, mathematics and language) at Grades 3, 5, 7 and 9 served as the dependent variable and "percent in attendance" was used as the quantity of schooling variable, with background equating variables of "mother's education," "family income," "cognitive ability," and "percent disadvantaged." Again, no appreciable effect of variations of quantity of schooling on academic achievement was found. Still other analyses that Karweit performed failed to reveal the powerful effects that W&H had claimed. Karweit arrived, somewhat reluctantly it seemed, at the following conclusion: "Whether we use the school as the unit of analysis and incorporate quantity as a mediating variable, whether we examine central city or suburban schools, whether we control or do not control for ability, whether we use the individual as the unit of analysis, in no case do we obtain the sizeable effects reported by Wiley and Harnischfeger."[11]

The Wiley-Harnischfeger and Karweit exchange did not end the matter of allocated time and achievement for researchers. Subsequent studies tended to confirm Karweit's findings that there is little relationship between small marginal variations in allocated time for schooling and measured academic achievement.

Learning Curves

Smith[12] correlated allocated time and achievement in social studies for about 70 sixth-grade classes and found no statistically significant relationship ($r = 0.17$ for allocated time and achievement gain). Brown and Saks[13] employed data from the Beginning Teacher Evaluation Study to fit "learning curves" relating allocated time to achievement. Their analysis showed small relationships between the two variables. When curves were fit separately for high-ability and low-ability students, the latter showed a slightly stronger relationship between allocated time and achievement.

The list of researchers who have found no important relationship between the length of the school day or school year and the achievement of students is long; a partial roster would include Blai,[14] Borg,[15] Cotton and Savard,[16] Fredrick and Walberg,[17] Honzay,[18] Karweit,[19] Lomax and Cooley,[20] Mazzarella,[21] and Walberg and Tsai.[22] It must be noted, however, that in every instance, the variation in the amount of allocated time is not great. No one has asserted, and no researcher believes, that students attending school for 100 days a year will achieve at the same level as students who attend school for 200 days a year.

Costs and Benefits

Proposals to increase the length of the school year must be looked at in terms of cost and returns on such expenditures. Odden[23] estimated that extending the school day to eight hours or lengthening the school year from 180 to 200 days (marginal increases of 11% in allocated time) would cost the nation more than $20 billion yearly in 1980 dollars (or roughly $40 billion in year 2000 dollars). In a quantitative synthesis of the existing research on the relationship of allocated time to student achievement, Glass,[24] Levin and Glass,[25] and Levin, Glass and Meister[26] sought to relate the cost of increasing allocated time to the returns in terms of grade equivalent gains on standardized achievement tests. Their analyses, using the results of prior research, simulated the addition of one hour to each school day for an entire school year; this hour would be used equally for instruction in reading and mathematics (30 minutes each). This additional time represents increases of between 25% and 50%, depending on subject and grade level, in baseline allocated time for basic skills instruction. These authors estimated that such increases in allocated time would result in yearly increases in achievement of less than one month in grade-equivalent units (seven-tenths of a month in reading and three-tenths of a month in mathematics). Levin[27] suggested that increasing teacher salaries, hiring remedial specialists, or buying new equipment are all superior in cost-effectiveness to increasing allocated time. Levin, Glass and Meister[28] went on to compare the effects of a fixed financial investment in lengthening the school day with the effects of three other possible interventions intended to increase achievement in elementary school basic skills: computer-aided instruction, class-size reduction, and cross-age tutoring. Of these four interventions, increasing allocated time showed the smallest return per dollar spent. Levin and Tsang[29] supported this conclusion with analysis that drew upon economic theory; they concluded that large and costly increases in allocated time would be needed to effect even small increases in academic achievement.

International Comparisons

As has been pointed out, children in typical public schools in the U.S. attend school for six hours each weekday for 180 days a year. Some other industrialized countries, e.g., the United Kingdom, operate schools for up to eight hours a day for as many as 220 days a year. The sensational character of international comparisons of educational achievement has done much to obscure the issue of allocated time for schooling and mislead the public and policy makers. Stigler and Stevenson[30] attributed the superiority of Japanese students in mathematics to their longer school year. Barrett,[31] in a journalistic account of the duration of school years in various countries, claimed that the cause of the low performance, particularly at higher grades, of U.S. students in algebra, calculus, and science was the relatively short U.S. school year. Such international comparisons as TIMSS (Third International Mathematics and Science Study) are frequently read as supporting the conclusion that certain high-scoring nations, which have longer school years than the U.S., owe their superior status to the greater amounts of allocated time for teaching and learning. In most cases, the differences between allocated time in the U.S. and in other nations are small and statistically insignificant. But more important, the assessments of achievement are undertaken in such non-standardized ways as to render any conclusions suspect, or patently invalid.

Bracey forcefully criticized the attempt to base policy decisions about America's schools on the TIMSS data.[32] For example, consider the TIMSS assessment in science and mathematics. Although the U.S. ranks relatively high in achievement at Grade 8, most public attention focuses on the poor performance of the U.S. at "Grade 12." When this poor standing is linked—rhetorically, not scientifically—to the relatively short U.S. school year, bad research is compounded by being invoked as the basis for bad policy recommendations. There are so many circumstances, particularly at the Grade 12 level, that differ among nations that little credibility is warranted for the TIMSS findings. For example, although the TIMSS assessment ostensibly assesses students in the "last year" of high school, the meaning of the "last year" differs from country to country, enrolling 19 year-olds in one nation and 17 year-olds in another; the U.S. high-school seniors are among the youngest assessed. The U.S. students were among a small minority of nations which chose to disallow the use of calculators on the TIMMS test. And to make matters worse, the U.S. is the only TIMSS assessment site in which most instruction is not in the metric system, although the TIMSS tests use only the metric system where measurements are involved. U.S. seniors score relatively low in international assessments of educational achievement, and they spend relatively fewer days in school during the year; but there are many other factors that intervene in this relationship, and the conclusion that small marginal increases in the length of the school year would lead to greater achievement is not warranted.

Conclusion Regarding Increasing Allocated Time and Student Achievement

The import of a couple of decades of research on the effect on student achievement of small, marginal increases in the amount of time allocated to schooling is clear. Such increases have virtually no benefits for student achievement, and what small benefits there might be would not be justified by the increased cost of small increases in the length of the school day or the number of days per school year. This conclusion has a counter-intuitive ring to it: if any amount of schooling is effective—as it surely must be, or else unschooled children would achieve at levels equal to their schooled counterparts—then why shouldn't more schooling be better? The answer probably lies in the intricacies of curriculum development and the organization of instruction. Virtually all of the research on allocated time for schooling has studied natural variation in the length of the school year and small differences therein. It is unlikely that an increase in the length of the school year of a few days (five or ten, for example) would prompt any important changes in the school curriculum. Most likely, teachers used the same textbooks and activities in the lengthened school year that they used in the shorter school year; more reviewing likely took place, and so on. Before major changes in curriculum and instruction take place, significant increases in the length of the school year would have to be attempted.

Changing the School Calendar (Year-Round Schools)

Given that increasing allocated time would likely yield small, insignificant increases in student achievement, are there ways of arranging the 180 days in the typical school year to promote greater academic achievement? Of all those ways of organizing a fixed amount of allocated time, only the proposals to deliver schooling on a "year-round" basis (equally spaced with intermittent vacations across twelve months) have gained much of a following among educators. Significantly, the original proposals to operate year-round schools (YRS) came from a consideration of the economics of school construction rather than any consideration of learning gains.

In year-round schools, as in traditional 9-month schools, students attend classes about 180 days spread throughout the twelve calendar months. Typically, the student body is divided into three, four or five groups; school year starting dates are staggered so that at any one time, between one-third and one-fifth of the students are on vacation. In the most popular year-round schedule, the 45–15 plan, four groups of students attend school for forty-five days, or about nine weeks, and then have fifteen days off. Building capacity can be increased 25% because one-quarter of the student body is always on vacation. The 45–15 plan is the most popular year-round attendance plan because all students have a summer vacation, even if it is shorter than the traditional 3-month summer recess of the 9-month/3-month calendar. It is not, however, favored by high schools because the short, three-week vacations limit summer job opportunities. In the Concept 6 year-round plan, the calendar year is divided into six 2-month blocks. The students, in three tracks, have classes for four consecutive months and then a vacation for two months. Concept 6 can accommodate a one-third increase in enrollment. Because the students attend two 4-month terms a year, the administrative burdens of scheduling classes and recording grades are not as heavy as in the 45–15 plan. One-third of the students will have no summer vacation at all; in areas with great seasonal temperature variations, this track will be unpopular. Concept 6, then, can meet with a great deal of community resistance when the students' tracks are mandated and not freely chosen.

Another year-round schedule is the quinmester. Five 45-day terms, or quins, make up the year; students attend four of the five quins. In some districts, the fifth quin is optional; students who desire acceleration or enrichment, or who need remediation, attend all five terms. Obviously, if many students take advantage of this option, the district does not save money, because the enrollment remains the same as in traditional schools. There are many other year-round schedules, such as the trimester or quarter systems. The rationale for most, however, is the same: to avoid construction of new schools by increasing enrollment at existing schools.

Determining which of the claimed advantages are in fact true requires a look at what has actually happened in year-round schools.

Do Year-Round Schools Improve Academic Achievement?

Year-round schools are principally a cost-cutting measure. Their success in reaching this goal and the many advantages and disadvantages that ensue from the change to a year-round calendar are the subject of some published policy studies.[33] But the subject of this review is the potential benefits to learning and achievement of converting schools on conventional 9-month/3-month calendars to year-round calendars.

Proponents of the year-round calendar claim several advantages:

1) Students retain more over shorter vacations.
2) Learning proceeds via the psychologically more effective "distributed" rather than "massed practice" schedule.
3) Teachers spend less time reviewing previously learned material because of less forgetting during shorter vacations.
4) Because breaks will be more frequent, teachers experience less burnout.

Dempster[34] argued, in support of calendars such as the 45–15 year-round calendar, that spaced (or "distributed") practice over several sessions is superior to the same amount of time concentrated into a single study session. These arguments often rely on data drawn from laboratory experiments where subjects memorize nonsense syllables or perform other non-meaningful tasks. The relevance of these studies to actual classroom practice is questionable.

Cherry Creek District 5 in the state of Colorado implemented year-round schools in 1974. After one year, student achievement in three year-round schools was compared to achievement in traditional calendar schools. Differences between standardized test scores in the two types of schools were found to be insignificantly small even after matching pupils on IQ. Similar findings are reported for other year-round programs in Colorado and across the country. For example, examination of three years of standardized test scores for Mesa County Valley School District (CO) indicates that the year-round schedule does not in any way enhance learning. A closer look at the Mesa County (CO) study reveals a pattern common in research on the academic benefits of the year-round calendar. In 1982, Chatfield Elementary School of the Mesa County Valley School District was converted from the conventional school calendar to the 45–15 year-round calendar. George and Glass[35] collected the SRA Achievement Test battery scores for all students at Chatfield who were tested in the spring of 1981 (before conversion to the year-round schedule) and again in the spring of

1982 (after one year on the year-round calendar). As a control, the district-wide SRA test scores were collected at the same two points in time; district averages were calculated after removing the scores of the Chatfield pupils. The results appear in the following table:

Table 4–1.   Average Percentile Gain (1981 to 1982) for Chatfield (YRS) and District-wide Pupils

	Reading	*Mathematics*	*Language*
Chatfield (YRS)	+3%	+5%	+1%
District-wide	–3%	+3%	+2%

These gains are statistically insignificant and should not be "over interpreted." They indicate no superiority of one calendar over the other. They are indistinguishable from the kinds of yearly variation that all schools and school districts experience normally.

Many teachers and parents who favor year-round schedules believe that students learn more and faster when the learning process is interrupted for only short periods of time, as it is on the 45–15 plan. Even in Concept 6 schools as in Colorado Springs, Colo., the most teachers in year-round schools rated their pupils' vacation learning loss as less severe than in traditional schools.[36] Smith and Glass[37] attempted to substantiate teachers' perceptions in Colorado's Cherry Creek District 5. They found that although teachers in year-round schools spent less time reviewing pre-vacation material than teachers in schools on the traditional calendar, the actual achievement differences were insignificant on tests designed specifically to measure district objectives.

Other YRS Studies

The early findings in Colorado were replicated across the U.S. when researchers sought to compare achievement of students in YRS with their counterparts in schools on the traditional 9-month/3-month calendar. Several studies—by Naylor,[38] Zykowski,[39] Carriedo and Goren[40]—reached the conclusion that there is no significant difference in achievement between students in YRS and students in traditional calendar schools. Campbell[41] reported finding no significant achievement benefits due to year-round schools when compared with the traditional 9-month/3-month calendar in several Texas elementary schools. Webster and Nyberg[42] concluded that no evidence existed for the superiority of the year-round calendar at the secondary school level: "There appear to be no trends in any of the districts describing either improvements or decline in standardized achievement test scores as measured by district-administered tests and the California Assessment Program. Further evidence produced from interviews and a

review of evaluation reports from Los Angeles Unified School District confirm that the impact of year-round education on achievement scores at the
high school level has been inconclusive."[43]

In a journalistic report on practitioners' assessments of the learning
benefits of the year-round calendar, Harp[44] cited the experiences of administrators in several states to the effect that the year-round calendar
appeared to have no appreciable benefits for academic learning. For
instance, Dr. N. Brekke, a Superintendent of Schools in Oxnard, reported
that 17 years of the year-round calendar failed to raise students' achievement to the California state average. Harp quoted administrators in
Orange County, Florida, as saying that "many of the benefits associated
with the year-round schedule have been more perceived than realized...
people want you to prove that test scores are going up, but that's a very difficult thing to do."[45]

Not all studies have failed to find achievement advantages for the year-
round calendar. Those that do claim advantages, however, stem disproportionately from an advocacy organization that has grown up around this
issue: the National Association for Year-Round Education (www.nayre.org).
(Institutional memberships range from $350 to $750 per year depending
on the number of students that a school or school district has enrolled in
year-round education.) NAYRE publishes its own research reports, and
avoids established peer-reviewed scholarly journals; copies of research
reports outlining the benefits of the year-round calendar sell for about $30.
"Negative" studies have tended to come from researchers working in uni-
versities.

The "Summer Forgetting" Argument for YRS

A primary argument in favor of YRS is that the long summer vacation of
the 9-month/3-month calendar causes a large negative effect on student
achievement. Allinder et al.[46] studied the summer break "forgetting" phenomenon for Grades 2 through 5. They found statistically significant losses
in spelling, but not in mathematics, at Grades 2 and 3; they also found
losses in mathematics, but not in spelling, for Grades 4 and 5.

Tilley, Cox, and Staybrook[47] studied summer regression in achievement
for students receiving no educational services for three months. They
found that most students experience some regression during the summer
recess. Cooper et al.[48] reviewed 39 such studies and found that achievement
test scores do indeed decline over the summer vacation. Their meta-analysis revealed that the summer loss equaled about one month on a grade-
level equivalent scale, or one tenth of a standard deviation relative to
spring test scores. The effect of summer break was more detrimental for
math than for reading and most detrimental for math computation and
spelling. Also, middle-class students appeared to gain on grade-level equiv-

alent reading recognition tests over summer while lower-class students lost on them. Possible explanations for the findings included the differential availability of opportunities to practice different academic material over summer (reading is much more easily practiced than mathematics) and differences in the material's susceptibility to forgetting (factual knowledge is more easily forgotten than conceptual knowledge).

Both the Allinder *et al.* and the Cooper meta-analysis of the summer forgetting phenomenon place estimates on the loss of achievement over the traditional 3-month vacation that are smaller than many expected. This may in part help explain why the YRS calendar does not produce the dramatic effects on achievement that some hoped to see.

Year-round schools can accomplish their principal goal of saving money by avoiding construction of new buildings. However, there is no credible evidence that the year-round calendar causes improved academic achievement. How is it, then, that an idea whose benefits have eluded all objective attempts to discover them nonetheless engenders enthusiasm and loyalty to such a degree that it has its own national organization? Perhaps the answer lies in the problems administrators have "selling" the idea of YRS to parents and teachers. YRS calendars can disrupt family life, including vacation schedules and traditional summer activities (baseball leagues, camping programs and the like). These problems can be particularly severe when one child in a family is on a year-round calendar and another attends school on a traditional calendar. Convincing parents that the inconveniences caused by the year-round calendar are worth the trouble is a task that falls to school principals. One argument used to make the case for conversion is that the year-round calendar is much superior to the traditional calendar in terms of academic learning. Unfortunately, this position lacks empirical support.

The Extended School Year

Of course, the obvious antidote to summer forgetting is to extend the school year throughout the summer. Without thinking much about it, parents in surveys give strong support (85%) to the idea that students who fail to meet academic standards should attend summer school.[49] Such an extension for all students would represent an astronomical increase in the cost of schooling in the U.S.—on the order of $80 billion in current dollars. No such proposals have been seriously advanced and no research exists to suggest the potential returns in terms of academic achievement. "Extended school year" proposals have been limited almost entirely to services for handicapped or disabled students.[50] Heyns's analysis of summer programs for at-risk students in Atlanta schools revealed gains in academic achievement, but at rates considerably slower than during the regular academic year.[51] The absence of research on the effectiveness of extending schooling through the summer months should not deter reasonable judgments of the potential success of such proposals, however. The elements in the successful delivery of schooling are not mysterious, after all. Well-trained and experienced teachers, good curriculum materials, adequate physical facilities—these ingredients in combination succeed day-in and day-out in teaching our nation's children. There is no reason to believe that the continuation with a high-quality program of the 9-month school year throughout the three months of the traditional summer recess would result in any less academic achievement than is observed during the regular school year. Cooper and his colleagues[52] have based their recommendations for quality summer school programs on a meta-analysis of the literature.

The absence of a relationship between small marginal increases in the length of the school year or the school day throughout the year must not be extrapolated to reach the conclusion that significant increases in allocated time for schooling (such as three months' instruction throughout the summer) would not result in significant increases in academic achievement.

RECOMMENDATIONS

The research conducted on time allocated for schooling yields three broad conclusions:

- Small—10–15%—increases in the time allocated for schooling would be expensive and would not be expected to produce appreciable gains in academic achievement.
- Furthermore, changes in the calendar by which those 180 days are delivered are very unlikely to yield higher levels of pupil achievement. To paraphrase a famous poet, "180 days is 180 days is 180 days." And, at least in terms of pupil achievement, it matters not at all whether those 180 days are interrupted by one long recess or four short ones.
- There is no reason *not* to expect—but little research to support—that three months summer school would result in the same rate of academic progress as any three months of the traditional academic calendar.

Within reason, the productivity of the schools is not a matter of the time allocated to them. Rather it is a matter of how they use the time they already have.

REFERENCES

1. G. Cawelti and J. Adkinsson, "ASCD study reveals elementary school time allocations for subject areas: other trends noted," *ASCD Curriculum Update*, April 1985, 1–10.

2. D. C. Berliner, "The half-full glass: A review of research on teaching," in *Using What We Know About Teaching*, ed. P. L. Hosford (Alexandria, VA: Association for Supervision and Curriculum Development, 1984), 51–77.

3. H. J. Walberg, R. A. Paschal and T. Weinstein, "Homework's powerful effects on learning," *Educational Leadership* 4, no. 27 (1985): 76–79.

4. H. Cooper, "Synthesis of research on homework," *Educational Leadership* 46 (November 1989): 85–91.

5. R. B. Cobb, S. Abate and D. Baker, "Effects on students of a 4 X 4 junior high school block scheduling program," *Education Policy Analysis Archives* 7, no. 3 (1999): <http://epaa.asu.edu/epaa/v7n3.html>.

6. W. R. Veal and J. Schreiber, "Block scheduling effects on a state mandated test of basic skills," *Education Policy Analysis Archives* 7, no. 29 (1999): <http://epaa.asu.edu/epaa/v7n29.html>.

7. D. E. Wiley and A. Harnischfeger, "Explosion of a myth: Quantity of schooling and exposure to instruction, major educational vehicles," *Educational Researcher* 3 (April 1974): 7– 12.

8. J. S. Coleman et al., *Equality of educational opportunity.* (Washington, DC: U.S. Government Printing Office, 1966).

9. D. E. Wiley and A. Harnischfeger, "Another hour, another day: Quantity of schooling, a potent path for policy," *Studies of Educative Processes, Report No. 3* (University of Chicago, 1973).

10. N. Karweit, "Quantity of schooling: A major educational factor?" *Educational Researcher* 5 (February 1976): 15–17.

    N. Karweit, "A reanalysis of the effect of quantity of schooling on achievement" *Sociology of Education* 49 (1976): 236–246.

11. N. Karweit, *Quantity of Schooling*, 17.

12. N. M. Smith, "Allocation of time and achievement in elementary social studies," *Journal of Educational Research* 72 (1979): 231–236.

13. B. W. Brown and D. H. Saks, "Measuring the effects of instructional time on student learning: Evidence from the Beginning Teacher Evaluation Study," *American Journal of Education* 94 (1986): 480–500.

14. B. Blai, "Educational reform: It's about 'time,'" *The Clearing House* 60 (1986): 38–40.

15. W. R. Borg, "Time and school learning," In *Time to Learn*, eds. Denham, C. and Lieberman, A. (Washington, DC: National Institute of Education, 1980).

16. K. Cotton and W. G. Savard, "Time factors in learning," (Portland, OR: Northwest Regional Educational Laboratory, 1981), ERIC, ED 214706.

17. W. C. Fredrick and H. J. Walberg, "Learning as a function of time," *Journal of Educational Research* 73 (1980): 183–194.

18. A. Honzay, "More is not necessarily better," *Educational Research Quarterly* 11 (1986–1987): 2–6.

19.   N. Karweit, "Should we lengthen the school term?" *Educational Researcher* 14 (1985): 9–15.

20.   R. G. Lomax and W. W. Cooley, *The student achievement-instructional time relationship* (Pittsburgh, PA: Learning Research and Development Center, University of Pittsburgh, 1979), ERIC, ED 179598.

21.   J. A. Mazzarella, "Longer day, longer year: Will they make a difference?" *Principal* 63, no. 1 (1984): 14–20.

22.   H. J. Walberg and S. Tsai, "Reading achievement and diminishing returns to time," *Journal of Educational Psychology* 76, no. 4 (1984): 442–451.

23.   A. Odden, "School finance reform: Past, present and future," *Issuegram #26* (Denver, CO: Education Commission of the States, 1983).

24.   G. V Glass, "A meta-analysis of effectiveness of four educational interventions," *IFG Project Paper* (Stanford, CA: Stanford University, Institute for Research on Educational Finance and Governance, 1984).

25.   H. M. Levin and G. V. Glass, "Cost-effectiveness of Computer Assisted Instruction," *Evaluation Review* 11 (1987): 50–72.

26.   H. M. Levin, G. V. Glass and G. R. Meister, "Different approaches to improving performance at school," *Zeitschrift für Internationale Erziehungs und Sozial Wissenschaftliche Forschung* 3 (1987): 156–176.

27.   H. M. Levin, "Length of school day and year," *ERS Bulletin* 11 (December 1983): 8.

28.   H. M. Levin, Glass, G.V., and Meister, G.R.

29.   H. M. Levin and M. C. Tsang, "The economics of student time," *Economics of Education Review* 6 (1987): 357–364.

30.   J. W. Stigler and H. W. Stevenson, "How Asian teachers polish each lesson to perfection," *American Educator* 15, no. 1 (1991): 12–20, 43–47.

31.   M. J. Barrett, "The case for more school days," *The Atlantic Monthly*, November 1990, 78–106.

32.   G. W. Bracey, "The TIMSS final year study and report: A critique," *Educational Researcher* 29, no. 4 (2000): 4–10.

33.   A. Kreitzer and G. V. Glass, "Policy considerations in conversion to year-round schools," *New Brunswick Educational Administrator* 19 (April 1990): 1–5.

      Sol H. Pelavin, "A study of Year-round Schools," *Volume I: Final Report* (Menlo Park, CA: Stanford Research Institute, 1979).

34.   F. N. Dempster, "Synthesis of research on reviews and tests," *Educational Leadership* 48, no. 7 (1991): 71–76.

35.   C. George and G. V. Glass, *Evaluation Report on the Mesa County Valley School District Year-Round School Program* (Boulder, CO: Laboratory of Educational Research, University of Colorado, 1982).

      C. George and G. V. Glass, *Evaluation Report on the Mesa County Valley School District Year-Round School Program, 1982–83* (Boulder, CO: Laboratory of Educational Research, University of Colorado, Boulder, Colorado, 1983).

36.   M. Shepard and M. Reed, *A Research Agenda for Year-Round Schools: Executive Summary. Volume I* (Cambridge, MA: Abt Associates Inc., 1975).

37. M. L. Smith and G. V. Glass, *Evaluation of Year-Round Schools, Cherry Creek District 5* (Boulder, CO: Bureau of Educational Field Services, University of Colorado, 1975).

M. L. Smith and G. V. Glass, *Evaluation of Year-Round Schools, Cherry Creek District 5 Second Year Final Report* (Boulder, CO: Evaluation Research Services, University of Colorado, 1976).

38. C. Naylor, "Do year-round schools improve student learning? An annotated bibliography and synthesis of the research," *BCTF Research Report* (Vancouver: British Columbia Teachers' Foundation, 1995), <http://www.bctf.bc.ca/ResearchReports/95ei03/>.

39. Zykowski et al., *A Review of Year-Round Education Research* (California Educational Research Co-operative, 1991).

40. R. A. Carriedo and P. D. Goren, *Year-Round Education Through Multi-Track Schools* (San Francisco, CA: Far West Laboratory, 1989), Brief No 10.

41. W. D. Campbell, "Year round schooling for academically At-Risk students: Outcomes and perceptions of participants in an elementary program," *ERS Spectrum* 12, no. 3 (1994).

42. W. E. Webster and K. L. Nyberg, "Converting a high school to YRE," *Thrust for Educational Leadership* 21, no. 6 (1992): 22–25.

43. Ibid., 25.

44. L. Harp, "Advocates of year round schooling shift focus to educational benefits." *Education Week*, 24 February 1993.

45. Ibid.

46. R. M. Allinder et al, "Effects of summer break on math and spelling performance as a function of grade level," *The Elmentary School Journal* 92, no. 4 (1992).

47. B. K. Tilley, L. S. Cox and N. Staybrook, "An extended school year validation study," *Report No. 86-2* (Seattle: Seattle Public Schools, 1986).

48. H. Cooper et al., "The effects of summer vacation on achievement test scores: A narrative and meta-analytic review," *Review of Educational Research* 66, no. 3 (1996): 227–268.

49. From a survey conducted in Fall 2000 by Public Agenda. See <http://www.publicagenda.org/issues>.

50. J. McMahon, "Extended school year programs," *Exceptional Children* 49 (1983): 457–461.

51. B. Heyns, "Educational effects: Issues in conceptualization and measurement," in *Handbook of Theory and Research for the Sociology of Education*, ed. J. G. Richardson (Westport, CT: Greenwood Press, 1978).

52. H. Cooper et al., "Making the most of summer school: A meta-analytic and narrative review," *Monographs of the Society for Research in Child Development* 65 (2000), 1, Serial No. 260.

CHAPTER 5

GROUPING STUDENTS FOR INSTRUCTION

Gene V Glass
Arizona State University

RESEARCH FINDINGS

Ability grouping has been found to have few benefits and many risks. When homogeneous and heterogeneous groups of students are taught identical curricula, there appear to be few advantages to homogeneous grouping in terms of academic achievement. More able students make greater academic progress when separated from their fellow students and given an accelerated course of study. Less able students who are segregated from their more able peers are at risk of being taught an inferior curriculum and consigned to low tracks for their entire academic career. Teachers assigned to higher tracks and parents of bright students prefer ability grouping. Teachers in lower tracks are less enthusiastic and need support in the form of materials and instructional techniques to avoid the disadvantages of tracking.

RECOMMENDATIONS

- Mixed or heterogeneous ability or achievement groups offer several advantages:
  1) less able pupils are at reduced risk of being stigmatized and exposed to a "dumbed-down" curriculum;

2) teachers' expectations for all pupils are maintained at higher levels;

3) opportunities for more able students to assist less able peers in learn-
    ing can be realized.

- Teachers asked to teach in a "de-tracked" system will require training,
  materials and support that are largely lacking in today's schools.

- Administrators seeking to "detrack" existing programs will require help
  in navigating the difficult political course that lies ahead of them.

The sorting of students into homogeneous ability and achievement
groups is nearly as old as universal compulsory education in the United
States. The grouping of students by ability or achievement forms a continuum that extends from "reading groups" (the redbirds, bluebirds, and
canaries) at one end to tracking and even segregation of students between
school districts at the other. While the one extreme may be a matter
strictly of professional pedagogical judgment, the other extreme may represent the impact of broad social forces outside the control of any one
educator or group of professionals. This review will touch on each point
across this continuum.

The seemingly simple notion of grouping pupils by their ability for
instruction proves, upon closer examination, to be very complex with many
variations. Within-class grouping, between-class grouping, the Joplin plan,
XYZ grouping, gifted classes, academic tracks, charter schools—the incli-
nation to sort students comes in many forms and has a long history. Otto
found evidence of homogeneous achievement grouping of pupils as far
back as the nineteenth century in America's schools.[1] The Santa Barbara
Concentric Plan of the early 1900s divided classes into A, B and C groups
who received three levels of curriculum based on their past performance.

The pedagogical justification for homogeneous grouping centers on the
role of the teacher: with students grouped by ability or achievement, the
teacher is able to focus more instruction at the level of all the students in
the group; thus, time is not wasted as bright students wait for elementary
explanations to be given to their slower classmates, and slow students are
not troubled with instruction that is over their heads. Bright students are
thought to need a faster pace and enriched material; low-ability students
are thought to require remediation, repetition, and more reviews. Slower
students, it is felt, will be better off shielded from competition with their
brighter classmates; more able students will not become complacent by
comparing themselves with slow students, and they will be spurred to
higher levels of achievement by competing with their own kind. These
images, not unfamiliar to teachers and parents alike, are rife with assumptions about the nature of human intelligence, the conditions of learning,
the development of students' self-perceptions, and the behavior of teachers, only a few of which are tested in the research literature.

Ability grouping enjoyed wide professional and public acceptance beginning in the heyday of the "scientific" movement in education (from Edward L. Thorndike, to Lewis M. Terman, to the post-WW II era) and extending to the post-Sputnik era of emphasis on enriching curriculum for the gifted.[2] Homogeneous grouping in the form of tracking received severe criticism in the last quarter of the 20th century. James Rosenbaum's *Making Inequality*[3] and Samuel Bowles and Herbert Gintis's *Schooling in Capitalist America*[4] saw ability grouping as not just perpetuating but creating disadvantages for poor and minority students. Jeannie Oakes's *Keeping Track*[5] prompted vigorous debate regarding the effects of homogeneous grouping. Tracking's detractors leveled charges of stigmatizing students, and consigning them to inferior and "dumbed-down" instruction. Homogeneous grouping was not completely without its supporters. Thomas Loveless concluded: "The primary charges against tracking are (1) that it doesn't accomplish anything and (2) that it unfairly creates unequal opportunities for academic achievement. What is the evidence? Generally speaking, research fails to support the indictment."[6]

STUDENT GROUPING RESEARCH

Researchers approaching this policy question from different points on the disciplinary compass have reached different conclusions about the value of homogeneous grouping. The issue of homogeneous grouping not only separates researchers and scholars, it separates social classes and ethnic groups as well. Ability grouping is nearly universally condemned by scholars from minority ethnic groups (e.g., Braddock,[7] Darling-Hammond,[8] Esposito[9]). Why these various groups have arrived at conflicting conclusions and what educators should make of their conflicting recommendations is the central question to be resolved in this review.

The Prevalence of Homogeneous Grouping

How common is it for teachers and schools to separate students into groups of similar ability or achievement for purposes of instruction?

In part, estimates of the incidence of homogeneous grouping depend on how one asks the question. Public sentiment and professional judgment have turned against strict ability (IQ) grouping of the XYZ-type that first made an appearance in the 1920s. Beginning in 1919, the Detroit public schools administered intelligence tests, divided the distribution of students into strictly ordered ability groups—X, Y and Z—and taught the same curriculum to all three groups. This Huxleyesque scheme, so reminiscent of the Alphas and Betas in *Brave New World*, would be found unconstitutional in the present day. (Indeed, in *Hobson v. Hansen*, the tracking of students into ability groups in the Washington, D.C. schools was ruled to be a violation of Fourteenth Amendment rights.[10]) Ask educators today if they track pupils into "ability groups," and they will probably say "No." Ask them if they group students homogeneously by achievement to facilitate instruction, and their answer is likely to be "Yes." While grouping is currently based on past performance rather than measured academic aptitude, the results are probably not much different, given the reasonably high correlation between achievement and aptitude.[11]

Hoffer[12] reported data from the Longitudinal Study of American Youth that addressed the incidence of tracking in mathematics and science in more than 50 middle schools of the late 1980s. About 40% of the schools tracked students for science teaching in Grade 7; this figure rose to 50% in Grade 8. For mathematics instruction, 80% tracked in Grade 7 and more than 90% tracked in Grade 8. These data are supported by Epstein and MacIver's[13] survey, also performed in the late 1980s. Survey respondents were asked "For which academic subjects are students assigned to homogeneous classes on the basis of similar abilities or achievement levels?" Homogeneous grouping was practiced in two-thirds of the middle schools in some or all subjects at Grade 5 and in three-quarters of the schools at Grade 8 (See Table 5–1). Surveys of homogeneous grouping in elementary grades would show even higher incidences, where the proverbial redbirds, bluebirds, and canaries are almost ubiquitous.

Table 5–1.   Middle Schools Classified by Tracking in Some or All Subjects: 1988 With Percents by Columns (After Epstein & MacIver, 1990)

Tracking in...	Grade 5	Grade 6	Grade 7	Grade 8
All Subjects	23%	22%	22%	23%
Some Subjects	40%	44%	47%	50%
No Tracking	37%	34%	31%	27%

These surveys may underestimate the incidence of homogeneous grouping in the nation's public schools. Even the most inexperienced administrator knows that this issue divides teachers, parents, and other stakeholders in our schools. Complete candor on questionnaires received in the mail or in reply to questions posed by some ephemeral visitor to one's school is not only unlikely, it could even be disruptive. Visitors to schools who enter them on different terms and who press for deeper answers might place the incidence of homogeneous grouping at levels even higher than these surveys. In an interview on his book *Savage Inequalities*, Jonathan Kozol remarked:

"Virtually every school system I visit, with a few exceptions, is entirely tracked, although they don't use that word anymore."[14] Whichever figure one might accept—two-thirds, three-quarters, or 100%—the conclusion seems inescapable that homogeneous grouping of students by ability or achievement is virtually endemic in American education.

Open enrollment plans in which students choose from among a set of courses also produces stratification of schools by ability groups. Sam Lucas has documented this phenomenon in his book *Tracking Inequality: Stratification and Mobility in American High Schools.*[15] Welner has observed the same pattern of sorting entering the school system in the form of choice programs:

> ...tracking under a choice regime resembles tracking under the more rigid tracking regimes of the past.[16]

> For many district students, choice was more apparent than real. Scheduling conflicts constrained some students' choices in ways that perpetuated tracking (e.g., taking a lower-level math class prevented scheduling of a higher-level English class). For other students, ... the course selection process amounted to little more than accepting the schools' recommendations.[17]

Who Wants to Group Students: Teachers or Parents?

A survey published by the National Education Association in 1968 indicated that at least 75% of teachers preferred to teach homogeneously grouped classes.[18] Teachers' affinity for ability grouping disappears among teachers who are assigned the lower-tracked classes.[19] Contemporary surveys, though lacking, would likely duplicate this finding. It is not difficult to understand why teachers' jobs are made easier by teaching students in groups of similar achievement levels. However, it is not clear whether homogeneous grouping is intrinsically more effective or whether it is preferred because of an absence of curriculum materials and instructional techniques designed for heterogeneous groups.

Teachers' preferences for homogeneous grouping must surely be matched or even exceeded by parents' preferences for the same, at least the preferences of educated and wealthier parents to have their children placed in the highest groups. Parents' interventions into tracking decisions are common. Highly educated parents have been found more likely to push for high track placements than other parents.[20] Oakes and Wells studied 10 middle schools and high schools in their research on "detracking" secondary education and found that middle-class suburban values and norms are strong reinforcers of tracking.[21]

Multiple Perspectives on the Effectiveness of Ability Grouping

The topic of grouping students for instruction has been studied by researchers from quite different perspectives. On the one hand, educational psychologists have focused on academic achievement narrowly construed as performance on paper-and-pencil tests and self-esteem scales. Sociologists have taken a broader view that encompasses students' academic careers, and the opportunities and services offered students in different groups and tracks. Indeed, on this particular topic, it is fair to say that two different disciplines—psychology, and particularly educational psychology on the one hand, and sociology on the other—have focused on different aspects of this phenomenon and have arrived at different conclusions.

Educational Psychologists' View

Research on ability grouping by educational psychologists has a very long history, dating from the very beginnings of educational research itself. As early as 1916, Whipple[22] studied students in the Urbana, Illinois, school system who had been grouped into homogeneous gifted classes. A handful of major studies—which themselves review and integrate the findings of dozens of primary studies extending over several decades—now forms the empirical basis of most persons' opinions about the effects of ability grouping on achievement: the Kulik and Kulik[23] and the Slavin[24] meta-analyses for elementary and secondary school ability grouping.

Since the meta-analyses[25] play a key role in forming an evaluation of the efficacy of homogeneous grouping, a brief explanation of this technique is in order. Meta-analysis is a statistical technique used to combine and integrate the findings—themselves expressed statistically—of many individual empirical studies. In its simplest form, as an example, a meta-analysis might collect a hundred studies of the correlation of achievement and ability and report that the correlation coefficients ranged from 0.25 to 0.85 with an average correlation of 0.62. When the primary research studies being "meta-analyzed" involve comparing two groups—for example, students taught in homogeneous (condition A) v. heterogeneous (condition B) groups—it is common to express the findings of each primary study in a form known as an *effect size*. An effect size that describes the difference between two groups is defined as a mean difference (between conditions A and B) in units of the within-condition standard deviation:

$$ES = \frac{\text{Mean}(A) - \text{Mean}(B)}{\sigma}$$

The value of *ES* reveals the degree of superiority of condition A over condition B (or, B over A in the event that *ES* has a negative value). Under the assumption of normally distributed scores, an average *ES* of +1.0 indicates that the average student in condition A scores above 84% of the students in condition B. The concept of the effect size applied to standardized achievement test data enjoys a fortuitous coincidence. It is an empirical fact that the standard deviation of most achievement tests is 1.0 years in *grade equivalent units*. Consequently, an effect size of 1.0 implies that the average superiority of condition A over condition B is one year in grade equivalent units. Likewise, an effect size of 0.50 implies that students in A achieve, on average, 5 months in grade equivalent units above students in condition B.

The Kuliks' Meta-analyses.   Kulik and Kulik[26] integrated the findings of 52 experimental and quasi-experimental studies of the effect of ability grouping on achievement of secondary school students. The results of their analysis showed that the benefits in terms of academic achievement of ability grouping were virtually absent in all cases, with the exception of the comparisons of high-ability students in gifted classes vs. their counterparts in mixed-ability classes. When the effects for different subjects (math, science, reading, social studies), standardized vs. locally relevant tests, and objective vs. non-objective tests were examined, no consistent benefits were seen for ability grouping. When Kulik and Kulik examined the effects of ability grouping at the elementary school level, they found small but positive effects in reading and mathematics for both within-class and between-class ability grouping. Effect sizes were approximately 0.30 for high-ability students and declined to less than 0.20 for low-ability students. There emerges in the Kuliks' meta-analyses the first hint that the benefits of ability grouping may be due to the fact that high-ability students receive an enriched curriculum in homogeneous classes (as described, for example, by Oakes[27]). This conclusion was given further substantiation in Kulik's meta-analysis of enrichment and accelerated programs for gifted and talented students that, when compared to gifted students in heterogeneous classes, yielded effects sizes of 0.40 for enrichment classes and 0.90 for accelerated classes. The Kuliks' meta-analyses were the first to challenge reviews like that of Good and Marshall[28] that recommended against all forms of ability grouping.

The Slavin Meta-analyses.   The Kulik and Kulik meta-analyses contrast somewhat with the meta-analyses (called "best evidence syntheses") published by Robert Slavin[29] in 1986 and 1990. Slavin, who relied on a good deal more selectivity in forming the database of studies on ability grouping before attempting to integrate their findings, drew conclusions from the body of work that questioned the efficacy of homogeneous grouping for instruction at the secondary school level:

"Comprehensive between-class ability grouping plans have little or no effect on the achievement of secondary students, at least as measured by standardized tests. This conclusion is most strongly supported in Grades 7–9, but the more limited evidence that does exist from Grades 10–12 also fails to support any effect of ability grouping."[30]

At the elementary school level, Slavin[31] concluded that the research supported modest but reliable benefits of within-class ability grouping for mathematics at the intermediate grades and benefits for reading achievement of the Joplin plan for all elementary grades. (In the Joplin plan, students are grouped *across grades* into intact classes for reading instruction, in which reading is taught in the same manner to the whole class, or at most two groups within the class; students then return to their principal grade assignment for all other instruction.) The seeming discrepancy between Slavin's and Kulik and Kulik's conclusions (Slavin being considerably more pessimistic about homogeneous grouping at the secondary school level than the Kuliks) is resolved when the criteria for inclusion of studies in the meta-analyses are examined. Whereas Kulik and Kulik threw a fairly broad net over the body of literature traditionally identified as ability grouping research, Slavin excluded studies that did not attempt to standardize curriculum among the various homogeneously formed groups that were compared. Slavin's interest was in isolating the unique effect of having students learn in homogeneous groups, not in evaluating how curriculum may become differentiated (enriched in high ability groups, "dumbed down" in low ability groups) among homogeneous groups. Indeed, Slavin issued a warning that is seldom acknowledged in brief or journalistic accounts of this research:

> ...there is an important limitation to this conclusion [of no beneficial effect of ability grouping]. In most of the studies that compared tracked to untracked grouping plans..., tracked students took different levels of the **same courses** (e.g., high, average, or low sections of Algebra 1). Yet much of the practical impact of tracking, particularly at the senior high school level, is on determining the nature and number of courses taken in a given area. The experimental studies do **not** compare students in Algebra 1 to those in Math 9.... The conclusions drawn ... are limited, therefore, to the effects of between-class grouping *within the same courses,* and should not be read as indicating a lack of differential effects of tracking as it affects course selection and course requirements."[32] [Added emphasis shown in boldface.]

The findings of the Kulik & Kulik and the Slavin meta-analyses are summarized in Table 5–2.

Table 5–2.   Average Effect Sizes from the Kulik & Kulik and Slavin Meta-Analyses of Ability Grouping Studies

Ability Grouping Type	Grade Level	Kulik & Kulik	Slavin
Within-Class	K–6	+.20	+.30
Joplin Plan	K–6	+.30	+.45
XYZ Ability Grouping	7–12	.00	.00
Enriched for Gifted	K–12	+.40	
Accelerated for Gifted	K–12	+.90	

What becomes clear from examination of the above results is that, whatever benefits may accrue from the grouping of students into homogeneous ability groups for instruction, these benefits pale beside the benefits that accrue to gifted students when they are separated from their classmates and given enriched and accelerated curricula.

Proponents of ability grouping have sometimes made extraordinary reaches to supply their position with empirical warrants. Allan reached toward the research on "peer modeling" from educational psychology:

> Further, the idea that lower ability students will look up to gifted students as role models is highly questionable. Children typically model their behavior after the behavior of other children of similar ability who are coping well with school. Children of low and average ability do not model themselves on fast learners.[33] It appears that "watching someone of similar ability succeed at a task raises the observer's feelings of efficiency and motivates them to try the task."[34] Students gain most from watching someone of similar ability "cope" (that is, gradually improve their performance after some effort), rather than watching someone who has attained "mastery" (that is, can demonstrate perfect performance from the outset).[35]

These are extraordinary claims, if true, because they seem to oversimplify the complex dynamics of children's lives in real classrooms. Indeed, the most generous thing that may be said for the research basis of this claim is that it is oversimplified and was never intended as justification for such positions. Schunk's review of "peer models and children's behavioral change" focuses entirely on short-term (a few minutes or hours), staged incidences in laboratories where children observe "models" performing artificial tasks, for the most part. In fact, Schunk excluded from his review studies of "natural peer interactions, [and] … tutoring or peer teaching."[36] Moreover, this literature lacks any definition of what a "peer" is. At one point, Schunk concluded that, of four experiments involving observational learning of cognitive skills or novel responses, "Each of these studies supports the idea that model competence enhances observational learning."[37] Schunk continues:

> Social cognitive theory [predicts both that] Children should be more likely to pattern their behaviors after models who perform successfully than to emulate less-successful models, [and that] models who are *dissimilar* in competence to observers exert more powerful effects on children's behavior. ... Similarity in competence may be more important in contexts where children cannot readily discern the functional value of behavior; for example, when they lack task familiarity, when there is no objective standard of performance, or when modeled actions are followed by neutral consequences.[38]

In other words, similar competence may be important—this theory seems to say—in those circumstances where children have no basis for inferring what the competence of the "model" is. If the reader thinks that this entire line of research bears scarcely a tenuous relationship to classroom practice and education policy, he or she is joined in those doubts by Schunk himself, who wrote: "Given the present lack of classroom-based research, drawing implications for educational practices is a speculative venture."[39] No research appeared to correct this "lack" between Schunk's review in 1987 and Allan's use of it in 1991.

Sociologists' View

Not surprisingly, psychologists acted like psychologists when they studied the effects of ability grouping: they contrived experiments, wrote paper-and-pencil tests, and sought objective evidence of superior test performance. When sociologists turned their attention to the tracking of students into ability groups, they acted like sociologists: spending time in schools observing; interviewing teachers, parents, and students; asking questions about opportunities, preconceptions; and wondering about what this form of schooling had to do with the larger society of which it was one small part.

Gamoran[40] found that students in low tracks or ability groups were less likely to attend college than students in higher tracks. That lower tracks receive a poorer quality curriculum, less experienced teachers, and teachers with lower expectations for their students' performance has been observed by several researchers, including Gamoran,[41] Oakes,[42] Persell,[43] Rosenbaum.[44]

Jeannie Oakes has been a consistent critic of homogeneous grouping of students at all levels of the educational system. Her research,[45] dating from the late 1970s, has drawn on the evidence accumulated in literally thousands of person-hours of observation of teachers and students in tracked classes and schools. She has presented her findings forthrightly and forcefully:

Tracking does *not* equalize educational opportunity for diverse groups of students. It does *not* increase the efficiency of schools by maximizing learning opportunities for everyone.... Tracking does *not* meet individual needs. Moreover, tracking does *not* increase student achievement.

What tracking does, in fact, appears to be quite the opposite. Tracking seems to retard the academic progress of many students—those in average and low groups. Tracking seems to foster low self-esteem among these same students and promote school misbehavior and dropping out. Tracking also appears to lower the aspirations of students who are not in the top groups. And perhaps most important, in view of all of the above, is that tracking separates students along socioeconomic lines, separating rich from poor, whites from non-whites. The end result is that poor and minority children are found far more often than others in the bottom tracks.[46]

Even proponents of tracking into ability groups have acknowledged that research "has verified again and again . . . that many low-track classes are deadening, non-educational environments."[47] What is more, assignment to a low track is seldom followed by later reassignment to middle or high tracks. The professed intention of assignment to lower tracks being a transitional remedial period for the purpose of bringing students back up to speed is seldom realized.[48]

In summarizing research on tracking from the sociological perspective, Welner and Mickelson wrote:

> In a nutshell, this substantial body of research demonstrates that low-track classes are consistently characterized by lowered expectations, reduced resources, rote learning, less-skilled teachers, amplified behavioral problems, and an emphasis on control rather than learning.... The extant empirical research has also demonstrated that low-track classes are rarely remedial; that is, students placed in a lower track tend not to move later to higher tracks and, in fact, suffer from decreased ambitions and achievement.... Track placements, while increasingly subject to parental and student choice, remain highly rigid and highly correlated to race and class-over and above measured academic achievement....[49]

Although he does not present himself as a sociologist, Jonathan Kozol has earned a reputation over nearly forty years as a perceptive and credible observer of America's schools, particularly the schools that suffer the multiple insults of severe poverty. Kozol's 1991 book, *Savage Inequalities: Children in America's Schools*, detailed his observations of the extreme inequities experienced by the poor and particularly the ethnic minority poor in U.S. schools. Tracking played a prominent role in most of the schools he visited. In an interview for the magazine *Educational Leadership*, Kozol was asked the following question:

Interviewer: Let's talk a little bit about curriculum innovations–for instance, the idea of reaching at-risk kids in ways that are usually reserved for the gifted. Teaching algebra to remedial students, for instance. Dissolving the tracking system. What are your opinions about these solutions to problems of inequity?

Kozol: Tracking! When I was a teacher, tracking had been thoroughly discredited. But during the past 12 years, tracking has come back with a vengeance. …We have these cosmetic phrases like "homogeneous grouping." It's tracking, by whatever name, and I regret that very much. It's not just that tracking damages the children who are doing poorly, but it also damages the children who are doing very well, because, by separating the most successful students–who are often also affluent, white children–we deny them the opportunity to learn something about decency and unselfishness. We deny them the opportunity to learn the virtues of helping other kids. All the wonderful possibilities of peer teaching are swept away when we track our schools as severely as we are doing today.[50]

Why Such Different Views?

Two groups of scholars—educational psychologists on the one hand and educational sociologists on the other—come to quite different conclusions on the value of homogeneous grouping of students for instruction. Why? The answer lies in what they look for and how they look for it. Psychologists have tended to focus on short-run comparisons of different ability groups exposed to the same curriculum; they have evaluated the effects of grouping with paper-and-pencil tests of achievement. For example, only nine of the 52 studies in the Kuliks' meta-analysis of secondary school ability grouping involved any *formal* adaptation of the curriculum to the ability level of the students.

Sociologists have taken a broader view of the various effects that ensue from the separation of students into homogeneous groups: the curriculum they receive, the type of instruction they are given, the social climate that is created and how it might shape their long-range plans, and the like. In large part, then, these two groups have been observing different phenomena, and operating with different disciplinary assumptions that have led them to draw conclusions that, if they don't contradict each other, at least place emphases on different outcomes. Psychologists' efforts to control independent variables have led them to focus on experiments that held curriculum constant and varied group composition: homogenously formed groups in one school, heterogeneously formed groups in another. Sociologists, by contrast, have employed methods more akin to naturalistic observation, finding tracked schools and observing all of the consequences that ensue, including markedly differentiated curricula between tracks. These different perspectives account, perhaps, for the relatively benign view of tracking taken by educational psychologists.

Conclusion

One's position on the ability grouping question will probably turn on the value one attaches to academic achievement of traditional types versus the broader goals of education. Those who construe the purpose of schooling as primarily preparing students—particularly the more academically able students—for higher education or the workforce, and who feel they see clearly the demands of those future roles, are likely to accept homogeneous grouping as an appropriate instructional strategy. On the other hand, those who see education as sorting children and reproducing social and economic class inequalities and protecting the privileges of already privileged social and ethnic groups are likely to regard homogeneous grouping as a principal means of achieving this goal. Loveless,[51] in his much cited book *The Tracking Wars,* sketches a view of education that virtually presupposes the superiority of ability grouping: Schools are "places for students to learn content that is designated, authoritatively, by someone else"[52] (p. 13). This authoritative designation involves "deciding what students should know (content), deciding what they are capable of learning (ability), and finally, reconciling the content with students' ability to learn it."[53] The educator's responsibility is that of "matching students with curriculum" and having "a legitimate party [decide what] students should learn."[54] This authoritarian, content-centered view of schooling has as many detractors and as it has supporters.

Welner summarized the situation with respect to tracking in language stripped of vagueness and euphemisms:

> Ultimately, tracking is philosophically premised on the belief that some children are so academically different from other children that these two (or more) groups should not be in the same classroom. Accordingly, the academically inferior children are placed in separate classrooms where, in theory, they catch up (remediate) but where, in practice, they usually fall further behind. Tracking, then, is about the rationing of opportunities. From the perspective of the low-track student, it's about deciding that this student should not be exposed to curriculum and instruction that would prepare him or her for subsequent serious learning. From the perspective of the high-track student, it's about enhancing the schooling environment for some students by shielding (segregating) them from other students.[55]

The teacher who worries about the potential injustice to poor and minority students of tracking them into homogeneous groups will find little support for dealing with the special challenges that heterogeneous grouping presents. Commercially available curriculum materials are unlikely to aim at the same goals while differentiating the approach for students of differing levels of ability. Cross-ability tutoring, which has the potential to significantly raise the achievement of the tutors as well as those students being tutored,[56] is seldom provided for in today's schools and almost never included among the techniques imparted during pre-service teacher training. Often, the most vocal and active parents in a school will request ability grouping, when their children stand a good chance of being assigned to the fast track. It is little wonder that teachers prefer homogeneous groups for instruction, unless they are confined to teaching the lowest tracks. However, the challenge that must be faced whenever students are separated into homogeneous achievement groups is to avoid the "dumbing down" of the curriculum, to make the content and activities of the class as engaging and interesting as the curriculum of the highest tracks, whether they are called "gifted," "accelerated," or "advanced." One of the few efforts to reverse the ill-effects of tracking at-risk students into low-achieving homogeneous groups is Henry Levin's[57] accelerated schools movement, in which curriculum and teaching methods thought to be appropriate only for high track students are adapted for the education of all students. Tomlinson has recently offered advice on how instruction can be differentiated in mixed-ability classrooms without suffering the many ills that can result from segregating students into homogeneous ability groups.[58]

Administrators wishing to "detrack" traditionally tracked schools will face a considerable challenge. Welner and Oakes have offered plans for navigating the choppy political waters that must be crossed when schools that have evolved to primarily serve the interests of the brightest students are transformed into schools that serve all students' needs.[59]

Ability grouping, achievement grouping, within-class, between-class, Joplin plan, gifted programs, tracking, advanced placement—all of these devices may spring from the same basic motivation. Since the empirical research on academic progress shows nothing much more than small benefits to bright students of any of these forms of grouping per se, and large benefits from enriching and accelerating the curriculum for select students, the prevalence of these forms themselves probably represents another expression of the wish of middle-class and upper-middle-class parents to secure some advantage or privilege for their children within the public school system. Is this bad? In a schooling system already markedly segregated on the basis of housing patterns and in which poor and academically deprived children already suffer not just from sub-standard schooling but from the indignity of racial and socio-economic segregation (as noted by Kozol[60] and by Orfield and Eaton[61]), the homogeneous grouping of students for instruction is one more advantage conferred on those who already enjoy many. Jonathan Kozol has called the tracking of poor and minority students into "special-needs" classes while white middle-class students are accelerated in classes for the gifted "one of the great, great scandals of American education."[62]

RECOMMENDATIONS

- Mixed or heterogeneous ability or achievement groups offer several advantages:
  1) less able pupils are at reduced risk of being stigmatized and exposed to a "dumbed-down" curriculum;
  2) teachers' expectations for all pupils are maintained at higher levels;
  3) opportunities for more able students to assist less able peers in learning can be realized.
- Teachers asked to teach in a "de-tracked" system will require training, materials and support that are largely lacking in today's schools.
- Administrators seeking to "detrack" existing programs will require help in navigating the difficult political course that lies ahead of them.

REFERENCES

1. H. J. Otto, "Elementary education–III. Organization and administration," in *Encyclopedia of Educational Research*, ed. W. S. Monroe (New York: MacMillan, 1950).

2. J. B. Conant, *The American High School* (New York: McGraw-Hill, 1959).

3. J. E. Rosenbaum, *Making inequality: The hidden curricula of high school tracking* (New York: John Wiley & Sons, 1976).

4. S. Bowles and H. Gintis, *Schooling in Capitalist America* (New York: Basic Books, 1976).

5. J. Oakes, *Keeping track: How schools structure inequality* (New Haven, CT: Yale University Press, 1985).

6. T. Loveless, *The Tracking and Ability Grouping Debate*, <http://www.edexcellence.net/library/track.html#anchor979998>.

7. J. H. Braddock, "The perpetuation of segregation across levels of education: A behavior assessment of the contact-hypothesis," *Sociology of Education* 53, no. 3 (1980): 178–186.

8. L. Darling-Hammond, "Inequality and access to knowledge," in *Handbook of research on multicultural education*, eds. J. A. Banks and C. A. M. Banks (New York: Macmillan, 1995).

9. D. Esposito, "Homogeneous and heterogeneous ability grouping: Principal findings and implications for evaluating and designing more effective educational environments," *Review of Educational Research* 43, no. 2 (1973): 163–179.

10. Hobson v. Hansen, 269 F. Supp. 401, 1967.

11. R. Dreeben and R. Barr, "The formation and instruction of ability groups," *American Journal of Education* 97, no. 1 (1988): 34–65.

12. T. B. Hoffer, "Middle school ability grouping," *Educational Evaluation and Policy Analysis* 14, no. 3 (1992): 205–227.

13. J. L. Epstein and D. J. MacIver, *Education in the Middle Grades: Overview of National Practices and Trends* (Baltimore, MD: Center for Research on Elementary and Middle Schools, 1990).

14. M. Scherer, "On Savage Inequalities: A conversation with Jonathan Kozol," *Educational Leadership* 50, no. 4 (1992–1993): 4–9.

15. S. Lucas, *Tracking Inequality: Stratification and Mobility in American Schools* (New York: Teachers College Press, 1999).

16. K. G. Welner, *Legal rights, local wrongs: When community control collides with educational equity* (New York: SUNY Press, 2001), 199.

17. Ibid., 202–203.

18. National Education Association, *Ability Grouping. Research summary 1968-53* (Washington, D.C.: National Education Association, 1968).

19. Welner.

20. E. L. Useem, "Middle schools and math groups: Parents involvement in children's placement," *Sociology of Education* 65, no. 4 (1992): 263–279.

21. J. Oakes, A. S. Wells and associates, *Beyond the Technicalities of School Reform: Policy Lessons from Detracking Schools* (Los Angeles: UCLA Graduate School of Education, 1996).

22. "The grouping of pupils," *Thirty-fifth Yearbook, Part I, National Society for the Study of Education*, ed. G. M. Whipple (Chicago: University of Chicago Press, 1936).

23. C. L. Kulik and J. A. Kulik, "Effects of ability grouping on secondary school students: A meta-analysis of evaluation findings," *American Educational Research Journal* 19, no. 4 (1982): 415–428.

    C. L. Kulik and J. A. Kulik, "Effects of ability grouping on elementary school pupils: A meta-analysis," Paper presented at the annual meeting of the American Psychological Association, Toronto, Ontario, Canada, 1984, ERIC, ED 255329.

    J. A. Kulik and C. L. Kulik, "Effects of accelerated instruction on students," *Review of Educational Research* 54, no. 3 (1984): 409–425.

    J. A. Kulik and C. L. Kulik, "Effects of ability grouping on student achievement," *Equity and Excellence* 23, no. 1-2 (1989): 22–30.

24. R. R. Slavin, "Ability grouping and student achievement in elementary schools: A best-evidence synthesis," *Review of Educational Research* 57, no. 3 (1987): 293–336.

    R. E. Slavin, "Synthesis of research on grouping in elementary and secondary schools," *Educational Leadership* 46, no. 1 (1988): 67–77.

    R. E. Slavin, "Achievement effects of ability grouping in secondary schools: A best-evidence synthesis," *Review of Educational Research* 60, no. 3 (1990): 471–499.

25. G. V Glass, B. McGaw and M. L. Smith, *Meta-analysis in social research* (Beverly Hills, CA: SAGE Publications, 1981).

26. C. L. Kulik and J. A. Kulik, "Effects of ability grouping on secondary school students"

27. J. Oakes.

28. T. Good and S. Marshall, "Do students learn more in heterogeneous or homogeneous groups?" in *The Social Context of Instruction: Group Organization and Group Processes*, eds. P. Peterson, L. C. Wilkinson and M. Halliman (New York: Academic Press, 1984), 15–38.

29. R. R. Slavin, "Ability grouping and student achievement in elementary schools: A best-evidence synthesis," *Review of Educational Research* 57, no. 3 (1987): 293–336.

    R. E. Slavin, "Achievement effects of ability grouping in secondary schools: A best-evidence synthesis," *Review of Educational Research* 60, no. 3 (1990): 471–499.

    R. E. Slavin, "Ability grouping in the middle grades: Achievement effects and alternatives," *Elementary School Journal* 93, no. 5 (1993): 535–552.

30. R. E. Slavin, *Achievement Effects*, 494.

31. R. R. Slavin.

32. R. E. Slavin, *Achievement Effects*, 487.

33. D. H. Schunk, "Peer models and children's behavioral change," *Review of Educational Research* 57, no. 2 (1987): 149–174.

34. J. P. Feldhusen, "Synthesis of research on gifted youth," *Educational Leadership* 46, no. 6 (1989): 6–11.

35. S. D. Allan, "Grouping and the gifted ability-grouping research reviews: What do they say about grouping and the gifted?" *Educational Leadership* 48 (March 1991).

36. D. H. Schunk, *Peer Models*, 152.

37. D. H. Schunk, *Peer Models*, 161.

38. Ibid.

39. D. H. Schunk, *Peer Models*, 169

40. A. Gamoran, "The stratification of high school learning opportunities," *Sociology of Education* 60 (1987): 135–155.

41. Ibid.

42. J. Oakes.

43. C. H. Persell, *Education and inequality: A theoretical and empirical synthesis* (New York: Free Press, 1977).

44. J. E. Rosenbaum, "Social implications of educational grouping," *Review of Research in Education* 8 (1980): 361–401.

45. J. Oakes, *Multiplying inequalities: The effects of race, class, and tracking on opportunities to learn math and science* (Santa Monica: RAND, 1990).

    J. Oakes, "Can tracking research inform practice? Technical, normative, and political considerations," *Educational Researcher* 21, no. 4 (1992): 12–22.

    J. Oakes, Gamoran, A. and Page, R., "Curriculum differentiation: Opportunities, outcomes, and meanings," in *Handbook of research on curriculum*, ed. P. Jackson (New York: Macmillan, 1992), 570–608.

46. J. Oakes, *Keeping Track*, 40.

47. T. Loveless, *The Tracking Wars: State Reform Meets School Policy* (Washington DC: Brookings Institution Press, 1999), 21.

48. K. G. Welner, 57–61.

49. K. Welner and R. A. Mickelson, "School reform, politics, and tracking: Should we pursue virtue?" *Educational Researcher* 29, no. 4 (2000): 22–26.

50. M. Scherer.

51. T. Loveless.

52. Ibid.,13.

53. Ibid.

54. Ibid.

55. K. G. Welner, 11–12.

56. H. M. Levin, G. V Glass and G. R. Meister, "A Cost-effectiveness Analysis of Computer-assisted Instruction," *Evaluation Review* 11, no. 1 (1987), 50–72.

57. H. M. Levin, "Accelerated schools after eight years," in *Innovations in Learning: New Environments for Education*, eds. L. Schauble and R. Glaser (New York: Lawrence Erlbaum Associates, 1996), 329–351.

58. C. A. Tomlinson, *How to Differentiate Instruction in Mixed-Ability Classrooms*, (Alexandria, VA: Association for Supervision and Curriculum Development, 1995).

59. K. G. Welner and J. Oakes, *Navigating the Politics of Detracking: Leadership Strategies* (Arlington Heights, IL: Skylight Training and Publishing Inc., 2000).

60. J. Kozol.

61. G. Orfield and S. E. Eaton, *Dismantling Desegregation. The Quiet Reversal of Brown v. Board of Education* (New York: The New Press, 1996).

62. M. Scherer, 9.

CHAPTER 6

PARENTAL AND FAMILY INVOLVEMENT IN EDUCATION

Douglas B. Downey
The Ohio State University

SUMMARY OF RESEARCH FINDINGS

This paper reviews the research evidence relevant to understanding the relationship between parental involvement and children's performance in school. Indicators of parental involvement with school (e.g., attendance at school events, parent/teacher conferences, PTO) have mixed associations with children's school performance. In contrast, measures of parental involvement at home (e.g., talking to children about school-related matters, high educational expectations, warm and consistent discipline) show consistent associations with children's school success. But even this evidence—based on correlations—may not represent causal relationships, and so some critics maintain that what parents do has little effect on children's school performance.

RECOMMENDATIONS

- Programs designed to promote parent/teacher interaction should be continued, but with greater emphasis on initiatives designed to improve the parent/child relationship.

113

- Programs should be promoted that increase the amount of time low-income children are exposed to school-based activities, whether through more after-school programs, summer activities, or year-round schooling.

By the age of eighteen, children have typically spent only 13% of their waking life at school,[1] and there are credible reasons for believing that parents have a role in shaping whether the remaining 87% is spent in a way that promotes school success. The current research evidence provides some guidance for understanding the kinds of parental involvement that most likely improves children's school performance, although limitations of this work merit attention.

PARENTAL AND FAMILY INVOLVEMENT RESEARCH

Research on parental involvement in their children's education covers two broad areas: the effects of parental interaction and involvement in the school, and the impact of parental involvement in the home. Research has examined both the norms of parental-school interaction at various levels of society, and the efficacy of special efforts to enhance parental involvement with school activities.

Parents at School

Parents and Teachers

There are several reasons for believing that good parent-teacher relationships are conducive to children's school performance. Izzo, Weissberg, Kasprow, and Fendrich[2] explain: "When parents communicate constructively with teachers and participate in school activities, they gain a clearer understanding of what is expected of their children at school and they may learn from teachers how to work at home to enhance their children's education"[3] When parents attend parent/teacher conferences, for example, it creates continuity between the two dominant spheres of influence in the child's life, home and school,[4] and likely signals to children the parents' value for education. In addition, some have argued that children learn more when they receive consistent messages from home and school.[5] Epstein[6] writes that the "main reason ... for better communications and exchanges among schools, families, and community groups is to assist students at all grade levels to succeed in school and in life."[7]

But what is the evidence that children's school performance is enhanced by a strong parent-teacher relationship? Stevenson and Baker report that children performed better in school (as measured by teacher ratings of how well the child performed in school and whether the child performed up to his or her ability) when teachers rated the parents as actively involved in school activities such as PTO and parent-teacher conferences in their sample of 179 children drawn from the Time Use Longitudinal Panel Study.[8] Similarly, Grolnick and Slowiaczek studied 300 11–14 year-olds and found a strong association between teachers' reports of parental involvement (measured as frequency of attendance at parent-teacher conferences, open school night, and school activities and events, such as the PTO) and teacher reported grades, controlling for parents' education.[9]

But several studies report the opposite pattern: an inverse relationship between parent/school contact and children's school success.[10] Desimone analyzed the National Education Longitudinal Study (NELS), a nationally representative sample of nearly 25,000 eighth graders collected in 1988, and found negative associations between parents' contact with the school regarding academic matters and students' math and reading test scores and grades.[11] Rigsby, Stull and Morse-Kelly suggest that one reason for this puzzling pattern is that parents may become involved with adolescents' schooling when the youths experience either behavioral problems or poor grades.[12] Unfortunately, cross-sectional data do not allow us to assess that possibility.

Some study designs avoid the limitations of correlational research by comparing children involved in an intervention program with those who did not experience the intervention. Moses et al. report the results of an intervention in which parents were involved in children's schooling in several ways: as project leaders, through informational meetings, through participation in workshops, and by acting as voluntary classroom helpers. In this study, students demonstrated a marked increase in math performance compared to the achievement of students from previous years lacking this parental involvement intervention.[13] Although it is impossible to know if the intervention program was the only major difference in the children's experiences across the different school years, the results of this study are consistent with the claim that nurturing parental involvement in the classroom can improve school performance.

School-Level Parental Involvement

Children may experience some benefits from their parents' involvement at school, but do they also fare better merely by attending a school where many other parents are highly involved? One argument is that children benefit from school-level parental involvement because it promotes information sharing and greater normative control over children's behavior. Coleman described how "social closure," i.e., environments in which parents know each other, facilitates children's identification with school.[14]

Podolny and Baron[15] explain that "a cohesive network conveys a clear normative order within which the individual can optimize performance, whereas a diverse, disconnected network exposes the individual to conflicting preferences and allegiances within which it is much harder to optimize."[16] As an illustration, if most parents strictly enforced homework rules then it becomes more difficult for any single child to resist because they are exposed to an environment where doing homework is normative. In this way, children benefit from their own parents' school involvement but also by attending a school where many parents are involved.[17]

While this argument has face validity, to date it receives only modest empirical support. Carbonaro found mixed support for Coleman's claims. He reported that social closure was related to better performance on mathematics test scores and a decrease in the probability of dropping out, but had no effect on reading test scores or grades.[18] Importantly, other researchers analyzing the same data concluded that social closure was associated with *lower* math test scores,[19] and so the debate regarding the benefits of social closure in school persists.[20]

Other researchers have asked how much variation in students' scores on achievement tests can be attributed to school-level differences in parental involvement. The answer, apparently, is very little. Sui-Chu and Willms analyzed NELS data and concluded that while schools did differ in the level of involvement associated with parental volunteers or attendance at parent-teacher conferences, school-level parental involvement plays only a very small role in explaining students' math and reading test scores.[21] They concluded that while schools vary in the degree to which parents are involved in school activities, relatively few schools have a strong influence in shaping the learning climate at home, the dimension of parental involvement most closely related to students' school success.[22]

Intervention studies also show little evidence that school-level parental involvement has any significant impact on students' school performance. For example, a recent intervention termed CoZi (Co for James Comer and Zi for Edward Zigler) involved:

1) parent and teacher participation in school-based decision making that is grounded in child development principles;
2) parent outreach and education beginning at the birth of the child;
3) child care for preschoolers and before- and after-school care for kindergarten through sixth graders; and
4) parent involvement programs.

In initial evaluations comparing one CoZi and one non-CoZi elementary school, the CoZi school had better school climate and parental involvement than the comparable non-CoZi school, but parent-child interactions and children's level of achievement were not improved.[23] Of course, it is possible that the children experienced no improvements in school performance because the program was only in effect one year.

Taken as a whole, the current research evidence suggests that parent involvement in children's schools via attending parent-teacher conferences, contacting school officials, attending school events, and developing a close-knit community where many parents know each other, probably has modest positive effects on children's school performance. If parents are serious about helping their children do well in school, improving their relationship with teachers and involvement in school activities are worthy goals. The bulk of research evidence, however, suggests that how parents interact with their children at home matters more.

Parents at Home

There are many reasons for believing that what parents do at home plays an important role in shaping children's school-related skills. One piece of evidence comes from the recently collected nationally representative *Early Childhood Longitudinal Study—Kindergarten Cohort of 1998–99.* Eighteen percent of children entering kindergarten in the U.S. in the fall of 1998 did not know that print reads left to right, where to go when a line of print ends, or where the story ends in a book.[24] At the other end of the spectrum, a small percentage of children beginning kindergarten could already read words in context. These large differences in beginning skills likely represent varying levels of exposure to print in the home. More evidence that what happens at home is important comes from researchers making seasonal comparisons—comparing students' cognitive gains during the summer and winter. Three independent longitudinal studies reach the same conclusion: disadvantaged children lose ground primarily during the summer, when school is not in session and parents' influence is primary.[25] But if home practices matter so much, what exactly do parents do that promotes children's school success?

Parenting Style

To the extent that school-related skills, both cognitive and social, are shaped by parenting approaches, parents play an important role in preparing children to meet teachers' demands. One characteristic of parents that is consistently related to children's school performance is the expectation parents have for their child's educational future. Children with parents who hope and expect them to do well are more likely to do well in school than their counterparts with parents who do not have high educational expectations for their children.[26]

But other work suggests that the best parenting approach combines high expectations with parental responsiveness or warmth. One idea popular among developmental psychologists is that an *authoritative* parenting style, characterized by a balance between parents' expectations and responsiveness, promotes children's self-esteem, mastery, and ultimately school success.[27] The argument is that children benefit from authoritative parenting because parents establish and consistently enforce rules and standards for their children's behavior using nonpunitive methods of discipline. Authoritative parents are warm and supportive and encourage communication with their children while validating the child's individual point of view. In contrast, children's development is said to be less consistent when exposed to *permissive* parenting (low expectations and high responsiveness) or *authoritarian* parents (high expectations and low responsiveness).

Some empirical evidence is consistent with this view. Dornbusch, Ritter, Leiderman, Roberts, and Fraleigh studied 7,836 high school students in the San Francisco Bay area and found associations between the parents' style of interaction (reported by the student) and students' grades that persisted despite statistical controls for parents' education, race, family structure, and the child's sex. Students describing their parents as employing an authoritative style performed best in school, while students with authoritarian and, to a lesser extent, permissive parents were more likely to have lower school grades, net of controls.[28] Similarly, in their study of adolescents in nine different high schools, Steinberg, Lamborn, Dornbusch, and Darling found that students with authoritative parents took greater responsibility for their school outcomes.[29]

Other studies, although not employing Baumrind's "authoritative/authoritarian" nomenclature, supplement our understanding of parental practices that are related to children's school success. The Children of the National Longitudinal Survey of Youth (CNLSY) and Infant Health and Development Program (IHDP) employ the Home Observation for Measurement of the Environment (HOME) scale to assess the quality of the child's home environment. The scale is based on interviewers' observations and questions of the mother. It includes measures of learning experiences outside of the home (e.g., trips to museums, visits to friends, trips to the grocery store), literary experiences within the home (e.g., child has more than ten books, mother reads to the child, family members read newspaper), cognitively stimulating activities within the home (e.g., materials that improve learning of skills such as recognition of letters, numbers, colors, shapes, and sizes), punishment (whether child was spanked during the home visit; maternal disciplinary style), maternal warmth (mother kissed, caressed, or hugged the child during the visit; mother praised the child's accomplishments during the visit), and the physical environment (whether the home is reasonably clean and uncluttered; whether the child's play environment is safe). A one standard deviation increase on the HOME scale was associated with a 9-point gain on the PPVT-R vocabulary test.[30] Phillips et al. conclude: "For parents who want their children to do well on tests (which means almost all parents), middle-class parenting practices seem to work."[31]

Similarly, in once-monthly observations of 40 families over a two and a half year period, Hart and Risely[32] found several dimensions of parenting style that were related to the child's subsequent performance on IQ tests. They conclude that three primary dimensions of parenting are what matter:

1) The absolute amount of parenting per hour (e.g., how often the parent is in the child's presence, the percentage of child activities in which the parent took a turn, the number of words the parent speaks to the child);

2) parents' social interaction with the children (e.g., the percentage of child's initiations the parent responds to); and

3) the quality of speech to the child (e.g., how often did the parent repeat child utterances, the percentage of parent utterances that were questions, and the absence of prohibitions such as "stop," "quit," or "don't").

The third factor, quality of speech to the child was the strongest predictor of the child's later IQ. They conclude that "[t]he major differences associated with differences in IQ were the extensive amount of time, attention, and talking that higher SES parents invest in their children and their active interest in what their children have to say."[33]

Clark's 1983 study also is consistent with Baumrind's emphasis on warm and responsive parenting. Clark studied 10 African-American children, half of whom were successful academically and half of whom were not. Clark reported that parents of high-achieving students had a distinct style of interacting with their children. They created emotionally supportive home environments and provided reassurance when the children encountered failure.[34]

Other studies also show evidence of parental involvement in the child's school planning as important. Using the NELS, Sui-Chu and Willms developed four dimensions of parental involvement: 1) home discussion, 2) home supervision, 3) school communication, and 4) school participation. They report that "of the four types of involvement, home discussion was the most strongly related to academic achievement."[35] The pattern they found was replicated by others.[36] This association may represent greater parental interest in the child's progress, greater involvement in negotiating course selection, guidance in how to handle school problems, or a number of other ways parents help their children with schooling.

Children whose parents provide structured, adult-supervised activities at home tend to do better on cognitive tests and earn better grades.[37] Clark found that parents of successful students actively helped them organize their daily and weekly schedules and monitored this schedule closely to ensure that it was followed.[38] Similarly, Taylor reports that family routines (e.g., "My family has certain routines that help our household run smoothly") are associated with success in school.[39] Children may benefit from structure because it promotes the development of school-related habits that teachers tend to reward (e.g., consistent attendance, attentiveness, consistently turning in homework, not disrupting class).

Parents' linguistic styles are also related to children's school success. Children do better in school when their parents verbalize instructions frequently and specifically.[40] Parents' use of verbal variety and detailed instruction are features of language associated with high academic achievement among children. Further, the parents of high-achieving children tend to be closely attuned to the cognitive level of their children and to respond more to individual cues their children give than to preconceived expectations or status rules for children.[41]

Reading to Children

Not surprisingly, several research strains suggest that children whose parents read to them 20 minutes or more a day during the pre-school years have substantially higher pre-reading skills when they enter kindergarten.[42] When analyzing the Children of the National Longitudinal Survey of Youth (CNLSY), Phillips et al. note that five- and six-year-olds' vocabulary scores are about 4 points higher (one-quarter of a standard deviation) when their mothers read to them daily as opposed to not at all, net background controls.[43] Furthermore, a British study suggests that parental reading may be more effective than reading with someone else. The authors report that children benefited more from being read to aloud two to four times a week from books sent home from school than did children receiving additional assistance at school from a tutor.[44]

Educational Opportunities

Some research suggests that children's school performance is better when the home has a variety of educational objects, such as books, newspapers, a computer, magazines, and a place to study.[45] While children would obviously not benefit from books in the home if never opened, the presence of books or a computer provide the child with the opportunity to develop school-related skills. In addition, there is an association between the amount of money parents save for children's educational future and school performance.[46] It is not clear whether this money directly influences children (by providing the message that they are expected to go to college) or if it is merely correlated with other parental characteristics that matter.

Homework

Finn suggests that helping with homework is a concrete way that parents demonstrate the commitment they have to education.[47] Surprisingly, however, there is little research support for this claim. Many studies based on the NELS sample of eighth graders show an inverse association between parents' help with homework (or rules about homework) and youths' performance in school,[48] although most suspect that this association is a result of parents deciding to help a struggling child. In addition, parents' effectiveness may depend on their level of education. Balli, Wedman, and Demo found that students whose parents held a college degree benefited more from parental involvement with homework than did students whose parents lacked a college degree.[49]

Cultural Capital

Bourdieu posited that students receive academic rewards not just for course knowledge, but also for signaling affiliation with elite groups (i.e., "cultural capital") through their speech, style, mode of dress, and other habits.[50] Bourdieu viewed cultural capital as arbitrary—he argued that the cultural practices of the elite are not inherently "better" than those of the disadvantaged—but cultural capital associated with elite culture tends to be rewarded in the classroom. From this perspective, some of the skills or habits children need to develop for school success are not necessarily "good" but are simply the ones rewarded by teachers.[51] Consistent with these claims, DiMaggio reported that U.S. high school students received higher grades, net of socioeconomic status, when they reported interests (e.g., interest in being a composer) and involvement (e.g., attending literature readings) in art, music, and literature.[52] Other researchers have also noted that children tend to do better in school when they have been exposed to events or activities outside of school such as art and history museums, or music and dance lessons.[53]

What are some of these cultural skills for which children are rewarded? Swidler describes a tool kit of cultural skills, habits, and styles as largely ingrained behaviors.[54] These might be as simple as understanding appropriate kinds of responses to teachers' questions about a book[55] or understanding that print reads left to right, where to go when a line of print ends, or where the story ends, three skills that nearly one in five children entering kindergarten in America lack.[56] This cultural tool kit may also contain non-cognitive skills that are important for negotiating the student role. For example, students who can demonstrate the appropriate level of attentiveness, persistence at tasks, eagerness to learn, and organizational skills are more likely to earn good grades.[57]

Low-Income Parents

Many of the parental practices described above are highly correlated with socioeconomic status, and so it is likely that one of the reasons children from disadvantaged backgrounds do less well in school than their more advantaged counterparts is because their parents' interaction style less successfully prepares them for school. Indeed, some scholars report that the typically positive effects of socioeconomic status on children's school performance are mediated entirely by parenting practices.[58] It is difficult to discern precisely how related parenting styles and socioeconomic status are, but it is clear that there is substantial overlap.

In his classic 1969 book, *Class and Conformity*, Melvin Kohn offers one reason for this overlap. He argued that parents' style of interaction with their children is influenced in important ways by the parents' occupations. Parents who work in jobs with little autonomy (e.g., data entry) and are rewarded for adherence to external standards (e.g., being on time, being neat, obedience to authority), tend to parent in ways that prepare their children for success in these same kinds of jobs. Kohn found that working-class parents put more emphasis on obedience than did middle-class parents. In contrast, parents in occupations that allow for more self-determined activities and decision-making tend to promote their children's skills for assuming these kinds of middle-class occupations. The middle-class parent, therefore, uses a less punitive style of discipline and puts greater emphasis on developing children's internal controls. From Kohn's perspective, both low- and high-socioeconomic parents want what is best for their children; they are simply teaching their children the skills they deem necessary for success in the world. Through the working-class parent's interaction style, however, he or she unwittingly increases the likelihood that the child will remain in the same social class position.[59]

Socioeconomic position is also related to how parents interact with teachers and school officials. Lareau observed parent/teacher relationships in a working-class and a middle-class community and reported that teachers in both communities made active efforts to involve parents, but that low-income parents were less involved. Working-class parents were less likely to attend parent-teacher conferences, for example, in part because the costs of attending—in terms of obtaining transportation, securing child care, and rearranging work schedules—were typically greater for working- than for middle-class parents. In addition, working-class parents were more likely than middle-class parents to espouse a view that it is the school's job to educate their children.[60] Lareau writes: "Working-class culture ... promotes independence between the spheres of family life and schooling."[61] In contrast, middle-class parents were more likely to view their child's education as partly their own responsibility, along with the school's. Working-class parents were less involved with teachers for other reasons too. They were less comfortable interacting with teachers, in part, because they reported feeling unqualified to discuss academic problems. When they did have contact with teachers, working-class parents often discussed non-academic issues such as bus schedules or playground activities.

Others note how language differences across class end up shaping success in school. Bernstein describes how parents of low socioeconomic status tend to use a "restricted" language code in which language is embedded in context, reflects the status of individuals, and minimizes the need to make one's meaning explicit. In contrast, higher socioeconomic parents use an "elaborate" code that is less context-based and more individualistic so that language is used to make meaning more explicit.[62] To illustrate this difference Bernstein offers two vignettes of a mother and a child riding a bus. In the lower socioeconomic pair, the mother's mode of control relies on commands with little explanation (e.g., "Hold on tight") and reflects the hierarchical view of the adult-child relationship ("I told you to hold on tight, didn't I?"). In the middle socioeconomic group, the interactions are less hierarchical, and the mother provides a learning opportunity by using language to explore the situation ("If you don't hold on tight, you will be thrown forward and you will fall," "If the bus stops suddenly, you'll jerk forward on to the seat in front.") Bernstein notes that an important educational consequence of these two different approaches to language is that the relatively context-independent style used by the middle-class parent matches that expected by school teachers.[63]

In addition, low-income parents experience greater financial stress and health-related problems than other parents, and both of these may impede their ability to develop consistent routines. Children perform better in school when their learning is not compromised by hunger, distracting physical ailments, lack of adequate sleep, unattended visual limitations, or other health related problems. Ear infections during the early years (before age four) pose a special problem because they can alter the functioning of the middle ear and thus affect the child's hearing and, consequently, language development. A report from the National Institute on Early Childhood suggests that treating middle ear infections is crucial to children's language development.[64] Kellaghan et al. note that iodine deficiency during pregnancy, zinc deficiency, and iron deficiency have long-lasting consequences for children's development.[65] There is also greater drug and alcohol abuse among the poor, factors that work against consistent routines. While some low-income parents may benefit from instruction on developing home routines, for those low-income parents who suffer from drug and alcohol abuse or experience stress related to financial problems, health problems, or both, it is unlikely that they will make substantial progress in developing home-based routines while these underlying problems persist.

Implications for Practice and Policy

The current evidence suggests that there may be some profit in improving parent/teacher relations, but that a more effective way to improve children's school performance involves improving parent/child relations. This is disconcerting news for policymakers, because parent/child relations are much more difficult to affect via policy than parent/teacher relations. And for low-income families, part of parents' interaction style—linguistic style, for instance—is likely rooted in class position and may not be fundamentally altered unless class position changes. If parents are unlikely to change what they do at home unless their class position is improved, one policy approach is to increase the amount of time that children are with teachers via after school programs or year-round schooling. Given what has been already noted from seasonal comparison research—that the gap in cognitive skills between advantaged and disadvantaged children emerges primarily during the summer—low-income children would likely benefit the most from more exposure to schooling.

The record for changing parents' home behaviors in ways that affect children's school performance is not encouraging. White, Taylor and Moss carefully reviewed the results of 172 studies ranging from those training parents to improve children's developmental skills (e.g., motor, language) to those where parents were classroom aides.[66] Surprisingly, they find little evidence that parental involvement matters. They conclude that "there is no convincing evidence that the ways in which parents have been involved in previous early intervention research studies result in more effective outcomes."[67]

However, one recent study shows success. Children participating in the Chicago Child-Parent Center Program enrolled in half-day preschool at ages three to four years and were exposed to rigorous reading lessons in small classes while their parents were involved in activities with other parents (e.g., educational workshops, reading groups, and craft projects), volunteered in the classroom, attended school events and field trips, and were encouraged to complete high school. Further, the program included health and nutrition services, health screening, speech therapy, and nursing and meal services. Results suggest that children in the program were more likely to graduate from high school and less likely to be arrested 15 years later than similarly matched children.[68] Because involvement in the program was not a result of parent initiative—parents were actively

recruited for the program—it is unlikely that the advantages for participants merely represent the selectivity of more involved parents.[69]

What Have Critics Said?

The vast majority of research on parenting practices is correlational, and
so an important concern is that the observed associations between parenting practices and students' school performance represent mere correlations, not causal relationships. This position has received considerable
attention lately from behavioral geneticists who assert that the role of parental behaviors has been overstated in the social sciences and that genetic
influences have been understated.[70] With respect to the impact parents
have on children through shaping the home environment, Scarr writes:

> It is clear that there are family differences, but it is also clear that most of
> those differences are not environmental. Among families in the mainstream
> of Western Europe and North American societies, differences in family envi-
> ronments seem to have little effect on intellectual and personality differences
> among their children, unless they are seriously deprived of opportunities
> and support... [g]ood enough, ordinary parents probably have the same
> effects on their children's development as culturally defined super-parents.[71]

For purposes of understanding how parental involvement influences
children's school performance, this debate is especially important because,
if the behavioral geneticists' position is correct, most parents cannot affect
their children's school success much.

An example of the problem of determining causality with correlational
studies can be illustrated with the frequently found negative relationship
between how often parents help with homework and children's school performance.[72] The idea that more help is associated with poorer performance strikes one as counterintuitive.[73] But this association probably
represents parents' response to children's need for help. The kinds of children needing help are different (probably poorer students) than the kinds
of children who easily complete their homework on their own. In a typical
correlational study, researchers try to address this possibility by statistically
equalizing the two groups on characteristics such as income, education,
family structure, race, urban/suburban/rural location, and other factors
they suspect might be different between the kinds of parents who supervise
children's homework versus those who do not. They would also statistically
control for the child's previous performance in school.

These attempts to isolate the unique effect of "parental involvement in
homework" are limited, however, because we usually cannot measure or
even conceive of all of the ways the two groups of parents and their chil-

dren may be different. As a result, despite statistical controls we probably fail to obtain unbiased estimates of the true effect of parental help with homework. Of course it is possible that children's school efforts really are hampered rather than helped by their parents, but few researchers espouse this view. A more likely explanation is that the statistical controls used to equalize the two groups are inadequate. But if this kind of problem affects our ability to estimate accurately the effects of parental involvement with homework, it likely affects our estimates of other parental behaviors too, casting doubt on nearly all of the parental involvement literature.[74]

Another example of the behavioral geneticists' position can be understood by considering the associations between "good" parenting practices and children's school success. Behavioral geneticists note that parents influence children in two ways, by providing their home environment but also by passing on genes. If parents who create good environments are also parents with good genes, associations between good parenting behaviors and students' school success may have little to do with parenting actions and may simply represent the genetic advantages typical of parents who also happen to use good parenting practices. This line of thinking posits that the correlation between "good" parenting (authoritative) and children's school success may be a function of parents with genetic advantages (high intelligence, easy disposition) having children with similar advantages and also parenting in the culturally prescribed way. Among middle-class Americans of European descent this means an authoritative approach. Because other racial/ethnic groups favor other parenting styles, genetically advantaged parents in other groups might not use authoritative parenting. Asian Americans, for example, more often use authoritarian parenting, yet Asian-American children often do well in school.[75] Correlations from most parenting studies could be reinterpreted as the effects of good genes rather than good parenting.

It is difficult to discern between environmental and genetic explanations with correlational data, so one approach is to look at whether adopted children are more like their adopted parents (who provide their environment) or their biological parents (who provide their genes). In terms of scores on intelligence tests, it appears that adopted children are more like their biological parents, even if they were adopted at birth.[76] Another analytically powerful comparison is to look at children who are similar genetically but who have experienced different environments: identical twins reared apart. Of course, identical twins are rare themselves and so finding identical twins raised apart is nearly impossible. Researchers at the University of Minnesota have collected data on more than 100 pairs, however. Analyses of these data show surprising results—the twins are more alike each other than we would expect, even when unaware of each other's existence for most of their lives.[77] While the position that children's outcomes are more readily understood via genetics rather than environment may strike many as unlikely, it is not easily dismissed based on the current empirical evidence.

The implications of this position—that parental involvement matters little—are clear for policy: Only programs designed to raise children out of the very worst environmental conditions would be effective.

Several important issues regarding heritability studies are still debated. For example, critics point out that it is not clear how much contact occurred between some of the identical twins raised apart in heritability studies. Identical twins in these studies vary in many ways (e.g., the age at which they were separated and the difference in the kinds of home environments they were raised); ideally all would have been separated at birth and raised in randomly different environments, but, of course, it would not be ethical to set up such an experiment prospectively. Another issue has to do with the attempt to neatly separate environmental and genetic effects. Critics claim that genetic and environmental effects interact and so typical heritability studies underestimate environmental contributions.[78] For example, a temperamentally difficult child may be difficult for genetic reasons, but this child also evokes harsh parenting. Perhaps identical twins reared apart are similar to each other because they end up evoking similar environments (they look alike), and only modestly so because of shared genes. If this interpretation of heritability studies proves true, then how parents interact with their children matters.

SUMMARY AND RECOMMENDATIONS

The research available to date on the subject of parental involvement in education yields conclusions about what we know as well as what we don't know.

It is unlikely that increasing parents' participation at PTA meetings and in helping with homework *alone* will have a substantial impact on children's school performance. Programs that successfully raise children's school performance via parental involvement do so by meeting the broad needs of parents. For example, the success of the Chicago Child-Parent Center Program is probably a function of the wide range of services provided to parents, including educational workshops, reading groups, and craft projects, health and nutrition services, health screening, speech therapy, and nursing and meal services.

There is little reason to believe that the kinds of policy initiatives employed in the past—even the Chicago Child-Parent Center Program— will dramatically affect the gap in performance among students from low-

and high-income families. After-school and year-round programs will probably benefit low-income children the most.

It is not clear that children's performance in school is solely or perhaps even primarily a function of parenting style. While children's school success is associated with parenting approaches, this association is culturally specific (e.g., authoritative parenting is used among the parents of successful white students but authoritarian parenting is used among the parents of successful Asian-American students in the U.S.) and may represent, in part, the genetic similarity between parent and child.

These conclusions support the following policy recommendations to enhance parental involvement:

- Programs designed to promote parent/teacher interaction should be continued, but with greater emphasis on initiatives designed to improve the parent/child relationship. Programs designed to meet the broad needs of parents (e.g., improving parents' reading skills, reducing financial stress, meeting health and nutritional needs) are likely to be the most successful.
- Programs should be promoted that increase the amount of time low-income children are exposed to school-based activities, whether through more after-school programs, summer activities, or year-round schooling.

REFERENCES

1. H. J. Walberg, "Families as Partners in Educational Productivity," *Phi Delta Kappan* 65 (1984): 397–400.
2. C. Izzo et al., "A Longitudinal Assessment of Teacher Perceptions of Parent Involvement in Children's Education and School Performance," *American Journal of Community Psychology* 27, no. 6 (1999): 817–839.
3. Ibid., 820.
4. J. L. Epstein and S. Lee, "National Patterns of School and Family Connections in the Middle Grades," in *The Family-School Connection, Vol. 2: Theory, Research and Practice,* eds. B.A. Ryan, G.R. Adams, T.P. Gullotta, R.P. Weissberg, & R. L. Jampton (Thousand Oaks, CA: Sage, 1995), 108–154.
5. J. L. Epstein, "Toward a Theory of Family-School Connections: Teacher Practices and Parent Involvement," in *Social intervention: Potential and constraints,* eds. K. Jurrelmann, F. Kaufmann, & F. Losel (New York: Degruyter, 1987), 121–136.
6. J. L. Epstein, "Advances in Family, Community, and School Partnerships," *New Schools, New Communities* 12, no. 3 (1996): 5–13.
7. Ibid., 5.
8. D. L. Stevenson and D. P. Baker, "The Family-School Relation and the Child's School Performance," *Child Development* 58 (1987): 1348–1357.

9. W. S. Grolnick and M. L. Slowiaczek, "Parents' Involvement In Children's Schooling: A Multidimensional Conceptualization and Motivational Model," *Child Development* 65, no. 1 (1987): 237–252.

10. Izzo et al, 1999.

    L. Desimone, "Linking Parent Involvement with Student Achievement: Do Race and Income Matter?" *The Journal of Educational Research* 93, no. 1 (1999): 11–30.

    L. Steinberg et al., "Impact of Parenting Practices on Adolescent Achievement: Authoritative Parenting, School Involvement, and Encouragement to Succeed," *Child Development* 63 (1992): 1266–1281.

    R. D. Taylor, "Adolescents' Perceptions of Kinship Support and Family Management Practices: Association with Adolescent Adjustment in African American Families," *Developmental Psychology* 32, no. 4 (1996), 687–695.

11. Desimone.

12. L. C. Rigsby, J.C. Stull, and N. Morse-Kelly, "School Performances: Complicating Explanatory Models by Incorporating Race and Gender" (Temple University, Philadelphia, 1995)

13. R. Moses et al., "The Algebra Project: Organizing in the Spirit of Ella," *Harvard Educational Review* 59, no. 4 (1989): 423–443.

14. J. R. Coleman, *Foundations of Social Theory* (Cambridge, MA: Harvard University, 1990).

15. J. M. Podolny and James N. Baron, "Resources and Relationships: Social Networks and Mobility in the Workplace," *American Sociological Review* 62 (1997): 673–693.

16. Ibid., 676.

17. B. Broh, "Linking Extracurricular Programming to Academic Achievement: Who Benefits and Why," Paper presented at the American Sociological Association Meetings, Washington, DC, 2000

    Broh noted that part of the reason children benefit academically from playing high school varsity sports is because this activity tends to bring parents together at school events.

18. W. J. Carbonaro, "Opening the Debate on Closure and Schooling Outcomes," *American Sociological Review* 64 (1999): 682–686.

19. S. L. Morgan and A. B. Sorensen, "Parental Networks, Social Closure, and Mathematics Learning: A Test Of Coleman's Social Capital Explanation of School Effects," *American Sociological Review* 64 (1999): 661–681.

20. Carbonaro.

    Desimone.

    M. T. Hallinan and W. N. Kubitschek, "Conceptualizing and Measuring School Social Networks," *American Sociological Review* 64 (1999): 687–693.

    Morgan and Sorensen. Morgan and Sorensen suggest that students benefit when parents do *not* know other parents in the school, and therefore know more adults outside of the school ("horizon-expanding" schools) because students are exposed to more varied expectations and opportunities.

21. E. H. Sui-Chu and J. D. Willms, "Effects of Parental Involvement on Eighth-Grade Achievement," *Sociology of Education* 69 (1996): 126–141.

22. Ibid.

23.   L. Desimone, M. Finn-Stevenson, and C. Henrich, "Whole School Reform in a Low-Income African American Community: The Effects of the CoZi Model on Teachers, Parents, and Students," *Urban Education* 35, no. 3 (2000): 269–323.

24.   J. West, K. Denton and E. Germino-Hausken, *America's Kindergartners: Findings from the Early Childhood Longitudinal Study, Kindergarten Class of 1998–99, Fall 1998*, NCES 2000-070 (Washington, DC: U.S. Department of Education, National Center for Education Statistics, 2000).

25.   D. R. Entwisle and K. L. Alexander, "Summer Setback: Race, Poverty, School Composition and Math Achievement in the First Two Years of School," *American Sociological Review* 57 (1992): 72–84.

   D. R. Entwisle and K. L. Alexander, "The Gender Gap in Math: Its Possible Origins in Neighborhood Effects," *American Sociological Review* 59 (1994): 822–838.

   B. Heyns, *Summer Learning and the Effects of Schooling* (New York: Academic Press, 1978).

   B. Heyns, "Schooling and Cognitive Development: Is There a Season for Learning?" *Child Development* 58 (1987): 1151–1160.

   N. Karweit and A. E. Ricciuti, *Summer Learning: Achievement Profiles of Prospects First Graders* (Washington, DC: Abt Associates, 1997).

26.   A. M. Milne, D. E. Myers, A. S. Rosenthal, and Alan Ginsburg, "Single Parents, Working Mothers, and the Educational Achievement of School Children," *Sociology of Education* 59 (1986): 125–139.

   N. M. Astone and S. S. McLanahan, "Family Structure, Parental Practices, and High School Completion," *American Sociological Review* 56 (1991): 309–20.

   A. C. Kerckhoff and R. T. Camp, "Black-White Differences in the Educational Attainment Process," *Sociology of Education* 50 (1977): 15–27.

27.   D. Baumrind, "Current Patterns of Parental Authority," *Developmental Psychology Monograph* 4, no. 1-1-3 (1971).

   D. Baumrind and A.E. Black, "Socialization Practices Associated with Dimensions of Competence in Preschool Boys and Girls," *Child Development* 38 (1967): 291–327.

28.   S. M. Dornbusch et al., "The Relation of Parenting Style to Adolescent School Performance," *Child Development* 58 (1987): 1244–1257.

   B. Schneider and Y. Lee, "A Model for Academic-Success: The School and Home-Environment of East-Asian Students," *Anthropology & Education Quarterly* 21, no. 4: 358–377.

   It is hard to argue that there is something we can call "good parenting" that applies universally. Dornbusch et al. found that the correlation between authoritative and permissive parenting styles and achievement was insignificant for all Asian students. Desimone and Steinberg et. al report similar patterns. In addition, Schneider and Lee report that Asian students are less influenced by the family-school link than are other students.

29.   Steinberg, Lamborn, Dornbusch, and Darling.

   The authors measured parenting style via adolescents' responses to questions about their parents' acceptance/involvement (e.g., "When [my mother or father] wants me to do something, [he or she] explains why"; " I can count on [him or her] to help out if I have some kind of problem") and strictness/supervision (e.g., My parents know exactly where I am most afternoons after school"; "In a typical week, what is the latest you can stay out on school nights?"). Twelve percent of the adolescents were categorized as living in authoritarian homes where the adolescents rated their parents in the upper third for both acceptance/involvement and strictness/supervision.

30. Meredith Phillips et al., "Family Background, Parenting Practices, and the Black-White Test Score Gap," in *The Black-White Test Score Gap*, eds. C. Jencks and M. Phillips (Washington DC: Brookings Institution, 1998).

31. Ibid., 127.

32. B. Hart and T. R. Risley, "American Parenting of Language-Learning Children: Persisting Differences in Family-Child Interactions Observed in Natural Home Environments," *Developmental Psychology* 28, no. 6 (1992): 1096–1105.

33. Ibid., 1104.

34. R. M. Clark, *Family Life and School Achievement* (Chicago: University of Chicago Press, 1983).

35. Sui-Chu and Willms, 138.

36. C. Muller, "Parent Involvement and Academic Achievement: An Analysis of Family Resources Available to the Child," in *Parents, Their Children, and Schools*, eds. B. Schneider and J. S. Coleman (Boulder, CO: Westview, 1993), 77–114.

Desimone.

37. Astone and McLanahan.

P. G. Fehrmann, T. Z. Keith, and T. M. Reimers, "Home Influence on School Learning: Direct and Indirect Effects of Parental Involvement on High School Grades," *Journal of Educational Research* 806 (1987): 330–337.

38. Clark.

39. Taylor.

40. R. D. Hess, and V. Shipman, "Early Experience and the Socialization of Cognitive Modes in Children," *Child Development* 36 (1965): 869–881.

41. J. E. Brophy, "Mothers as Teachers of Their Own Preschool Children: The Influence of Socioeconomic Status and Task Structure on Teaching Specificity," *Child Development* 41 (1970): 79–94.

In one of the most impressive studies of a generalizable sample, Desimone employed the NELS data and constructed 12 different measures of parental involvement: (1) discussion with child about high school, (2) talk with parents about post-high school plans, (3) parent volunteering or fund-raising, (4) parent has rules about homework, GPA, and chores, (5) PTO involvement, (6) parent attends PTO meetings, (7) parent has rules about TV, friends, and chores, (8) parent checks homework, (9) parent contacts school about academics, (10) student reports discussing school matters with parent, (11) student reports talking to father about high school program, (12) parents report knowing parents of child's friends. The most consistent positive influence on students' math and reading test scores and grades was students' reports of discussing school matters with parents (talks to mother about planning high school program, discussed program at school with parents, discusses school activities with parents, discusses thing studied in class with parents). Parents knowing the parents of their child's friends also consistently predicted math and reading test scores and grades, although this benefit did not generalize to low-income families. In addition, Desimone (1999) reports that parental involvement measures account for twice as much variance in student grades than in student test scores.

42.   E. W. Ball and B. A. Blachman, "Does Phoneme Awareness Training in Kindergarten Make a Difference In Early Word Recognition and Developmental Spelling?" *Reading Research Quarterly* 26, no. 1 (1991): 49–66.

I. Lundberg, J. Frost, and O. Petersen, "Effects of an Extensive Program for Stimulating Phonological Awareness in Preschool Children," *Reading Research Quarterly* 23 (1988): 263–284.

43.   Phillips et al.

44.   J. Tizard, W. Schofield, and J. Hewison, "Collaboration Between Teachers and Parents in Assisting Children's Reading," *British Journal of Educational Psychology* 52, no. 1 (1982): 1–11.

45.   J. D. Teachman, "Family Background, Educational Resources, and Educational Attainment," *American Sociological Review* 52 (1987): 548–57.

D. B. Downey, "When Bigger is not Better: Family Size, Parental Resources, and Children's Educational Performance," *American Sociological Review* 60 (1995): 746–761.

46.   Downey.

47.   J. D. Finn, "Parental Engagement that Makes a Difference," *Educational Leadership* (May 1998): 20–24.

48.   Milne et al.

T. Madigan, "Parent Involvement and School Achievement." Paper presented at the meeting of the American Educational Research Association, New Orleans, 1994.

Desimone.

49.   S. J. Balli, J. F. Wedman, and D. H. Demo, "Family Involvement With Middle-Grades Homework: Effects of Differential Prompting," *The Journal of Experimental Education* 66, no. 1 (1997): 31–48.

50.   P. Bourdieu, *Reproduction in Education, Society, and Culture* (Beverly Hills, CA: Sage, 1977).

51.   Ibid.

52.   P. J. DiMaggio, "Cultural Capital and Schooling Success: The Impact of Status Culture Participation on the Grades of U.S. High School Students," *American Sociological Review* 47 (1982): 189–201.

53.   V. J. Roscigno and J. W. Ainsworth-Darnell, "Race, Cultural Capital, and Educational Resources: Persistent Inequalities and Achievement Returns," *Sociology of Education* 72 (1999): 158–178.

54.   A. Swidler, "Culture in Action: Symbols and Strategies," *American Sociological Review* 51 (1986): 273–286.

55.   S. B. Heath, "What No Bedtime Story Means: Narrative Skills at Home and School," *Language in Society* 11, no. 2 (1982): 49–76.

56.   West, Denton and Germino-Hausken.

57.   G. Farkas et al., "Cultural Resources and School Success: Gender, Ethnicity, and Poverty Groups Within an Urban School District," *American Sociological Review* 55 (1990): 127–142.

J. W. Ainsworth-Darnell and D. B. Downey, "Assessing the Oppositional Culture Explanation for Racial/Ethnic Differences in School Performance," *American Sociological Review* 63 (1998): 536–553.

58.   Stevenson and Baker.

Stevenson and Baker's indicator of parental involvement was based on teachers' responses to the questions, "To what extend did his/her parents get involved in the activities of the school such as PTO and parent-teacher conferences?" Their indicator of socioeconomic status was the mother's education.

59.   M. L. Kohn, *Class and Conformity* (Chicago: Chicago University Press, 1969).

S. Bowles and H. Gintis, *Schooling in Capitalist America* (New York: Basic Books, 1976).

Bowles and Gintis argue that schools in working-class neighborhoods also promote obedience and vocational skills that will likely ensure the reproduction of class position. Middle-class schools, they argue, allow students greater responsibility and put less emphasis on obedience to external standards–practices that prepare them for middle-class jobs.

60.   A. Lareau, "Social Class and Family-School Relationships: The Importance of Cultural Capital," *Sociology of Education* 56 (April 1987): 73–85.

61.   Ibid., p. 82.

62.   B. Bernstein, *Class, Codes and Control* (New York: Schocken Books, 1975).

63.   Ibid.

64.   *Reconsidering Children's Early Learning and Development: Toward Shared Beliefs and Vocabulary*, eds. S. L. Kagan, E. Moore, and S. Bredecamp, (Washington, DC: National Education Goals Panel, 1995).

65.   T. Kellaghan et al., *The Home Environment and School Learning* (San Francisco: Jossey-Bass, 1993).

66.   K. R. White, M. J. Taylor, and V. D. Moss, "Does Research Support Claims About the Benefits of Involving Parents in Early Intervention Programs?" *Review of Educational Research* 62, no. 1 (1992): 91–125.

67.   Ibid., 91.

68.   A. J. Reynolds et al., "Long-term Effects of an Early Childhood Intervention on Educational Achievement and Juvenile Arrest," *Journal of the American Medical Association* 285, no. 18 (2001): 2339–2346.

69.   For a more detailed description of the intervention, see: A.J. Reynolds, *Success In Early Intervention: The Chicago Child-Parent Centers* (Lincoln: University of Nebraska Press, 2000).

70.   J. R. Harris, *The Nurture Assumption: Why Children Turn Out the Way They Do* (The Free Press: New York, 1998).

D. C. Rowe, *The Limits of Family Influence: Genes, Experience, and Behavior* (New York: The Guilford Press, 1994).

S. Scarr, "How People Make Their Own Environments: Implications for Parents and Policy Makers," *Psychology, Public Policy, and Law* 2, no. 2 (1996): 204–228.

R. Plomin, M. J. Owen, and P. McGuffin, "The Genetic Basis of Complex Human Behaviors," *Science* 264 (17 June 1994): 1733–1739.

71.   Scarr, 220–221.

72.   Milne et al.

Madigan.

73.   Some studies suggest that parents help their children more with homework when they are young and so it is possible that the studies based on the NELS eighth graders simply reflect that most parents are helping little at that point unless their child is struggling. It would be a mistake to conclude that parental involvement with homework, especially at young ages, is detrimental.

74.   Arguably, research that looks at how changes in parental involvement are associated with changes in children's school performance, are less vulnerable to this criticism. For example, Izzo et al. estimated children's standardized test scores at Time 2 while controlling for Time 1 measures, and still found that parental involvement variables predicted test scores. There are important limitations to this study, however. See: Izzo et al.

75.   L. Steinberg, S. M. Dornbusch, and B. B. Brown, "Ethnic Differences in Adolescent Achievement: An Ecological Perspective," *American Psychologist* 47 (1992): 723–729.

76.   R. Plomin, "The Role of Inheritance in Behavior, Science," 248 (1990): 183–188.

77.   T. J. Bouchard, Jr., "Genes, Environment, and Personality," *Science* 264 (17 June 1994): 1700–1701.

Plomin (1990) suggests that roughly 70% of the variance in intelligence is likely due to inherited characteristics and 30% to environment. Given how important intelligence is for school performance, if this ratio is correct then it is likely that a reasonably large part of the typically observed association between parenting practices and children's school success represents parents' genetic contribution to children's development.

78.   W. A. Collins et al., "Contemporary Research on Parenting: The Case for Nature and Nurture," *American Psychologist* 55, no. 2 (2000): 218–232.

CHAPTER 7

PUBLIC SCHOOLS AND THEIR COMMUNITIES

Catherine Lugg
Rutgers University

SUMMARY OF RESEARCH FINDINGS

Although limited largely to case studies, research has documented a wide range of programs that have expanded public schools' involvement with the communities in which they operate. Such programs face a variety of challenges that range from institutional rivalries to competition for scarce financial resources. Operated effectively, however, than can contribute to improved achievement by students living in poverty.

RECOMMENDATIONS

- Basic parental involvement programs should be enhanced to include multiple opportunities for formal and informal communication between school personnel and parents.
- Parental involvement programs should be developed that embrace the ethnic, linguistic, cultural, racial, and religious diversity of the parents.
- Parental involvement programs should be designed to be sensitive to the special needs of poor parents, single parents, parents with large families, and those families where both parents work outside of the home.

- Written materials should be provided in the language with which parents are the most familiar.
- Schools and other social organizations wishing to provide school-linked services should carefully consider the scope, funding needs, organizational and professional complexities, and types of services to be offered.
- Funding for new community involvement projects should be kept consistent and stable. The bigger and more complex the project, the greater the need for adequate funding.
- Extra-curricular programs should be kept vital to help foster strong parental involvement.
- Educational leaders and policy makers should be encouraged to reconceptualize the public school as a vital economic resource that must be nurtured.

The interplay between public schools, their respective communities, and child welfare has been an area of public policy concern for well over a century. From as early as the late 19th century, various educational and social reformers have sought to strengthen the ties between schools and communities in hopes of bolstering better outcomes for children, as well as building stronger, more functional communities.[1] Yet, many of the same problems reformers faced over a century ago stubbornly remain: low parental involvement, the deleterious effects of concentrated poverty, inappropriate pedagogy and policy, racial and ethnic economic isolation, dysfunctional families, and ineffectual political leadership.[2] Each issue can hinder an individual child's educational achievement, but the interaction of multiple factors can be devastating.[3]

This report seeks to map out this history and the contemporary research literature regarding the interaction of public schools, their communities, and student outcomes, especially academic achievement. It reviews some of the major consistencies within the research literature, particularly during the past 15 years. It also notes some of the major criticisms regarding school to community outreach, including some of the lingering paradoxes. This report pays particular attention to what reforms seem to work best with poor children and concludes with recommendations for the best choices in educational practice and policy making.

SCHOOLS AND COMMUNITY RESEARCH

An Historical Overview

During the late 19th and early 20th centuries, educational and social reformers pushed for an expanded role for public education. Many were deeply concerned by the exploding numbers of poor and destitute children who seemed to overwhelm local schools, particularly in the nation's booming urban centers. Cities were also faced with an ever-enlarging immigrant population, many of whom had little education or economic resources.[4] In hopes of improving the lives of children, educators and social reformers sought to expand the mission of the public school. Not only would the public school educate, but it would also bathe, feed, and inoculate needy children. Their mission did not stop there: all children, many of whom were either immigrants themselves or children of recent immigrants, would be "Americanized." They would learn the dominant social, political, and cultural norms of mainstream—and at that time, largely Anglo—America.[5] Reformers of the era viewed the public school as a linchpin in the process of "child-saving."[6] By the 1910s, numerous city schools offered gyms, school nurses, playgrounds, shower facilities, and even school lunches.[7] Some locations offered adult education classes for parents, held typically at night, not only to build their own language skills and knowledge base, but also to learn new parenting skills. In other instances, teachers would visit their students' homes in hopes of fostering better communication between the school and parents, as well as building a consistency of academic and behavioral expectations. Urban districts began to use the "school newsletter" as a means of communication with parents and the public at large.[8]

These efforts to better link the schools with their communities were rooted in the late 19th century sociological notion of building "social ecology," or improving the overall environment in which children and their parents lived. For many children, their lives did improve. Public schools not only ameliorated the harshest effects, but also offered children the promise of a way out of poverty. Attendance rates soared as immigrant children in particular streamed into the public schools. By 1908, a larger percentage of immigrant children attended public schools than did their "native-born" peers.[9]

These services came at costs that were both personal and fiscal, however. The personal costs were generally borne by those who were receiving the help. To become "Americanized" meant that children had to relinquish the cultural practices and norms from the "old country." In practical terms, it meant that many immigrant children were taught that their heritage (and by implication, their parents) were inferior. Accordingly, teachers and administrators treated immigrant parents with more than a whiff of condescension. As one educator explained:

> They must be *made* to understand what it is we are trying to do for the children. They must be *made* to realize that in forsaking the land of their birth, they were also forsaking the customs and traditions of that land; and they

must be *made* to realize an obligation, in adopting a new country, to adopt the language and customs of that country.[10]

In addition to problematic relations between the schools and parents, both the textbooks and teachers could be hostile towards non-Anglo children, with more than a few hurling racial, ethnic, and religious slurs.[11] In 1903, reporter Adele Marie Shaw recounted that one elementary teacher bellowed at one child, "You dirty little Russian Jew, what are you doing?"[12]

Finally, the help tended to be imposed whether or not students and their parents believed they needed assistance.[13] The assumption of the era was that professional educators were far better prepared to assess the welfare of children than were their immigrant parents.

The greatest drawbacks to extending more services to "children at risk," though, were fiscal, and these financial drawbacks were rooted in the politics of the era. These efforts were subjected to intense scrutiny on the heels of the 1917 Russian Revolution, with some commentators noting that such social programs were dangerously "socialistic."[14] For years, public education had been under the policy microscope regarding its seeming lack of fiscal accountability, possible political radicalism,[15] and instructional inefficiencies. Thanks to the churning political environment, much of the tax money for greater social services, which, in some places, was extensive and expensive, evaporated.[16] In hopes of maintaining political and fiscal support, public school leaders scrambled to deflect criticism, and many embraced the new "science" of public relations, touting public education's ever-increasing efficiency.[17] Until the late 1980s, efforts to do community outreach and communication to bolster student academic outcomes would become largely one-way—with information flowing only from the schools to the families.[18]

Schools and Communities Today

By the late 1980s and early 1990s, researchers, educators, social service providers, and policy makers were alarmed at the rising number of children in crisis, particularly in poor urban areas. Many states had curtailed social service provisions to offset budget shortfalls. Additionally, the federal government had greatly reduced its level of fiscal involvement with poor children beginning in the early 1980s.[19] Concurrently, the number of children in poverty was rising. As researcher Joy Dryfoos observed in 1994:

By 1991, more than fourteen million children—22 percent of all children— lived in families below the poverty line, the highest number and rate since 1965. As in no other period of time, disadvantage shifted from the oldest people to the youngest. And those children living in mother-only households have become the most deprived of all, with more than 55 percent living in poverty.[20]

Such social and economic turbulence was adversely affecting many students and their academic achievement. This turbulence was also coupled with increased political concern regarding public education and its possible adverse effects on the nation's economic competitiveness.[21] Public schools leaders, community members, social service providers, policy makers and researchers took a renewed interest in rebuilding the social ecology of local public schools in hopes of fostering better academic outcomes, and in turn, stabilizing the social environment—thus revitalizing a national economy.[22]

States and the federal government began to explore the notion of "systemic reform," or coordinating the various governmental policies that affect children in a more holistic fashion to improve both their current lives and their long-term life chances.[23] For education, and urban education in particular, this meant involving various branches of government in efforts to better link schools to the communities they serve.[24]

Many of these new reform efforts drew on the work of the sociologist James S. Coleman. In the early to mid-1980s, Coleman and his colleagues had studied the academic effectiveness of urban Catholic schools. He theorized that the reason Catholic schools seemed to generate better outcomes for their students was that these schools and their students enjoyed a high degree of "social capital." Coleman further theorized that these schools in their particular communities were "functional communities," because their members shared a high degree of what he called "intergenerational closure." Additionally, the communities and the schools shared a strong interest in the general welfare of the students. Parents knew each other and each other's children. The implications were that these schools functioned in relatively close-knit communities. Parents, school personnel, and community members cultured the relationships and shared norms (i.e. the social capital) that were critical to successful child rearing and schooling.[25]

There were criticisms of the Coleman studies, particularly regarding their possible utility and applicability for public schools. The critics noted three key differences between Catholic urban and public urban schools. First, Catholic schools tended to "cream" the academically strongest students (and their parents) away from the distressed urban schools. Additionally, students who attended Catholic schools did so voluntarily, unlike many of their public school peers. Finally, Catholic schools were free to expel students who failed to conform to either academic or behavioral expectations.[26]

Nevertheless, researchers and policy makers began to explore the possibilities that public schools, in conjunction with other community and social service groups, could build, rebuild or even expand the social capital of their communities. Reformers also drew on the earlier efforts of Progressive-Era reformers to strengthen the social ecology of school neighborhoods. Subsequently, multiple and various blueprints were designed; all aimed at bringing various stakeholders together.[27]

Full-Service Schools

By the early 1990s, well over 800 projects were aimed at fostering greater ties between schools and their communities.[28] States from California to New Jersey were experimenting with vastly expanded social service provision as well as experimenting with differing organizational structures, including interagency collaboration and full-service school programs. These terms, as well as school-linked services, have been used in the research literature. They describe efforts to bring various social service providers together within a formal organizational structure—sometimes sharing a building, typically a public school—to share staff, resources, and responsibilities. All were to better serve children, their parents, and the larger community.[29] In an age of continuing budget constraint, some early proponents of this approach argued that providers might even realize budgetary cost savings if the collaborating agencies could eliminate needless service duplication.[30]

These projects tended to be idiosyncratic in nature. As Joy Dryfoos noted in 1994, full-service schools, by design, were to be highly sensitive to the local contexts. There has been no one model of a "full-service school." The disparate interagency collaborations have included personnel from public schools, child protective services, juvenile justice agencies, mental health agencies, public health departments, the medical system, as well as parents and other community members.[31]

Most of the extant evaluation research of these projects has been in the form of single-case or multi-case studies. However, common similarities across project sites include better attendance rates, lower substance abuse, and lower dropout rates. Additionally, "[s]tudents, parents, teachers, and school personnel report a high level of satisfaction with school clinics and centers and particularly appreciate their accessibility, convenience, and caring attitude."[32]

Despite the encouraging signs, stubborn organizational and legal issues have been hard to resolve in these expansive undertakings. Some of the most vexing issues have been those of professional "turf," client confidentiality, and budgetary authority.[33] In the area of professional turf, for example, some school counselors have felt threatened by the presence of social workers from child protective services and were reluctant to share information.[34] Furthermore, child protective agencies and the criminal justice system at times were barred by law from sharing crucial information regarding children with school officials.[35] Finally, a number of collaborative efforts got snarled in various budgetary directives, many of which demanded single, rather than shared, lines of fiscal accountability.[36]

Another issue facing proponents of full-service schools has been maintaining consistent funding. A mixture of state and federal funds and private foundation grants has paid for many of these collaborative projects. These projects have been particularly vulnerable to shifting political winds. For instance, the movement suffered a setback by the withdrawal of funding by one major foundation. After a disappointing preliminary evaluation of an inter-organizational collaboration in June of 1994, the Pew Charitable Trust withdrew from a highly ambitious 10-year, $60 million project dubbed The Children's Initiative. Pew concluded that to realize the positive changes envisioned by the initial project, even greater expansion of social service provision was needed. For the initiative to have even greater influence on children's lives, it was going to move into areas such as housing, employment, and drug abuse. It was already a large-scale and highly complex initiative that called for various service providers to fundamentally reconceptualize their professional roles and behaviors, while they continued to work in traditional bureaucratic environments. The weak initial evaluations regarding student outcomes in a political climate that had been hostile to tax-based social service provision made the project too politically risky for Pew to maintain its presence.[37]

Disappointing as this has been, the demise of Pew's Children's Initiative is congruent with what we know about educational reform. Historians David Tyack and Larry Cuban surveyed more than 100 years of educational and social reforms to determine which ones had staying power. They concluded the reforms that were institutionalized all had the following characteristics:

1) The reforms were adaptable to local circumstances.
2) Successful reforms were modest in approach and design.
3) Policy makers and regulators solicited and incorporated continuous input from those who had to implement the reforms (teachers, administrators, parents, etc.).
4) Successful reforms enjoyed strong and consistent political and fiscal support. Popular at the grassroots, these reforms encountered little opposition.
5) Successful reforms were relatively easy to implement and maintain (for example, structural or programmatic add-ons—adding kindergarten programs, the development of the junior high school,

expanding the school lunch program to include a breakfast program, offering computer classes to parents after hours, etc.).[38]

Given these findings it is understandable that the Pew initiative was not sustainable. Yet, as Tyack and Cuban have demonstrated, there are effective reform efforts targeted at community building and parental outreach, which this report now explores.

Successful Efforts at Linking Schools and Communities

Parental Involvement

In bolstering school community outreach, public school educators have used numerous strategies. Many of these are centered on increasing parental involvement in their children's education and school. As researchers Daniel J. McGrath and Peter J. Kuriloff observe:

> For policy makers, parent involvement in schools represents a method for, first, improving schools' services to families by making schools more accountable to parents; second, strengthening ties between schools and families traditionally underserved by schools; and, third, better serving students by taking advantage of parents' rich stores of knowledge about their children.[39]

Additionally, the research base regarding the efficacy of parental involvement is strong, and these findings have generally demonstrated that parental involvement can have positive effects on student academic achievement. Students whose parents are involved with their education tend to have fewer behavior problems in school, fewer absences, and higher rates of academic achievement and graduation than those students whose parents do not get involved.[40] Additionally, those students who are failing can improve dramatically if parental assistance is cultivated by school personnel. In particular, ethnic minority students or those with learning disabilities can enjoy significant benefits if their parents are involved with their schooling.[41]

Many public schools use the traditional methods of soliciting parental involvement: hosting the open house or "parents' night," soliciting parent volunteers to help work during a special event, maintaining a PTA/PTO, sending parents a school newsletter, using infrequent notes and phone calls, and of course, issuing a regular report card. While these efforts are a good start, they have significant limitations. First, the more traditional approaches to cultivating parental involvement can lead to parents being *guided* and sometimes manipulated by teachers and administrators. Parents are carefully steered away from voicing concerns around contentious professional issues like grading policies and teaching style. The second criticism is that the traditional forms of parental involvement tend to be *constrained*. By design, the information is to flow in one tightly controlled direction—from the school to the parents. Parents tend to be viewed as "non-professionals" and hence have limited value in shaping the larger policy issues of the school. The third criticism is that the traditional forms of parental involvement tend to be *representational*, since many contemporary parents cannot participate. The traditional forms assume a stable, two-parent family, with one parent (typically the mother) working full-time as a homemaker. Given that the vast majority of adults with children work outside of the home (whether they are parents, grandparents, aunts, uncles, etc.), only a few "representative" parents can participate. The parents who can participate tend to be white and middle- to upper-middle-class. And finally, the fourth criticism of the traditional forms of parental involvement is they expect parents to be *passive*. Parents are to receive information from the school, but the school does not seem to want much information from the parents.[42]

While the traditional forms of parental involvement do include some parents, there remains the potential to do more. Additionally, the traditional forms of parental involvement are strikingly ineffective at reaching out to families that are: (a) large, (b) headed by a single-parent (usually female), (c) poor, (d) non-English speaking, (e) abusive, or (f) include parents and older siblings who dropped out of school.[43]

Experiments to Expand Participation

Recognizing the problems of the traditional forms, public educators have experimented with a variety of reforms to encourage greater parental participation. One of the more recent innovations is the "open school." In this approach, the school opens itself up to each member of the community and actively seeks their input. This has been called the "warts-and-all" approach, because community members get to see the school staff at their best, and possibly at their worst. Parents and other adults can drop in at any time of the day, to see how their children are doing, what else is going on within the school, and have meaningful conversations with teachers and educational leaders regarding their child's education. Contemporary parents and guardians may not have schedules or consistently reliable transportation that permit them to visit the school during a scheduled (and formal) meeting. The open school demands a fair measure on flexibility on the part of the school personnel, many who have been socialized to view "their" school as a pedagogical island, removed from external forces and pressures, including parents. Yet, an open school grants parents and the community greater and very real access. It also provides parents with a meaningful sense of ownership, not only of the school, but also of their children's education.[44]

Parental Education

Another reform aimed at boosting parental involvement is parental education. Some parents, particularly those who have had poor school experiences themselves, may need experiences as a co-learner, advocate, and decision-maker, so they can become their child's educational advocate. Parent education programs encourage parents to become their children's resident teacher, as well as the critical caretaker and nurturer.[45]

For example, Norwood and her colleagues designed a model program of parental involvement through the University of Houston's Graduate School of Social Work and College of Education. They provided parent education to a school within the Houston public school system. The school had a high-percentage of students who were considered at risk for academic failure and came from poor socioeconomic backgrounds. All were African-American. Their parents were recruited to participate in an experimental parental education program that was focused on skills and that was also culturally and linguistically sensitive. Additionally, a sense of community among the researchers and participating parents was carefully cultivated, and the researchers took pains to blur distinctions between parents and the researchers. Participants were surveyed prior to the beginning of the program to determine what their needs and concerns were. Soliciting detailed input from parents also helped to establish ownership of the program by parents.[46]

The actual program focused on building parenting skills, as well as parents' teaching or coaching skills. Throughout the sessions, parents were invited to share their knowledge and experiences in raising their children. This helped to validate parents' knowledge and broadened the knowledge base of all participants. The parents also engaged in role-playing and various school- and home-related scenarios with Norwood and colleagues, so parents could practice their newly acquired skills.[47]

Six months after the program concluded, parents were asked to evaluate the program. All were very enthusiastic, and they had put their newly acquired skills immediately to work. As one woman explained:

> Most parents just run up to the school, but she [the instructor] helped us to see there are two sides to every story. We did role-playing, one was the parent and one of us was the teacher. We also practiced how to ask teachers for the things we need. I used this when my little boy didn't have homework. I went to his teacher and she gave me some homework for him. (Ms. C)[48]

Another participant noted:

> I felt the information on the parent-teacher conferences was very good. Now when I have to talk to my child's teacher, I am not as timid or afraid as I used to be. I have some say in his education. (Ms. W)[49]

The researchers then examined the subsequent academic achievement of these parents' children. They scored significantly higher on standardized measures of achievement, in math and reading, than did the children whose parents did not participate in the program. The degree of difference surprised Norwood and her colleagues, since they were expecting only modest academic gains at best.[50]

The Houston parental education program succeeded in large part because it was attentive to the needs and concerns of urban, minority parents, as well as being respectful of their backgrounds. Parents were treated with respect and their cultural, linguistic, and racial backgrounds honored. This result is consonant with other researchers' recommendations—that public school personnel who solicit parental involvement need be sensitive to the needs of an increasingly multicultural parent population to have greater and meaningful parental involvement with the schools.[51]

School-Based Management

Another parental involvement program that has been part of a larger school reform effort is school-based management (SBM). In this model, the authority for most decisions is delegated to the school site. In turn, the individual school establishes an SBM committee or council that is typically composed of teachers, parents, administrators, and perhaps, additional community members. The idea behind the reform is that those closest to real students know what policies, programs and budget expenditures will serve them best. Hence, the SBM council is empowered to make most of the policy decisions that affect that specific school. The ultimate goal is to improve the decision-making process and empower those closest to children to such an extent that student achievement improves. The research regarding SBM's effectiveness in bolstering student achievement is conflicted, although it does seem to improve the morale of the teachers who participate.[52]

A final note is in order regarding some of the more overlooked and undervalued parental involvement programs. Extra-curricular offerings have been a traditional form of parental involvement, perhaps the most popular of all informal forms of parental involvement. These programs, which range from athletics, music, drama, and arts programs to various student interest clubs, have historically involved highly disparate students. In terms of socioeconomic status, race, ethnicity, religion, gender, etc., these activities have produced enthusiastic parental involvement, regardless of background. Additionally, members from the larger community tend to get involved, if only as spectators. Research indicates that extra-curricular activities promote student academic achievement, in that they inhibit students from dropping out. The direct influence on improving student achievement is more tenuous.[53] In many distressed urban areas, extra-curricular venues are most vulnerable to budget reductions. This may be unwise given the strong connections that appear to be generated by these activities among students, their families, the schools, and members of the larger community.

Community Development

A more recent notion of strengthening school, community, and parental interaction views the public school system as a critical economic resource. That is, like any other industry or business, it provides both services and employment to individuals located within a certain geographic area.[54] Researcher Charles Kerchner argues that instead of viewing school systems as a sometimes-crushing municipal burden, cities should aggressively support their public schools.

> Schools build cities in two ways. They develop the economy, both indirectly by adding to a location's stock of human capital and directly through programs that enhance neighborhoods. Schools become part of a microeconomic policy. Schools also serve as agents for community development, the creation of cohesion and civic relations among neighbors.[55]

Kerchner theorizes that a public school system could greatly enhance a community's economic stability in four ways, by:

1) providing jobs for professional and service staff;
2) enhancing the human capital of the children in the community through quality education;
3) encouraging local businesses through targeted contracts for goods and services; and
4) enhancing property values while concurrently holding down property taxes.[56]

This economic vitality, in turn, can rebuild the social stability of the area. A stronger local economy reduces many of the social pathologies faced by urban areas.

Greater social and economic stability for parents also has a direct positive influence on student achievement, since the social capital of the area is enhanced. An additional benefit is that more people, those with and without children, will move to the area because of its relative economic health and growing social stability. When these new residents become involved in the services that the school district offers, such as concerts, plays, athletic events, computer classes, and the like, the community's social appeal is further enhanced.[57]

When Lawrence Picus and Jimmy Bryan examined the economic and fiscal influences that the Los Angeles area school systems have on both the local and state economies, they discovered public education in the LA region to be an enormous enterprise:

> In Los Angeles County, the school districts provide education for nearly 1.6 million children, spend almost $6.9 billion, and employ some 133,500 people. As a business concern, the Los Angeles County schools would rank 190th on the *Fortune 500*, larger than such companies as Northrop Grumman (192), Coca-Cola (196), Levi Strauss (198), and even Microsoft (219). On its own, the Los Angeles Unified School District (LAUSD), with its $4.9 billion budget, 55,767 employees, and 650,000 students, would rank 270 on the Fortune 500.[58]

Obviously, large urban school systems have a far greater economic influence on an area's economy and possible social stability than many businesses—including professional sports franchises.

A New Conceptual Lens

Viewing the public school system as a major community economic resource, as well as a social service, may provide local and state educational policy makers with a new conceptual lens. Public schools will no longer be seen as a never-ending drain on the community, but as a source of the community's economic and social well-being. This vision of the public schools will also enable community members to view the system as *critical* to the welfare of the local economy and, therefore, a vital social institution. While there is much research to be done in this specific area, these initial explorations do offer intriguing possibilities regarding building stronger links between public schools, their communities, and student academic achievement.

What Cannot be Concluded from the Research

This report has presented historical and contemporary overviews of the research pertaining to schools, their communities, and student academic achievement. While much of this research is stimulating and offers school personnel and policy makers various conceptual plans, a basic problem in the research base is that it is almost entirely comprised of single or multi-case studies. This is not surprising given the degree of autonomy that some districts have in developing and implementing community outreach programs. Additionally, since public education is largely a state responsibility, there is great variation among the 50 states and Washington, DC. Fragmentation is a hallmark of the US educational system. Unfortunately, this makes conducting large scale, experimental studies most difficult. While case studies do provide us with some compelling insights and broad guidelines, they make specific and highly prescriptive recommendations difficult.

SUMMARY AND RECOMMENDATIONS

Public schools have been reaching out to parents and communities since their inception. With over 100 years of data, we know what programs can enhance student academic achievement. The challenge is to devise the right mixture of services and programs in organizational situations that are highly idiosyncratic.[59] As Joy Dryfoos notes, there is no model for social service provision.[60] This is congruent with educational historian David Tyack's observation that there is "no best system" for public education.[61] Yet there is enough information to permit informed decisions regarding what might be feasible to implement.

Despite the limitations of the case-study approach, the documented results of efforts to create deeper ties between schools and the communities in which they operate and which they serve warrant efforts to further enhance school-community relationships. The history of more than 100 years of research and experience in involving schools in community life points to several potential policy initiatives:

- Basic parental involvement programs should be enhanced to include multiple opportunities for formal and informal communication between school personnel and parents. Open, engaged, mutual, and honest communication should be encouraged. As much as possible, public schools should move towards an *open*, or "warts and all," approach to school-community relations.
- Parental involvement programs should be developed that embrace the ethnic, linguistic, cultural, racial, and religious diversity of the parents.
- Parental involvement programs should be designed to be sensitive to the special needs of poor parents, single parents, parents with large families, and those families where both parents work outside of the home. This might mean providing transportation and child care for some, while planning meetings around work/home schedules for others.
- Written materials should be provided in the language with which parents are the most familiar.
- Schools and other social organizations wishing to provide school-linked services should carefully consider the scope, funding needs, organizational and professional complexities, and types of services to be offered. While perhaps not as compelling or intellectually stimulating, incremental types of school-linked services should be pursued if providers are dedicated to institutionalizing the project.[62]

- Funding for new community involvement projects should be kept consistent and stable. The bigger and more complex the project, the greater the need for adequate funding.
- Extra-curricular programs should be kept vital to help foster strong parental involvement.
- Educational leaders and policy makers should be encouraged to reconceptualize the public school as a vital economic resource that must be nurtured.

What Works Best with Poor Urban Children?

In addition to the above recommendations, programs particularly targeted to assist children and communities living in poverty should take into account the following principles:

- Programmatic offerings need to be stable, consistent, and long-lived. Poor urban children's lives are marked by chaos. Public schools and the services they provide may be the only stable "thing" in many children's lives.
- New services should be carefully expanded, ensuring they become institutionalized over time. For example, it might be advantageous to expand the free lunch program to include all students. Once this has been established and consistently maintained over several years, it might be time to include or expand a school breakfast program.
- Schools facing a budget shortfall should focus on maintaining extra-curricular activities that are relatively low cost and can serve broader numbers of students. This logic might make the choral program more appealing than the more expensive and litigation-prone football program.
- Parental education programs should focus on parents' knowledge and skills in child raising and work to build on this foundation. School personnel and other service providers must be aware of the parents' own needs and wishes for their children, and design programs so these are addressed.
- Parental education programs need to be sensitive to the racial, ethnic, cultural, and religious backgrounds of participating parents. These programs must also attend to the realities that families in poverty confront. This might include offering transportation to the program and offering on-site child care, and even providing an evening meal for the families attending.
- City and educational leaders need to view the public school system as a foundation for community revitalization initiatives.

REFERENCES

1. D. Tyack, "Health and Social Services in Public Schools: Historical Perspectives," *The future of Children: School-Linked Services* (Los Altos, CA: The Center for the Future of Children, 1992).

    D. Tyack, *The One Best System: A History of American Urban Education* (Cambridge, MA: Harvard University Press, 1974).

2. J. Anyon, *Ghetto Schools* (New York, NY: Teachers College Press, 1997).

    L. Delpit, *Other People's Children: Cultural Conflict in the Classroom* (New York, NY: The New Press, 1995).

    C. N. Stone, "Civic Capacity and Urban Education," *Urban Affairs Review* 36, no. 5 (May 2001): 595–619.

    G. Orfield, S. E. Eaton and the Harvard Project on School Desegregation, *Dismantling Desegregation: The Quiet Reversal of Brown* v. Board of Education (New York, NY: The New Press, 1996).

    Tyack, *The One Best System.*

3. Anyon; Tyack, *The One Best System.*

    J. G. Dryfoos, *Full-Service Schools: A Revolution in Health and Social Services for Children, Youth, and Families* (San Francisco, CA: Jossey-Bass, 1994).

4. Tyack, *Health and Social Services, The One Best System.*

    D. H. Bennett, *The Party of Fear: The American Far Right from Nativism to the ilitia Movement* (New York, NY: Vintage Books, 1995).

5. D. Tyack and L. Cuban, T*inkering Toward Utopia: A Century of Public School Reform* (Cambridge, MA: Harvard University Press, 1995).

    Tyack, *The One Best System.*

6. D. Nasaw, *Schooled to Order: A Social History of Public Schooling in the United States* (New York, NY: Oxford University Press, 1979).

    See also, L. E. Teitelbaum, "Family History and Family Law," *Wisconsin Law Review,* 1985 Wis. L. Rev. 1135 (September-October 1985).

7. Nasaw, 96–98.

8. R. E. Callahan, *Education and the Cult of Efficiency* (Chicago: University of Chicago Press, 1962).

9. Tyack, *The One Best System,* 244.

    Tyack cites U.S. Immigration Commission data. The "Foreign-born" category is an aggregate figure. Desegregated, students who were classified as "Russian Jew," "Southern Italian" and "Polish" had lower attendance rates than their "Native-born" peers. However, students who were classified as "German" and "Swedish" had dramatically higher attendance rates. Readers should be cautioned, however, that most U.S. students eventually dropped out of school. It was not until the 1950s, that over 50% of all students graduated from high school. Two other factors that drove increased attendance were the development of child labor and compulsory attendance laws, both of which, when enforced, also drove up attendance rates. However, these laws would be haphazardly enforced until the Great Depression.

10. Tyack, *The One Best System,* 231. Emphasis added.

11. Tyack, *The One Best System,* 237.

12. See Tyack, *The One Best System;* Anyon.

D. Tyack and E. Hansot, *Managers of Virtue, Public School Leadership in America, 1820–1980* (New York: NY: Basic Books, 1982).

13.   B. M. Franklin, "'Something Old, Something New, Something Borrowed...': A Historical Commentary on the Carnegie Council's Turning Points," *Journal of Educational Policy* 5, no. 3 (1990): 265–272.

14.   Tyack, *Health and Social Services.*

15.   K. Rousmaniere, *City Teachers: Teaching and School Reform in Historical Perspective* (New York, NY: Teachers College Press, 1997).

16.   Joy Dryfoos observes that foundations continued to support experimentation in social service provision throughout the Depression-era. The most frequently cited example was the project located in Flint, Michigan, which provided after-school and summer recreation, and later health and nutrition services. Yet it is doubtful that such an effort would have survived without strong support from the Charles Mott Foundation. See Dryfoos, 30.

17.   Callahan.

18.   This does not imply that public educators and researchers were only concerned with the "marketing" of public education. But as Robert Crowson observed, "Community-relations proponents of the 1960s and 1970s recognized clearly the value of a greater opening of communications between home and school, and the benefits of parental involvement in the schools. Nevertheless, there was still an important sense of separation—a sense that in the interest of professionalism, the school must guard carefully an independence from the pressures and politics of the clientele." See:

R. L. Crowson, *School-Community Relations, Under Reform* (Berkeley, CA: McCuthan Publishing, 1992), 31.

19.   B. A. Jones, "Schools in the Community and Urban Context: Incorporating Collaboration and Empowerment," in *Investing in U.S. Schools: Directions for Educational Policy*, eds. Bruce Anthony Jones and Kathryn M. Borman (Norwood, NJ: Ablex Publishing, 1994), 5–23.

20.   Dryfoos, 2.

21.   C. A. Lugg, *For God and Country: Conservatism and American School Policy* (New York: Peter Lang, 1996).

J. Murphy, *Restructuring Schools: Capturing and Assessing the Phenomena* (New York: Teachers College Press, 1991).

22.   R. L. Crowson and W. L. Boyd, "Coordinating Services for Children: Designing Arks for Storms and Seas Unknown," *American Journal of Education* 101, no. 2 (February 1993).

23.   M. S. Smith and J. A. O'Day, "Systemic School Reform," in *The Politics of Curriculum and Testing*, eds. S. Fuhrman and B. Malen (Bristol, PA: Falmer Press, 1991). Since the 1990s, there have been numerous and conflicting definitions of "systemic reform." However, Smith and O'Day are the originators of the term.

24.   Dryfoos.

A. I. Melaville and M. J. Blank. *What It Takes: Structuring Interagency Partnerships to Connect Children and Families with Comprehensive Services* (Washington, DC: Education and Human Services Consortium, January 1991).

A. I. Melaville and M. J. Blank, *Together We Can: A Guide for Crafting a Profamily System of Education and Human Services* (Washington, DC: U.S. Department of Education, Office of Educational Research and Improvement (OERI), 1993).

25. See: J. S. Coleman, "Schools and the Communities They Serve," *Phi Delta Kappan* 66, no. 8 (April 1985).

   J. S. Coleman, "Families and schools," *Educational Researcher* 16, no. 6 (August-September 1987).

   J. S. Coleman, T. Hoffer and S. Kilgore, "Cognitive Outcomes in Public and Private Schools," *Sociology of Education* 55 (1982).

26. For an overview of the criticisms of Coleman's work, see Crowson, 108–109.

27. R. L. Crowson and W. L. Boyd, "Achieving Coordinated School-Linked Services: Facilitating Utilization of the Emerging Knowledge Base," *Educational Policy* 10, no. 2 (June 1996).

   See Melaville and Blank, *What it Takes, Together We Can*; Dryfoos.

28. S. L. Kagan, *Integrating Services for Children and Families: Understanding the Past to Shape the Future* (New Haven, CT: Yale University Press, 1993).

29. C. A. Lugg and W. L. Boyd, "Leadership for Collaboration: Reducing Risk and Fostering Resilience," *Phi Delta Kappan* 75, no. 3 (November 1993): 253–258.

30. Crowson and Boyd.

31. Dryfoos. More generally, see:

   E. Schorr, *Within Our Reach* (New York, NY: Doubleday, 1988).

   S. L. Kagan, "Support systems for Children, Youths, Families, and Schools in Inner-City Situations," *Education and Urban Society* 29 (May 1997).

32. Dryfoos, 135.

33. Lugg and Boyd.

34. Dryfoos.

35. Lugg and Boyd.

36. *The Politics of Linking Schools and Social Services*, eds. L. Adler and S. Gardner, (Washington, DC: Falmer, 1974).

   See also M. W. Kirst, J. E. Koppich and C. Kelley, "School-Linked Services and Chapter I: A New Approach to Improving Outcomes for Children." in *Rethinking Policy for At-Risk Students*, eds. K. K. Wong and M. C. Wang (Berkeley, CA: McCutchan, 1994).

37. C. Smrekar, "The Organizational and Political Threats to School-Linked Integrated Services," *Educational Policy* 12, no. 3 (May 1998).

   J. Cibulka, "Toward an Interpretation of School, Family, and Community Connections: Policy Challenges," in *Coordination Among Schools, Families, and Communities: Prospects for Educational Reform*, eds. J. Cibulka and W. Kritek (Albany: SUNY Press, 1996).

   Other large-scale social reform efforts have also generated disappointing or ambiguous results. See:

   The Annie E. Casey Foundation, *The Path of Most Resistance: Reflections on Lessons Learned from New Futures* (Washington, DC: The Annie E. Casey Foundation, 1995).

38. Tyack and Cuban.

39. D. J. McGrath, P. J. Kuriloff, "'They're Going to Tear the Doors Off This Place': Upper-middle-class Parent School Involvement and the Educational

Opportunities of Other People's Children," *Educational Policy* 13, no. 5 (November 1999).

40. Diane E. Karther and Frances Y. Lowden, "Fostering Effective Parent Involvement," *Contemporary Education* 69, no. 1 (Fall 1997).

Joyce L. Epstein, "Perspectives and Previews on Research and Policy for School, Family, and Community Partnerships," in *Family-school links: How Do They Affect Educational Outcomes?* eds. A. Booth and J. E Dunn (Mahwah, NJ: Lawrence Erlbaum, 1996).

Natasha K. Bowen and Gary L. Bowen, "The Mediating Role of Educational Meaning in the Relationship Between Home Academic Culture and Academic Performance," *Family Relations* 47, no. 1 (January 1998).

41. L. Floyd, "Joining Hands: A Parental Involvement Program," *Urban Education* 33, no. 1 (March 1998).

Crowson, 195.

Families and Schools in a Pluralistic Society, ed. N. Chavkin (Albany, NY: State University of New York Press, 1993).

42. Crowson, 184–188.

K. Nakagawa, "Unthreading the Ties That Bind: Questioning the Discourse of Parent Involvement," *Educational Policy* 14, no. 4 (September 2000).

McGrath & Kuriloff.

A. G. Dworking and M. L. Townsend, "Teacher Burnout in the Face of Reform: Some Caveats in Breaking the Mold," in *Investing in U.S. Schools: Directions for Educational Policy*, eds. B. A. Jones and K. M. Borman (Norwood, NJ: Ablex, 1994), 81–83.

For a discussion on contemporary families, see S. Coontz, *The Way We Really Are: Coming to Terms with America's Changing Families* (New York, NY: Basic Books, 1997).

43. Karther and Lowden.

44. Crowson.

45. P. M. Norwood et al., "Contextualizing Parent Education Programs in Urban Schools: The Impact on Minority Parents and Students," *Urban Education* 32, no. 3 (September 1997).

see also J. Epstein, "What Principals Should Know About Parent Involvement," *Principal* 66 (1987).

46. Norwood, Atkinson, Teller and Saldana.

47. Ibid.

48. Ibid.

49. Ibid.

50. Ibid.

51. Ibid.

Delpit; Nakagawa; Floyd.

52. *Handbook on Educational Research, 3rd Edition*, eds. S. Smith and P. K. Piele (Eugene, OR: ERIC Press, 1996).

53. J. W. Alspaugh, "The Relationship of School and Community Characteristics to High School Drop-out Rates," *The Clearing House* 71, no. 3 (January-February 1998).

J. K. Urice "Implications of the REAP Report on Advocacy," *Arts Education Policy Review* 102, no. 5 (May-June 2001).

A. Aprill, "Toward a Finer Description of the Connection Between Arts Education and Student Achievement," *Arts Education Policy Review* 102, no. 5 (May-June 2000).

54.   C. T. Kerchner, "Education as a City's Basic Industry," *Education and Urban Society* 29, no. 4 (August 1997).

L. O. Picus and J. L. Bryan, "The Economic Impact of Public K–12 Education in the Los Angeles Region," *Education and Urban Society* 29, no. 4 (August 1997).

55.   Kerchner.

56.   Kerchner, 1997. He observes in a footnote that, "At the traditional real estate rule of thumb of $9/$1,000 in mortgage, the parent(s) in the 30% bracket contemplating $4,000 in private school tuition could afford an extra $75,000 for a house in order to send their children to a desirable public school."

57.   Kerchner notes the converse is also true; witness the destruction of the Detroit public school system, which was followed by the hollowing out of the community. American suburbs are a positive example of a school district's influence on the community's economy.

58.   Picus and Bryan.

59.   Dryfoos.

60.   Ibid.

61.   Tyack, *The One Best System.*

62.   Tyack and Cuban.

CHAPTER 8

TEACHER CHARACTERISTICS

Gene V Glass
Arizona State University

SUMMARY OF RESEARCH FINDINGS

Traditional psychometric techniques (using ability, achievement, other paper-and-pencil tests, GPAs, and the like) to predict teaching effectiveness (in terms of student achievement) have failed. Certification status appears to be causally related to improved student achievement: regularly certified teachers produce higher student achievement than non-certified or emergency certified teachers. Teacher experience generally has been shown to be positively related to student achievement when other variables are statistically controlled. Little research has been published on the unique characteristics of teachers that make them successful in teaching children in poverty.

RECOMMENDATIONS

- Paper-and-pencil tests are not useful predictors of teaching candidates' potential to teach successfully and accordingly should not be used for that purpose.
- A teaching candidate's academic record (e.g., GPA) is not a useful predictor of his or her eventual success as a teacher. A candidate's record of success in pre-service (undergraduate) technical courses (mathematics and science, for example) may contain useful information about that candidate's success in teaching secondary school mathematics and science.

- Other things equal, 1) students of regularly licensed teachers achieve at higher levels than students of emergency certified teachers; and 2) more experienced teachers produce higher student achievement than less experienced teachers. Teacher selection policies should reflect these facts.
- The selection of teachers who will best contribute to their students' academic achievement should focus on peer and supervisor evaluation of interns, student teachers, substitute teachers and teachers during their probationary period.

INTRODUCTION

How can one identify in advance of a decision to hire which teachers will most improve their students' measured achievement? What are the characteristics of promising teachers that will permit an accurate prediction of their ability to teach children well?

This review deals with those characteristics of teachers that might be identified and used in the initial hiring of teachers to increase their students' achievement. These characteristics can include qualities of teachers that are viewed as personal—such as mental ability, age, ethnicity, gender and the like—or as "experiential"—such as certification status, educational background, previous teaching experience and the like. Some characteristics are combinations—in unknown amounts—of personal and experiential qualities, e.g., candidates' performance on teacher-certification tests such as the National Teacher Examinations and state-mandated tests.

This review will not examine characteristics of teachers that would be impractical to assess in the initial hiring and selection process, such as deep personality traits. The term "teacher characteristics" typically refers to qualities of teachers that can be measured with tests or derived from their academic or professional records. It does not generally refer to the direct observation of their impact on students' learning in terms of either students' test performance or teaching behaviors (both of which are addressed elsewhere in the present work). Rather, the approaches dealt with here are those that fall traditionally into the province of personnel psychology or personnel selection.[1] These distinctions are particularly important because of the conclusions at which the present review arrives, namely, that psychometric selection is inappropriate in the initial selection of teachers and should defer to the evaluation of probationary teachers (teachers in the first few years of their employment).

RESEARCH ON TEACHER CHARACTERISTICS

Micro-Studies and Macro-Studies

The research literature on teacher characteristics and student achievement encompasses two quite different kinds of study. One type—here referred to as *micro-studies*—uses individual teachers as the unit of analysis. Correlation coefficients are calculated from data descriptive of individual teachers and their students' achievement (usually expressed as a class average). Studies of this type yield findings most relevant to the question whether there are characteristics of teachers that predict their ability to improve the achievement of their students.

The second type of study is here called *macro-studies*. These studies measure characteristics of groups of teachers, such as "percentage of teachers in the school district who hold Masters degrees." Macro-studies attempt to exercise statistical controls by means of complex multiple regression analyses, often taking account of the multiple levels (states, districts, schools) of organization that tie individual teachers together. Macro-studies often inform policy at high levels but give limited direction to administrators who face individual selection decisions. Frequently, they do not express relationships in a form that permits the calculation of the actual benefits of selecting an elementary school teacher in terms of increased student achievement. Moreover, these macro-studies—useful though they are for addressing state or national level policy questions—seldom achieve the levels of control needed to reach consensus among their readers. In spite of their contribution, macro-studies of the relationship between teacher characteristics as a school, district, or state "input" and student achievement as an "output" have several limitations: they must rely on imperfectly measured "background characteristics" of students to equate unequal conditions; they can not, without substantial and seldom realized extensions, resolve the ambiguity of the direction of the causal influence (Does a high percentage of Masters degrees raise student achievement, or do districts with able students who learn quickly and easily attract teachers with Masters degrees?); they typically fail to address the ambiguities present in ecological *correlation analysis*. (For instance, it is unclear whether the teachers holding the Masters degrees in the school district are the teachers actually responsible for the increased student achievement). Nevertheless, macro-studies of the relationship between teacher characteristics and student achievement are visible and influential at policy levels and will be reviewed here.

The Micro-Studies

Aptitude and Intelligence

Two major reviews of research[2] on the relationship of teachers' measured intelligence and their students' achievement arrived at the same conclusion: there is no important correlation between the two variables. Various explanations have been advanced for the failure to find a relationship that many expected would exist: the truncated variability of the intelligence scale for a population of teachers already highly selected for academic aptitude; the unreliability and lack of content validity of measures of student achievement; as well as the essential irrelevance of high levels of measured intelligence for effective teaching, particularly at the elementary school level.

Academic Preparation

Research suggests that there is a modest relationship between teachers' college course work in the subject area in which they subsequently teach and their students' achievement.[3] Monk[4] analyzed data for almost 3,000 high school students from the Longitudinal Study of American Youth. Students took tests in mathematics and science, and supplied information on their backgrounds. Their math and science teachers were also questioned. Monk correlated teacher characteristics with student achievement, taking into account students' earlier achievement, background characteristics, and teacher inputs. The greater the number of college-level mathematics or science courses (or math or science teaching courses) teachers had taken, the better their students did on the mathematics and science tests. Goldhaber and Brewer[5] found similar relationships in a secondary analysis of more than 5,000 high school sophomores and their teachers. College-level math courses taken by the teachers was the only variable that accounted for any appreciable variation in students' achievement.

The National Teacher Examinations (NTE)

The National Teacher Examinations (NTE), developed and administered by the Educational Testing Service of Princeton, New Jersey, are widely used and an influential model for the state-level paper-and-pencil licensure exams that are currently proliferating throughout the United States. The validity of the NTE was the subject of an extensive review published in 1973 by Quirk, Witten, and Weinberg.[6] Subsequent reviews have not substantially added to nor altered their conclusions. Quirk et al. documented the nearly 30-year history of NTE research attempts to correlate NTE scores with such "concurrent validity" measures as high school GPA, undergraduate GPA, graduate GPA, ability tests (GRE-V, GRE-Q), as well as grades in specialized education courses. (Such correlations are referred to as "concurrent validity" coefficients because the two measures correlated are taken at roughly the same stage, in this case, during a prospective teacher's pre-service career.) Such criteria are only presumptively related to student learning; but even so, the concurrent validity evidence was not impressive. The highest correlations were with paper-and-pencil tests of academic ability and were in the region of 0.60. Paper-and-pencil tests correlate with other paper-and-pencil tests; that much might have been expected. Correlations of NTE scores with GPAs were in the region of 0.30. Most significantly, the two studies that produced correlations of NTE with grades in practice teaching yielded the following results: Shea[7] correlated NTE scores with grades in practice teaching for 110 pre-service teachers who had graduated from Worcester State Teachers College and obtained a r of −0.01; Walberg[8] correlated performance on the NTE with practice teaching grades for 280 pre-service teachers and found an r of −0.04. These are sobering findings indeed for those who hope for paper-and-pencil test information that will predict teaching effectiveness.

The usefulness of the NTE for predicting principals' ratings of various qualities of in-service teachers is similarly wanting. Research over 30 years in a wide variety of settings has shown correlations of NTE test scores and principals' ratings ranging from −0.15 to 0.50 with an average r of about 0.10.[9] In the face of these discouraging results, researchers have been prone to blame the professionals' evaluations of their peers and subordinates, suggesting that they are unreliable or biased or distorted by friendships or prejudices or unsophisticated views of quality teaching. The fault, however, may lie more with the inadequacies of paper-and-pencil tests as measures if teachers' abilities to manage the complex demands of educating groups of children.

Quirk, Witte and Weinberg found only a single study in which NTE scores were correlated with students' average gain in performance from pretest to posttest, and this study by Lins,[10] published in 1946, produced data on only seven teachers. The correlation of NTE score with pupils' gain scores was 0.45; unfortunately, one can only assert with reasonable statistical confidence that a much larger sample would produce a validity coefficient somewhere between −0.50 and +0.90.[11]

The State of Massachusetts has instituted one of the most controversial paper-and-pencil teacher licensure tests. Haney and his colleagues found no empirical evidence that the Massachusetts teacher tests could predict student learning.[12]

Certification (Licensure)

A job candidate's certification status has become a visible consideration in recent decades as a result of a variety of reforms and economic pressures placed on the educational system. Class-size reduction efforts, most notably in California in the mid-1990s, not surprisingly created an acute need for teachers that could not be met by the existing supply of regularly certified personnel. The difficulty of recruiting certified teachers for schools in the deteriorating core of large cities prompted the hiring of college graduates without pre-service training or teaching experience—"Teach for America" being the most visible program of this type.[13] In addition, the market ideology that has influenced both the discussion and the implementation of education policy proposals since the 1980s questioned the need for state-operated systems of teacher certification. Some believe that any educated person, with or without a college degree, can teach.[14] Educators are left with the question, what value is represented by the teacher license? Should certification status be considered in the hiring of new teachers?

Darling-Hammond wrote that "…reviews of research over the past thirty years, summarizing hundreds of studies, have concluded that even with the shortcomings of current teacher education and licensing, fully prepared and certified teaches are … more successful with students than teachers without this preparation."[15] Ashton[16] noted that teachers with regular state certification receive higher supervisor ratings and student achievement than teachers who do not meet standards, but this observation was based on data with virtually no statistical controls having been imposed. In spite of the quantity of research on the benefits of teacher certification for student learning that Darling-Hammond refers to, little of the past research exercised controls over student "inputs" that would give the critical reader confidence in the findings. One recent study addressed the effect of certification status with a series of controls that engendered this missing confidence.

Laczko and Berliner[17] studied the impact of certification status on student achievement in two large urban school districts. These school districts provided information about teachers hired for the 1998–1999 and 1999–2000 school years. Information included the school where they were currently teaching, the grade level taught, the teacher's certification status, highest degree earned, date and institution where it was achieved, age, and number of years teaching experience. Teachers were eliminated from the sample if they taught a grade level or subject that was not assessed (e.g., art and music) by the Stanford Nine (SAT 9) achievement test battery, the measure of achievement used in the study.

Emergency certified teachers were matched with regularly certified teachers in the following manner: matches were first made by grade level; secondarily, matching was based on highest degree attained; whenever possible, matches were made within the same school, otherwise, matches were made within the same school district; cross-district matching was not allowed. Matching the two samples produced 23 pairs of teachers for the 1998–1999 school year and 29 pairs of teachers for the 1999–2000 school year.

Stanford Achievement Test-Version 9 scores aggregated at the class level for the 52 matched pairs of teachers were collected. Correlated t-tests were conducted to analyze the difference in the student achievement scores between emergency certified and standard certified teachers. The principal findings from the Laczko and Berliner study appear in Table 8–1.

Table 8–1.   NCE Differences and Effect Sizes (ES)[18] for 1998–1999 and 1999–2000 (After Laczko & Berliner, 2001)

SAT 9 Sub-Test	1998–1999	1999–2000	Mean ES
Reading	13.9	9.2	0.50
Math	–0.2	11.1	0.24
Language	9.4	10.7	0.44

Note. The NCE differences are between certified and emergency teachers. Effect sizes (ES) were calculated with a standard deviation of 23 NCE units.

Using the NCE (Normal Curve Equivalent) scale to express the results, Laczko and Berliner found, for example, that in the 1998–99 school year, students taught by certified teachers outscored their counterparts taught by uncertified teachers by almost 14 NCE points in Reading. The similar margin in the 1999–2000 school year was greater than 9 points. Expressed as a proportion of the standard deviation of the NCE scale, these differences averaged across the two years yield an effect size of one-half (0.50) standard deviation (equivalent to five months grade-equivalent units). One would expect, based on these findings, then, that the students of certified teachers would make an additional five months academic growth in reading when compared to the students of uncertified teachers across an entire school year. The advantage for students of certified teachers in mathematics and language is one-quarter (0.25) standard deviation (about 2.5 months in grade-equivalents) and four-tenths (0.40) a standard deviation (about four months GE), respectively. These are, perhaps, the most convincing data yet produced by research on the effect of teacher certification on student achievement. (It should be noted that these differences in means expressed in standard deviation units correspond to correlations between certification status and student achievement of roughly 0.25, for effect sizes of 0.50, and 0.15, for effect sizes of 0.30 to 0.25.[19])

Successful Teachers of Poor Students

Poor students are disproportionately taught by less experienced teachers who are less likely to be licensed and who leave the profession sooner than teachers of the children of middle-class or wealthy families. Researchers have largely ignored the question of whether there are special characteristics of teachers who will be successful in teaching poor children.

One of the few quantitative studies of the relationship between teacher characteristics and student achievement for poor children is due to Murnane and Phillips.[20] Using data collected in a study of a federal welfare reform project in a large midwestern city, the researchers fit regression equations to account for the variability of vocabulary scores on the Iowa Test of Basic Skills in terms of teacher behaviors and other characteristics. The teachers were predominantly black, female and held Masters degrees. The researchers concluded: "Overall, the results ... suggest that variables describing teacher behavior and variables describing teacher characteristics are both important in predicting teacher effectiveness."[21] Teacher characteristics of race, prestige of the undergraduate college, whether the teacher earned a Masters degree and verbal ability were not significantly related to students' achievement. However, "years of teaching experience" was related to student achievement. This relationship for Grades 4 and 6 is depicted in Figure 8–1. The relationship for Grade 1 was weaker, but still positive, and non-existent for Grade 5. No reasonable explanation for the interaction of the relationship with grade level exists, and a prudent conclusion would hold that teacher experience and student achievement are positively related in these circumstances.

Another one of the very few attempts to address this question was made by Martin Haberman in his book *Star Teachers of Children in Poverty*.[22] Drawing on years of interviewing hundreds of teachers in poor urban schools,

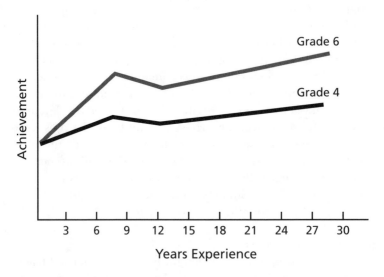

Figure 8–1.   Teacher experience and student achievement for inner-city children (After Murname, 1981).

Haberman advanced a view of what makes for success for a teacher of poor children. These successful teachers, which he named "star teachers," display the following characteristics: star teachers do not punish students, but instead use "logical consequences" to direct students to learn appropriate behaviors; star teachers believe that discipline problems are best handled by making learning interesting, meaningful, and engrossing; star teachers are persistent. Haberman saw these teachers dealing with the organization of the school in a uniquely productive way. They did not attempt to undermine the school's administration, nor did they ignore the directives of officials; however, they did not use bureaucratic directives as excuses to keep from achieving their objectives in the classroom. Star teachers engaged in what Haberman called "gentle teaching." Gentle teaching promotes kindness in classroom interactions; it pointedly avoids the discord that can characterize interactions in schools that emphasize compliance with rules instead of learning.

Haberman suggested that there may be ways to predict which teachers will be the star teachers. Candidates for teaching positions should be selected on the basis of criteria other than good grades and high test scores. New teachers, if they are to develop into Haberman's star teachers, should not be judgmental; they should be tolerant and avoid moralistic attitudes; they must be open, understanding, and not easily shocked; and they must be capable of open and authentic communication with their superiors and colleagues.

Haberman has produced one of the few research-based works aimed at understanding the characteristics of teachers that make for success with poor children, and yet, his work has been criticized as methodologically weak.[23] No demographic description of the group of teachers interviewed is given; no explanation of the criteria by which the star teachers were recognized as successful is offered. Haberman may well be right, but the path traveled to reach his understandings is hidden from view.

THE MACRO-STUDIES

Large-scale studies that use school districts or states as the unit of analysis and attempt with multiple regression analysis to control for pre-existing differences among these units have addressed many of the same concerns analyzed in the micro-studies. The first large study of this type was Coleman's *Equality of Educational Opportunity*.[24] Coleman *et al.* measured seven characteristics of teachers: years of experience, highest degree attained, vocabulary test performance, ethnic group, parents' educational attainment, whether the teachers grew up where they were teaching, and the teacher's attitude toward teaching middle-class students. These teacher characteristics accounted for less than 1% of the variation in student achievement—meaning that a correlation of teacher characteristics with student achievement, holding other factors constant, would be less than +0.10. Coleman et al., as well as Bowles and Levin,[25] felt that they detected slight relationships between teachers' verbal intelligence and student achievement. Summers and Wolfe[26] indicated that this relationship, though quite weak in statistical terms, was more important in some areas of the curriculum than in others. Hanushek[27] joined these early researchers in finding no strong relationship between teacher characteristics and student achievement.

A pair of meta-analyses of macro-level studies arrived at differing conclusions on the question whether teachers' measured ability influences student achievement. Greenwald, Hedges, and Lane[28] reviewed a number of studies of the relationship between school inputs and student outcomes and concluded that teacher ability, teacher education, and teacher experience appeared to be related to student achievement. Hanushek's[29] synthesis of research studies arrived at a contrary conclusion regarding the relationship between teacher characteristics and student achievement. Less than a year later, Hanushek[30] published an "update" of his 1996 article in which he reported the following summary of studies that investigated the relationship (in terms of regression coefficients) between student achievement and their teacher's "years of experience."

Table 8–2.   Direction and Statistical Significance of Regression Coefficients for Student Achievement Related to Teacher Experience (After Hanushek, 1997)

Ind. Var.	# of studies	Stat. Significant		Non. Significant		
		+	−	+	−	?
Teacher Experience	207	29%	5%	30%	24%	12%

Although a statistically significant regression coefficient for "teacher experience" was six times more likely to be positive than negative, Hanushek nonetheless read the results of Table 8–2 as negative for the effects of teacher experience on achievement. He wrote of the results: "A higher [than class size or teacher education] proportion of estimated effects of teacher experience are positive and statistically significant: 29%. Importantly, however, 71% still indicate worsening performance with experience or less confidence in any positive effect."[31] The logic of this conclusion is illusive. Of results that reach statistical significance, 85% (60/70) are positive, indicating that students of more experienced teachers achieve at higher levels. Of the statistically non-significant results that can be determined, 55% are positive, but fail to reach conventional levels of significance. Hanushek creates an impression of no effect of teacher experience by lumping together the category "indicative of worsening performance or less confidence of beneficial performance" all significant but negative coefficients (5%), all non-significant coefficients whether positive or negative (30% + 24%) and, remarkably, the 12% of the coefficients that were so incompletely reported that it could not be determined whether they were positive or negative. The treatment of these data is hardly even-handed. By such logic, ten "positive studies," "no negative studies" and 100 studies so poorly reported that the results could not be discerned would lead to a conclusion of no confidence in a positive result. This author's reading of Table 8–2 is much different from Hanushek's. The data therein can be reasonably interpreted as evidence that regression studies have generally shown a positive relationship between teacher experience and student achievement.

Fetler[32] investigated the relationship between measures of mathematics teacher skill and student achievement in California high schools. Test scores are analyzed in relation to teacher experience and education and student demographics. The results are consistent with the hypothesis that there is a shortage of qualified mathematics teachers in California and that this shortage is associated with low student scores in mathematics. After controlling for poverty, teacher experience and preparation significantly predict test scores.

Darling-Hammond[33] utilized data from a survey of all 50 states' policies, the 1993–1994 Schools and Staffing Surveys of the U.S. Department of Education, and the National Assessment of Educational Progress to study the relationship between teacher qualifications and student achievement. The findings suggested that policy investments in the quality of teachers may be related to improvements in student performance. Measures of teacher preparation and certification were the strongest correlates of student achievement in reading and mathematics, both before and after controlling for student poverty and language status (limited English fluency v. full English fluency). "The most consistent highly significant predictor of student achievement in reading and mathematics in each year tested is the proportion of well-qualified teachers in a state: those with full certification and a major in the field they teach (r between 0.61 and 0.80, $p<0.001$). The strongest, consistently negative predictors of student achievement, also significant in almost all cases, are the proportions of new teachers who are uncertified (r between –0.40 and –0.63, $p < 0.05$) and the proportions of teachers who hold less than a minor in the field they teach (r between –0.33 and –0.56, $p < 0.05$)." (It must be noted that these correlation coefficients, in the area of 0.50 and above, are calculated on state-level aggregated data and are much higher than would be obtained if similar variables were correlated at the level of individual teachers.) Darling-Hammond's analyses suggest that state policies regarding teacher education, licensing, hiring, and professional development may make an important difference in the qualifications and capacities of teachers, and, as a consequence, in the achievement of their students.

Implications for Personnel Selection

Correlations and Base Rates

It is common in research on the relationship of teacher characteristics and student achievement to express the relationship in terms of correlation coefficients. Such coefficients have distinct disadvantages in communicating the benefits of selecting teachers on the basis of their entry characteristics (such as college GPA, NTE scores, scores on teacher certification exams, Teacher Perceiver profiles and other similar measures of potential). Correlations of beginning teacher characteristics and their students' eventual achievement are typically in the range of 0.15 to 0.35, as was seen in the research reviewed above. The lay reader is frequently misled into thinking that such relationships possess a practical benefit when the finding is referred to as "statistically significant." This may not and—in the present application of psychometrics—probably is not the case. "Statistical significance" is a quality of statistical findings that refers only to their reliability or "inferential stability," that is, the likelihood that a particular finding has not arisen by chance sampling from a population in which the two variables correlated are completely unrelated. Statistical significance results from taking large samples, and generally means nothing more than that the statistical finding was based on a large sample. The finding itself could be of no practical value and still be "statistically significant." Persons' heights and their IQs might correlate 0.02 in a sample of 100,000 persons and be deemed "statistically significant"; but that finding will be of no value whatsoever.[34]

The benefits, if there are any, of selecting teachers on the basis of such weak correlational evidence—validity coefficients in the range of 0.35 and below—are not clearly seen in correlation coefficients. The meaning of these relationships is more clearly seen in statistics such as "hit rates" or measures of "false positives" and "false negatives"—for example, the differences in percentages of teachers who will not survive their probationary evaluation between those who score high on some characteristic, such as college GPA, and those who score low on that characteristic.

Consider what will prove to be a typical situation: the district's assistant superintendent for personnel has available the college GPA of all applicants for openings in elementary education. There are twice as many applicants as there are openings, so she selects the top half of the applicants on the basis of their GPA. Suppose further that the correlation between teaching candidates' GPA and their students' learning is 0.35—a not unreasonable assumption, surely not an underestimate. Furthermore, suppose that 5% of the probationary teachers in this district are not rehired after two years and that the rehire decision is based solely on their ability to engender student learning.[35]

Table 8–3.   Hypothetical Relationship Between Selection Criterion and Success Criterion

	Re-Hired	Not re-hired	Totals
Selected	490	10	500
Rejected	460	40	500
Totals	950	50	1,000

Table 8–3 shows counts of teaching candidates selected or rejected on the basis of their college GPAs and the result of the decision to continue employment after their probationary period. The data in Table 8–2 correspond to a correlation of GPA and "teaching success" of approximately 0.35 with a selection rate of 50% and a success rate of 5%. Meehl and Rosen[36] pointed out nearly 50 years ago that the utility of a correlation in predicting an event (like success in teaching as evidenced by continuing employment) depends on: a) the size of the correlation, b) the costs of errors in prediction (of rejecting a person who would succeed or accepting a person who will eventually fail), and c) the "base rate" of the event being predicted. (Also see Wainer's application of these concepts to the Massachusetts Teacher Tests).[37] The major implication of Meehl and Rosen's argument is this: if the event being predicted has a very low incidence of occurring (a "low base rate"), then very large correlations of predictors with the criterion are needed or else one makes fewer errors by using no predictor whatsoever.

One can see this phenomenon at work in the above table. If teaching candidates are selected because they have high (top half) GPAs, 10 out of 500 candidates will not be re-hired, and 460 out of 500 who would have succeeded if they had been hired will never get a chance to show that they could have succeeded. Applicants with a high GPA (and who are selected) have a 2% probability of "failing" (i.e., not being rehired). But applicants with a low GPA (who would not have been selected) have only an 8% probability of failing (i.e., not surviving the probationary period). The use of the GPA in selecting new teachers represents a gain in detecting "success" of from only 2% to 8%, but this gain comes at the cost of rejecting 92% of new hires would eventually would prove to be successful. In most people's system of values, rejecting 92% of potentially successful applicants in order to achieve a 98% success ratio in prediction is unfair to a large number of applicants. Psychometricians say that in these circumstances the cost of "false negatives" is too high.

Furthermore, when an administrator can control the overall rate of "success" (say, for example, when 95% of teachers receive "merit pay" bonuses and the discretion exists to raise that rate to 100%), it is frequently the case that even a good predictor of that 95% will create more erroneous decisions than declaring all 100% of teachers successful, hence using no selection criterion at all. Validity coefficients are not sufficient for evaluating the practical utility of a test or other selection technique: "...when the base rates of the criterion classification deviate greatly from a 50 percent split, use of a test sign having slight or moderate validity will result in an *increase* of erroneous clinical decisions."[38]

Between and Within District Variation

A second problem exists in translating the research on teacher characteristics into the real world of personnel decisions. In research studies, an effort is made to sample a full range of subjects (persons) along the continuum of the characteristics being correlated with student learning. But in the real world of schools, teacher applicants and students are clustered into schools and districts that represent selected portions of these continua. It may often be the case that a teacher characteristic that has shown modest correlations with student achievement in research studies will have no relationship with achievement *within* the particular school district attempting to select the best teachers for its students. This possibility—which is a highly likely circumstance—is illustrated in Figure 8–2.

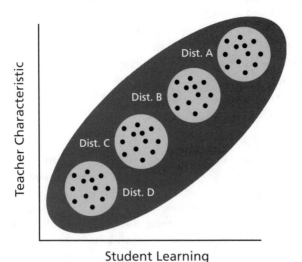

Figure 8–2.   Illustration of between and within school district relationships of a teacher characteristic and student learning.

Figure 8–2 illustrates a hypothetical situation in which 12 teachers are measured in each of four school districts on a characteristic (such as college GPA, for example) and on their contribution to their students' learning. It should be noted that the degree of relationship between a teacher characteristic and student learning depicted in Figure 8–2 is far greater than anything ever demonstrated in an actual research study, but this exaggeration will strengthen rather than vitiate the point being illustrated. Within each school district there is zero correlation between the measured teacher characteristic and the students' learning; however among the four districts, the teacher characteristic and student learning are highly correlated, perhaps as high as a coefficient of 0.80. The import of this situation is significant, however. What this arrangement of variation between and within districts implies is that the teacher characteristic is of no use whatsoever for selecting teachers within any one school district. And since it is within particular school districts that administrators live and work, knowledge of the teacher characteristic is of no value to them in selecting teachers who will enhance their students' learning.

This point may appear to be simply argumentative and counter-intuitive. The implication of this observation is real, however, and not simply some statistical sleight of hand. It dampens enthusiasm for the meager correlations that have been found; and coupled with the earlier observation on the relationship between correlation coefficients and hit ratios, it underlies the ultimate recommendation made here on the matter of initial teacher selection.

Finally, one more point must be raised that will further temper one's expectations of finding here clear statistical evidence for selecting teachers who can promote student learning. A proper predictive validity study would involve randomly assigning students to groups (or some careful matching of students across groups to ensure their initial equivalence), then randomly assigning groups to teachers, measuring teacher characteristics, allowing instruction to proceed for some substantial period, measuring student learning, and then correlating the groups' learning gains with the teacher characteristics for many teachers. It would be crucial to measure student learning by means of their *gains* in performance from before to after instruction. Simply to correlate teacher characteristics with students' achievement, as has been done repeatedly in the research literature, would not accomplish the purpose of relating teacher characteristics to student learning. Because of the many factors that influence which teachers are employed in which schools in the world outside the research laboratory—teachers with higher GPAs, and measured aptitude, perhaps, are employed in schools whose students enjoy many advantages over schools that face the challenges of poverty and discrimination—the correlation of teacher characteristics with (uncorrected) student achievement test scores measures little more than the often remarked upon sorting of more able teachers into privileged schools. Nothing like this research has ever been published, in part because of the obvious expense, the impracticality of arbitrarily constituting actual school classes of students and randomly assigning them to teachers, and, perhaps, because of researchers sense that the payoff in terms of useful predictive information would be meager. (The "micro-teaching" studies of the 1960s and early 1970s at Stanford University approximate this ideal design in terms of controls, but the focus there was on teacher behaviors that promote student learning.) A thorough literature review in the preparation of the current work revealed a single study that even approached the conditions stated above for a proper study, and that study[39] was published more than 50 years ago.

SUMMARY AND RECOMMENDATIONS

The early promise of psychometric techniques for the initial selection of teachers seems to have all but disappeared from the agenda of researchers; it may never have held a prominent place in the actual practice of educators.[40] Though rare exceptions can be found (e.g., the Montgomery County, Va., schools in the 1980s, as described by Wise et al.[41]), actual selection of teachers in America's schools is today based on interviews and personal interactions that reveal evidence of the candidate's appearance, enthusiasm, personal style and similar attributes. Measurement of ability, past achievements, or the candidate's ability to produce learning gains for students plays virtually no role in the selection of new teachers. This is not to say that the current practice is to be disapproved of. Current practice in teacher selection probably reflects an understanding that the cohesiveness of a school's staff is more critical to the success of the school and its students than is the level of teachers' performance on paper-and-pencil tests of dubious validity.

The customary procedure for selecting new teachers is based more often on first-hand experience with the candidate's teaching than it is on psychometric evidence in the form of test scores, GPAs or other evidence of personal characteristics believed to be predictive of successful teaching.[42] Schools often choose their new teachers from among interns and student teachers for whom the teaching staff has direct knowledge of their teaching abilities. Alternatively, substitute teachers are observed and evaluated as potential candidates. The arguments marshaled here against psychometric selection of new teachers, because of low correlations of teacher characteristics with student learning and very low base rates of releasing probationary teachers, have already worked their way into the existing system of evaluating candidates for new hires. The need is not for better instruments to measure initial teachers' aptitudes and dispositions, but for better methods of evaluating more directly the ability of probationary teachers to foster learning in their students.

The measurement of the direct contribution that a teacher makes to the learning of his or her students is an enormously difficult technical problem that, in the opinion of the author, has no adequate solution that can be applied with confidence under real world conditions. The attempt to base teachers' rewards (salary increases, for example) on measured student progress is even more problematic,[43] as is noted elsewhere in this report.

The claim that psychometric measures of teacher characteristics are not useful for initial teacher selection implies that candidates be selected by other means—staff interviews, recommendations by peers or past supervisors, and the like. Some might think that this approach is an abrogation of responsibility; but instead, it is a realization of the limits of psychometric approaches to personnel selection. The true abrogation of responsibility is when professional educators—whether they are tenured teachers, administrators or professors engaged in pre-service education of teachers—fail to conduct adequate evaluations of pre-service and in-service teachers who are practicing their profession under the supervision of their superiors.

These findings, then, yield the following recommendations:

- Paper-and-pencil tests are not useful predictors of teaching candidates' potential to teach successfully and should not be used as such.
- Teaching candidates' academic record (e.g., GPA) is not a useful predictor of their eventual success as teachers. A candidate's record of success in pre-service (undergraduate) technical courses (mathematics and science, for example) may contain useful information about that candidate's success in teaching secondary school mathematics and science.
- Other things equal, 1) students of regularly licensed teachers achieve at higher levels than students of emergency certified teachers; and 2) more experienced teachers produce higher student achievement than less experienced teachers. Teacher selection policies should reflect these facts.
- The selection of teachers who will best contribute to their students' academic achievement should focus on peer and supervisor evaluation of interns, student teachers, substitute teachers and teachers during their probationary period.

NOTES

1. L.J. Cronbach and G.C. Gleser, *Psychological Tests and Personnel Decisions,* 2nd ed. (Urbana: University of Illinois Press, 1965).

2.   D. Schalock, "Research on Teacher Selection," in *Review of Research in Education, Vol. 7*, ed. D. C. Berliner (Washington, D.C.: American Educational Research Association., 1979).

   R. S. Soar, D. M. Medley, and H. Coker, "Teacher Evaluation: A Critique of Currently Used Methods," *Phi Delta Kappan* 65, no. 4 (1983): 239–246.

3.   C. A. Druva and R. D. Anderson, "Science Teacher Characteristics by Teacher Behavior and by Student Outcome: A Meta-Analysis of Research," *Journal of Research in Science Teaching* 20, no. 5 (1983): 467–479.

   See also: V. A. Perkes, "Junior High School Science Teacher Preparation, Teaching Behavior, and Student Achievement," *Journal of Research in Science Teaching* 6, no. 4 (1967–1968): 121–126.

4.   D. H. Monk, "Subject Matter Preparation of Secondary Mathematics and Science Teachers and Student Achievement," *Economics of Education Review* 13, no. 2 (1994): 125–145.

5.   D. D. Goldhaber and D. J. Brewer, "Why Don't Schools and Teachers Seem to Matter? Assessing the Impact of Unobservables on Educational Productivity," *Journal of Human Resources* 32, no. 3 (1996): 505–520.

6.   T. J. Quirk, B. J. Witten, and S. F. Weinberg, "Review of Studies of Concurrent and Predictive Validity of the National Teacher Examinations," *Review of Educational Research* 43 (1973): 89–114.

7.   J. A. Shea, *The Predictive Value of Various Combinations of Standardized Tests and Subtests for Prognosis of Teaching Efficiency* (Washington, D.C.: Catholic University of America Press, 1955).

8.   H. J. Walberg, "Scholastic Aptitude, the National Teacher Examinations, and Teaching Success," *Journal of Educational Research* 61 (1967): 129–131.

9.   Quirk *et al*, Table 2.

10.   L. Lins, "The Prediction of Teaching Efficiency," *Journal of Experimental Education* 15 (1946): 2–60.

11.   G. V Glass and K. D. Hopkins, *Statistical Methods in Education and Psychology*, 3rd ed. (Boston: Allyn & Bacon, 1996), 357.

12.   W. Haney et al., "Less Truth Than Error? An Independent Study Of The Massachusetts Teacher Tests," *Education Policy Analysis Archives* 7, no. 4 (1999), <http://epaa.asu.edu/epaa/v7n4/.>.

13.   W. Kopp, "Teach for America: Moving Beyond the Debate," *The Educational Forum* 58, no. 4 (1994): 187–192.

14.   G. W. McDiarmid and S. Wilson, "An Exploration of the Subject Matter Knowledge of Alternative Route Teachers: Can We Assume They Know Their Subject?" *Journal of Teacher Education* 42, no. 2 (1991): 93–103.

15.   L. Darling-Hammond, *The Right to Learn: A Blueprint for Creating Schools That Work* (San Francisco, CA. Jossey-Bass, 1997), 308

16.   P. Ashton, "Improving the Preparation of Teachers," *Educational Researcher* 25, no. 9 (1996): 21–22.

17.   I. I. Laczko and D. C. Berliner, "The Effects of Teacher Certification on Student Achievement: An Analysis of the Stanford Nine," paper presented at the Annual Meeting of the American Educational Research Association, Seattle, WA, 2001.

18.   The practical significance of a study is often expressed in a form known as an effect size. An effect size that measures the amount of difference

between two groups is defined as a mean difference (between conditions A and B) in units of the within-condition standard deviation:

$$ES = \frac{\text{Mean}(A) - \text{Mean}(B)}{\sigma}$$

The value of *ES* reveals the amount of superiority of condition A over condition B (or, B over A in the event that *ES* has a negative value). Under the assumption of normally distributed scores, an *ES* of +1.0 indicates that the average student in condition A scores above 84% of the students in condition B. When the effect size is calculated on standardized achievement test data, a fortuitous coincidence gives the measure added meaning. It is an empirical fact that the standard deviation of most achievement tests is 1.0 years in *grade equivalent units*. Consequently, an effect size of 1.0 implies that the average superiority of condition A over condition B is 1.0 in grade equivalent units. Likewise, an effect size of .50 implies that students in A achieve, on average, 5 months in grade equivalent units above students in condition B.

19.   Glass and Hopkins, 1996

20.   R. J. Murnane and B. R. Phillips, "What Do Effective Teachers Of Inner-City Children Have In Common?" *Social Science Research* 10, no. 1 (1981): 83–100.

21.   Ibid., 91.

22.   M. Haberman, *Star Teachers of Children in Poverty* (Bloomington, IN: Kappa Delta Pi, 1995).

23.   E. L. Brown, review of *Star Teachers of Children in Poverty*, by Martin Haberman, *Education Review* (July 22, 1999), <http://coe.asu.edu/edrev/reviews/rev64.htm>.

24.   J. S. Coleman et al., *Equality of Educational Opportunity* (Washington, DC: U.S. Government Printing Office, 1966).

25.   S. Bowles and H. M. Levin, "The Determinants of Scholastic Achievement—An Appraisal of Some Recent Evidence," *Journal of Human Resources* 3 (1968): 3–24.

26.   A. A. Summers and B. L. and Wolfe, *Which School Resources Help Learning? Efficiency and Equality in Philadelphia Public Schools* (Philadelphia, PA: ED 102, February 1975), 716.

       A. A. Summers, and B. L. Wolfe, "Do Schools Make a Difference?" *American Economic Review* 67 (September 1977): 639–652.

27.   E. A. Hanushek, "Teacher Characteristics and Gains in Student Achievement: Estimation Using Micro Data," *The American Economic Review* 61, no. 2 (1971): 280–288.

28.   R. Greenwald, L. V. Hedges, and R. D. Laine, "The Effect of School Resources on Student Achievement," *Review of Educational Research* 66 (1996): 361–396.

29.   E. Hanushek, "A More Complete Picture of School Resource Policies," *Review of Educational Research* 66, no. 3 (1996): 397–409.

30.   E. Hanushek, "Assessing the Effects of School Resources on Student Performance: An Update," *Educational Evaluation and Policy Analysis* 19, no. 2 (1997): 141–164.

31.   Hanushek, 144.

32.   M. Fetler, "High School Staff Characteristics and Mathematics Test Results," *Education Policy Analysis Archives*, 7, no. 9 (1999), <http://epaa.asu.edu/epaa/v7n9.html>.

But also see:

E. J. Fuller, *Does Teacher Certification Matter? A Comparison Of TAAS Performance in 1997 Between Schools with Low and High Percentages of Certified Teachers* (Austin, TX: Charles A. Dana Center, University of Texas at Austin, 1999).

L. Darling-Hammond, "Teaching and Knowledge: Policy Issues Posed by Alternate Certification for Teachers," Peabody Journal of Education 67, no. 1 (1990): 123–154.

33.   L. Darling-Hammond, "Teacher Quality and Student Achievement: A Review of State Policy Evidence," *Education Policy Analysis Archives* 8, no. 1 (2000), <http://epaa.asu.edu/epaa/v8n1/>.

34.   Glass and Hopkins, 269.

35.   This estimate is actually higher than the prevailing figures in public schools. An informal survey of teacher educators and administrators conducted in June 2001 on the AERA Division K listserv fixes the true figure at 5% or less.

36.   P. E. Meehl and A. Rosen, "Antecedent Probability and the Efficiency of Psychometric Signs, Patterns, or Cutting Scores," *Psychological Bulletin* 52 (1955): 194–216.

37.   H. Wainer, "Some Comments on the Ad Hoc Committee's Critique of the Massachusetts Teacher Tests," *Education Policy Analysis Archives* 7, no. 5 (1999), <http://epaa.asu.edu/epaa/v7n5.html>.

38.   Meehl and Rosen, 215.

39.   Lins.

40.   W. Haney, G. Madaus, and A. Kreitzer, "Charms Talismanic: Testing Teachers for the Improvement of American Education," in *Review of Research in Education*, vol. 14., ed. E. Z. Rothkopf, (Washington, D.C.: American Educational Research Association, 1987), 169–238.

41.   A. E. Wise et al., *Effective Teacher Selection: From Recruitment to Retention—Case Studies* (Santa Monica, CA: The RAND Corporation, 1987).

42.   Ibid.

L. Darling-Hammond, A. E. Wise, and S. R. Pease, "Teacher Evaluation in the Organizational Context: A Review of the Literature," *Review of Educational Research* 53 (1983): 285–337.

43.   G. V Glass, "Using Student Test Scores To Evaluate Teachers," in *New Handbook of Teacher Evaluation*, eds. J. Millman, and L. Darling-Hammond (Beverly Hills, CA: SAGE, 1989).

CHAPTER 9

CONVERGING FINDINGS ON CLASSROOM INSTRUCTION

Barak Rosenshine
University of Illinois at Urbana

SUMMARY OF RESEARCH FINDINGS

The past 30 years have seen major advances in research on cognitive processing; in studies of teachers whose classes made the highest achievement gains compared to other classes; and in research on helping students learn and apply cognitive strategies in their learning. The research on cognitive processing underlies a major goal of education: helping students develop well-organized knowledge structures. A number of strategies have been found that consistently help students effectively acquire strong knowledge structures.

RECOMMENDATIONS

- Present new material in small steps so that the working memory does not become overloaded.
- Help students develop an organization for the new material.
- Guide student practice by supporting students during initial practice, and providing for extensive student processing.
- When teaching higher-level tasks, support students by providing them with cognitive strategies.

- Help students learn to use the cognitive strategies by providing them with procedural prompts and modeling the use of these procedural prompts.
- Provide for extensive student practice.

The past 30 years have seen three major advances in research on instruction and teacher behavior. These advancements are:

1) research on cognitive processing,
2) studies of teachers whose classes made the highest achievement gain compared to other classes, and
3) research on helping students learn and apply cognitive strategies in their learning.

This report examines the impact that teacher behavior can have on the achievement of students, particularly of students living in poverty.

CLASSROOM INSTRUCTION RESEARCH

Cognitive Processing: The Importance of Well-Connected Knowledge Structures

A major area of research, one with important implications for teaching, has been the research on cognitive processing, research on how information is stored and retrieved. It is currently thought that the information in our long-term memory is stored in interconnected networks called knowledge structures. The size of these knowledge structures, the number of connections between pieces of knowledge, the strength of the connections, and the organization and richness of the relationships are all important for processing information and solving problems.

There is no underestimating the importance of background knowledge. Simon and Hayes wrote that "there is no substitute for having the prerequisite knowledge if one is to solve a problem."[1] In discussing how expertise is acquired, Chase and Chi wrote:

> The most obvious answer is practice, thousands of hours of practice. For the most part, practice is by far the best predictor of performance. Practice can produce two kinds of knowledge ... a storage of patterns and a set of strategies or procedures that can act on the patterns.[2]

It is easier to learn new information and easier to solve new problems when one has 1) a rich, well-connected knowledge structure and 2) stronger ties between the connections, when the knowledge structure on a particular topic is large and well-connected, new information is more readily acquired and prior knowledge is more readily available for use. When information is "meaningful" to students, they have more points in their knowledge structures to which they can attach new information. Education is a process of developing, enlarging, expanding, and refining our students' knowledge structures.[3]

Helping students to organize information into well-connected patterns has another advantage. When a pattern is unified, it only occupies a few bits in the working memory. Thus, having larger and better-connected patterns frees space in our working memory. This available space can be used for reflecting on new information and for problem solving. For example, when U.S. history is organized into well-connected patterns, these patterns occupy less space in the working memory and the learner has additional space in the working memory to use to consider, assimilate, and manipulate new information. A major difference between an expert and a novice is that the expert's knowledge structure has a larger number of knowledge items, the expert has more connections between the items, the links between the connections are stronger, and the structure is better organized. A novice, on the other hand, is unable to see these patterns, and often ignores them. This development of well-connected patterns and the concomitant freeing of space in the working memory is one of the hallmarks of an expert in a field.[4]

To summarize, well-connected and elaborate knowledge structures are important because they allow for easier retrieval of old material; they permit more information to be carried in a single chunk, and they facilitate the understanding and integration of new information.

Helping Students Develop Background Knowledge

What can be done to help students develop well-connected bodies of knowledge? One important instructional procedure is providing for extensive reading, review, practice, and discussion. These activities serve to help students increase the number of pieces of information that are the long-term memory, organize those pieces, and increase the strength and number of these interconnections. The more one rehearses and reviews information, the stronger these interconnections become. Thus, the research on cognitive processing supports the need for a teacher to assist students by providing for extensive reading of a variety of materials, frequent review, testing, and discussion and application activities.

Providing for Student Processing

New material is stored in the long-term memory when one processes it. The quality of storage can depend on the "level of processing." For example, the quality of storage is stronger when we read a passage and focus on its meaning than it would be if we read to find a single word answer. Similarly, the quality of storage would be stronger if one summarized or compared the material in the passage, rehearsed, reviewed, and drew connections. The connections would be weaker if one hurriedly skimmed the material.

Thus, the research on cognitive processing supports the importance of a teacher initiating activities that require students to process and apply new information. Such processing strengthens the knowledge network that the student is developing. Classroom discussion and projects that require students to organize information, summarize information, or compare new material with prior material are all activities that should help students develop and strengthen their cognitive structures. In addition, Palincsar and Brown wrote:

> Understanding is more likely to occur when a child is required to explain, elaborate, or defend his position to others; the burden of explanation is often the push needed to make him or her evaluate, integrate, and elaborate knowledge in new ways.[5]

Other examples of such processing activities include asking students to do any of the following: read a variety of materials; explain the new material to someone else; compare material from different sources; justify their conclusions; write papers and engage in inquiry; or write daily summaries.

Helping Students Organize Knowledge

Information is organized into knowledge structures. Without these structures, new knowledge tends to be fragmented and not readily available for recall and use. However, students frequently lack these knowledge structures when they are learning new material. Without direction, there is the danger that students will develop a fragmented, incomplete, or erroneous knowledge structure.

Graphic Organizers.   One way of helping students expand their knowledge structures in content areas and also allowing for a check on misconceptions is to teach students to use graphic organizers and develop concept maps. These structures allow a student to show connections between concepts. An outline is an example of such an organizer; concept maps are another example. These structures help students organize the elements of the new learning and such organization can serve to facilitate retrieval. In addition, having such organizers can enable the student to devote more working memory to the content.

Another approach is to teach students how to develop their own graphic organizers for new material. Providing students with a variety of structures that they can use to construct their own graphic organizers facilitates this process. When teaching students to develop a graphic organizer, it is useful for the teacher to model the process and also provide models of thinking and thinking aloud while constructing the maps.

When students are encouraged to construct ideas and develop conclusions, there is also a danger they will develop misconceptions. Research shows we sometimes develop misconceptions in an effort to make sense of our environment.[6] (A notorious example is the belief that the sun is closer to the Earth during summer.) Allowing students to work independently before they are ready increases the danger that they may develop misconceptions. Therefore, teachers need to supervise students when they are working independently and to check their understanding before they begin independent work.

In summary, the research on cognitive processing has identified the importance of developing well-connected knowledge structures. Encouraging extensive reading and practice might develop such structures, student processing of new information, and helping students organize their new knowledge.

Research on Teacher Effects

A second important body of research is the teacher effects studies. This line of research, which took place in the 1960s and 1970s, used extensive classroom observation in an attempt to identify those teacher behaviors that were most related to student achievement gain.

Design of the Studies

There were three parts to the design of these studies. The first part consisted of systematic observation of the instructional behaviors of teachers and students. Observers sat in a number of existing classrooms, usually 20 to 30 classrooms, and observed and recorded the frequency with which those teachers used a variety of instructional behaviors such as the cause, frequency, and type of praise, the cause frequency and type of criticism, the number and type of questions that were asked, the quality of the student answers, and the responses of a teacher to a student's answers. Many investigators also recorded how much time was spent in activities such as review, presentation, guided practice, and supervising seatwork. Others recorded how the teachers prepared students for seatwork and homework, and the attention-level during teacher-led discussion and during seatwork.

At the end of the observation period or at the end of the semester, each class took a posttest in the subject that was observed, usually reading or mathematics. These class posttest scores were then statistically adjusted, using a variety of regression techniques, for initial or pretest scores of these students. That is, the pretest was used as the independent variable in the analysis, and was used to statistically adjust the posttest scores, the dependent variables, for initial standing. In the final step, each of the observed teacher and student behaviors, in each classroom were then, correlated with the adjusted posttest scores.

In effect, these are studies of master teachers. That is, based on the test scores, the investigators were able to identify those teachers whose classrooms made the greatest adjusted achievement gain during the semester, and those teachers whose classrooms made the least adjusted gain during the semester. The investigators were able to take the results of their systematic observation and use this to identify the instructional procedures that the master teachers used and compare these instructional procedures with those procedures used by the less-effective teachers. The significant results are described later in this section.

Usually 20–30 classrooms were in each study, although the study by Stallings and Kascovitz[7] involved 108 first grade and 58 third grade classrooms, and studies by Robert Soar and Ruth Soar involved 55 middle grade classrooms,[8] 59 fifth grade classrooms,[9] and 289 Follow-Through and comparison classrooms.[10]

Although a number of studies of this type were conducted as early as 1948 by Barr,[11] the two most famous studies that initiated the teacher-effects research were those by Flanders[12] and by Medley and Mitzel.[13] The best known of the later studies were those by Stallings and Kascovitz[14] in Follow-Through classrooms, Good and Grouws[15] in fourth-grade mathematics, and Brophy and Evertson[16] in first grade reading.

These correlational studies were frequently followed by experimental studies in which one group of teachers—the experimental group—was taught to use the findings of the correlational studies in their teaching and another group of similar teachers continued to teach in their usual manner. By and large, these studies were successful in that the teachers in the experimental groups used more of the new behaviors and the posttest scores of their classrooms—adjusted by regression for their initial scores—were significantly higher than scores in classrooms taught by the control teachers.

Rosenshine summarized the earliest studies in 1971.[17] The correlational studies and the experimental studies in this tradition are described in detail by Brophy and Good,[18] and the experimental studies are also described by Gage and Needles.[19]

Validity

One argument for the validity of these findings is that the correlational results were replicated in subsequent correlational studies. These studies represented cumulative research. Second, the correlational results were also replicated in a number of experimental studies. Finally, the instructional findings that emerged from this research also appear in an independent line of research, that of cognitive strategy instruction, a topic which will be covered later.

Rosenshine and Stevens concluded that those teachers whose classrooms made the greatest gains in reading or mathematics usually used the following procedures:[20]

- Begin a lesson with a short review of previous learning.
- Begin a lesson with a short statement of goals.
- Present new material in small steps, providing for student practice after each step.
- Give clear and detailed instructions and explanations.
- Provide a high level of active practice for all students.
- Ask a large number of questions, check for student understanding, and obtain responses from all students.
- Guide students during initial practice.
- Provide systematic feedback and corrections.
- Provide explicit instruction and practice for individual exercises and, where necessary, monitor students during their individual work.

Rosenshine and Stevens further grouped these instructional procedures under six teaching "functions" as shown in Table 9.1.[21]

Table 9–1.   Functions for Teaching Well-Structured Tasks

1. Review

Review homework
Review relevant previous learning
Review prerequisite skills and knowledge for the lesson

2. Presentation

State lesson goals or provide outline
Present new material in small steps
Model procedures
Provide positive and negative examples
Use clear language
Check for student understanding
Avoid digressions

3. Guided Practice

Spend more time on guided practice
High frequency of questions
All students respond and receive feedback
High success rate
Continue practice until students are fluent

Table 9-1.   Functions for Teaching Well-Structured Tasks (Cont.)

4. Corrections and Feedback

Provide process feedback when answers are correct but hesitant
Provide sustaining feedback, clues, or re-teaching when answers are incorrect
Re-teach material when necessary

5. Independent practice

Students receive overview and/or help during initial steps
Practice continues until students are automatic (where relevant)
Teacher provides active supervision (where possible)
Routines are used to provide help for slower students

6. Weekly and monthly reviews

Small Steps, Practice, and Success

Four strategies that are particularly relevant to teaching are:

1)   teaching in "small steps,"
2)   guiding student practice,
3)   ensuring a high student success rate, and
4)   providing extensive practice.

Present New Material in Small Steps

When the most effective teachers in these studies taught new material, they taught it in "small steps." That is, they only presented small parts of new material at a single time, and then guided students in practicing this material. In contrast, the least effective teachers in these studies would present an entire lesson, and then pass out worksheets and tell students to work the problems.

The importance of teaching in small steps fits well with the findings from cognitive psychology on the limitations of our working memory. Our working memory, the place where we process information, is small. It can only handle a few bits of information at once—too much information swamps our working memory. The procedure of first teaching in small steps and then guiding student practice represents an appropriate way of dealing with the limitation of our working memory.

Guide Student Practice

A second major finding from the teacher effects literature was the importance of guided practice.[22]

As noted, the most effective teachers presented only small amounts of material at a time. After this short presenting, these teachers then guided student practice. This guidance often consisted of the teacher working a few problems at the board and discussing the steps out loud. This instruction served as a model for the students. This guidance also included asking students to come to the board, work problems, and discuss their procedures. Through this process the students at their seats would see additional models.

In contrast, the least effective teachers would present an entire lesson, and then pass out worksheets and tell the students to work the problems. When this happened, it was observed that many students were confused and made errors on the worksheets and the teachers would be seen going from student to student and explaining the material. In this case, the amount of material that was presented was too large, and swamped the working memory.

The process of guiding practice also includes checking the answers of the entire class in order to see whether some students need additional instruction. Guided practice has also included asking students to work together, in pairs or in groups, to quiz and explain the material to each other. Guided practice may occur when a teacher questions and helps a class with their work before assigning independent practice.

Guided practice also fits the cognitive processing findings on the need to provide for student processing. Guided practice is the place where the students—working alone, with other students, or with the teacher—engage in the cognitive processing activities of organizing, reviewing, rehearsing, summarizing, comparing, and contrasting. However, it is important that all students engage in these activities. The least effective teachers often asked a question, called on one student to answer, and then assumed that everyone had learned this point. In contrast, the most effective teachers attempted to check the understanding of all students and to provide for processing by all students.

Another reason for the importance of guided practice comes from the fact that we construct and reconstruct knowledge. We cannot simply repeat what we hear word for word. Rather, we connect our understanding of the new information to our existing concepts or "schema," and we then construct a mental summary: "the gist" of what we have heard. However, when left on their own, many students make errors in the process of constructing this mental summary. These errors occur, particularly, when the information is new and the student does not have adequate or well-formed background knowledge. These constructions are not errors so much as attempts by the students to be logical in an area where their background knowledge is weak. These errors are so common that there is a literature on the development and correction of student misconceptions in science. Providing guided practice after teaching small amounts of new material, and checking for student understanding, can help limit the development of misconceptions.

Provide for Extensive Practice

The most effective teachers also provided for extensive and successful practice. As noted in the cognitive processing research, students need extensive practice in order to develop well-connected networks. The most effective teachers made sure that such practice took place after there has been sufficient guided practice, so that students were not practicing errors and misconceptions.

Provide for a High Success Rate

In two of the major teacher-effects studies the investigators found that students in classrooms of the more effective teachers had a higher success rate as judged by the quality of their oral responses and their individual work. The need for a high success rate follows from the previous research on the need to provide extensive and successful practice.

Yet, teachers often struggle to obtain a high success rate, particularly when they are teaching whole-class to heterogeneous students. One solution is the above-mentioned "teaching in small steps." Another solution is for students to meet in heterogeneous groups during the independent practice and work problems together. In these settings, students who have learned the material re-explain the material to the other students.

Other schools have dealt with this problem by regrouping students, by achievement, across classrooms, for reading and for mathematics. In such settings, it is easier for the teachers to explain, supervise, and re-teach to the entire class because all the students in this setting are at similar levels.

The need for a high success rate, and the need for students to master one step before they proceed to the next step is the major idea behind Mastery Learning. In Mastery Learning there is explicit provision for bringing all students to mastery on one section of the material before they proceed to the next section.

Teaching Cognitive Strategies

The third, major instructional advance has been the development and teaching of cognitive strategies. Cognitive strategies are guides that support learners as they develop new internal procedures, procedures that enable them to perform higher-level operations in areas such as reading comprehension and scientific problem solving.

Until the late 1970s, students were seldom provided with any help in reading comprehension. Durkin[23] observed 4,469 minutes of reading instruction in fourth-grade classrooms and noted that only 20 minutes of this total was spent in comprehension instruction. Durkin found that teachers spent almost all of the instructional time asking questions, but spent little time teaching students comprehension strategies they could use to answer the questions. Duffy and Roehler[24] noted a similar lack of comprehension instruction in elementary classrooms:

> There is little evidence of instruction of any kind. Teachers spend most of their time assigning activities, monitoring to be sure the pupils are on task, directing recitation sessions to assess how well children are doing and providing corrective feedback in response to pupil errors. Seldom does one observe teaching in which a teacher presents a skill, a strategy, or a process to pupils, shows them how to do it, provides assistance as they initiate attempts to perform the task and assures that they can be successful.[25]

As a result of these astonishing findings, and as a result of emerging research on cognition and information processing, investigators began to develop and validate cognitive strategies that could help students. For example, one approach that has been used successfully to help students improve their reading comprehension has been to teach students to ask themselves questions about their reading. In these studies students would read passages and use prompts such as "who" and "why" to ask questions about the passage. And, as a result of this practice, comprehension improved when the students were tested on new passages.

What happened? Asking oneself a question, obviously, does not lead directly to improved comprehension on new passages. Rather, it is believed that the process of asking questions changed the way students read—it led them to search the text and combine information—and it was this change in processing that led to improved comprehension on new passages.

Throughout the 1980s, investigators began to develop and teach students specific cognitive strategies such as question-generation and summarization that could be applied to reading comprehension.[26] Cognitive strategy procedures have also been developed and taught in mathematics problem solving,[27] physics problem solving,[28] and in writing.[29] These intervention studies, in reading, writing, mathematics, and science, together with a description of the cognitive strategies and the instructional procedures were used, has been assembled in an excellent volume by Pressley et al.[30]

The concept of cognitive strategies provides a general approach that can be applied to the teaching of higher-order tasks in the content areas. The profession has made much progress. In place of Durkin's observation that there was little evidence of cognitive strategy instruction in reading, there are now studies that have succeeded in providing instruction in cognitive strategies in a number of content areas.

Instructional Elements in Teaching of Cognitive Strategies

The process of teaching students cognitive strategies is distinctive in that the investigators used a variety of supports, or scaffolds, to teach students to use the strategies. Many of these instructional elements had not appeared in the teacher-effects literature. These elements—which are described in this section—can now be used by teachers, profitably, to help students not only in the learning of cognitive strategies, but also in variety of other learning situations.

Scaffolds. Cognitive strategies are taught by providing students with cognitive supports or scaffolds.[31] A scaffold is a temporary support that is used to assist a learner during initial learning. Scaffolds operate to reduce the complexities of the problems and break them down into manageable chunks that the child has a real chance of solving.[32] Scaffolds help students bridge the gap between their current abilities and the goal. The scaffolds are gradually withdrawn as learners become more independent, although some students may continue to rely on scaffolds when they encounter particularly difficult problems. Scaffolds include simplified problems, modeling of the procedures by the teacher, thinking aloud by the teacher as he or she solves the problem, prompts, suggestions, and guidance as students work problems. Scaffolds may also be tools, such as cue cards or checklists, or a model of the completed task against which students can compare their work.[33]

Collins, Brown, and Neuman originated the term Cognitive Apprenticeship to refer to the entire process of teaching cognitive strategies and providing scaffolds to aid students.[34] Students are learning strategies during this apprenticeship that will enable them to become competent readers, writers, and problem solvers. They are aided by a Master who models, coaches, provides supports, and withdraws the supports and scaffolds as the students become independent.

A number of these supports and scaffolds, drawn from the research, are presented here.

1) Provide Procedural Prompts That Can Guide Student Processing.

In these studies, the first step in teaching a cognitive strategy was the development of a procedural prompt.[35] Procedural prompts are concrete aids that supply the students with specific procedures or suggestions that facilitate the completion of the task. Learners can temporarily rely on these hints and suggestions until they create their own internal structures.[36]

As noted, the words "who," "what" "why" "where" "when" and "how" are procedural prompts that help students learn the cognitive strategy of asking questions about the material they have read.[37] These prompts are concrete references on which students can rely for support as they learn to apply the cognitive strategy.

Another example of procedural prompts comes from a study by King,[38] who also taught students to generate questions. In her studies, however, she provided students with a list of question stems:

How are _____ and _____ alike?
What is the main idea of _____?
What do you think would happen if _____?
What are the strengths and weaknesses of _____ ?
In what way is _____ related to _____?
What do you think causes _____?
How does _____ tie in with what we have learned before?
What do I (you) still not understand about . . .?

Students practiced in groups, using these stems to ask each other questions about passages. King found that students who practiced using these prompts were superior to control students in comprehension of new material. Apparently, using these stems to develop and answer questions led the students to develop new internal approaches to reading text, and these approaches helped them when they now read new material.

A wide variety of excellent procedural prompts have been developed for reading comprehension, for writing, and for vocabulary. Investigators have also developed a number of "concept maps" and "graphic organizers" that have been shown to help students learn from text. Twenty-four of these procedural prompts and details on their use—mostly derived from successful studies—have been assembled in a useful book published by the Wisconsin State Department of Public Instruction.[39]

2) Demonstrate use of the prompt through modeling and thinking aloud.

On one hand, demonstration of use of the procedural prompts is similar to traditional demonstrations by a teacher. What is new is the addition of two cognitive supports: modeling of the cognitive strategy, and "thinking aloud" that provides an insight into how experts solve problems. These supports would seem useful in a variety of instructional situations.

Provide Models of the Appropriate Responses.   The literature on cognitive strategies has introduced us to the concept of a teacher modeling appropriate responses. Excellent teachers have undoubtedly modeled difficult learning for centuries, but it was the cognitive strategy literature that highlighted this important instructional procedure.

As noted, prompts were "who," "what" and "where," then a teacher would model questions starting with those words. This modeling occurred at the start of the lessons and also during the lesson when students were having problems developing questions.[40]

Modeling is particularly appropriate when using prompts for writing essays or arguments. The author once watched a class where the teacher spent the entire period modeling and leading the class as he completed an essay prompt using material from the play *Macbeth*, which the class had read and discussed. The next day, he led the class as they completed the prompt using a second argument. The third day, he supervised the students as they worked alone and used the prompt to develop a third argument.

Think Aloud, as Choices are Being Made.   Another scaffold, similar to modeling, is thinking aloud: literally vocalizing the internal thought processes one goes through when using the cognitive strategy. A teacher might think aloud while summarizing a paragraph—illustrating the thought processes that occur as one first determines the topic of the paragraph then uses the topic to generate a summary sentence.

Thinking aloud by the teacher and more capable students provides novice learners with a way to observe "expert thinking" that is usually hidden from the student. Garcia and Pearson (1990) refer to this process as the teacher "sharing the reading secrets" by making them overt.[41] Indeed, identifying the hidden strategies of experts so that they can become available to learners has become a useful area of research.[42]

Anderson[43] worked with adolescent readers who were competent decoders but poor in comprehension. These readers were reluctant to identify or to attempt to solve problems that occurred during their reading. The students met in groups, read somewhat difficult passages, and attempted to make sense of the passages. Anderson illustrated the procedure she was trying to teach by modeling how one might attempt to clarify a difficult passage:

> I don't get this. It says that things that are dark look smaller. I know that a white dog looks smaller than a black elephant, so this rule must only work for things that are about the same size. Maybe black shoes would make your feet look smaller than white ones would.

Anderson also modeled how they might summarize important information:

> I'll summarize this part of the article. So far, it tells where the Spanish started in North America and what parts they explored. Since the title is "The Spanish in California," the part about California must be important. I'd sum up by saying that Spanish explorers from Mexico discovered California. They didn't stay in California, but lived in other parts of America. These are the most important ideas so far.

3)   Guide Initial Practice through Techniques That Reduce the Difficulty of the Task.
Typically, after the modeling, the teacher guided students during their initial practice. As they worked through text, the teacher gave hints,

reminders of the prompts, reminders of what was overlooked, and suggestions of how something could be improved.[44]

Much of this guided practice is similar to the guided practice that emerged from the teacher effects research.[45] Now, however, the guided practice is being applied to the learning of higher-level tasks. A number of investigators also developed procedures that facilitate practice by reducing the initial demands on the students. These procedures, described next, would seem useful for teaching a variety of skills, strategies, and concepts, not just those illustrated here.

Regulate the Difficulty of the Task.   One approach to guided practice has been to regulate the difficulty of the material by having the students begin with simpler material and then gradually move to more complex materials. For example, when Palincsar taught students to generate questions, the teacher first modeled how to generate questions about a single sentence.[46] This was followed by class practice. Next, the teacher modeled and provided practice on asking questions after reading a paragraph. Finally, the teacher modeled and then the class practiced generating questions after reading an entire passage. Similar procedures were used by other investigators.[47]

The same simple to complex procedure was used to teach the strategy of summarizing.[48] Students first learned to write summaries of single paragraphs, and then progressed, with guidance and modeling from the teacher, to producing a summary of longer passages.

In another study where summarization was taught, the initial difficulty was reduced by starting the practice with material that was one or two grade levels below the students' reading level.[49] In a study by Blaha,[50] the teacher divided up the strategy. She first taught a part of a strategy, then guided student practice in first identifying and then applying the strategy. After that, the teacher taught the next part of the strategy, and guided student practice. Finally, the parts of the strategy were combined. In many of these studies, the prompts were diminished after students had learned the task. In all these examples, the initial difficulty of the higher-level task was reduced by beginning with simpler materials or by teaching the strategy in small steps.

Anticipate and Discuss Potential Difficulties.   One characteristic of experienced teachers is their ability to anticipate student errors prior to instruction and then focus instruction around these potential problems. This practice occurred in some of these studies. For example, in a study by Palincsar the teacher anticipated the inappropriate questions that students might generate.[51] After the students had read a paragraph, the students were shown a question that was too narrow, that focused only on a small detail, and the students discussed why it was a poor question. The teacher then showed the students a question that could not be answered by the information provided in the paragraph, and the students discussed why it was a poor question. They continued through the exercise discussing whether each question was too narrow, too broad, or appropriate.

Provide a Cue Card when Appropriate.   Another support used in these studies was providing a cue card containing the procedural prompt. A cue card might support a student during initial learning by reducing the strain upon the working memory. In a number of studies, the students were given cards that contained the procedural prompts. In all these studies, the investigators modeled the use of the cue card.

4)   Provide Feedback and Self-Checking Procedures.
    Teacher feedback and corrections occurred during the guided practice as students attempted to generate questions. Feedback typically took the form of hints, questions, and suggestions.

Provide and Teach a Checklist.   In some of the studies, students were taught to use another scaffold, a self-evaluation checklist. In a study by Davey and McBride[52] a self-evaluation checklist was introduced in the fourth of five instructional sessions. The checklist listed the following questions:

> How well did I identify important information?
> How well did I link information together?
> How well could I answer my questions?
> Did my "think questions" use different language from the text?
> Did I use good signal words?

In another study[53] the students were taught specific rules to discriminate a question from a non-question and a good question from a poor one:

> A good question starts with a question word.
> A good question can be answered by the story.
> A good question asks about an important detail of the story.

Provide Models of Expert Work.   In some studies, students would view an expert's model after they had completed their own work.[54] The intent of this model was to enable the students to compare their efforts with that of an expert.[55]

Suggest Fix-Up Strategies.   Fix-up strategies are strategies students learn to use when their writing or reading or project is not going well. In two studies, student reading comprehension improved when they were taught fix-up strategies.[56] Some of the fix-up strategies that were taught included:

Re-read the difficult portion of the text.
Read ahead to see if the problems clear up.
Formulate the difficulty as a problem.

These strategies came from studies of expert readers, and teaching these strategies resulted in improved comprehension.

Feedback in Groups.   Another form of guided practice occurred when students met in small groups of two to six, without the teacher, and practiced asking, revising, and correcting questions and provided support and feedback to each other.[57] Such groupings allow for more support when revising questions and for more practice than can be obtained in a whole-class setting. Nolte and Singer applied the concept of diminishing support to the organization of groups.[58] Students first spent three days working in groups of five or six, followed by three days working in pairs, and then began to work alone.

5)   Provide Independent Practice with New Examples
Extensive and successful independent practice is required for learning cognitive strategies. Such practice can lead to "automatic responding," which means that the students use the strategy automatically and do not have to stop to recall it. Another result of extensive practice is "unitization" of the strategy, that is, the blending of elements of the strategy into a unified whole. This extensive practice, and practice with a variety of material, also frees the learning from its original limited context so that it can be applied easily and unconsciously to various situations.[59] One can also practice transfer during independent practice. For example, in a study by Dermody[60] the last phase of the study involved application of cognitive strategy to a different content area than was used for the original instruction.

Increase Student Responsibilities.   As students become more competent during guided practice and independent practice, the teacher diminishes the use of models and prompts and other scaffolds, and also diminishes the support offered by other students. The responsibilities of the individual student and the complexity and difficulty of the material are gradually increased. In reading, for example, one begins with well-organized, reader-friendly material and then increases the difficulty of the material. That way, students receive practice and support in applying their strategies to the more difficult material they can expect to encounter in their regular reading.

Assess Student Mastery. After guided practice and independent practice, some of the studies assessed whether students had achieved a mastery level, and provided for additional instruction if that level had not been reached. On the fifth and final day of instruction, Davey and McBride required students to generate three acceptable questions for each of three passages and re-teaching was provided.[61] Smith stated that student questions at the end of a story were compared to model questions, and re-teaching took place when necessary.[62] Wong, Wong, Perry, and Sawatsky required that students achieve mastery in applying the self-questioning steps; students had to continue doing the exercises, with assistance, until they achieved mastery.[63] Unfortunately, the other studies cited in this review did not report the level of mastery students achieved in generating questions.

Table 9–2.   Instructional Elements in Teaching Cognitive Strategies.

1. Provide procedural prompts that can guide student processing.

2. Demonstrate the use of the prompts through modeling and thinking aloud.

Model the use of the prompt.
Think aloud as choices are being made.

3. Guide initial practice.

Regulate the difficulty of the task.
Anticipate and discuss potential difficulties.
Provide a cue card when appropriate.

4. Provide feedback and self-checking procedures.

Provide and teach a checklist.
Suggest fix-up strategies.
Arrange for feedback in groups.

5. Provide independent practice with new examples.

Increase student responsibility.
Assess student mastery.

RECOMMENDATIONS

Since the publication of the first *Handbook of Research on Teaching*[64] nearly 40 years ago, and with the investment of public and private funds in research, we have undertaken an extensive program of research and development in education. The profession has come a long way. How might the results from these three areas of research fit together?

The research on cognitive processing underlies a major goal of education: helping students develop well-organized knowledge structures. In well-organized structures the parts are well-organized, the pieces are well-connected, and the bonds between the connections are strong.

We also know something about how to help students acquire these structures.

- Present new material in small steps so that the working memory does not become overloaded.
- Help students develop an organization for the new material.
- Guide student practice by supporting students during initial practice, and providing for extensive student processing.
- When teaching higher-level tasks, support students by providing them with cognitive strategies.
- Help students learn to use the cognitive strategies by providing them with procedural prompts and modeling the use of these procedural prompts.
- Provide for extensive student practice.

REFERENCES

1.   H. A. Simon and J. R. Hayes, "The Understanding Process: Problem Isomorphs," *Cognitive Psychology* 8, no. 2 (1976): 165–190.

2.   W. G. Chase and M. T. H. Chi, "Cognitive Skill: Implications for Spatial Skill in Large-scale Environments," in *Cognition, Social Behavior, and Environment*, ed. J. Harvey (Potomac, MD: Erlbaum 1980), 12.

3.   M. Pressley and C. B. McCormick, *Advanced Educational Psychology For Educators, Researchers, And Policy Makers* (New York: Harper Collins, 1995): 48–109.

4.   Ibid.

5.   A. S. Palincsar and A. L. Brown, "Reciprocal Teaching of Comprehension-fostering and Comprehension-monitoring Activities," *Cognition and Instruction* 2 (1984): 117–175.

6.   B. J. Guzzetti, T. E. Snyder, and G. V. Glass, "Promoting Conceptual Change in Science: Can Texts be Used Effectively?" *Journal of Reading* 35 (1992): 642–649.

7.   J. A. Stallings and D. H. Kaskowitz, *Follow Through Classroom Observation Evaluation (1972–1973)* (Menlo Park, CA: Stanford Research Institute, 1974).

8.   R. S. Soar, *An Integrative Approach to Classroom Learning* (Philadelphia: Temple University, 1966), ERIC, ED 033749.

9.   R. S. Soar and R. M. Soar, *Classroom Behavior, Pupil Characteristics, and Pupil Growth for the School Year and the Summer* (Gainesville: University of Florida, Institute for Development of Human Resources, 1973).

10.   R. S. Soar, *Follow-Through Classroom Process Measurement and Pupil Growth (1970–1971)* (Gainesville: University of Florida, Institute for Development of Human Resources, 1973), ERIC, ED 106297.

11.   A. S. Barr, "The Measurement and Prediction of Teaching Efficiency: A Summary of the Investigations," *Journal of Experimental Education* 16 (1948): 203–283.

12.   N. A. Flanders, *Teacher Influence, Pupil Attitudes and Achievement* (Minneapolis: University of Minnesota, 1960).

13.   D. M. Medley and H. E. Mitzel, "Some Behavioral Correlates Of Teacher Effectiveness," *Journal of Educational Psychology* 50 (1959): 239–246.

14.   Stallings and Kascowitz.

15.   T. Good and D. Grouws, "Teaching Effects: A Process-Product Study of Fourth Grade Mathematics Classrooms," *Journal of Teacher Education* 28 (1977): 49–54.

16.   J. Brophy and C. Evertson, *Learning From Teaching: A Developmental Perspective* (Boston, MA: Allyn & Bacon, 1976).

17.   B. Rosenshine, *Teaching Behaviors and Student Achievement* (Slough, England: National Federation for Eucational Research, 1971).

18.   J. Brophy and T. Good, "Teacher Effects Results," in *Handbook of Research on Teaching*, 3rd ed., ed. M. C. Wittrock (New York: Macmillan, 1986).

19.   N. L. Gage and M. C. Needles, "Process-Product Research on Teaching: A Review Of Criticisms," *Elementary School Journal* 89 (1989): 253–300.

20.   B. Rosenshine and R. Stevens, "Teaching Functions," in *Handbook of Research on Teaching*, 3rd ed., ed. M. C. Wittrock (New York: Macmillan, 1986).

21.   Ibid.

22.   M. Hunter, *Mastery Teaching* (El Segunda, CA.: TIP Publications, 1982).

23.   D. Durkin, "What Classroom Observations Reveal About Reading Comprehension," *Reading Research Quarterly* 14 (1979): 581–544.

24.   G. Duffy and L. R. Roehler, "Improving Reading Instruction Through The Use Of Responsive Elaboration," *The Reading Teacher* 40 (1987): 514–521.

25.   Ibid.

26.   S. C. Paris, D. R. Cross, and M. Y. Lipson, "Informed Strategies for Learning: A Program to Improve Children's Reading Awareness and Comprehension," *Journal of Educational Psychology* 76 (1984): 1239–1252.

      T. E. Raphael and P. D. Pearson, "Increasing Student Awareness of Sources of Information for Answering Questions," *American Educational Research Journal* 22 (1985): 217–237.

      D. E. Alvermann, "The Compensatory Effect of Graphic Organizers on Descriptive Text," *Journal of Educational Research* 75 (1981): 44–48.

27.   A. H. Schoenfeld, *Mathematical Problem Solving* (New York: Academic Press, 1985).

28.   J. H. Larkin and F. Reif, "Analysis and Teaching of a General Skill for Studying Scientific Text," *Journal of Educational Psychology* 72 (1976): 348–350.

29.   C. S. Englert and T. E. Raphael, "Developing Successful Writers Through Cognitive Strategy Instruction," in *Advances in Research on Teaching, Volume I*, ed. J. Brophy (Newark, NJ: JAI Press, 1989).

      M. Scardamalia and C. Bereiter, "Fostering the Development of Self-Regulation in Children's Knowledge Processing," in *Thinking And Learning Skills: Research And Open Questions*, eds. S. F. Chipman, J. W. Segal, and R. Glaser (Hillsdale, NJ: Lawrence Erlbaum Associates, 1985).

30.   M. Pressley et al., *Cognitive Strategy Instruction*, 2nd ed. (Cambridge, MA.:Brookline Books, 1995).

31.   Palincsar and Brown.

      B. Rosenshine and C. Meister, "Scaffolds for Teaching Higher-Order Cognitive Strategies," in *Teaching: Theory into Practice*, ed. A. C. Ornstein (Boston: Allyn & Bacon, 1995).

      D. J. Wood, J. S. Bruner, and G. Ross, "The Role of Tutoring in Problem Solving," *Journal of Child Psychology and Psychiatry* 17 (1976): 89–100.

32.   M. H. Bickhard, "Scaffolding and Self-scaffolding: Central Aspects of Development," in *Children's Development Within Social Context*, vol. 2, eds. L. T. Winegar and J. Valsiner (Hillsdale, NJ: Lawrence Erlbaum, 1992).

33.   A. Collins, J. S. Brown, and S. E. Newman, "Cognitive Apprenticeship: Teaching The Crafts Of Reading, Writing, And Mathematics," in *Knowing, learning, and instruction: Essays in honor of Robert Glaser*, ed. L. Resnick (Hillsdale, N.J.: Erlbaum Associates, 1990).

      Palincsar and Brown.

34.   Collins, Brown and Newman.

35.   Scardamalia and Bereiter.

36.   Ibid.

37.   B. Rosenshine, C. Meister, and S. Chapman, "Teaching Students to Generate Questions: A Review of the Intervention Studies," *Review of Educational Research*, 66 (1996): 181–221.

38.   A. King, "Improving Lecture Comprehension: Effects Of A Metacognitive Strategy," *Applied Cognitive Psychology*, 4 (1990): 1–16.

39.   Wisconsin Department of Public Instruction, *Strategic Learning in the Content Areas* (Madison, WI: Publication Sales, Wisconsin Department of Public Instruction, 1999).

40.   Palincsar and Brown.

      A. S. Palincsar, "Collaborating for Collaborative Learning of Text Comprehension," paper presented at the annual conference of the American Educational Research Association, April, Washington, D.C., April 1987.

41.   G. E. Garcia and P. D. Pearson, "Modifying Reading Instruction To Maximize Its Effectiveness For All Students," Technical Report #489 (Champaign, IL: Center for the Study of Reading, University of Illinois, 1990).

42.   A. Collins, J. S. Brown, and A. Holum, "Cognitive Apprenticeship: Making Thinking Visible," *American Educator* 15, no. 3 (1991).

43.   V. Anderson, "Training Teachers to Foster Active Reading Strategies in Reading-Disabled Adolescents," paper presented at the annual meeting of the American Educational Research Association, Chicago, April 1991.

44.   R. Cohen, "Students Generate Questions as an Aid to Reading Comprehension," *Reading Teacher* 36 (1983): 770–775.

      Palincsar.

      Y. L. Wong et al., "The Efficacy of a Self-questioning Summarization Strategy for Use by Underachievers and Learning-disabled Adolescents," *Learning Disability Focus* (1986).

45.   Rosenshine and Stevens.

46.   Panlincsar.

47.   M. D. A. Andre and T. H. Anderson, "The Development and Evaluation of a Self-Questioning Study Technique," *Reading Research Quarterly* 14 (1978–1979): 605–623.

M. J. Dreher and L. B. Gambrell, "Teaching Children to use a Self-Questioning Strategy for Studying Expository Text," *Reading Improvement* 22 (1985): 2–7.

Wong, Wong, Perry, and Sawatsky.

48.   M. Dermody, "Metacognitive Strategies For Development Of Reading Comprehension For Younger Children," paper presented at the annual meeting of the American Association of Colleges for Teacher Education, New Orleans, February, 1988.

49.   R. B. Lonberger, "The Effects Of Training In A Self-Generated Learning Strategy On The Prose Processing Abilities Of Fourth And Sixth Graders" (Ph.D. diss., State University of New York at Buffalo, 1988).

50.   B. A. Blaha, "The Effects Of Answering Self-Generated Questions On Reading" (Ph.D. diss., Boston University School of Education, 1979).

51.   Palincsar.

52.   B. Davey and S. McBride, "Effects of Question-Generation on Reading Comprehension," *Journal of Educational Psychology* 78 (1986): 256–262.

53.   Cohen.

54.   Andre and Anderson; Dreher and Gambrell.

55.   Collins, Brown, and Newman.

56.   Lonberger.

C. Bereiter and M. Bird, "Use of Thinking Aloud in Identification and Teaching of Reading Comprehension Strategies," *Cognition and Instruction* 2 (1985): 131–156.

57.   R. Y. Nolte and H. Singer, "Active Comprehension: Teaching a Process of Reading Comprehension and its Effects on Reading Achievement," *The Reading Teacher* 39 (1985): 24–31.

A. King, "Effects of Self-Questioning Training on College Students' Comprehension of Lectures," *Contemporary Educational Psychology* 14 (1989): 366–381.

King.

H. Singer and D. Donlan, "Active Comprehension: Problem-solving Schema with Question Generation of Complex Short Stories," *Reading Research Quarterly* 17 (1982): 166–186.

58.   Nolte and Singer.

59.   Collins, Brown and Newman.

60.   Dermody.

61.   Davey and McBride.

62.   N. S. Smith, "The effects of training teachers to teach students different reading ability levels to formulate three types of questions on reading comprehension and question generation ability" (Ph.D. diss., University of Georgia, 1977).

63.   Wong, Wong, Perry, and Sawatsky.

64.   *Handbook of Research on Teaching*, ed. N. L. Gage (Chicago, Il: Rand McNally, 1963).

CHAPTER 10

TEACHER UNIONS AND STUDENT ACHIEVEMENT

Robert M. Carini
Indiana University Bloomington

RESEARCH FINDINGS

While only 17 prominent studies have looked at the teacher union-achievement link, the evidence suggests that unionism raises achievement modestly for most students in public schools. These favorable patterns on unionism include higher math and verbal standardized test scores, and very possibly, an increased likelihood of high school graduation. Although most studies were conducted on high-school students, favorable union effects were also found at the elementary level. At the same time, a union presence was harmful for the very lowest- and highest-achieving students. Research to date is only suggestive as to why unions may improve achievement for most students. Two promising explanations include the possibility that unions standardize programs, instruction, and curricula in a way that benefits middle-range (most) students, and that unions "shock" schools into restructuring for greater effectiveness by improving connections and communication among district administrators, principals and teachers.

RECOMMENDATIONS

- Policy makers should view teacher unions more as collaborators than as adversaries.
- Policy makers and school districts should reconsider current union proposals for educational improvement. Given the empirical evidence, unions have a solid track record of supporting policies that boost achievement for most students.
- In unionized school districts, policy makers should direct particular attention to programs for very low- and high-achieving students, and should ensure that appropriate resources and specialized curricula are available.

One of the most dramatic events in education over the past few decades has been the rise of teacher unions. Until the early 1960s, virtually no teachers were unionized, i.e., covered by collective bargaining agreements. Today, the National Education Association (NEA) claims 2.5 million members, and the American Federation of Teachers (AFT) another 1 million.[1] Given the extensive growth and influence of teacher unions, observers often wonder if unionism affects students' academic performance. Unlike most other topics in this Report, unionism is not typically considered a key factor in promoting greater achievement. In fact, public opinion is split as to whether teacher unionism is harmful or helpful to educational outcomes.[2] Considering both this general perception and the considerable rhetoric from both critics and supporters of unions, it is surprising that so little research exists on the unionism-achievement link. Still, the overall pattern in the research is increasingly clear; teacher unionism favorably influences achievement for most students in public schools.

TEACHER UNIONISM RESEARCH

Development of Teacher Unions

The vast majority of unionized teachers are members of either the NEA or the AFT. The NEA traces its roots to 1857. The NEA, or National Teachers' Association as it was originally known, was formed to provide a collective voice for educators who were concerned about the movement toward centralization in public schools.[3] At its onset, the NEA was led not by classroom teachers, but a cadre of educational elites, primarily administrators, who pressed for the increased professionalization of teachers. In contrast, the AFT was formed in 1916 by rank-and-file teachers with a mindset not unlike that found in industrial unions.[4] The AFT was granted an American

Federation of Labor (AFL) charter membership in 1917, and stayed with the AFL after its merger with the Congress of Industrial Organizations in 1955. Despite interest by their members, it was not until the early 1960s that teachers engaged in collective bargaining. The AFT embraced the concept more quickly than the NEA. At first, NEA leadership held that collective bargaining was incompatible with professionalism. The NEA was compelled to alter its position on collective bargaining, however, when it began losing ground to the AFT in the mid-1960s. Due to possible conflicts of interest, administrators were pushed out of the NEA with the onset of collective bargaining. Although serious merger talks began as early as the late 1960s, the two unions have maintained their separate identities.

The proliferation of teacher unions is even more impressive against a backdrop of overall union decline in the United States since the 1960s.[5] Membership gains were especially strong for teacher unions during the initial expansion of collective bargaining in the 1960s and 1970s. Since the 1980s, membership growth has continued at a more moderate yet steady pace. The expansion of teacher unionism has not been uniform across all regions of the country. Teacher unionization in the South has noticeably lagged that in other regions. Weaker unionization is reflected in state laws on union rights,[6] as well as in the proportion of teachers covered under collective bargaining agreements.[7] This weakness for teacher unions in the South parallels that of industrial unions in this region.[8]

Why Unionism Might Decrease Achievement

In considering whether teacher unions affect achievement, it is helpful to examine why they might do so. There are compelling cases made both against and for unions. Many of these arguments mirror those put forth regarding unions in general. Whether these differences actually influence student achievement as the arguments assert is an empirical question requiring further exploration.

Critics of unions argue that efforts to improve compensation and working conditions for teachers compromise student achievement. Some common arguments against teacher unionism include:[9]

- Unions raise the costs of education, thereby draining resources away from inputs that raise achievement.
- Unions remove incentives for teachers to improve instruction—for example, by shielding ineffective teachers from dismissal and by tying salaries to seniority rather than merit.
- Increased formalization as a result of unionization hampers principals' ability to manage their schools.

- Unions encourage distrustful relationships between teachers and principals.
- Due to their political clout, teacher unions can block promising educational reforms that threaten union interests.
- Teacher union strikes, or even their threat, disrupt instruction, lower morale, and damage community relations.

Some of the differences suggested above between unionized schools and their non-unionized counterparts have been documented. For example, that teacher unions raise the costs of education, especially teacher salaries, is well established.[10] Some studies have reported that unionism made it more difficult for principals to remove ineffective teachers.[11] And in some studies, unionism was linked to more conflicted relationships among teachers, principals, and district administrators.[12]

Why Unionism Might Boost Achievement

While the higher costs associated with teacher unionism are confirmed, supporters of unions assert that these additional costs are a worthwhile investment, i.e., educational gains are worth the higher costs. Several of these arguments assume that unions ultimately enhance teacher instruction. Teacher interests and educational needs of children are not viewed as incompatible, but in fact, intertwined. Others hold that unions should make schools more effective organizations. Some common arguments for teacher unionism include:[13]

- The higher salaries and benefits associated with unionism attract and retain superior teachers.
- Unions offer teachers a greater sense of professionalism and dignity.
- Unions provide teachers with a collective "voice" to express ideas and concerns.[14]
- Unions enhance teacher morale and job satisfaction
- Unions support practices purported to boost student achievement, e.g., smaller class sizes and designated instructional planning time.
- Unions "shock" management, schools, or both, into becoming more effective organizations.

As with arguments against unionism, some of the differences suggested above between unionized schools and their non-unionized counterparts are documented. For example, teacher unions have attained many of their bread-and-butter goals such as greater compensation and security.[15] Evidence suggests that school structures become more formalized after unionization.[16] Several studies show that unionized schools tend to have smaller class sizes[17] and teachers who engage in more instructional preparation time.[18]

Research on Achievement

Despite the considerable scrutiny of teacher unions, and speculation on why they might affect student achievement, few empirical studies exist. While the studies scrutinized here may not reflect the entire population of empirical work, the 17 selected have been the most widely cited. In contrast, consider that there are literally hundreds of studies on factors covered in other chapters in this report. Still, despite the relatively small research base, there is an emerging consensus in the literature that teacher unionism favorably influences achievement for most students, as measured by a variety of standardized tests. These patterns hold at both the elementary and high school levels. Fewer researchers have looked at whether unionism affects the probability of graduation from high school—while the findings are somewhat mixed, the bulk of the evidence points toward a small positive impact of unions. In addition, some studies have examined unions' impact on educational attainment, as measured by high school graduation or dropout. Despite the overall pattern of favorable union impacts, five studies have reported that unionism depresses educational outcomes. As will be seen in the next section, several of these studies reach questionable conclusions given their analyses.

Research: Unions Decrease Achievement

Two of the three studies with negative union findings attempted to explain the decline of college entrance scores from the 1960s until 1980. Teacher unions seemed a plausible culprit due to their rapid development over this same period. Accordingly, Kurth tested whether several factors were responsible for changes in state Scholastic Assessment Test (SAT) scores between 1972 and 1983.[19] He concluded that unionism was more responsible than any other factor for declines in state SAT scores (both math and verbal). Kurth's work did not go unchallenged. Nelson and Gould of the AFT, citing measurement and methodological problems in Kurth's analysis, reanalyzed the same data and concluded just the opposite—that greater state unionism led to higher SAT scores.[20] As others have pointed out, this research debate is inconclusive.[21]

Peltzman conducted a similar study on state SAT and ACT (American College Test) scores from 1972 to 1989.[22] Curiously, he analyzed the NEA and AFT memberships separately—in essence, testing not a general effect of unionism, but particular union effects. Summarizing his findings, Peltzman reported: "I found that the growth of teacher unions has contributed to the student test score decline."[23] Indeed, Peltzman's study is often cited as one that found harmful union effects. Upon closer inspection, however, Peltzman's results are more mixed than he suggested. As noted by others,[24] Peltzman's analysis finds that greater NEA strength *boosted* scores from 1972 to 1981, while greater AFT strength contributed to declines in scores. Given that the NEA had a much larger share of teachers under collective bargaining than the AFT, the overall union effect over this period should be considered mixed or even positive. During the period from 1981 to 1989, Peltzman found that stronger NEA and AFT unionization lowered scores. Peltzman's work has been further criticized on methodological grounds,[25] such as whether he included appropriate statistical adjustments, especially measures of family background that are strongly linked to achievement.[26]

The two studies discussed so far focused on academically superior students—those who took college entrance exams. To gain insight into how unionism might affect students of lower achievement, Peltzman conducted a second study.[27] Specifically, he studied applicants to the United States military who completed the standardized Armed Forces Qualifying Test (AFQT)—most of whom never attend college. He tested whether changes in state unionization from 1971 to 1991 led to changes in state scores. Peltzman concluded that increased unionization decreased state scores. In addition, the negative effects of unionization held for two particular student populations: African-Americans and those who scored in the lowest quartile. As in Peltzman's earlier work involving college entrance exams, these findings are more mixed than he concluded. In particular, stronger unionization was not associated with lower test scores over half of the period (the 1970s). However, increased unionization was associated with lower scores during the 1980s, but even then, not for all measures of unionization examined.

Fuller, Mitchell, and Hartmann examined trends in the Milwaukee Public School District from 1964 to 1996.[28] Milwaukee's teachers first unionized in 1964, and the authors attempted to link the union's presence to subsequently disappointing student achievement. Unlike other studies on the unionism-achievement link discussed in this chapter, this one does not control for possible confounding factors. The switch to unionism certainly was not the only change in the district over the 32-year period that might have affected achievement. For instance, changes in student demographics alone might have been responsible for the disappointing test scores. The authors themselves noted that the proportion of disadvantaged students served by the district increased dramatically over the period. The authors are unable to make a compelling argument that unionism was responsible for declining achievement during the period.

While Fuller and associates looked at test scores, Caroline Hoxby's research covered high school dropouts. Hoxby found that unionized districts had higher dropout rates than non-unionized districts from 1970 to 1990.[29] Of the five studies examined in this section, Hoxby's may offer the strongest evidence, although like the others, it too can be challenged on methodological grounds. In particular, Hoxby reported that she analyzed 10,509 school districts, and asserted that her sample constituted 95% of all districts in the United States in 1990. Given that there were 15,552 school districts in 1990,[30] Hoxby's research only covered 68% of the districts, not the 95% that she reported. It is not clear why nearly one in three districts were lost. More important, the missing districts were likely fiscally dependent districts, the bulk of which are located in strongly unionized Northeastern states. This is a potentially critical omission that may completely change her findings, particularly given the small gap in dropout rates that she found. Albert Shanker, the late President of the AFT, asserted this very critique of Hoxby's study in the *Wall Street Journal*.[31] In her response, Hoxby offered rebuttals to nearly all of his points, but did not offer a clarification on the missing districts.[32]

Research: Unions Boost Achievement

The studies mentioned in the prior section focused on achievement at either the state or district level. For example, Kurth looked at state SAT scores, while Hoxby examined district dropout rates. Some have argued that state-level analyses are appropriate since this is where educational policy originates, including laws on collective bargaining.[33] Others have used the district level as a "natural" unit of analysis. Still others have argued that the impact of unions should be measured precisely where learning occurs—at the student level. Indeed, studies of unionism at the state or district level clearly have merit. However, if studies using highly aggregated levels of analysis are not conducted carefully, they are more prone to erroneous conclusions about student achievement than studies conducted at the student level.[34] Many of the studies that find favorable effects of unionism are conducted at the student level.

In contrast to the five studies that find harmful effects of unionism, 12 prominent studies (including Nelson and Gould) report generally beneficial effects of unionism. In general, the studies that report beneficial effects of unionism are more methodologically sound than those that report negative findings. In particular, studies that report beneficial effects tend to employ more extensive statistical controls, thereby increasing our confidence that the findings are real.

These studies are organized below as to whether they were conducted at the student or state level. Each study is summarized to provide insights into the issues, student outcomes, and notable findings.

Student-Level Research.   In their pioneering study, Eberts and Stone looked at the improvement in standardized math test scores of fourth-graders over a school year in both unionized and non-unionized schools.[35] Overall, they found that students in unionized schools improved more than counterparts in non-unionized schools. Others have reported similarly favorable findings for unionism at the student-level:

1) Milkman on high school sophomores into their senior year on a standardized math test;[36]
2) Grimes and Register on high school seniors on the SAT;[37]
3) Grimes and Register on high school seniors on the Test of Economic Literacy, a standardized test of mastery of economics;[38]
4) Zigarelli on high school sophomores' improvement on a composite standardized test (vocabulary, reading, writing, and math) into their senior year;[39] and
5) Argys and Rees on eighth-graders' improvement through their sophomore year in high school on a standardized math test.[40]

Others have considered whether unionism has favorable effects for all types of students. Eberts and Stone found that unionism had different impacts on students depending on their achievement level (as measured by a pretest).[41] For middle-range fourth-graders, unionized schools raised scores higher than in non-unionized schools. However, the very lowest and the very highest achievers actually fared *worse* in unionized schools than in non-unionized ones. This pattern was corroborated by two studies at higher grades on test improvements in math: 1) Milkman on high school sophomores into seniors,[42] and 2) Argys and Rees on eighth-graders' into high school sophomores.[43]

Researchers have begun to examine other student characteristics that might lead to differential unionism impacts, such as race and sex. For example, Grimes and Register found that African-American seniors in unionized schools scored higher on the SAT than comparable African-Americans in non-unionized schools.[44] In another study that focused on race, Milkman analyzed gains in standardized math scores for minority students between the sophomore and senior years in high school.[45] He reported that minority students overall had larger gains in unionized schools than in non-unionized schools. Among schools with mostly minority students, minority students showed higher gains in unionized schools. In contrast, among schools with mostly majority students, minority students showed *smaller* gains in unionized schools. In contrast, Zwerling and Thomason tested if unionism had the same impact on women's and men's probabilities of dropping out of high school after the sophomore year.[46]

While unionization lowered the probability of dropping out for men, it did not offer similar protection for women.

State-Level Research.   In a study that covered similar territory as those by Kurth and Peltzman, Kliner and Petree found that increases in state unionization from 1972 to 1982 generally led to increases in state SAT and ACT scores.[47] They measured unionization in two ways; one measure led to higher SAT scores, but another was unrelated. Unlike Hoxby, the authors found that unionization led to improved high school graduation rates. However, like Kurth and Peltzman, it is not clear if or how the authors adjusted raw state scores for the participation rate, i.e., the proportion of students in a state who took the exam. Powell and Steelman demonstrated that using raw SAT or ACT scores for interstate comparisons can result in misleading conclusions.[48] States vary widely in their student participation rates. For example, SAT participation rates ranged from a low of 4% (Mississippi and North Dakota) to a high of 81% (Connecticut and New Jersey) in 2000.[49] When increasing numbers of students take the SAT in a state, that state's score generally drops. This occurs because increasing numbers of lower-achieving students now contribute to the state's score. Thus, states with low participation rates likely have artificially high raw SAT scores, and vice versa. Adjusting for each state's participation rate accounts for the bulk of state differences in SAT scores.[50] Others have reported that using raw SAT scores underestimates the union effect on SATs;[51] the union effects on SATs reported by Kliner and Petree may then be understated.

In the most recent study at the state level, Steelman, Powell, and Carini found favorable linkages between unionization and state SAT scores in 1993, and ACT scores in 1994.[52] They also found that greater unionization led to higher eighth-grade NAEP math scores. Like Kliner and Petree, they reported lower dropout rates with greater unionization. To a greater extent than other studies, the authors measured unionization in several ways, and found the same patterns regardless of the measure used. Interestingly, they reported that weak unionization in the South explained much of why the South lagged other regions on the SAT and ACT. However, the authors acknowledged the difficulties of making conclusions based on single point in time. Nelson and Rosen found similar results in a state-by-state analysis on SAT and ACT scores.[53] In addition, this study found that greater unionization was associated with higher NAEP scores for fourth-graders.

Research: Why Unions Boost Achievement

While there are relatively few studies on the unionism-achievement link, there are even fewer that have systematically examined *why* unionism appears to boost achievement. Indeed, unions may raise achievement by their association with other factors discussed in this report, such as reduced class size. The most promising explanations to date for unionization's positive effects are: 1) standardization of the school environment, and 2) more tightly-coupled schools.

Standardization of Schools

There is accumulating evidence that teacher unions do, as is generally assumed, produce more standardized work environments.[54] We focus our attention on how standardization might directly affect the character of instruction students receive. Eberts and Stone find that unionism tends to standardize math instruction and math programs for fourth-graders.[55] Specifically, students spend less time learning math with specialists, tutors, or in independent study programs in unionized schools. Standardization in the classroom tends to enhance the performance of middle-range students.[56] Standardization may also lead to the funneling of resources away from specialized programs and techniques that would benefit the lowest- or highest-achieving students. The upshot is that, while standardization may boost achievement of middle-range students in unionized environments, similar gains do not accrue to those outside the middle-range. In fact, the achievement gains of the many may come at the expense of the lowest and highest achievers. Given that disadvantaged students are disproportionately represented among the lowest-achieving students, unionization will likely have disproportionately harmful effects for these students.

Stone has suggested that the differential impacts of unionism by student achievement-level unifies much of the research to date.[57] In particular, it is consistent with the findings that unionism boosts average standardized test scores when students of all abilities are grouped together. Further, Stone has argued that Hoxby's finding that unionism led to higher drop-out rates is not necessarily inconsistent with research documenting favorable union effects. The argument is that, with a focus on high school dropouts, Hoxby essentially limited the scope of her study to lower-achieving students. In any case, three other studies discussed previously have reported that unionism did not increase dropout rates.[58] Stone's proposed explanation also appears consistent with Peltzman's findings that unionism wields negative effects on those who scored in the lowest quartile on the AFQT exam. We might expect that Stone's findings should hold for high-achievers, e.g., those who take college entrance exams. Yet, several studies using college entrance exams (Kliner and Petree, Steelman et al., and Nelson and Rosen) do not find negative impacts of unionism. Stone may still be correct on high-achieving students—given the increased number of students attending college since the 1960s, the average achievement level of the test-taking pool dropped accordingly. Researchers might find that unionism lowers college entrance test scores if test-takers with only the highest achievement-levels were examined.

More Tightly-Coupled Schools

Some scholars have characterized schools as loosely-coupled organizations.[59] In other words, interactions between principals and teachers are infrequent on a day-to-day basis. Compared to many types of employees in other workplaces, teachers enjoy considerable autonomy and discretion within the classroom. Direct supervision and evaluation by principals is relatively infrequent. The overall quantity and quality of communication may suffer in such an environment. In particular, it may be difficult for principals to communicate and enforce goals with few formal organizational ties. By definition, interdependency is reduced among loosely-coupled school personnel. The exact meaning of coupling may seem diffuse—at this point, there is not complete agreement on exactly what constitutes coupling, or how it should be measured empirically.[60]

One argument discussed earlier was that unions might "shock" schools into becoming more effective organizations. Schools might become more effective if unionization results in tightened couplings, that is, increased connections and interdependencies between district administrators, principals, and teachers. Zigarelli found that compared with non-unionized schools, unionized schools had tighter couplings.[61] Moreover, tighter coupling helped explain why unionized schools had higher test scores in Zigarelli's study.

In a similar vein, Eberts and Stone found that the time a principal spent on instructional leadership had different impacts on achievement in unionized and non-unionized schools.[62] Specifically, increased time spent on instructional leadership (defined here as curriculum design, program needs evaluation, and program planning and assessment), led to higher test scores in unionized schools, but *lower* scores in non-unionized schools. It was not that principals in unionized schools devoted more time to instructional leadership. Rather, the time invested resulted in a much greater payoff (positive versus negative) in test scores in unionized schools. Eberts and Stone speculated that greater leadership productivity stemmed from the collective voice function of unions.[63] In other words, teachers could communicate their views via formal channels to their principals. Principals, in turn, may have used this feedback to tailor future leadership activities. Clearly, Eberts and Stone's finding and proposed explanation on instructional leadership are also consistent with the idea of a more tightly-coupled organization.

Union Contracts and Administrative Flexibility

Even though the effect of teacher unions appears positive overall, there might be aspects of unions that contribute to lower achievement for most students. In particular, provisions of union contracts may reduce administrators' flexibility to make key decisions—perhaps to the point that effectiveness is compromised.[64] For example, provisions on greater teacher participation in decision-making, reduction-in-force (RIF) procedures, involuntary transfer scenarios, guidelines for teacher removal, and maximum class size may well decrease administrative discretion in the allocation of resources, the shaping of the personnel mix, and in rendering policy decisions. A decrease in administrative flexibility may prove especially problematic in rapidly changing environments that require adaptation. Overall, the evidence suggests that union contracts often constrain the flexibility of principals.[65] However, decreased flexibility does not necessarily mean that principals' effectiveness is also curtailed.

Considerable evidence suggests that union contracts constrain principals' autonomy to manage their corps of teachers. In particular, it is difficult for principals to remove incompetent teachers under union contracts.[66] The procedural hurdles to remove a teacher can be extensive. Further, unions are bound by law to defend members against procedural violations of their contract.[67] Even successful attempts to remove teachers are typically long and drawn-out processes.[68] Ironically, the protection of incompetent teachers is considered an obstacle to the professionalization of unions by some teachers.[69] In addition, principals often express frustration with RIF and involuntary transfer procedures that protect teachers with seniority, instead of those who are most effective.[70]

At the same time, these decreases in flexibility do not necessarily hamper the ability of principals to effectively manage their schools. To the contrary, these decreases in flexibility may provide an impetus to greater efficiency. For example, McDonnell and Pascal report that:

> Truly effective principals usually accept collective bargaining and use the contract both to manage their building more systematically and to increase teacher participation in school decision-making. Less effective principals may view the contract as an obstacle to a well-run school and then use it as an excuse for poor management.[71]

The particular approach that principals adopt appears to shape their effectiveness in unionized environments. Effective principals are likely those who can capitalize on the tighter coupling that follows union contracts.[72] Ironically, while the contract decreases discretion of principals, it simultaneously may strengthen their authority through its emphasis on the application and enforcement of rules.[73]

The extent to which superintendents are affected by union contracts is less clear. Some suggest that many superintendents are reluctant to oppose contract provisions for fear of losing their job.[74] Others argue that the authority of superintendents may increase with unionization.[75] Union contracts tend to centralize relations within districts, which generally enhance superintendents' ability to enforce rules. In some cases, superintendents may use union rules to strengthen their control over principals.[76]

Union contracts also shape the allocation of financial resources, both within and without schools. Eberts and Stone find that contract provisions have a cumulative effect in lowering administrative discretion.[77] In other words, administrators may be able to compensate for a loss in flexibility in one area by increasing their use of discretion in other areas not limited by the contract. However, as the number of contract provisions increases, administrators will be less able to compensate as they lose flexibility in complementary areas. The number of contract provisions may be interpreted as a measure of contract strength; administrators tend to lose more financial flexibility as the contracts strengthen. With increasing numbers of provisions, administrators direct more money toward instruction, teacher salaries, and benefits, and away from other budgetary considerations.[78] In addition to shaping the within-school allocation of resources, an increasing number of contract provisions generally lead to larger school budgets, thereby impacting the allocation of resources within communities as well.

SUMMARY OF FINDINGS

The often negative perception of teacher unionism on achievement is misplaced—unionism does not appear to lower student achievement for most students in public education. Instead, the evidence suggests that unionism leads to modestly higher standardized achievement test scores, and possibly enhanced prospects of graduation from high school. Further, favorable student outcomes hold for students from the fourth-grade level through high school. It is not known if unionism has similar impacts for the very youngest children. However, the favorable effects of unionism do not extend to all types of students. In particular, very low- or very high-achieving students fare worse on standard tests in unionized schools. Disadvantaged children are disproportionately represented among the lowest-achieving students, and may be among those least served by unionism. There is evidence to suggest that unions exert different effects depending on the student's race and sex. But given the small number of studies involved, it is too early to draw conclusions.

There is little research on why unions enhance the scores of most students. Two promising explanations exist, however. First, there is evidence to suggest that unionism standardizes instruction and curricula and directs the flow of resources away from specialized programs. Increased standardization helps students of middle-range achievement, but lowers the achievement of students with distinct needs—the lowest and highest achievers. This standardization mechanism explains two consistent research findings: 1) unionism leads to higher standardized test scores for students overall because it helps most students, and 2) unionism depresses scores of the lowest and highest achievers. Further, unionization may transform schools from loosely-coupled environments into more effective, tightly-coupled organizations.

Clearly, unions are not antithetical to student achievement. Yet considerable work remains so as to better inform policy decisions. First, until the mechanisms by which unions raise achievement are better understood, it is difficult to know precisely where to focus policy efforts. Second, as is the case with all school reforms, there is the issue of whether the gains from unionism are worth the associated costs. As always, there are other promising vehicles to higher achievement to choose from—as evidenced by other chapters in this report. In fact, future collaboration with teacher unions should enable policy makers to better evaluate other reform proposals.

The foregoing research points to the following policy recommendations:

- Policy makers should view teacher unions more as collaborators than as adversaries.
- Policy makers and school districts should reconsider current union proposals for educational improvement. Given the empirical evidence, unions have a solid track record of supporting policies that boost achievement for most students.
- In unionized school districts, policy makers should direct particular attention to programs for very low- and high-achieving students, and should ensure that appropriate resources and specialized curricula are available.

REFERENCES

1. *National Education Association Handbook 2000–2001* (Washington, D.C.: National Education Association, 2000).
    American Federation of Teachers Web Site, <http://www.aft.org>.

2. L. C. Rose and A. M. Gallup, "The 30th Annual Phi Delta Kappa/Gallop Poll of the Public's Attitudes Toward the Public Schools," *Phi Delta Kappan* 80 (1998): 41–56.

    D. Haselkorn and L. Harris, *The Essential Profession: American Education at the Crossroads* (Belmont, MA: Recruiting New Teachers, Inc., 2001).

3. M. Murphy, *Blackboard Unions: The AFT and the NEA, 1900–1980* (Ithaca: Cornell University Press, 1990).

4. D. S. Selden, *The Teacher Rebellion* (Washington, D.C.: Harvard University Press, 1985).

    Murphy.

    See also:

    M. R. Berube, *Teacher Politics: The Influence of Unions* (Westport, CT: Greenwood Press, 1988).

5. R. W. Eberts and J. A. Stone, *Unions and Public Schools: The Effect of Collective Bargaining on American Education* (Lexington, MA: Lexington Books, 1984).

    W. A. Streshly and T. A. DeMitchell, *Teacher Unions and TQE: Building Quality Labor Relations* "Thousand Oaks, CA: Corwin Press, 1994"

6. R. G. Valetta and R. B. Freeman, "Appendix B: The National Bureau of Economic Research Public Sector Collective Bargaining Law Data Set," in *When Public Sector Workers Unionize,* ed. R. B. Freeman and C. Ichiowsi (1988), 399–419.

    J. L. Lund and C. L. Maranto, "Public Sector Labor Law: An Update." in *Public Sector Employment: In a Time of Transition,* ed. D. Belman, M. Gunderson, and D. Hyatt (Madison, WI: Industrial Relations Research Association, 1996), 21–57.

7. National Center for Educational Statistics, *Schools and Staffing Survey, 1993–1994* (Washington, D.C.: U.S. Department of Education, 1994).

8. S. Aronowitz, *Working Class Hero: A New Strategy for Labor* (New York: Adama Books, 1983).

9. See, for example:

    Streshly and DeMitchell.

    P. Brimelow and L. Spencer, "The National Extortion Association?" *Forbes* (7 June 1993): 72–83.

    C. J. Sykes, *Dumbing Down our Kids: Why America's Children Feel Good about Themselves but Can't Read, Write, or Add* (New York: St. Martin's Press, 1995).

    M. Lieberman, *The Teacher Unions: How the NEA and AFT Sabotage Reform and Hold Students, Parents, Teachers, and Taxpayers Hostage to Bureaucracy* (New York: The Free Press, 1997).

    G. G. Moo, *Power Grab: How the National Educational Association is Betraying our Children* (Washington, D.C.: Regnery Publishing, 1999).

10. See, for example:

    W. H. Baugh and J. A. Stone, "Teachers, Unions and Wages in the 1970s: Unionism Now Pays." *Industrial and Labor Relations Review* 35 (1982): 368–376.

    R. W. Eberts and J. A. Stone, "Teacher Unions and the Cost of Public Education," *Economic Inquiry* 24 (1986): 631–643.

C. M. Hoxby, "How Teachers' Unions Affect Education Production." *Quarterly Journal of Economics* 111 (1996): 670–718.

11.   S. M. Johnson, *Teacher Unions in Schools* (Philadelphia: Temple University Press, 1984).

12.   H. L. Fuller, G. A. Mitchell, and M. E. Hartmann, "Collective Bargaining in Milwaukee Public Schools," in *Conflicting Missions? Teachers Unions and Educational Reform,* ed. T. Loveless (Washington, D.C.: Brookings Institution Press, 2000): 110–149.

13.   See, for example:

Eberts and Stone.

M. A. Zigarelli, "The Linkages Between Teacher Unions and Student Achievement." *Journal of Collective Negotiations* 23 (1994): 299–319.

S. Feldman, "Where We Stand," *Phi Delta Kappan* (November 1998): 233–236.

N. Bascia, "The Other Side of the Equation: Professional Development and the Organizational Capacity of Teacher Unions," *Educational Policy* 14 (2000): 385–404.

S. Feldman, "Where we Stand: Everyone Wins," *The New York Times* (1 April 2001).

14.   R. Freeman and J. Medoff, *What do Unions do?* (New York: Basic Books, 1984).

Eberts and Stone.

15.   L.M. Mcdonnell and A. Pascal, *Teacher Unions and Educational Reform* (Santa Monica, CA: RAND, 1988).

16.   Eberts and Stone.

17.   Eberts and Stone.

M. M. Kleiner and D. L. Petree, "Unionism and Licensing of Public School Teachers: Impact on Wages and Educational Output," in *When Public Sector Workers Unionize,* eds. R. Freeman and C. Ichiowsi (Chicago: University of Chicago Press, 1988), 305–319.

Hoxby.

18.   Eberts and Stone.

19.   M. Kurth, "Teacher Unions and Excellence in Education: An Analysis of the Decline in SAT scores," *Journal of Labor Research* 8 (1988): 351–387.

20.   F. H. Nelson and J. C. Gould, "Teacher Unions and Excellence in Education: Comment," *Journal of Labor Research* 9 (1988): 379–387.

21.   Zigarelli.

22.   S. Peltzman, "The Political Economy of the Decline of American Public Education," *The Journal of Law & Economics* 36 (1993): 331–370.

23.   S. Peltzman, "Political Factors in Public School Decline," *The American Enterprise* 4 (1993): 46.

24.   C. R. Sunstein, "Against Interest-group Theory: A Comment on Peltzman—The Political Economy of the Decline of American Public Education," *The Journal of Law & Economics* 36 (1993): 371–378.

25.   D. D. Friedman, "Comments on Peltzman—The Political Economy of the Decline of American Public Education," *The Journal of Law & Economics* 36 (1993): 371–378.

26. C. Hurn, *The Limits and Possibilities of Schooling*, 3rd ed. (Boston: Allyn and Bacon, 1993).

27. S. Peltzman, "Political Economy of Public Education: Non-College-Bound Students," *Journal of Law and Economics* 39 (1996): 73–120.

28. Fuller, Mitchell, et al.

29. Hoxby.

30. U.S. Census Bureau, *Statistical Abstract of the United States: 2000*, 120th ed. (Washington, DC, 2000), 164.

31. A. Shanker, "Strong Teacher Unions, Better Teachers," *The Wall Street Journal*, 17 October 1996, p. A23.

32. C. Hoxby, "Unions' Effect on Schools," *The Wall Street Journal*, 31 October 1996, p. A23.

33. Kleiner and Petree.

     Peltzman.

34. E. A. Hanushek, S. G. Rivkin, and L. L. Taylor, "Aggregation and the Estimated Effects of School Resources," National Bureau of Economic Research, Working Paper No. 5548. (Cambridge, MA: National Bureau of Economic Research, 1996).

35. R. W. Eberts and J. A. Stone, "Teacher Unions and the Productivity of Public Schools." *Industrial and Labor Relations Review* 40 (1987): 354–363.

36. M. Milkman, "Teacher Unions and High School Productivity" (Ph.D. diss., University of Oregon. Eugene, OR, 1989).

37. P. G. Grimes and C. A. Register, "Teacher Unions and Black Students' Scores on College Entrance Exams," *Industrial Relations* 30 (1991): 492–500.

38. P. G. Grimes and C. A. Register, "Teachers' Unions and Student Achievement in High School Economics," *Journal of Economic Education* 21 (1990): 297–306.

39. Zigarelli.

40. L. M. Argys and D. I. Reese, "Unionization and School Productivity: A Reexamination," *Research in Labor Economics*, vol. 14, ed. S. Polacheck (Greenwich, CT: JAI Press, 1995), 49–68.

41. Eberts and Stone.

42. Milkman.

43. Argys and Reese.

44. Grimes and Register.

45. M. Milkman, "Teachers' Unions, Productivity, and Minority Student Achievement," *Journal of Labor Research* 18 (1997): 137–150.

46. H. L. Zwerling and T. Thomason, "The Effects of Teacher Unions on the Probability of Dropping out of High School," *Journal of Collective Negotiations* 23 (1994): 239–250.

47. Kleiner and Petree.

48. B. Powell and L. C. Steelman, "Variations in State SAT Performance: Meaningful or Misleading?" *Harvard Educational Review* 54 (1984): 389–412.

     B. Powell and L. C. Steelman, "Bewitched, Bothered, and Bewildering: The Use and Misuse of State SAT and ACT Scores," *Harvard Educational Review* 66 (1996): 27–59.

49.   *News 2000–2001*, Table 3: SAT Averages by State for 1990 and 1997–2000, *The College Board web site*, <http://www.collegeboard.org >.

50.   Powell and Steelman.

51.   L. C. Steelman, B. Powell, and R. M. Carini, "Do Teacher Unions Hinder Educational Performance? Lessons Learned from State SAT and ACT Scores," *Harvard Educational Review* 70 (2000): 437–466.

52.   Steelman, Powell et al.

53.   F. H. Nelson and M. Rosen, *Are Teacher Unions Hurting American Education? A State-by-State Analysis of the Impact of Collective Bargaining Among Teachers on Student Performance*, Technical Report (Milwaukee, WI: The Institute for Wisconsin's Future, 1996).

54.   Johnson.

55.   Eberts and Stone.

56.   S. Michelson, "The Association of Teacher Resources with Children's Characteristics," *How do Teachers Make a Difference?* (Washington, D.C.: Office of Education, OE-58042, 1970), 55–75.

57.   J. A. Stone, "Collective Bargaining and Public Schools," in *Conflicting Missions? Teachers Unions and Educational Reform*, ed. T. Loveless (Washington, D.C.: Brookings Institution Press, 2000), 47–68.

58.   Kleiner and Petree.

      Zwerling and Thomason.

      Steelman, Powell, et al.

59.   K. E. Weick, "Educational Organizations as Loosely Coupled Systems," *Administrative Science Quarterly* 21 (1976): 1–19.

      J. W. Meyer and B. Rowan, "The Structure of Educational Organizations," *Environments and Organizations*, ed. M. W. Meyer and Associates (1978), 78–109.

60.   Zigarelli.

61.   Zigarelli.

62.   Eberts and Stone.

63.   Eberts and Stone.

64.   See, for example:

      J. R. Cochren, "Teacher Unions: A Career Educator's Perspective," *Contemporary Education* 69 (1998): 214–217.

      Moo.

      Fuller, Mitchell, Hartmann.

65.   For one of the earliest studies on this issue, see:

      L. Cunningham, "Implication of Collective Negotiation for the Role of the Principal," in *Collective Negotiations in Public Education*, ed. S. M. Elam, M. Lieberman and M. H. Moskow (Chicago: Rand McNally, 1967), 298–313.

66.   S. M. Johnson, *Teacher Unions in Schools* (Philadelphia: Temple University Press, 1984)

      Fuller, Mitchell, Hartmann.

67.   S. M. Johnson.

68.   S. M. Johnson.

69.   McDonnell and Pascal.

70. McDonnell and Pascal.

71. L. M. Mcdonnell and A. Pascal, *Organized Teachers in American Schools* (Santa Monica, CA: RAND, 1979), 83.

72. C. T. Kerchner and D. E. Mitchell, *The Changing Idea of a Teachers' Union* (London: The Falmer Press, 1988)

73. Kerchner and Mitchell.
    Zigarelli.

74. G.Geisert and M. Lieberman, *Teacher Union Bargaining: Practice and Policy* (Chicago: Precept Press, 1994).

75. Kerchner and Mitchell.

76. Kerchner and Mitchell.

77. Eberts and Stone.

78. Eberts and Stone.

CHAPTER 11

VALUE-ADDED ASSESSMENT OF TEACHERS

The Empirical Evidence

Haggai Kupermintz
University of Colorado at Boulder

RESEARCH FINDINGS

The Tennessee Value-Added Assessment System (TVAAS) employs a sophisticated statistical methodology to estimate the aggregated yearly growth in student learning, as reflected in changes in test scores in five tested academic subjects. It assumes that changes in test scores from one year to the next accurately reflect student progress in learning. By tracking progress and linking it to schools and teachers, the model asserts that the educational effects of these schools and teachers can be evaluated. Estimates of aggregated gains are used as indicators of how effective teachers and schools have been in raising student performance. Yet, the model's empirical base is weak and fails to document adequately its efficacy as a teacher evaluation instrument. It remains unclear how other variables that may affect achievement as much as teacher effectiveness will determine the evaluation results. Much more research is needed in order to rationally judge the system's strength and weaknesses.

RECOMMENDATIONS

- Develop and implement a program evaluation plan to define and monitor value-added assessment program outcomes. Program evaluation oversight should be maintained by the state and developed and implemented by an independent contractor.
- In order to support and provide guidance for the development and implementation of the program evaluation plan, the state should establish an independent technical panel of experts in measurement, statistics, and educational research methodology.
- The TVAAS database should be made available, along with all technical documentation pertaining to the operations of the TVAAS model, to interested researchers.
- National standards and mechanisms should be developed for the approval of statistical procedures and models to be used in high-stakes accountability systems. Such standards should have the force of a professional code. The task of developing them should be led by the American Educational Research Association (AERA).

The evaluation of teaching has been a major concern in attempts to improve education because "[a] conceptually sound and properly implemented evaluation system for teachers is a vital component of an effective school."[1] Efforts to develop and implement useful and trustworthy systems of teacher evaluation, however, have frustrated education leaders and policy makers, especially when the evaluation attempted to measure teacher performance by assessing what students have learned. Shrinkfield and Stuffelbeam went so far as to declare that "there is no topic on which opinion varies so markedly as that of the validity of basing teacher effectiveness on student learning."[2] Various proposals for outcome-based teacher evaluations have been examined under the headings of "process/product" research, school effectiveness research, merit pay and career ladder schemes, public education accountability programs, and private-sector performance contracting.[3] Still, persistent substantive and methodological shortcomings of the proposed systems have contributed to "teacher skepticism and growing criticism of attempts to link learning gains to teacher work."[4]

Recent efforts to reform American education by emphasizing student testing, coupled with significant developments in the statistical modeling and analysis of longitudinal test score data, have sparked a renewed interest in the notion of basing teacher evaluations on measured outcomes of student learning. Whereas traditional school and teacher performance indicator systems have relied on measures of the current level of student achievement, the new systems have shifted their focus to the assessment of year-to-year progress in measured achievement. The assessment of growth is typically achieved by using some variant of an emerging family of statistical models, collectively known as "value-added assessment."[5] The most visible among these contemporary approaches is the Tennessee Value-Added Assessment System (TVAAS), developed in the late 1980s by Dr. William L. Sanders at the University of Tennessee and implemented as the keystone of the Tennessee Education Improvement Act in 1992.

The purpose of this chapter is to describe the TVAAS approach to teacher evaluation and to offer a critical review of the empirical research base that addresses the validity of estimates of teacher effectiveness. It concludes with a set of recommendations intended to strengthen the empirical base of TVAAS and similar programs.

VALUE-ADDED ASSESSMENT RESEARCH

An Overview of TVAAS

TVAAS is the centerpiece of an ambitious educational reform effort implemented by the Tennessee Education Improvement Act of 1992. Inequalities in school funding, followed by a lawsuit brought against the state by a coalition of small rural districts, led to a comprehensive reform of the Tennessee educational system. Under pressure from business, the legislature adopted a strong accountability model that required schools to show concrete evidence of satisfactory year-to-year improvements in student achievement, measured down to the classroom level. Relying on pilot studies that Sanders and his colleagues conducted on the value-added model during the 1980s, the Tennessee legislature embraced the model as its methodology of choice for measuring the performance of students, teachers, schools, and school systems. The legislation defines TVAAS as a "statistical system for educational outcome assessment which uses measures of student learning to enable the estimation of teacher, school, and school district statistical distributions," and requires that the "system will use available and appropriate data as input to account for differences in prior student attainment, such that the impact which the teacher, school and school district have on the educational progress of students may be estimated on a student attainment constant basis."[6]

The TVAAS model, referred to as "the Sanders model' in some sections of the legislation, employs a sophisticated statistical methodology to estimate the aggregated yearly growth in student learning, as reflected in changes in test scores in five tested academic subjects. Estimates of average student achievement progress are calculated for each school and teacher for each of Tennessee's school systems. The results are then summarized in a series of reports that show the estimated growth in student achievement attributed to each school system, each school, and each individual teacher in Tennessee. System and school report cards are made public while teacher reports are only shared with their supervisors.

The details of the statistical calculations are too complex to describe in this chapter,[7] but the idea behind value-added assessment is straightforward. It assumes that changes in test scores from one year to the next accurately reflect student progress in learning. By keeping track of this progress across several years and linking it to the particular schools and teachers who taught the student during that period, the model asserts that the educational effects of these schools and teachers can be evaluated. The larger the aggregated gains attributed to a school or a teacher, the more "value" is said to have been added by them to their students' learning. Estimates of aggregated gains are used as indicators of how effective teachers and schools have been in raising student performance.

The statistical "mixed model" methodology employed in TVAAS offers several important advantages over competing methods. First, it ensures that all available data will be used in the calculations; other techniques often include in the analysis only students for whom complete records exist. The statistical calculations take into account the correlation among each student scores across different subjects and across grade levels to provide improved estimates of growth in measured achievement. In addition, the estimation of teacher effects takes into account the amount of data available so that teachers with less data (implying less accurate estimation) are assumed to perform at their system level until more data become available. The model is quite flexible and can be expanded to include different outcome measures and input variables.

Using annual data from the norm-referenced tests that make up the Tennessee Comprehensive Assessment Program (TCAP), schools and school systems are expected to demonstrate progress at the level of the national norm gain (as determined by a national sample of students who took the same tests) in five academic subject areas: math, science, social studies, reading, and language arts. Beginning in 1993, reports have been issued to educators and the public on the effectiveness of every school and school system in Tennessee. Teacher reports are not part of the public record; rather, value-added assessment of teacher effectiveness has been provided only to teachers and their administrators.

TVAAS and Teacher Evaluation

Value-added methodology is increasingly becoming a prominent component in emerging educational accountability systems. The shift in attention from assessing current level of performance to showing systematic progress in learning has enriched and refined the way in which policy makers conceptualize educational outcomes. Consequently, many systems now require schools and teachers to exhibit adequate yearly growth for their students, regardless of how strong or weak the current level of incoming student performance is. TVAAS represents a pioneering effort to implement a comprehensive statewide value-added assessment system to determine the merit of every school system, school, and teacher in fostering student achievement. Since its inception, TVAAS's advocates have made remarkable claims asserting its effectiveness as an educational accountability tool for teacher evaluation and have promised that TVAAS can provide precise and fair quantitative estimates of the impact of any particular teacher on the academic growth of their students. The system developers have consistently argued that these claims are supported by a strong research base, relying on the massive TVAAS database containing millions of merged longitudinal records of student achievement.

Three major assertions have been offered in support of the TVAAS methodology as a teacher evaluation instrument. In the next section, we will examine the empirical evidence supporting these assertions:

1) Teacher effectiveness is by far the most important factor in determining the outcomes of the learning process and TVAAS estimates of teacher effects provide accurate indicators of teacher effectiveness.

2) TVAAS estimates of teacher effects measure the independent and unique contribution a particular teacher makes to his or her students' growth, regardless of a student's background.

3) TVAAS teacher effects are independent of students' prior ability; therefore teacher effectiveness does not depend on the student's aptitude for learning.

It is clear that any teacher evaluation program possessing these attributes would, indeed, be able to gauge the precise contributions teachers make to students' academic progress—the "value added." In doing so, such an evaluation program would represent a revolution in accountability. After decades of heroic efforts to disentangle the effects of schooling from the social context in which it is inevitably embedded, the TVAAS system promises to do exactly that. Moreover, it proposes to do so without measuring any of the background variables that have persistently frustrated generations of researchers and policy makers—variables that led sociologist James Coleman to dismiss the effects of schooling relative to broader social influences more than 30 year ago.[8] In short, the TVAAS claims that by simply using the student's past achievement record as a starting point from which to measure progress, and then by keeping track of who teaches the student what, all of the possible influences on this student's learning—except for those of the teacher, the school, and the school system—can be filtered out or taken into account. No other educational assessment system has ever made such a bold claim. As Education Week's Jeff Archer noted: "In the current craze for accountability in education, that's like inventing a state-of-the art mining tool during a gold rush."[9] This report now turns to examine the scientific basis that has been offered to validate the above claims.

TVAAS and Peer-Reviewed Research

The scientist's prime communication tool is the peer-reviewed journal article. Through published articles, innovative methodologies or applications are subjected to rigorous and independent examination by others in the research community. For example, the application of multi-level modeling to the study of school effectiveness (a methodology sharing much in common with TVAAS) has been discussed in countless articles published in educational research journals. Frequently, preliminary findings from the early stages of program development will be presented and discussed in less formal venues. Occasional research reports, working papers, and presentations in workshops or scientific conferences are useful intermediary means to facilitate discussion and to obtain timely feedback. But ultimately, the rigor of the peer-review process is universally accepted in the scientific community (in both the natural and social sciences) as the public forum for the examination of scientific claims. Prominent methodologists Lee Cronbach and Paul Meehl have concluded: "A claim is unsubstantiated unless the evidence for the claim is public, so that other scientists may review the evidence, criticize the conclusions, and offer alternative explanations. Reference to something 'observed by the writer in many clinical cases' is worthless as evidence."[10] Clearly, the more radical the claim, the more rigorous should be the public examination of evidence, interpretations, and conclusions.

Given the revolutionary nature of the claims advanced by TVAAS developers, it is surprising to find that research findings from TVAAS that specifically pertain to claims regarding teacher effectiveness have been discussed in only three peer-reviewed journal articles, two book chapters, and three unpublished research reports, all of them authored by TVAAS staff. Moreover, out of these, only one journal article and two unpublished reports actually present findings from original empirical studies. Other publications, as well as numerous presentations and newspaper interviews with Sanders and other TVAAS staff, typically repeat these findings and their implications or provide general descriptions of the statistical methodology, program operations, and the variety of reports produced by the system.

The only independent investigations of TVAAS claims and supporting evidence come from two external evaluations of the system. In 1995, teacher concerns about the imminent release of individual teacher reports prompted the Office of Educational Accountability to commission an evaluation study, which indicated several problematic aspects of TVAAS.[11] A second external evaluation was initiated in response to the first evaluation and resulted in a report by researchers D. Bock and D. Wolfe[12] dealing with statistical issues, and a companion report by assessment expert T. Fisher addressing implementation and policy issues. The Bock and Wolfe report contains some limited empirical investigations. In addition, two unpublished dissertation studies, one by a former TVAAS staff member and the other by one of the authors of the 1995 evaluation, provide additional analyses.

A note on publications related to the statistical mixed-model methodology employed in the TVAAS is in order here. The theory of mixed-models and related techniques have been among the most productive areas in statistics and have been successfully applied to many practical problems across diverse substantive areas. A vast volume of theoretical expositions and applied research reports documents the validity and utility of mixed-model methodology. The Tennessee Educational Improvement Act makes specific reference to six such publications, furnished by Sanders as support for the TVAAS model.[13] No one knowledgeable about the issues doubts the soundness of the statistical theory of mixed models, although debate continues about issues such as the efficiency of calculations or estimation algorithms.

The critical point, however, is the validation of any particular application of the general statistical theory. In this regard, reference to the general statistical literature offers no relief. Over the last two decades more and more educational applications have been developed that employ variants of mixed-models methodology, each having to show public evidence for the specific claims, interpretations, and conclusions submitted for consideration. The following section examines the public empirical record concerning TVAAS claims.

TVAAS Research Findings

This section describes the empirical studies that have been offered to support the three key claims of TVAAS as a system of teacher evaluation, as presented above.

Claim No. 1: *Teachers are by far the most important factor determining the outcomes of the learning process, and TVAAS teacher effects provide accurate estimates of teacher effectiveness.*

One of the most visible TVAAS findings comes from a 1996 study conducted by Sanders and Rivers[14] in two large Tennessee metropolitan school systems. Results were summarized in an unpublished research progress report. The researchers used longitudinal test scores in mathematics from a cohort of students who started as second graders in 1991–92 and were followed through their fifth grade in 1994–95. Using a simplified version of the full TVAAS model, Sanders and Rivers calculated teacher effects for Grades 3–5 and then arbitrarily grouped teachers into five effectiveness levels according to their relative ranking among their peers. Each group comprised 20% of the teacher sample (referred to by statisticians as "quintiles"). This classification scheme resulted in 125 possible teacher sequences across the three grades—from low-low-low to high-high-high. Fifth grade scores were then used to compare the cumulative effects of seven of these sequences, controlling for second-grade scores. This analysis revealed that the average scores of fifth graders who were assigned the two extreme teacher sequences (low-low-low and high-high-high) differed by about 50 percentile points. Furthermore, for students with comparable teachers in the fifth grade, differences in previous grades' teacher sequences were still apparent. For example, the differences between the low-low-high and the high-high-high sequences were around 20 percentile points. The researchers concluded that the effects of teachers on student achievement are additive and cumulative, with little evidence for any compensatory effects."[15]

A dissertation study by J. Rivers, one of the authors of the previous study, used a similar analytic strategy. Rivers used fourth-grade math scores and TVAAS teacher effects in Grades 5–8 to predict ninth-grade math competency scores. Although no exact number of students included in the analysis was given, computer outputs presented in the dissertation suggest that the sample size was 2,612. Analyses indicated that teacher effects from Grades 5 to 8 had significant impact on ninth-grade math achievement. In addition a significant interaction effect indicated stronger fifth- and sixth-grade teacher effects on ninth-grade achievement for students with lower prior achievement. These findings held for the original scale scores on the ninth-grade math competency test and on passing probabilities calculated using a number of different cut scores.[16]

In a separate study of a sample of third-, fourth-, and fifth-grade student gains in five subject areas (math, reading, language, social studies, and science) from 1994 to 1995, several context effects were examined in addition to teacher effects: intra-classroom heterogeneity, student achievement level, and class size.[17] Using a simplified version of the TVAAS model, the researchers examined data from 54 school systems in Tennessee. The study addressed classroom context effects. For each grade and subject area, the researchers employed a model that predicted student gains from 12 different factors including school system, classroom heterogeneity, student achievement level (the average of the 1994 and 1995 scores), class size, and various interactions among these terms. The result was a series of 30 separate analyses, one for each grade and subject combination. After comparing the levels of statistical significance of the different effects in the model, the researchers concluded that "the two most important factors impacting student gain are the teacher and the achievement level for the student."[18] Teacher effects were found to have the largest effect size in two-thirds of the different analyses.[19]

Claim No. 2: *TVAAS teacher effects measure the independent and unique contribution a particular teacher makes to his or her students' growth, regardless of student socioeconomic or ethnic background.*

In an article summarizing research findings from TVAAS, Sanders and Horn[20] reported that "the cumulative gains for schools across the entire state have been found to be unrelated to the racial composition of schools, the percentage of students receiving free and reduced-price lunches, or the mean achievement level of the school." No source or further details were provided to support this statement. The same assertion has been repeated numerous times in reports and presentations by TVAAS staff, as well as in media coverage of the system. These alleged results have been taken to verify "the contention that by allowing each student to serve as his or her own control (the longitudinal aspect of TVAAS) the inclusion of exogenous co-variables to ensure fairness in the estimates of system, school, and teacher effects is not necessary."[21]

This contention distinguishes TVAAS from other similar methodologies, as no other contemporary value-added system has reached the same conclusion. Accordingly, such systems typically include an explicit statistical adjustment for competing factors that may influence student progress (over and above their influence on student current level of achievement). In an exposition of value-added indicators of school performance, Robert Meyer explains:

> The key idea is to isolate statistically the contribution of schools from other sources of student achievement. This is particularly important in light of the fact that differences in student and family characteristics account for far more of the variation in student achievement than school-related factors. Failure to account for differences across schools in student, family, and community characteristics could result in highly contaminated indicators of school performance.[22]

The contention that merely by including in the analysis the student's previous test scores, the system is able to control adequately for all exogenous influences—without actually measuring them—is a radical departure from the conclusions reached by other researchers, as well as from basic intuitions about schooling. It is counter-intuitive for most educators to assume that student, family, or community resources will have only negligible impact on a student's rate of progress, even after prior achievement has been accounted for. Extraordinary claims demand extraordinary evidence. Such a radical assertion requires reliable and strong empirical evidence if it is to be trusted to serve as a working assumption for school or teacher evaluations. The only evidence that has been offered to date to support this contention, however, comes from an unpublished report circulated by the University of Tennessee Value-Added Research and Assessment Center.[23] The document, whose authors are unidentified, displays scatter plots of the percentage of minority students in each of some 1,000 Tennessee schools against the three-year cumulative average gains in each school for the five TCAP-tested subjects, as calculated by TVAAS. The report does not provide any formal statistical analysis of these patterns, leaving the reader to evaluate its conclusions by eyeballing the scatter plots. The report concludes that "the graphs show that the effectiveness of a school cannot be predicted from a knowledge of the racial composition."[24] Yet a closer inspection of the graphs reveal that while they do not display a clear downward trend, schools with more than 90% minority enrollment seem to exhibit lower cumulative average gains. For example, about 70% of the schools with high minority enrollment showed gains that were below the national norm; comparable patterns can be observed for reading, language, and social studies. Similar graphs for school systems reveal an even stronger relationship between average system gains and percentage of students eligible for free or reduced-price lunch, despite the authors' claim to the contrary.

The Sanders and Rivers 1996 report provides further indirect evidence for the role family background factors may play in influencing student progress. Table 3 of the report gives the frequency with which white and black students, respectively, were assigned to teachers in each effectiveness level. Generally, white students were more often assigned to more effective teachers than were black students. Of white third-grade students in one of the school systems, 15.9% were assigned to teachers in the lowest effectiveness group, compared with 26.7% of the black students who were assigned to similar teachers. In contrast, 22.4% of the white students, and 14.4% of the black students, were assigned to teachers in the highest effectiveness level. These findings echo the well-documented severe inequalities in resources and opportunities characteristic of the American educational system.[25] The link between teacher effectiveness, as measured by TVAAS, and student ethnicity further underscores the fragility of the contention that value-added indicators are unrelated to the racial composition of the student body.

Another dissertation study provides additional demonstration of the relationships between TVAAS value-added scores and exogenous factors. Hu has documented substantial and significant correlations at the school level between per-pupil expenditure, percent minority students, and percent of reduced-price/free lunch students with average TVAAS value-added scores in both math and reading.[26] Taken together, these variables explained a sizable proportion of the variability in the value-added three-year average gains.

Claim No. 3: *TVAAS teacher effects are independent of student prior ability; therefore teacher effectiveness does not depend on students' aptitude for learning.*

There is a growing recognition that "[e]ffective instruction begins with what learners bring to the setting."[27] Students bring powerful general and domain-specific ideas, knowledge, and skills to the classroom environment. These initial knowledge and skills are resources for further learning and are ingrained in internal mental representations and dispositions, but also in socially determined patterns of participation, within and outside of school. Prior knowledge and conceptions, both formal and informal, play an important role in student performance and later development.

The study of the relationship between teacher effectiveness and student abilities as determinants of student academic progress faces two major challenges. The first concerns the question of clarifying what role each of these two influences plays in the progress of any individual student. The second concerns the potential confusion that may arise when certain teachers are consistently assigned lower- or higher-ability students. The studies described above show a rather consistent pattern in which higher-ability students tended to achieve lower gains, regardless of teacher effectiveness level as estimated by TVAAS. This phenomenon has been labeled "a shed pattern," raising concerns about lack of adequate instructional support for high-ability students. TVAAS presentations also describe different patterns, labeled "reverse shed" (whereby higher gains are made by higher-ability students) and "tee-pee" (whereby higher gains are made by students of average ability). No study to date has examined the relative prominence of these different patterns of growth and initial achievement across classrooms and schools.

Some empirical evidence that illustrates the difficulty of isolating the role of teacher effectiveness from that of student prior achievement comes from data presented in the Sanders and Rivers report. Kupermintz, Shepard, and Linn[28] re-analyzed data from Table 1 of the report to demonstrate a sizable correlation between estimates of teacher effectiveness and student prior ability. Among students who hadn't done well in the past, nearly one-third were then assigned to teachers who were later rated to be the least effective, while among the highest-achieving students, more than one-half were assigned to teachers later found to be "highly effective." These findings suggest that higher-ability students were assigned to teachers that

TVAAS analysis identified as more effective, thereby complicating the claims attributing student progress solely to the teacher.

Similarly, independent analyses conducted by Bock and Wolfe for their evaluation report examined the correlations between students' average score levels and their average gains in a sample of the Tennessee data.[29] Bock and Wolfe have commented:

> "Although the magnitude of all of the correlations is less than 0.3, a good number of them are large enough to have implications for the comparison of gains between teachers whose students differ in average achievement level... [A]djustments for expected gain as a function of student score level should be included when the magnitude of the correlation exceeds, say 0.15."[30]

When students with higher or lower prior achievement are likely to differ systematically in the amount of progress they can demonstrate relative to their peers due to factors outside of the teacher's control, a potential for biased teacher evaluations exists if some teachers consistently get lower- or higher-achieving students. Under such circumstances, it becomes increasingly difficult to differentiate between learning gains that should be attributable to the teachers and those that reflect the superior aptitude of their students.

A Critical Examination of the Evidence

An examination of the empirical record to date reveals a number of issues in methodology and interpretation that call into question the validity of the major TVAAS claims. The available empirical base consistently documents considerable variations among teachers in estimated TVAAS teacher effects. The studies reviewed in this chapter convincingly demonstrate that students of certain teachers show substantially greater or lower gains on average than the students of other certain teachers. The analyses, however, fail to explain clearly and conclusively why such differences exist.

The causal attribution of student gains to teacher effectiveness, as well as the conclusion that teacher effects are additive, cumulative, and largely irreversible, cannot be dismissed as a plausible hypothesis to explain average achievement gain differentials among teachers. Other untested hypotheses remain equally plausible, however. If observed patterns of academic progress are a function of complex interactions between instructional practices, student readiness to learn, and school and community context factors, then teacher effectiveness should be seen as one component of estimated teacher effects. Because there have been no studies that credibly isolate teacher effects from these other factors, however, the question remains open. The current TVAAS model, by default, attributes to the teacher *all* the effects of the possible factors, which in reality are probably confounded with or interacting with teaching practices.

At least two studies have documented the importance of student ability on academic progress and suggested more complex interactions with teacher effects than has been acknowledged by the authors. The issue of the relationships between student aptitude, student actual achievement, and academic progress is a complicated one. "Shed patterns," for example, indicate that students with higher prior achievement tend to exhibit smaller gains. Such patterns may result from inefficient instruction for these students, but they may also reflect statistical artifacts like "ceiling effects" (high ability students scoring at the highest levels of the measurement scale, leaving little room for observed improvement) or "regression to the mean" (the statistical tendency of extreme scores to converge to the mean in subsequent measurements). It is unclear to what extent such artifacts may affect the TVAAS model. A contrasting growth pattern will be expected if students lacking in aptitude also tend to make lower gains. Because of the high correlation between aptitude and achievement these trends would result in contradictory findings. Furthermore, potential systematic inequalities in the assignment of teachers to students would complicate the problem further if teachers are systematically assigned to students with different potential to show progress, regardless of a teacher's efforts. To date, no systematic analysis addresses this crucially important question. Indeed, TVAAS has shown inconsistent results in this regard. It is not sufficient to insist that in any case the pattern of gains exhibited by students differing in ability reflects the efficacy of teachers in addressing low- or high-achieving students. Rival hypotheses remain competent contenders. An informative validation would document teacher practices to determine how well they address students with different abilities, and the extent to which TVAAS estimates reflect these practices.

A major source of confusion appears to be the circular nature of the line of argumentation that attempts to define teacher effectiveness in terms of estimated teacher effects. This has been noted by other researchers.[31] Statements like "differences in teacher effectiveness were found to be the dominant factor affecting student academic gain"[32] are highly misleading. It leaves the reader with the impression that "teacher effectiveness" and "student academic gain" are two different variables and that the former predicts the latter. If fact, teacher effectiveness is *defined* by student academic gain. The only defensible interpretation of the various findings is that teachers vary as to the extent of their students' average academic gain. Causal attribution, almost by default, of this variability to "teacher effectiveness" has to remain suspect until further validation studies become available. At a minimum, such studies should employ independent measures of teacher effectiveness, such as teaching practices, supervisor evaluations, scores from teacher tests, and so on.

SUMMARY AND RECOMMENDATIONS

The idea of evaluating schools and teachers on the basis of the "value added" to students' education each year has wide appeal for policy makers. Instead of ranking schools or teachers from best to worst, the intention is to monitor the amount of gain in student achievement from one grade to the next. This approach has obvious advantages over the traditional alternatives when coupled with a sophisticated statistical modeling apparatus capable of handling massive cumulative longitudinal data. Technical and methodological sophistication, however, are only part of the full array of considerations that form a comprehensive evaluative judgment. Ultimately, the value of any proposed methodology and the information it produces heavily depend on the soundness of the claims made by the system's advocates. A validity argument assembles and organizes the empirical evidence as well as the logical line of reasoning linking the evidence to favored inferences and conclusions. A useful and valid model must begin with a sound theory.

Learning and development are arguably the most complex and intriguing phenomena explored by social science. An emerging learning science has started to make tentative inroads into understanding the many facets of the interactions of teaching and learning. Providing effective teaching to support and cultivate learning is therefore the most complex design problem facing educators. Yet the TVAAS model represents an overly simplistic description of teaching and learning. It is in stark contrast to a very rich body of research on learning and teaching that has demonstrated the enormous importance of student learning histories and contextual factors on the rate of academic progress. It seems to ascribe to the teacher an unrealistic responsibility for student learning. No doubt, teachers can make a critical difference in student academic growth, but so can student preparation, the support they receive outside of school (tutoring and summer school are obvious examples), the school context, and the community context—that is, the resources available to the school. Not measuring these factors does not mean they don't have important effects, only that their effects don't get a chance to show through. Unmeasured factors could potentially bias the evaluation results to the extent they play a role in determining learning outcomes. Teachers who operate in a supportive environment at the school and community levels, where students have access to a wealth of resources and enriched learning experiences, will likely be evaluated more favorably than their similarly able counterparts who struggle with harsher conditions. The TVAAS model controls only for prior student achievement, yet empirical evidence is lacking to document the assertion that prior achievement may serve as a reasonable proxy for all the other factors that matter to student learning.

The simplicity of the TVAAS model poses an interesting policy paradox. An implicit assumption of the model is that teachers, not students, are responsible for learning and that teachers hold the responsibility to produce measurable progress in learning outcomes. This is a common theme in interpreting TVAAS results. This assumption contradicts an opposite emphasis on student accountability. If indeed, as TVAAS has purported to show, "teachers are the single most important factor affecting student growth," then a student's failure to pass a gateway or graduation exam is mainly the responsibility of the teacher. This passive view of students seems unrealistic and may send conflicting messages to teachers and students.

An examination of the TVAAS model's empirical base shows that much more research is needed in order to arrive at a rational judgment of the system's strength and weaknesses. Currently, only a few sketchy empirical studies have been relied upon to substantiate strong claims of the system's merits. In light of this weakness, the recommendations below are intended to establish proper mechanisms to ensure the validity and usefulness of current and future educational accountability systems that use the TVAAS model.

- Develop and implement a program evaluation plan to define and monitor value-added assessment program outcomes. The plan should specify the intended goals for the program and how they will be measured. Periodic program evaluation reports should be required to monitor program performance. The plan should also include specifications of potential unintended consequences and a mechanism to ensure that they are kept at an acceptable minimum. Program evaluation oversight should be maintained by the state and developed and implemented by an independent contractor.
- In order to support and provide guidance for the development and implementation of the program evaluation plan, the state should establish a technical panel of experts in measurement, statistics, and educational research methodology. The panel would be asked to provide routine input into the evaluation process and help policy makers with the technical issues. The panel should also be actively involved in the design and analysis of the various studies and data analyses performed by the independent contractor.
- The TVAAS database should be made available, along with all technical documentation pertaining to the operations of the TVAAS model, to interested researchers. The state should seek proposals from independent researchers for studies that address the validity of

the major claims advanced by TVAAS developers. The technical panel can provide input as to the merit of the various proposals and suggest improvements.

- National standards and mechanisms should be developed for the approval of statistical procedures and models to be used in high-stakes accountability systems. Such standards should have the force of a professional code. The task of developing them should be led by the American Educational Research Association (AERA).

REFERENCES

1. J. H. Stronge, "Improving Schools Through Teacher Evaluation," in *Evaluating Teaching: A Guide to Current Thinking and Best Practice*, ed. J. H. Stronge (Thousand Oaks, CA: Corwin Press, 1997), 1.
2. A. J. Shinkfield and D. L. Stufflebeam, *Teacher Evaluation: Guide to Effective Practice* (Boston: Kluwer Academic Publishers, 1995).
3. See J. Millman and H. D. Schalock "Beginnings and Introduction," in *Grading Teachers, Grading Schools: Is Student Achievement A Valid Measure?* ed. J. Millman (Thousand Oaks, CA: Corwin Press, 1997), 6–7. Table 1.1 for a summary
4. Ibid., 7.
5. For reviews, see H. Meyer, "Value-Added Indicators of School Performance," in *Improving America's Schools: The Role of Incentives*, eds. E. A. Hanushek and D. W. Jorgenson (Washington, DC: National Academy Press, 1996), 200.
    L. Saunders, "A Brief History of Educational 'Value Added': How Did We Get to Where We Are?" *School Effectiveness and School Improvement* 10, no. 2 (1999): 233–256.
6. State of Tennessee, Education Improvement Act (1992), §49-1-603
7. For a detailed description of the TVAAS model, see W. L Sanders, A. M. Saxton and S. P. Horn, "The Tennessee Value-Added System: A Quantitative Outcomes-Based Approach To Educational Assessment," in *Grading Teachers, Grading Schools: Is Student Achievement A Valid Measure?* ed. J. Millman (Thousand Oaks, CA: Corwin Press, 1997), 137–162.
8. J. S. Coleman et al., *Equality of Educational Opportunity* (Washington, DC: U.S. Government Printing Office, 1966).
9. J. Archer, "Sanders 101," *Education Week* 18, no. 34 (5 May 1999): 26–28.
10. L. J. Cronbach and P. E. Meehl, "Construct Validity In Psychological Tests," *Psychological Bulletin* 52 (1955): 281–302.
11. A. P. Baker and D. Xu, *The measure of education: A review of the Tennessee Value Added Assessment System* (Nashville: Tennessee Comptroller of the Treasury, Office of Education Accountability, 1995).
12. R. D. Bock and R. Wolfe, *Audit and Review of the Tennessee Value-Added Assessment System (TVAAS): Final Report, 1996* (Nashville: Tennessee Comptroller of the Treasury, Office of Education Accountability, 1996).

13. State of Tennessee, Education Improvement Act (1992), §49-1-604. Mixed model methodologies.

14. W. L. Sanders and J. C. Rivers, *Cumulative And Residual Effects Of Teachers On Future Student Academic Achievement, Research Progress Report* (Knoxville, TN: University of Tennessee Value-Added Research and Assessment Center, 1996).

15. Ibid.

16. It is interesting to note that an error message from the computer run presented in Table 2 of Rivers' dissertation suggests that estimates from the analyses may be biased. A possible reason for this error is the inclusion of highly correlated variables in the same analyses.

17. S. P. Wright, S. P. Horn, and W. L. Sanders, "Teacher And Classroom Context Effects On Student Achievement: Implications For Teacher Evaluation," *Journal of Personnel Evaluation in Education* 1, no. 1 (1997): 57–67.

18. Ibid.

19. This study used a statistical technique to compare the magnitude of the different factors affecting student achievement, citing Rosenthal as a supporting reference. However, Rosenthal suggests the technique for comparing results *across different studies* (a methodology known as "meta-analysis) and not for comparing the magnitude of effects within the same study. The authors offer no justification for this unconventional application of the technique.

20. W. L. Sanders and S. P. Horn, "Research Findings From The Tennessee Value Added Assessment System (TVAAS) Database: Implications For Educational Evaluation And Research," *Journal of Personnel Evaluation in Education* 12, no. 3 (1998): 247–256.

21. W. L. Sanders, "Value-Added Assessment," *The School Administrator* 55, No. 11 (December 1998).

22. H. Meyer, "Value-Added Indicators of School Performance," in *Improving America's Schools: The Role of Incentives,* eds. E. A. Hanushek and D. W. Jorgenson (Washington, DC: National Academy Press, 1996), 200.

23. *Graphical Summary of Educational Findings From the Tennessee Value-Added Assessment System* (Knoxville, TN: University of Tennessee Value-Added Research and Assessment Center, 1997).

24. Ibid.

25. L. Darling-Hammond and L. Post, "Inequality in Teaching and Schooling: Supporting High-Quality Teaching and Leadership in Low-Income Schools," in *A Notion at Risk: Preserving Public Education as an Engine for Social Mobility,* ed. R.D. Kahlenberg (The Century Foundation / Twentieth Century Fund Inc. 2000).

26. D. Hu, "The Relationship of School Spending and Student Academic Achievement When Achievement is Measured by Value-Added Scores" (Ph.D. diss., Nashville, TN: Vanderbilt University, 2000).

27. *How People Learn: Brain, Mind, Experience, and School,* eds. J. D. Bransford, A. L. Brown and R. R. Cocking, (Washington, DC: National Academy Press, 1999), xvi.

28. H. Kupermintz, L. Shepard, and R. Linn, "Teacher Effects as a Measure of Teacher Effectiveness: Construct Validity Considerations in TVAAS (Tennes-

see Value Added Assessment System)," in *New Work on the Evaluation of High-Stakes Testing Programs,* chair D. Koretz, Symposium at the National Council on Measurement in Education (NCME) Annual Meeting, Seattle, WA, April 2000.

29.   Bock and Wolfe.

30.   Ibid., 27

31.   G. W. Bracey, "The Ninth Bracey Report On the Condition Of Public Education", *Phi Delta Kappan* 81,no. 2 (October 1999): 147.

L. Darling-Hammond, "Toward What End? The Evaluation of Student Learning for the Improvement of Teaching," in *Grading Teachers, Grading Schools: Is Student Achievement A Valid Measure?* ed. J. Millman (Thousand Oaks, CA: Corwin Press, 1997).

32.   Sanders and Horn, 251.

CHAPTER 12

PROFESSIONAL DEVELOPMENT

Ulrich C. Reitzug
University of North Carolina at Greensboro

SUMMARY OF RESEARCH FINDINGS

Current predominant staff development practice is limited, fragmented, and marginalized. The complexity of teaching and learning is incompatible with the narrow focus of much of traditional staff development. Evidence abounds of the significance of the relationship between the content of staff development, the quality of the staff development, and student achievement, so long as staff development adheres to certain principles that emphasize school-level control, focus on student learning and instruction, a commitment of time and resources to implement development over an extended period of time, and the development of professional development styles that engage teachers collaboratively rather than focusing on them as individuals. Effective professional development requires that continuous inquiry be embedded in the daily life of the school.

RECOMMENDATIONS

- Professional development should be viewed as an on-going part of the daily life of the school.
- More time and resources should be devoted to professional development.

- When a specific curricular or instructional initiative is being implemented in a school, training should be supplemented by coaching and the initiative should be the subject of the on-going inquiry in the school.
- The perceived relationship between professional development of any sort and teacher growth should not be left to chance. The relationship between professional development initiatives and teacher growth should be clearly articulated.
- Schools should be cognizant of the relationships between professional development initiatives and other parts of the system. Time schedules, curricular goals, student and teacher evaluation, curricular materials, and expectations must all be brought in line with the focus of professional development initiative.
- State laws mandating schools' curriculum content and school time and governing school financing should be revised to accommodate more extensive and sophisticated professional development efforts.
- Principals should be prepared to be instructional leaders not only through traditional practices such as teaching them about teacher supervision and evaluation and curricular alignment, but also by preparing them to initiate and facilitate the development cultures of inquiry in their schools.

Professional development can be thought of as "processes and activities designed to enhance the professional knowledge, skills, and attitudes of educators so that they might, in turn, improve the learning of students."[1] The definition implies that staff development consists of a broad range of processes and activities that contribute to the learning of educators. However, when most educators hear the words "staff development" they associate them much more narrowly with only workshops and in-services.[2] Unfortunately, the narrow conceptions many educators have of staff development[3] mirror staff development practices in most schools and districts in the United States.

Current predominant staff development practice is limited, fragmented, one-shot or short term and pre-packaged. It occurs on the margins and is focused on "training over problem solving."[4] Specifically, most educators participate in a very limited amount of staff development. They may attend a workshop or two during the year, as well as participating in their school district's one or two annual staff development days. In all likelihood, the focus of the workshops and the staff development days are unconnected to each other. The staff development days likely are centrally-planned and either do not match the needs of most schools in the district, or consist of a smorgasbord of brief, one-hour "sit and get" presentations. The effect of such staff development efforts on teacher practice and student achievement reflects the financial and mental investment in them—minimal, at best. Judith Warren Little, the author of a number of significant staff development studies, concludes that most traditional staff development "communicates a relatively impoverished view of teachers, teaching, and teacher development."[5]

Recent research on teaching and learning has established that teaching and learning is not a simple cause and effect relationship, but rather a complex process in which learning is co-constructed by teachers and students in a *specific* classroom context with instruction at any point in time reflecting the teacher's analysis of the various elements in play at that moment[6]—what Brown has called the "nowness" of teaching.[7] The complexity of teaching and learning is incompatible with the narrow, short-term, episodic, special-project focus of much of traditional staff development. Additionally, Little argues that the complexity of current reforms (e.g., authentic instruction and assessment, curricular integration, achieving equity) often do not lend themselves to simple skill training, but rather require professional growth cultures in schools that permit teachers to function as intellectuals rather than technicians.[8]

The focus of this literature review is to examine what are the various "processes and activities" that might "enhance the professional knowledge, skills, and attitudes of educators" and to explore their impact on teaching practice and student achievement.

PROFESSIONAL DEVELOPMENT RESEARCH

Types of Professional Development

There are many forms that professional development may take. "Training" is the traditional, and still dominant, form and includes workshops, presentations, and other types of in-service activities. Training typically includes a direct instruction/lecture component, skill demonstration and modeling, and may also include simulated skill practice, and even workplace coaching and consultation.

Opportunities to learn that are "embedded" in the work setting are a second form of professional development. Embedded professional development includes processes such as inquiry, discussion, evaluation, consultation, collaboration, and problem solving. It may be stimulated by new roles for teachers (e.g., teacher leader, peer coach, teacher researchers), new structures (e.g., problem-solving groups, decision-making teams, common planning periods, self-contained teams), or new tasks (leading an in-house workshop, journal writing, collaborative case analysis, grant writing, curriculum writing, school improvement team membership).

Networks are a third, recently emerging form of professional development. Networks are collections of educators from across different schools who interact regularly to discuss and share practices around a particular focus or philosophy of schooling (e.g., new math standards; authentic instruction). They are held together by a typically loose organizational structure that facilitates their interaction across schools. They interact via such means as in-person sharing meetings, cross-school or cross-classroom visitations, professional institutes, critical friends groups, and electronic forms of communication. Pennell and Firestone found that networks were effective in helping teachers get students more actively involved in learning,[9] and Lieberman and Grolnick found networks to have a number of positive effects on the professional development of teachers.[10]

Professional Development Schools are a fourth, also fairly recent, form of professional development. Professional Development Schools (PDS) are schools in which university faculty, PDS teachers, and student teachers work collaboratively to enhance the student teaching experience and to improve the professional development of the PDS teachers and staff. These goals are met through active involvement of the university faculty in the school, formal professional development experiences (e.g., teacher study groups, curriculum writing, peer observation, case conferences, workshops),[11] and through school-based collaborative research.

Outcomes of Staff Development

There are several outcome areas that are potentially affected by professional development. These include:

- teacher knowledge,
- teacher attitudes and beliefs,
- teaching practice,
- school-level practice, and
- student achievement.

Professional development's impact on *teacher knowledge and skill* includes imparting knowledge about content or content standards and skills in instruction, classroom management, or assessment. Developing teacher knowledge and skill, however, is about more than acquiring existing skills and knowledge; it also includes enabling teachers to reflect critically on their practice and fashion new knowledge and beliefs about content, pedagogy, and learners.[12] Smylie[13] notes, "In order to *change practice* in significant and worthwhile ways, teachers must not only learn new subject matter and new instructional techniques, but they must alter their *beliefs* and conceptions of practice, their 'theories of action'."[14] Guskey argues that change in *beliefs and attitudes* occurs subsequent to change in practice, and results from teachers' observing the impact of changes in their practice on student outcomes.[15] Finally, the impact of professional development on *stu-*

dent achievement should not be limited to an examination of only standardized test scores. Other measures of student achievement include teacher made exams and quizzes, students' attendance, involvement in class sessions, student motivation for learning, attitudes toward school & learning,[16] authentic assessment of student work, homework completion rates, and classroom behaviors.[17]

Challenges in Studying Professional Development and Student Achievement

Although a great deal has been written on the topic of professional development, the empirical literature on the topic is much less extensive. This is particularly so when only studies that link professional development and student achievement are considered (see related discussion below). Indeed, much of the research empirically linking professional development to specific outcomes has not appeared in the major refereed scholarly journals, but has, as often as not, appeared in ERIC research reports, or in reports produced by school districts, foundations, or other organizations. The conceptual and theoretical work on professional development that has appeared in the major academic journals is typically thoughtfully argued and pulls from a variety of sources and bodies of knowledge (e.g., from research on adult learning) to develop arguments for specific forms of professional development.

Although the ultimate objective of professional development is improving student achievement as a result of increased teacher learning, testing the relationship between professional development and student achievement is problematic. Due to a variety of confounding variables, there is great difficulty in establishing a direct relationship between professional development activities, improvements in teaching, and increases in student achievement.[18] This is particularly problematic when there are a variety of other "new" programs, materials, or interventions occurring simultaneously with professional development activities (which is essentially all the time in most schools). Further increasing the difficulty of testing the professional development–student achievement relationship are forms of professional development that go beyond the traditional training workshop format and are embedded in the daily life of the school (see subsequent discussion). Guskey and Sparks observe that to explore the professional development–student achievement relationship, the content ("what?"), process ("how?"), and context ("who, when, where, why?") of professional development need to be considered in the study.[19] Given that each one of these factors is likely to include multiple variables, empirically testing this relationship becomes extremely unwieldy.

Linking Staff Development and Student Achievement

Theoretically, enhancing the knowledge, skills, and attitudes of teachers should translate into improved teaching practices, which, in turn, should improve student achievement. Dennis Sparks and Stephanie Hirsh, the executive directors of the National Staff Development Council, note that "a growing body of research shows that improving teacher knowledge and teaching skills is essential to raising student performance."[20] Indeed, in a study of 900 school districts, Ferguson found that teacher expertise accounted for 40% of the difference in student achievement in reading and math.[21] A second study found that differences in teacher qualifications accounted for more than 90% of the variance in student achievement in a large urban district.[22]

It should be noted, however, that the relationship between professional development and student achievement is a function of both the quality of the professional development *processes and activities*, and the efficacy of the *substance* of the professional development (i.e., the content, skills, or attitudes that the professional development is attempting to influence). That is, professional development's impact can improve student achievement only to the extent to which its *content focus* can do so. The relationship might be portrayed as follows:

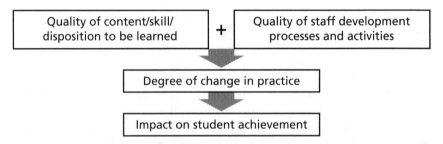

A study by Shymanksy, Yore, and Anderson provides an illustrative example.[23] Shymanksy and colleagues studied the impact of a high-quality science professional development program on teaching practice and student achievement. The professional development program included an initial problem-centered workshop, development and subsequent field-testing of science materials in participating teachers' classrooms, follow-up workshops, and sharing with colleagues—a total of 110 hours of in-service over a four-year period. While teachers changed their teaching to more regularly use the methods and objectives the professional development program advocated, student achievement in science did not improve subsequent to the professional development initiative.[24] This suggests that it is not professional development processes and activities alone that influence student achievement. Rather, it is the *content and methods* being advocated in the professional development program in combination with the *quality of the professional devel-*

opment processes and activities that influence student achievement. An alternative explanation in this case may be that the student achievement assessment strategy that was used may not have been congruent with the content and methods being advocated in the staff development program. Although some evidence exists to the contrary,[25] it is reasonable to assume that a staff development program advocating authentic means of instruction may not show an impact on student achievement when the student achievement measure being used is scores on standardized tests—which typically do not focus on testing the types of higher-level thought processes that result from authentic teaching and other constructivist-oriented learning processes.[26]

In any case, perhaps the single most comprehensive source of evidence for the significance of the relationship between the content of staff development, the quality of the staff development, and student achievement is found in *Student Achievement through Staff Development,* by Joyce and Showers.[27] The book reviews, synthesizes, and interprets research from a variety of sources: some empirical, some theoretical, and some conceptual. Joyce and Showers devote an entire chapter to exploring practices that have been empirically documented to be effective and that might serve as sources for staff development efforts geared toward improving student achievement.

What Works in Professional Development

Professional development does make a difference in the quality of teaching in schools and in the achievement of students. Even given the paucity of much current professional development practice, in a national survey almost two-thirds of teachers report that professional development activities have caused them to change their teaching.[28] A second national survey found that teachers who participated in professional development focused on standards were more likely to describe teaching in ways consistent with the standards than teachers who did not participate in the professional development activities.[29] Similarly, Cohen and Hill found that professional development that was carefully focused on particular objectives resulted in more teaching practices consistent with the objectives. Additionally, they found that the greater the amount of professional development, the more practice was influenced.[30] In a study of a long-term professional development effort, the researchers found a significant correlation between teachers' level of use of the strategies promoted by the professional development effort and students' cognitive gain (as measured by a cognitive assessment instrument).[31] Cognitive gain was also directly linked to subsequent gain in academic achievement.[32] Finally, Greenwald, Hedges, and Laine found that there is a greater increase in student achievement for money spent on professional development than for money spent on reducing class size or raising teachers' salaries.[33]

Professional Development Implications of Other Research

Research focused on other aspects of education has also produced findings with a bearing on professional development.

Professional Development and Effective Class-Size Reduction: Wisconsin's SAGE Program.

In an evaluation of a reduced class size initiative in Wisconsin, Molnar, Smith, Zahorik, Palmer, Halbach, and Ehrle found that reduced class size resulted in improved student achievement.[34] In order to analyze changes in teaching that occurred as a result of reduced class sizes, they interviewed 28 teachers who participated in the reduced-class-size initiative. The teachers noted that as a result of lower class sizes they were able to know and understand their students better, spend less time on discipline, individualize instruction more to meet the needs of individual students, and increase the amount of student-centered instruction. Student-centered instruction included more hands-on activities, more enrichment activities, more interest centers, and more cooperative groups. The researchers concluded that the teachers did not necessarily adopt totally new teaching practices as a result of the smaller class sizes, but rather that the lower class sizes permitted them to more frequently use the teaching practices that they had always wanted to use. Seemingly, the addition of professional development would be fruitful for these teachers since large class size would not be a factor that prohibits them from implementing newly learned practices. Indeed, many of the interviewed teachers expressed a desire for more in-service.

Professional Development and Teacher Quality: The Wenglinsky Study.

Correlating achievement data from over 7,000 eighth graders who took the National Assessment of Educational Progress (NAEP) Mathematics and Science exams with data from accompanying surveys completed by their teachers, resulted in a number of significant findings in a study conducted by Wenglinsky.[35] Survey data measured three types of teacher quality: teacher inputs (such as education levels and years of experience); classroom practices (such as use of small-group instruction or hands-on learning); and professional development (such as training to support classroom practices). Wenglinsky's study yielded the following findings.

In Mathematics:

- Of the six professional development topics in math, students whose teachers received professional development—in working with different student populations and in higher-order thinking skills—outperformed students whose teachers lacked such professional development. Students whose teachers received professional development in ongoing forms of assessment performed worse than students of teachers who did not receive such professional development (the three topics which did not have an influence in math included classroom management, cooperative learning, and interdisciplinary instruction).

- Teachers with more professional development were more likely to engage students in hands-on learning activities. Students who frequently engaged in hands-on learning activities as well as students who were frequently engaged in activities that required higher-order thinking skills outperformed students who spent less time in such activities.

In Science:

- Of the eight professional development topics in science, students whose teachers received professional development in laboratory skills outperformed students whose teachers lacked such professional development. Students whose teachers received professional development in classroom management performed worse than students of teachers who did not receive such professional development (the 6 topics which did not have an influence in science included cooperative learning, working with different student populations, higher-order thinking skills, on-going forms of assessment, interdisciplinary instruction, and integrating science instruction).
- As in math, students who frequently engaged in hands-on learning activities outperformed students who spent less time in such activities.
- As in math, teachers with more professional development were more likely to engage students in hands-on learning activities.

Overall, although the study found that student socioeconomic status was the single most influential measure that impacted student achievement, when the influential measures of teacher quality (i.e., professional development factors and classroom practices) were added together, they outweighed the influence of socioeconomic status (0.76 for SES, 0.86 for teacher quality inputs).

Related Findings.   A study by Dunne, Nave, and Lewis[36] found that the teaching of teachers who participated in critical friends groups became more student-centered. If hands-on learning is an aspect of student-centered teaching, then an indirect link could be argued to exist between critical friends groups as a form of professional development and student achievement. (Critical Friends Groups consist of a small group of teachers who get together to "identify student learning goals that make sense in their schools, look reflectively at practices intended to achieve those goals, and collaboratively examine teacher and student work in order to meet their objectives."[37] A national Critical Friends Group initiative is being conducted by the National School Reform Faculty of the Annenberg Institute for School Reform.)

Sanders and Rivers, cited in Wenglinsky,[38] found that the top 20% of teachers boosted the scores of low-achieving students over a one year period by an average of 53 percentile points, which was 39 percentile points higher than the 14-percentile point gain experienced by students assigned to the bottom 20% of teachers.[39]

Although the research indicates that professional development can make a difference in changing teaching practice and in improving student achievement, the research is clear that these effects are more likely to occur when professional development is characterized by certain principles. The remainder of this review will discuss eight principles that emerge from the professional development literature as key to effective professional development. These principles reflect an overwhelming consensus that is found in the literature on the subject. While only a limited amount of the work on professional development is based on empirical research, most of the remaining work is nonetheless research-based[40]—the work of noted scholars who have grounded their findings in a broad synthesis and thoughtful consideration of large quantities of research and research-based literature on a variety of related topics and from a variety of fields. In the absence of more empirical research, it is the best available literature on the topic, and is well grounded in its own right.

Principle 1: **Decisions about professional development should be made within schools rather than at the district level.**[41]

There is a broad consensus in the organizational theory literature that planning that is solely top-down alienates teachers.[42] Additionally, as Little observes, there is little value in the one-size-fits-all model of staff development that exposes teachers with different backgrounds and from different schools to the same material.[43] Thus, professional development initiatives should reflect participant input.[44] Sparks, however, cautions that professional development should not be based only on the perceptions of educators regarding their needs, but rather should begin with an assessment of student needs and learning outcomes and work backwards to what the results of that assessment mean for staff development.[45] Little echoes this sentiment, noting that professional development must make connections between students' experiences, teachers' classroom practice, and school-wide structures and cultures.[46] Professional development has been found to be most effective when it is based on student learning goals that reflect the challenges and uniqueness of the particular school whose staff is participating in the professional development.[47] It should be driven by a "clear, coherent strategic plan" rather than being a "fragmented, piecemeal improvement effort...with no thought given to follow-up or to how the new technique fits in with those that were taught in previous years."[48]

Totally bottom-up planning, however, is also not advisable. Such planning is unlikely to engender the support of district leadership.[49] District backing is important for a number of reasons, including that research has found a degree of correlation between district backing and teachers' willingness to undertake an initiative.[50] Thus, decisions about professional development should be made within schools rather than at the district level, but planning should include participation from the district level.

Principle 2: **Professional development must be focused on instruction and student learning.**[51]

Joyce, Wolf, and Calhoun[52] note that they did not find a single instance in the literature on professional development and school improvement initiatives "where student learning increased but had not been a central goal."[53] Sparks argues that staff development must begin not with teacher or district needs and desires, but rather "with a clear sense of what students need to learn and be able to do,"[54] and recommends that staff development be connected to assessable student learning outcomes.[55] As Elmore and Burney note: "It's about instruction...and only about instruction."[56]

To be about instruction, staff development must focus on both deeper forms of content knowledge *and* on the most effective instructional strategies in a discipline.[57] In the *National Plan for Improving Staff Development* published by the National Staff Development Council, Sparks and Stephanie Hirsh note that effective staff development must result in teachers being "deeply immersed" in subject matter and teaching methods[58] and must be curriculum-centered and standards-based. Providing empirical support, Cohen & Hill found that there were higher average student standardized test scores in schools where staff development was specifically focused on the objectives of the school improvement initiative effort (in this case, the California Mathematics Framework), and where staff development linked curriculum with assessment.[59] Using data from a 1994 survey of California elementary school teachers and the 1994 California Learning Assessment System, they found that student achievement on standardized tests improves when teachers' learning opportunities are grounded in the curriculum students study, deal with the connections between multiple elements of the instructional system (e.g., curriculum, instruction, *and* assessment), and occur over an extended time period.

Principle 3: **Professional development initiatives must take place over an extended period of time.**[60]

As we know from research and practice, change is a long, slow process.[61] If the objective of professional development is change in teaching practice, then it is clear that professional development must be sustained over time if change is to be realized. Sparks and Hirsh note that professional development should be "sustained, rigorous, and cumulative."[62] The importance of professional development extending over a period of time is also supported by empirical research. The National Center for Education Statistics found that teachers who participated in staff development programs that lasted eight hours or more were three to five times more likely to report that the staff development had significantly improved their teaching than teachers who participated for lesser amounts of time.[63] Cohen and Hill found that there were higher average student standardized test scores in schools where teachers received a greater amount of staff development than in schools where teachers received a lesser amount of professional development.[64]

Principle 4: **Professional development activities should model effective pedagogy.**[65]

Little observes that professional development must offer "meaningful intellectual, social, and emotional engagement with ideas, with materials, and with colleagues..."[66] This, in a nutshell, summarizes effective pedagogy. More specifically, modeling effective pedagogy in professional development includes two primary components: professional development must be consistent with what we know about constructivist teaching and learning, and professional development must follow the principles of adult learning. Constructivism holds that learners connect new information to their existing knowledge in order to create new knowledge.[67] This is in contrast to merely having knowledge transmitted from someone else to them. Constructivist staff development might encompass activities such as "action research, conversations with peers about the beliefs and assumptions that guide their instruction, and reflective practices (e.g., journal keeping)."[68] Principles of adult learning include learning in varied settings and circumstances; problem-oriented learning that relates to the adult learners' lives; adult learners playing an active role in their own learning; and connecting new learning to the adults' existing knowledge, skills, and beliefs from past experiences (also a key aspect of constructivism).[69]

Principle 5: **Professional development workshops must be supported by modeling and coaching in order to attain a higher degree of effectiveness.**[70]

Implementation of practices advocated in staff development workshops is most effective when professional development includes both staff training activities and staff support activities. Guskey notes that few teachers can go from workshop to practice without experimentation, classroom-based modeling, and other follow-up support.[71] Additionally, teachers must be helped to endure and persist past the anxiety of initial failures.[72]

Research has found that when they were well conducted, workshops combined with coaching and related follow-up support produced sustained student achievement gains and teacher adherence to project methods and objectives. By contrast, training alone produced only short-term achievement gains, there was less fidelity in implementation to project objectives, and adherence to project methods did not persist. The types of related follow-up support that led to desirable outcomes included local resource personnel to assist teachers with project implementation, outside consultants, and regular project meetings that included teachers, were collaborative, and focused on collective problem-solving and sharing of expertise.[73]

Joyce and Showers found that a "dramatic increase of transfer in training … occurs when in-class coaching is added to an initial training experience comprised of theory explanation, demonstration, and practice with feedback."[74] They found that acquiring new skills requires understanding the theoretical base of the skill, viewing numerous demonstrations (they suggest about 20), practicing the skills with feedback, and receiving on-the-job coaching.[75] Similarly, Joyce, Wolfe, and Calhoun, assessing several bodies of research as well as their own extensive experience as staff developers, argue that staff development initiatives require 10 to 15 days of training (rather than the one or two days of training that are typically provided), about 20 demonstrations of the strategies to be learned, workshop opportunities to practice, and a redesigned workplace that supports the new initiative, in order to be effective.[76]

***Principle 6:* Professional development should focus on communities of practice rather than on individual teachers.**[77]

Traditionally staff development efforts are an individual endeavor. Often, a teacher uses a professional day to attend a workshop in which she or he is interested while teacher colleagues remain at the school to fulfill teaching responsibilities. Where a workshop is offered to an entire school, each teacher typically retreats to his or her classroom afterward to implement the new practices in isolation. Unfortunately, teachers, over time, have tended to think in terms of only their classrooms and their students. Such traditional perspectives and professional development practices fail to recognize the significance of collective and interdependent effort and effect.[78] Sparks, drawing conclusions from his long experience as director of the National Council of Staff Development and as editor of the *Journal of Staff Development*, notes that a paradigm shift is needed in staff development that requires a movement from individual development to individual development *and* organizational development.[79] He argues that the success of students depends not only on the learning of individual adults in the school, but also on the capacity of the school "to solve problems and renew itself."[80]

Arguing largely from case studies (which, given the complexity of studying the impact of professional development, may often be the more appropriate methodology than more quantitative research), Little and colleagues echo this sentiment, asserting the necessity of considering professional development in school-wide institutional terms.[81] Similarly, Elmore and Burney observe that, "Deep and sustained change requires that people feel a personal commitment to each other" and that instructional improvement as a result of professional development is not "a collection of management principles" but rather the development of "a culture based on norms of commitment, mutual care, and concern."[82]

Research supports the opportunity to work together and learn from each other as one of the most effective forms of professional development.[83] For example, Stein observed that in the New York City schools professional development effort she studied, teachers returned to their school after collectively attending an off-site workshop, engaged in conversations with other teachers about the practices on which the workshop focused, and observed each other teaching using the practices. The result, she found, created a "community-based expectation that they would implement the newly-learned practices in their daily work."[84] Stevens found that of six professional development strategies, teachers cited collaboration and networking as the most helpful to their professional development, noting that this permitted them to share their best practices and benefit from those of others.[85] Although the study did not prove a direct empirical link, test scores improved in the schools that were subjected to the professional development strategies. By contrast, participants in school renewal work in New York City's District 2 cited isolation as "the enemy of instructional change."[86] Little found that working collaboratively is important not just in training, but also in implementing new initiatives.[87] In a study of two schools, each of which experienced a similar, highly-rated staff development program, the difference between the school that effectively implemented the initiative and the school that was unsuccessful in doing so was that the successful school continued to work collaboratively during the implementation process, while in the less successful school teachers worked individually during the implementation process. The successful school committed to a three-year implementation process, rather than simply to five to eight days of training, and developed habits of shared work and problem-solving during the implementation process. Additionally, the principal became a fully involved, proactive change agent, rather than simply permitting or approving the change.

Principle 7: **Effective professional development requires that continuous inquiry be embedded in the daily life of the school.**[88]

This principle, perhaps more than any other, reflects the paradigm shift that is necessary (and is occurring in some quarters) in professional development. The paradigm shift requires a move away from the traditional staff development "adult pull-out" model in which staff development is an "event" that occurs primarily at a site away from teachers' workplace (usually in a workshop), to thinking of professional development as something that is embedded in multiple ways in the daily life of the school (e.g., through action research, school-based study groups, peer observation, coaching, journaling, involvement in school improvement processes, joint lesson planning, collective problem-solving, collaborative critiquing of students' work, or collective student-oriented case conferences).[89] Sparks and Hirsh note: "In a learning school, all staff members are engaged in sustained, intellectually rigorous study of what they teach and how they teach it."[90] Smylie observes that schools will not improve "until we acknowledge the importance of schools not only as places for teachers to work but also as places for teachers to learn."[91]

Research indicates that school cultures in which inquiry is prevalent are characterized by norms of collegiality, openness, and trust; opportunities and time for disciplined inquiry; reconstruction of leadership roles; and networking and collaboration.[92] Shared work, shared problem-solving, mutual assistance, and teacher leadership in curriculum and instruction are the cornerstones for building such a culture of inquiry in a school.[93] Indeed, Deborah Meier, former director of the highly acclaimed Central Park East Secondary School in New York City, observes in writing about the school, "continuing dialogue, face to face, over and over, is a powerful educative force. It is our primary form of staff development."[94]

Collaborative, school-wide forms of inquiry-oriented professional development increase teacher learning and change schools more than simply attending workshops or in-services.[95] Little found that when teachers observed each other in classrooms, had time to talk about their teaching, and worked collaboratively to find solutions for problems, their professional lives were "transformed."[96]

Little's study was based on interviews with 105 teachers and 14 administrators and included extensive operation of both average-achieving and "high success" schools. The latter, she found, were characterized by a norm of collegiality that encompassed an expectation for shared discussion and shared work among teachers. High success schools were also characterized by a norm of experimentation in which continuous improvement as a result of analysis, evaluation, and experimentation was an expectation. In the high success schools, teachers engaged in frequent and continuous talk about teaching practice, in frequent and mutual observation and critique of teaching, evaluated teaching materials together, and taught each other how to be better teachers through such practices as being instructors for school-based in-services.

Little later concluded that the power of professional development lies less in the opportunities it provides teachers to *consume* research and knowledge and more in the capacity it develops for teachers to "*generate* knowledge and to *assess* the knowledge claimed by others."[97]

In a study of 78 schools, Rosenholtz found that in the 13 schools classified as effective and progressing, teachers learned from one another as well as from outside sources.[98] Improvement in teaching was "a collective rather than individual enterprise, and...analysis, evaluation, and experimentation in concert with colleagues are conditions under which teachers improve."[99]

Among specific inquiry-oriented practices, Larson et al. found that *action research* was an effective, but time-consuming, form of professional development that resulted in teachers generating new knowledge in their self-selected area of inquiry, and changing their teaching practices.[100] Dunne and Honts reported that participants in *critical friends groups* cited their participation in the groups as the most powerful form of professional development they had ever experienced.[101] The groups consisted of faculty and administrators working collaboratively toward agreed upon student learning goals and meeting at least once a month for two hours. During the meetings they discussed teaching practices that would help them move closer to their goals, examined curriculum and student work, and identified school culture issues that could affect student achievement. In still another study, 52% of teachers who participated in weekly *common planning sessions* subsequent to professional development workshops believed the staff development significantly improved their teaching, while only 13% of the teachers who occasionally participated in collaborative planning sessions reported staff development as significantly improving their teaching.[102]

In summary, a school wide "press" for daily learning and on-going inquiry is important for teachers to access the potential power of professional development to impact their practice and improve student achievement.

Principle 8: **Principals and other school leaders must provide proactive support for professional development and the initiatives upon which it is focused.**[103]

Many of the decisions and structures that create support for professional development are within the control of school leaders.[104] The norms and expectations that are held for professional growth and the extent to which a culture of inquiry develops in a school are directly related to the words, actions, and decisions of principals and to the structures they develop in the school. Reitzug and O' Hair, for example, found that even actions such as the structures principals create for teachers to share with colleagues the substance of workshops that they have attended affects the culture of inquiry that develops in a school.[105] Additionally, they found that when principals went beyond simply letting teachers participate in a professional development initiative to actually being proactive supporters of the initiative, the initiative was much more likely to be successfully implemented in the school. Stein describes the practices of three principals who created supportive structures to facilitate cross-grade collaboration.[106] The principals' actions included creating multi-grade classrooms; hiring a resource teacher to identify interdisciplinary, cross-grade curricular themes; and initiating cross-grade curriculum articulation conferences.

Supportive school structures should focus on providing ways for teachers to get feedback on their performance, to communicate with colleagues, and to move outside the isolation of their classrooms to share practices, observe other teachers, and communicate with professional colleagues.[107] Little found that the successful schools in her study created support structures (e.g., teaming, schedules, room assignments, faculty meeting agendas, governance structures) that provided teachers with common space and time and permitted them to work with each other.[108] Cross-school networks, mentioned previously, are one increasingly popular structure that facilitates these practices intentionally across schools and unintentionally within schools.

RECOMMENDATIONS

In addition to the self-evident policy recommendations suggested by the principles of professional development discussed in this review, the following policy recommendations are implied by the research that has been reviewed.

- Professional development should be viewed as an an-going part of the daily life of the school, whether or not a specific initiative is being implemented.
- More time and resources should be devoted to professional development. Current school structures and schedules include little time for in-school collaboration, inquiry, and discourse.
- When a specific curricular or instructional initiative is being implemented in a school, training should be supplemented by coaching and the initiative should be the subject of the on-going inquiry in the school.
- The perceived relationship between professional development of any sort and teacher growth should not be left to chance. The biggest

motivation for teachers to participate in and implement professional development initiatives is their perception that they will grow professionally and that their students will benefit.[109] Consequently, the relationship between professional development initiatives and teacher growth should be clearly articulated.

- Schools should be cognizant of the relationships between professional development initiatives and other parts of the system.[110]   Time schedules, curricular goals, student and teacher evaluation, curricular materials, and expectations must all be brought in line with the focus of professional development initiative,[111] and the initiative should be consistent with the school's values and beliefs. For example, professional development focused on constructivist teaching makes little sense if there is concurrent pressure to teach-to-the-test as a result of a high-stakes testing environment.
- State laws mandating schools' curriculum content and school time and governing school financing should be revised to accommodate more extensive and sophisticated professional development efforts.
- Principals should be prepared to be instructional leaders not only through traditional practices such as teaching them about teacher supervision and evaluation and curricular alignment, but also by preparing them to initiate and facilitate the development cultures of inquiry in their schools.

REFERENCES

1.   T. R. Guskey, *Evaluating Professional Development* (Thousand Oaks, CA: Corwin Press, 2000), 16.

2.   D. Sparks, "Focusing Staff Development on Improving Student Learning," in *Handbook of Research on Improving Student Achievement*, ed. G. Cawelti (1995), 163–172, ERIC, ED 394629.

3.   The terms "staff development" and "professional development" will be used synonymously in this review

4.   J. W. Little, "Teachers' Professional Development in a Climate of Educational Reform," *Educational Evaluation and Policy Analysis* 15, no. 2 (1993): 129–151, 143.

5.   Ibid., 148.

6.   M. McLaughlin, "Enabling Professional Development," in *Staff Development for Education in the '90s*, ed. A. Lieberman and L. Miller (1991), 61–82.

7.   J. S. Brown, *Remarks at a Stanford Center for Organizational Research Seminar*, 13 January 1989.

8.   Little.

9.   J. Pennell and W. A. Firestone, "Changing Classroom Practices Through Teacher Networks: Matching Program Features with Teacher Characteristics and Circumstances," *Teachers College Record* 98, no. 1 (1996): 46–76.

10. A. Lieberman and M. Grolnick, "Networks And Reform In American Education," *Teachers College Record* 98, no. 1 (1996): 7–45.

11. A. Lieberman and L. Miller, "Teacher Development in Professional Practice Schools", 1992, ERIC, ED 374098.

12. L. Darling-Hammond and M. W. McLaughlin, "Policies that Support Professional Development in an Era of Reform," *Phi Delta Kappan* 76 (1995): 597–604.

13. M. A. Smylie, "Teacher Learning in the Workplace," in *Professional Development in Education: New Paradigms and Practices,* ed. T.R. Guskey and M. Huberman (New York: Teachers College Press, 1995), 92–113.

14. Ibid., 93.

15. T. R. Guskey, "Staff Development and the Process of Teacher Change," *Educational Researcher* 15, no. 5 (1986): 5–12.

     D. P. Crandall et al., *People, Policies, and Practices: Examining the Chain of School Improvement* (Andover, MA: The NETWORK, Inc., 1982).

16. Guskey.

17. T. R. Guskey and D. Sparks, "Exploring the Relationship Between Staff Development and Improvements in Student Learning," *Journal of Staff Development* 17 (1996): 34–38.

18. J. E. Mullens et al., *Student Learning, Teaching Quality, and Professional Development: Theoretical Linkages, Current Measurement, and Recommendations for Future Data Collection,* 1996, ERIC, ED 417158.

19. Guskey and Sparks.

20. D. Sparks and S. Hirsh, *A National Plan for Improving Professional Development,* 2000, 1, ERIC, ED 442779.

21. R. Ferguson, "Paying for Public Education: New Evidence on How and Why Money Matters," *Harvard Journal of Legislation* 28 (1991).

22. T. E. Armour et al., *An Outlier Study of Elementary and Middle Schools in New York City: Final Report* (New York: New York City Board of Education, 1989).

23. J. A. Shymansky, L. D. Yore, and J. O. Anderson, *A Study of the Impact of a Long-Term Local Systemic Reform on the Perceptions, Attitudes, and Achievement of Grade 3 / 4 Students,* 1999, ERIC, ED 429820.

24. Ibid.

25. See, for example:

     F. M. Newmann and G. G. Wehlage, *Successful School Restructuring* (Madison, WI: University of Wisconsin, Center on Organization and Restructuring of Schools, 1995).

     F. M. Newmann and Associates, *Authentic Achievement: Restructuring Schools for Intellectual Quality,* San Francisco: Jossey-Bass, 1996).

26. Newman and Wehlage describe *authentic instruction* as teaching and learning that 1) involves disciplined inquiry, 2) construction of knowledge, and 3) learning tasks that have a "value beyond school" (i.e., students see the relationship between the task and things that happen in the real world). *Constructivist learning* and construction of knowledge refer to a body of cog-

nitive research that has found that students learn by attaching new knowledge to which they are exposed to existing knowledge they already hold. The product is a reconstruction of what they know – essentially, the old and new knowledge combine to create a different form of knowledge. *Disciplined inquiry* refers to gathering information and data. In essence, it can be thought of as the new material that students gather to add to their existing foundation of knowledge, which they then cognitively process to create new knowledge.

27. B. Joyce and B. Showers, *Student Achievement Through Staff Development* (New York: Longman, 1988).

28. National Center for Education Statistics, *Toward Better Teaching: Professional Development in 1993–94* (Washington, D.C.: US Department of Education, 1998).

29. National Center for Education Statistics, *Status of Education Reform in Public Elementary And Secondary Schools: Teachers' Perspectives* (Washington, D.C.: US Department of Education, 1998).

30. D. K. Cohen and H. C. Hill, *State Policy and Classroom Performance: Mathematics Reform in California*, 1998, ERIC, ED 418842.

    D. K. Cohen and H. C. Hill, *Instructional Policy and Classroom Performance: The Mathematics Reform in California*, 1998, ERIC, ED 417 942.

31. P. S. Adey, *Factors Influencing Uptake of a Large Scale Curriculum Innovation*, 1997, ERIC, ED 408672.

    P. S. Adey, and M. Shayer, "An Exploration of Long-Term Far-Transfer Effects Following an Extended Intervention Programme in the High School Science Curriculum," *Cognition and Instruction* 11, no. 1 (1993):1–29.

    P. S. Adey, and M. Shayer, *Really Raising Standards: Cognitive Intervention and Academic Achievement* (London: Routledge, 1994).

    M. Shayer and P.S. Adey, "Long-Term Far-Transfer Effects of a Cognitive Intervention Program: A Replication," paper presented at the Annual Meeting of the American Educational Research Association, New York, 1996.

32. Adey and Shayer.

33. R. Greenwald, L.V. Hedges, and R.D. Laine, "The Effect of School Resources on Student Achievement," *Review of Educational Research* 66, no. 3 (1996): 411–416.

34. A. Molnar et al., "Evaluating The SAGE Program: A Pilot Program in Targeted Pupil-Teacher Reduction in Wisconsin," *Educational Evaluation and Policy Analysis* 21, no. 2 (1999): 165–177.

35. H. Wenglinsky, *How Teaching Matters: Bringing the Classroom Back into Discussions of Teacher Quality* (Princeton, NJ: Educational Testing Service, 2000).

36. F. Dunne, B. Nave and A. Lewis, "Critical Friends Groups: Teachers Helping Teachers to Improve Student Learning," *Phi Delta Kappa Center for Evaluation, Development, and Research*, December 2000, <www.pdkintl.org/edres/resbul28.htm>.

37. Ibid., 1.

38. Wenglinsky.

39. W. L. Sanders and J. C. Rivers, "Cumulative and Residual Effects of Teachers on Future Student Academic Achievement," *Education Trust, Thinking K-16:*

Good Teaching Matters: How Well Qualified Teachers Can Close the Gap (1998), cited in Wenglinsky.

40. A quick count of references indicates that 13 come from refereed journals; 17 from books published by national/international academically-oriented or university presses; 15 from ERIC reports; eight from research lab, school district, or government reports; four from non-refereed national or international journals; and a handful from a variety of other sources.

41. W. D. Hawley and L.Valli, "The Essentials of Effective Professional Development: A New Consensus," in *Teaching as the Learning Profession*, eds. L. Darling-Hammond and G. Sykes (San Francisco: Jossey-Bass, 1999), 125–150.

Little.

D. Sparks, *A Paradigm Shift in Staff Development*, 1995, ERIC, ED 381136.

M. G. Visher, P. Teitelbaum, and D. Emanuel, *Key High School Reform Strategies: An Overview of Research Findings*, 1999, ERIC, ED 430271.

42. For example, Michael Fullan repeatedly points out the ineffectiveness of top-down planning in his two highly regarded and research-based works on change:

M. Fullan, *The New Meaning of Educational Change* (New York: Teachers College Press, 1991).

M. Fullan, *Change Forces* (Londan and New York: RoutledgeFalmer, 1993).

43. Little.

44. Hawley and Valli; Mullens et al.

45. Sparks, *A Paradigm Shift*.

46. Little.

47. D. Sparks, "A New Vision for Staff Development," *Principal* 77, no. 1 (1997): 20–22.

48. Sparks, *Paradigm Shift*, 3.

49. P. Berman, and M. W. McLaughlin, *Federal Programs Supporting Educational Change/ Volume 8, Implementing and Sustaining Innovations* (Santa Monica: Rand Corporation, 1978).

McLaughlin.

50. Berman and McLaughlin.

51. Darling-Hammond and McLaughlin.

W. Doyle and G. Ponder, "The Practical Ethic and Teacher Decision Making," *Interchange* 8, no. 3 (1977): 1–12.

R. F. Elmore and D. Burney, *Investing in Teacher Learning: Staff Development and Instructional Improvement in Community School District #2, New York City*, 1997, ERIC, ED 416203.

Hawley and Valli; Sparks and Hirsh.

J. W. Little, "Seductive Images and Organizational Realities in Professional Development," *Teachers College Record* 86, no. 1 (1984): 84–102.

G. Sykes, "Teacher and Student Learning: Strengthening the Connection," in *Teaching as the Learning Profession*, eds. L. Darling-Hammond and G. Sykes (San Francisco: Jossey-Bass, 1999), 151–179.

P. Zigarmi, L. Betz, and D. Jensen, "Teachers' Preferences in and Perceptions of In-Service," *Educational Leadership* 34 (1977), 545–551.

52.   B. Joyce, J. Wolfe, and E. Calhoun, *The Self-Renewing School* (Alexandria, VA: Association for Supervision and Curriculum Development, 1993).

53.   Ibid., 19.

54.   Sparks, 21.

55.   Sparks, *A Paradigm Shift.*

56.   Elmore and Burney, 8.

57.   Sparks, *A Paradigm Shift.*

D. Sparks, "A New Form of Staff Development is Essential to High School Reform," *The Educational Forum* 60 (1996): 260–266.

58.   Sparks and Hirsh, 5

59.   Cohen and Hill, *State Policy.*

Cohen and Hill, *Instructional Policy.*

60.   Cohen and Hill, *State Policy.*

Cohen and Hill, *Instructional Policy.*

Darling-Hammond and McLaughlin; Elmore and Burney; Hawley and Valli; Little; Mullens et al.

Sparks, *A Paradigm Shift.*

Visher et al.

61.   M. G. Fullan, *The New Meaning of Educational Change,* 2nd ed. (New York: Teachers College Press, 1991).

M. G. Fullan, *Change Forces: Probing the Depths of Educational Reform* (Bristol, PA: Falmer Press, 1993).

Guskey.

62.   Sparks and Hirsh, 5.

63.   National Center for Education Statistics, *Teacher Quality: A Report on the Preparation and Qualifications of Public School Teachers* (Washington, D.C.: US Department of Education, 1999).

64.   Cohen and Hill, *State Policy.*

Cohen and Hill, *Instructional Policy.*

65.   Little; Mullens et al.

Sparks, *A Paradigm Shift.*

Sparks.

66.   Little, 138.

67.   See, for example:

L. B. Resnick and L. E. Klopfer, *Toward the Thinking Curriculum: Current Cognitive Research* (Alexandria, VA: Association for Supervision and Curriculum Development, 1989).

D. Walker and L. Lambert, "Learning and Leading Theory: A Century in the Making," in *The Constructivist Leader,* eds. L. Lambert, D. Walker, D. P. Zimmerman, J. E. Cooper, M. D. Lambert, M. E. Gardner, and P. J. Ford Slack (New York: Teachers College Press, 1995), 1–27.

68.   Sparks, *A Paradigm Shift,* 3.

69.   S. Brookfield, *Understanding and Facilitating Adult Learning* (San Francisco: Jossey-Bass, 1986).

70. Darling-Hammond and McLaughlin; Elmore and Burney; Guskey; Joyce and Showers.

71. Guskey.

72. M. L. Cogan, "Current Issues in the Education of Teachers," in *Teacher Education: Seventy-Fourth Yearbook of the National Society for the Study of Education*, ed. K. Ryan (Chicago: University of Chicago Press, 1975).

73. McLaughlin; Berman and McLaughlin.

74. Joyce and Showers, 112.

75. See Joyce & Showers, 81–94 , for a more extensive discussion of coaching and the research supporting its effectiveness.

76. Joyce, Wolfe and Calhoun.

77. Cohen and Hill, *State Policy*.

   Cohen and Hill, *Instructional Policy*.

   Darling-Hammond and McLaughlin; Elmore and Burney; Hawley and Valli; Little; Mullens et al.

   Sparks, *A Paradigm Shift*.

   M. K. Stein, *High Performance Learning Communities District 2: Report on Year One Implementation of School Learning Communities*, High Performance Training Communities Project, 1998, ERIC, ED 429263.

78. J. W. Little et al., *Staff Development in California* (San Francisco: Far West Laboratory for Educational Research and Development and Berkeley, CA: University of California at Berkeley, 1987).

79. Sparks, *A Paradigm Shift*.

80. Ibid., 3.

81. Little et al.

82. Elmore and Burney, 13.

83. Sparks and Hirsh.

84. Stein, 7.

85. F. I. Stevens, *Case Studies of Teachers Learning and Applying Opportunity to Learn Assessment Strategies in Two Urban Elementary Schools*, 1999, ERIC, ED 437487.

86. Elmore and Burney, 9.

87. Little.

88. Cohen and Hill, *State Policy*.

   Cohen and Hill, *Instructional Policy*.

   Darling-Hammond and McLaughlin; Elmore and Burney; Hawley and Valli.

   B. Joyce, "Prologue," in *Changing School Culture Through Staff Development*, ed. B. Joyce (Alexandria, VA: Association for Supervision and Curriculum Development, 1990), xv-xviii.

   A. Lieberman, "Practices That Support Teacher Development: Transforming Conceptions of Professional Learning," *Phi Delta Kappan* 76 (1995): 591–596.

   J. W. Little, "Norms of Collegiality and Experimentation: Workplace Conditions of School Success," *American Educational Research Journal* 19 (1982): 325–340.

   Little; Little et al.; McLaughlin; Mullens et al.

S. Rosenholtz, *Teachers Workplace: The Social Organization of Schools* (New York: Longman, 1989).

Sparks, *A Paradigm Shift*; Stein.

Little et al.; Sparks, *A Paradigm Shift*; Sparks; Sparks and Hirsh; Stein; Visher et al.

89.   Darling-Hammond and McLaughlin; Lieberman and Miller.

Sparks, *A Paradigm Shift*; Sparks.

90.   Sparks and Hirsh, 11.

91.   Smylie, 92.

92.   Lieberman and Miller.

93.   Ibid.

94.   D. Meier, *The Power of Their Ideas: Lessons for America from a Small School in Harlem* (Boston: Beacon Press, 1995), 109.

95.   Sparks and Hirsh.

96.   Little.

97.   Little, 139. Italics in original

98.   Rosenholtz.

99.   Ibid., 73.

100.   J. O. Larson et al., *Narrowing Gaps and Formulating Conclusions: Inquiry in a Science Teacher Action Research Program*, 1998, ERIC, ED 417976.

101.   F. Dunne and F. Honts, "That Group Really Makes Me Think!" *Critical Friends Groups and the Development of Reflective Practitioners*, 1998, ERIC, ED 423228.

102.   NCES.

103.   Berman and McLaughlin; Little; McLaughlin; Meier.

U. C. Reitzug and M. J. O' Hair, "From Conventional School to Democratic School Community: The Dilemmas of Teaching and Leadership," in *School as Community: From Promise to Practice*, ed. Gail Furman-Brown (New York: State University of New York Press, in press).

Sparks; Stein.

104.   McLaughlin.

105.   Reitzug and O'Hair.

106.   Stein.

107.   McLaughlin; Meier.

108.   Little.

J. W. Little, "What Teachers Learn in High School: Professional Development and the Redesign of Vocational Education," *Education and Urban Society* 27, no. 3 (1995): 274–293.

109.   McLaughlin; Berman and McLaughlin.

110.   Sparks, *A Paradigm Shift*; Sparks; Visher et al.

111.   J. Bellanca, *Designing Professional Development for Change: A Systematic Approach* (Arlington Heights, IL: IRI/Skylight Training and Publishing, 1995).

CHAPTER 13

CHARTER SCHOOLS, VOUCHERS, AND EMOs

Gerald W. Bracey, Ph.D.
Independent Researcher

RESEARCH FINDINGS

Of three proffered approaches to privatizing public education—charter schools, private school vouchers, or private management of public schools or charter schools—none has yet uncovered or established any factors that can be systematically applied to increase children's achievement. Privatization alternatives have shown little accountability, despite promises to do so, and achievement data that have been reported have been inconsistent at best and suspect at worst.

RECOMMENDATIONS

- No existing charter school or private school voucher program funded by public money should be expanded. The existing evidence fails to support such expansion.
- Policy makers seeking to implement or expand voucher or charter school experiments should first design and implement rigorous evaluation programs that comprehensively examine the impact of such programs both on the students who participate in them and on the larger school districts in which they are operating.

- School districts and state legislatures should institute monitoring systems to ensure that for-profit Education Management Organizations fulfill the obligations they undertake when they contract to manage local public schools, including conventional public schools as well as charter schools, and should rigorously enforce contract compliance.

The years since *A Nation At Risk* appeared in 1983 have seen an unprecedented level of effort at school reform. "Risk" urged public schools do more: more rigorous courses, more hours in the day, more days in the school year. Other reforms, though, are aimed at fundamentally changing the nature of how schools are funded or how they operate. Among the most popular of these attempts are *charter schools, vouchers* funded either by public funds or private charity, and the management of schools or parts of schools by private, mostly for-profit businesses referred to as *Educational Management Organizations,* or EMOs. This chapter examines what research has found about the ability of each of these three proposed reforms to increase student achievement, particularly the achievement of students in schools with high concentrations of poverty.

SCHOOL PRIVATIZATION RESEARCH

Charter Schools

The concept of a "charter school" was first put forth by Massachusetts teacher Ray Budde in the 1970s[1] and was adopted and popularized by Albert Shanker, President of the American Federation of Teachers in the 1980s.[2] In return for a charter freeing a school from many of the rules and regulations that applied to regular public school, the charter school would promise to raise achievement. If it failed, it would lose its charter. The change is often referred to as shifting from accountability by compliance to accountability by performance. The charter idea quickly became popular and advocates saw it as a way of stimulating education. Charter advocate Joe Nathan's 1996 book *Charter Schools* described the idea this way:

> Charter schools are public, non-sectarian schools that do not have admissions tests but that operate under a written contract, or *charter,* from a school board or some other organization, such as a state school board. These contracts specify how the school will be held accountable for improved student achievement, in exchange for a waiver of most rules and regulations governing how they operate. Charter schools that improve achievement have their contracts renewed. Charter schools that do not improve student achievement over the contract's period are closed.[3]

Charter Schools and Accountability

Although Nathan's exposition presents accountability as a simple conse-quence of achievement, the concepts of accountability and of achievement have proven to be much more complex in practice. Early on, charter-school advocates Chester E. Finn, Jr., and colleagues acknowledged that they had "yet to see a single state with a thoughtful and well-formed plan for evaluating its charter school program."[4] Earlier, Jeffrey Henig of the George Washington University observed that charter schools "show few signs of interest in systematic empirical research that is ultimately needed if we are going to be able to separate bold claim from proven performance. Premature claims of success, reliance on anecdotal and unreliable evi-dence are still the rule of the day."[5]

By 1999, the situation had not improved much, which Finn's colleague Manno attributed to the newness of the charter strategy, and the conse-quent absence of data; underdeveloped charter accountability systems; and the failure of charter authorizers and operators to embrace detailed and rigorous accountability systems.[6] Meanwhile, other charter advocates have already complained, in the words of one, about "the ever-growing load of regulatory and reporting requirements" charter operators face.[7] Moreover, charter advocates at the Center for Education Reform, in rating states' charter schools laws, consider the "strongest" to be those with the fewest regulations and requirements.[8]

Finn, Manno, and Gregg Vanourek prescribe an accountability proce-dure that they call "Accountability Via Transparency—a regimen where so much is visible in each school that its watchers and constituents routinely 'regulate' it through market-style mechanisms, rather than command-and-control structures."[9] These authors adapt the Generally Accepted Account-ing Principles from the private sector into what they propose as the Gener-ally Accepted Accounting Principles in Education. Yet the system they propose appears to call for more information than either traditional public or charter schools produce currently in the form of routine, timely and complete disclosure of details about their programs, performance, organi-zations and finances—requiring so much information and efforts to dis-seminate the information as to raise the question of whether it eviscerates the concept of charter school.

Some who have attempted to evaluate charter schools have not always found the schools responsive to inquiries on what data do exist, even when such data fall under the provisions of various states' Freedom of Informa-tion Acts.[10] The lack of responsiveness seems stronger in charter schools that are operated by Educational Management Organizations.

Others have found that charter school operators challenge the validity of data even when the data is routinely published at the state level. For instance, charter schools in Ohio spend a great deal more on administration and operating costs and less on instruction than do public schools. Charter defenders claimed that charter schools define categories of spending differently than do public schools.[11]

The charter schools themselves have not taken the lead in becoming "transparent." The Fourth Year Report on the Condition of Charter Schools from the U. S. Department of Education found that only 37.3% of charters sent a progress report to the chartering agency. Some 60.9% did send a report to the school governing board, but only 41.2% sent one to the students' parents and only 25.3% sent one to the community.[12]

Without a great deal of technical assistance from outside agencies, the quality of reports is unlikely to be high. In Massachusetts, for instance, the State Department of Education (SDE) specifies what the charter schools' annual reports must contain. It is probably the clearest and most extensive set of specifications in any state. The Massachusetts SDE, though, does not specify the reports' format. As a consequence, the same information appears in quite different places in reports from different schools and, in fact, not all of the required data are present in all reports. For example, City on a Hill Charter School's 1999–2000 annual report was 68 pages long and cast mostly in narrative form. It did not report teacher experience. Murdoch Middle School's annual report was 28 pages long and provided a brief biography of its teachers, but no summary tabulations. Other charters provide teacher experience in tabular form.

Charters and Achievement

In the absence of much data about achievement, little can be said about whether or not charter schools increase student achievement. The most typical evaluation has been a comparison of test scores in charters and those in traditional public schools. Some of those comparisons have not favored charters.[13] These comparisons are not conclusive and might be misleading, however. Many charter schools are established to educate "at risk" or special-needs students who, by definition, are not scoring well on tests or may not be taking them at all. A simple charter-public comparison cannot determine whether or not the charter school is instructionally deficient or if it has selected a more difficult student population. To be more definitive, a comparison would need to have test scores for charter school students before they entered the charter school or, alternatively, would need to study growth in achievement over time in comparison to demographically similar public schools.

On occasion, press releases generated by charter advocates have been accepted uncritically or without sufficient care to what the reports actually said. For instance, of an evaluation of Pennsylvania charter schools, *USA Today* wrote that "Western Michigan University researchers found that Pennsylvania charter public schools posted gains on state assessments of more than 100 points in just two years, outpacing the gains of their host school districts by 86 points over the same period of time. The study examined 48 of the state's 65 charter schools."[14] This statement is virtually a verbatim quote from a press release from the Pennsylvania Secretary of Education, an advocate of both charters and vouchers. In fact, the two-year data came from only four of the 48 schools examined and, overall, charters scored lower than their host districts.[15]

Evaluations of charter school achievement at the state level have been conducted in Arizona,[16] Michigan,[17] California,[18] and Pennsylvania.[19] A similar evaluation in Connecticut is near completion and an evaluation has been conducted on charter schools in the District of Columbia.[20]

Arizona.   In March, 2001, the Center for Market-Based Education at the Goldwater Institute in Phoenix released a study purporting to show larger test score gains in reading for Arizona students who stayed in charter schools two or three years compared to those who remained in traditional public schools for two or three years.[21] Gains in mathematics were not significantly different. The study takes advantage of the Arizona student database, which can track a student over the years as long as the student is somewhere in the Arizona public school system. The test used to measure gains was the Stanford Achievement Test, ninth edition (SAT9). The gains are measured in percentile ranks. However, Gene V Glass, Associate Dean of Research at Arizona State University, and Douglas Harris, an economist at the Economic Policy Institute, both have indicated that the methods used in reaching the report's conclusions are too unclear to be independently assessed.[22]

Moreover, the gains, if we accept them, are relatively small, and, in fact, leave the charter students still scoring below traditional public school students at the end of three years.

The Goldwater researchers also analyzed changes in test scores for students who moved between the two types of schools, reporting that students do better when they start in a charter and move to a traditional public school than when they spend two years in a traditional public school or start in a traditional public school and then move to a charter.[23] Their report, however, obscures the fact that the test scores of students who moved from a charter school to a traditional public school increased the year after transition, while the test scores of those who moved from a traditional school to a charter school declined the year after the transition. They also ignore other, equally plausible, interpretations for changes at a very small scale—one or two percentile ranks. Those include the possibility that in moving back to traditional schools, charter students might simply have been more comfortable in their old school and among old friends. There is also substantial question about a standardized, norm-referenced test such as the SAT9 to measure growth.[24] Finally, the drop in scores for students who enter charters does not accord with the results claimed for other choice experiments. These studies (of private voucher programs, which will be discussed later in this report) make contradictory claims: that either no change occurs until several years have passed,[25] or that positive outcomes resulted after a single year.[26] Furthermore the variety of reasons for which Arizona charter schools were started would suggest that judging them as a single category of "charter schools" and evaluating them with a single instrument, the SAT9 lacks any sound rationale.

California.   The first evaluation of charters in California found there was too little information to report on student outcomes and that accountability goals were often vague, ill-defined, and difficult or impossible to assess.[27] Another evaluation, by Amy Wells and colleagues at UCLA, found that, contrary to claims that charter schools would be more efficient and produce more achievement with fewer resources, that they required more resources and relied on private charity as well as public funds to survive.[28]

   An evaluation of 13 Los Angeles Unified School District charters by West Ed, although hampered by disruptions in the state testing program, found more positive results, concluding that "charter schools maintain or slightly improve their performance over time with respect to students in a comparison group of non-charter schools, with a few exceptions."[29]

Michigan.   Michigan differs from most states in that 71% of its charter schools, which account for 75% of charter schools students, are operated by private Educational Management Organizations, almost all of which are for-profits.[30] Teams conducting two separate evaluations—one (PSC) of charters in Detroit, Flint, and Lansing[31] and the other (WMU) of suburban and rural charters[32]—agreed that scores from the Michigan Educational Assessment Program (MEAP) were not appropriate for evaluating the achievement of all charter schools because, as in California, some charters' goals were not related to changes in test scores. Both evaluations, though, acknowledged the importance of MEAP in public thinking about schools and, therefore, analyzed MEAP data.

   PSC found gains somewhat higher for charters than for comparison public schools. Eighty-three percent of the charters made satisfactory progress in math compared to 58% of the public comparison schools. In reading the figure was 63% and 46%, respectively. Seventy-one percent of the charters had larger gains than the comparison school in math, but only half has larger gains in reading. The study did not address possible factors that may have given charters an advantage, including reliance on drills that can improve elementary mathematics skills in the short term, and the fact that most charter schools are small and have small classes.

In their 2000 evaluation, Horn and Miron found charters did not score as high on MEAP as regular public schools in their districts, but noted that such comparisons are not always appropriate because some charters serve at-risk students.[33] Passing rates for charters fell from 1995–96 to 1996–97, rose the next year, the fell again. Over the same period of time, regular publics showed a gain in passing rates from 49.4% to 68%.[34] Horn and Miron concluded that state charter schools produced "few and limited innovations", that most lacked comprehensive accountability plans, and that increased EMO involvement was moving decision-making far from the school level.[35]

Bettinger found charter school students scored no higher on average, and may be doing worse, than students in public schools with similar characteristics.[36] Bettinger also found that scores of students in public schools near charter schools declined. Because the charters drew students with lower scores initially, their leaving the public schools would have been expected to raise the public schools' scores.[37] Eberts and Hollenbeck's conclusions were consistent with the other evaluations, finding that charter school students scored lower on reading, math, science, and writing tests. The researchers used a model that controlled for characteristics of school districts, buildings, and students.[38]

A contrary finding came from Hoxby, who concluded that Michigan public schools were more productive in districts where they had to compete with charter schools.[39] She calculates productivity by dividing a state-wide test scores for a school by its per-pupil spending.[40] Some may question whether such a measure of productivity captures the complexity of a school, however. Hoxby also included untested assumptions, such as that "charter schools were likely to form in districts that had unproductive public schools."[41]

Pennsylvania. In their study of Pennsylvania charter schools, Miron and Nelson reported that the newness of the state's charters, along with a lack of data from charters and on student achievement rates before they began attending charter schools, precluded "conclusive statements about charter schools' impacts on student learning..."[42] Despite that they reported that charter schools typically scored lower than their host districts on the Pennsylvania System of School Assessment.[43] Meanwhile, high attrition rates may thwart the collection of more definitive data from Pennsylvania: In a "non-random" survey of charter schools of those reporting lost an average of 38% of their students.[44]

Washington, D.C. As with the other evaluations, the authors of the analysis of Washington, D.C. charter schools caution that the data from charters is not strictly comparable to data from other D.C. public schools (hereafter,

DCPS) because charters typically serve a lower income population.[45] They note, though, that in spite of this the D.C. charter schools have fewer special education students. Nonetheless, comparisons of Stanford Achievement Test Series, Ninth Edition (SAT9), scores showed large differences in favor of DCPS students, even when schools are grouped by categories including percent of students from low-income homes, percent with language needs and percent in special education. Only the outcome for schools with 10–15% special education students are comparable, and only for reading. For this same group of schools, 33.6% of the DCPS students scored below basic in math, compared with 66.8% of the charter students.[46]

Differences were generally larger for mathematics than for reading. For instance, in schools with 75% or more of the students from low income families, 26.6% of the DCPS students scored below basic in reading and 52.8% score below basic in math. For charter students, the figures are 52.8% and 78.4%, respectively.[47] Similar results were found at the "Proficient" and "Advanced" levels. Authors of the study suggest that teacher turnover due to longer school days and school years in charters than in DCPS created an additional barrier to student achievement.[48]

Vouchers

The arguments for school vouchers are very similar to those for charter schools: that giving parents the ability to choose alternatives to conventional public schools will encourage greater innovation and spur schools to achieve higher standards and better student outcomes.

Publicly Funded Vouchers

To date, most voucher programs have been small experiments in low-income urban areas. As such, the results, no matter how positive, cannot be generalized to the larger system. Some who favor vouchers acknowledge that limitation.[49] Some, however, argue for allowing voucher programs to operate in ways that would likely make attempts to draw universal conclusions nearly impossible. Paul E. Peterson of Harvard[50] has suggested that voucher schools in Milwaukee (which are required to choose students randomly) should have been allowed to select those students who seemed most compatible with the school's instructional program.[51] His complaint reflects an intractable conflict between those who advocate vouchers and those who research the impact of vouchers. Researchers favor random assignment whenever it is possible to ensure that there is no selection bias. (In his use of random assignment in his later studies, Peterson appears to have abandoned this objection.)

Milwaukee. "The Milwaukee case" is the oldest of the voucher experiments and its results are among the most contentious. The Wisconsin legislature created the Milwaukee voucher program in 1990, permitting 1% of the children in Milwaukee's low-income schools to attend private schools that would accept the voucher. The cap has been raised to 15% and the Wisconsin Supreme Court has declared that it is constitutional for the vouchers to be used at sectarian schools (the U. S. Supreme Court declined to hear the case).

John Witte of the University of Wisconsin conducted an evaluation for each of the first five years of the program. Witte and his co-authors concluded in the fifth-year evaluation that public school students and voucher students did not differ on measures of achievement.[52] Peterson challenged these conclusions; his reanalysis found differences in both reading and mathematics favoring the voucher students.[53] Economist Cecilia Rouse of Princeton also reanalyzed the data using different assumptions about how it should be treated statistically. She found voucher students scored higher in mathematics, but not reading.[54] Rouse's treatment is the most complete in terms of testing alternative assumptions about sampling and missing data. Most of the difference occurred from declining scores of public school students, not increases by voucher students. Rouse has since suggested that the voucher students benefited from having smaller classes.[55]

Cleveland. A second well-known voucher program was developed in 1995 in Cleveland through the initiative of then-Ohio governor George Voinovich. The Ohio legislature approved the use of state funds for vouchers and permitted them to be used at sectarian as well as secular schools. The program is currently before the US Supreme Court, while students in the program at the time of a lower court ruling striking down the program have been permitted to continue.

Greene, Peterson and Howell examined tests administered in the fall of 1996 and the spring of 1997 and concluded that the voucher students had gained 5.6 percentile ranks in reading and 11.6 in math.[56] This study was criticized for using fall-to-spring testing, which can be misleading for a variety of reasons, including that phenomenon of "summer loss"—when fall-to-spring gains have disappeared by the following fall, appears to be particularly strong for low-income students. The Greene, Peterson, and Howell study was also criticized for only studying students in two of the schools, two Hope schools that had been newly created by Ohio entrepreneur, David Brennan.[57] A second test, again of only two Hope schools, by Peterson and colleagues in the fall of 1998 found smaller, but still statistically significant, gains in math and reading, and an insignificant decline in language scores.[58]

A separate evaluation of the Cleveland program by researchers at Indiana University found "no significant differences" in achievement between voucher and public school students.[59] Peterson, Howell and Greene criticized the Indiana study on a number of methodological grounds. For one thing, the Indiana group had tried to control for prior achievement by factoring in the students' performance in the second grade. Peterson, Greene and Howell found these scores implausible because they were much higher than comparable percentile ranks in the third grade (the second grade tests had been administered by Cleveland Public Schools, while the Indiana researchers had overseen the third grade test administration). In addition, the second grade tests had low correlations with family background characteristics, an unusual result.[60]

Peterson and colleagues reanalyzed the data once excluding second-grade scores as a control variable, and once with those scores incorporated. With the second-grade scores excluded, statistically significant results were found in reading, mathematics, language skills, social studies and science. With the second grade scores included, effects were smaller and only those for language skills and science were statistically significant.[61] Metcalf subsequently rebutted Peterson and colleagues,[62] who rebutted Metcalf in turn,[63] each defending their research and impugning the other's.

Other Publicly Funded Programs.   No large-scale voucher experiment exists in the United States. Proposals for such in Michigan and California were defeated in the 2000 election by wide margins.

A potentially statewide program exists in Florida, but it has only 55 students. Florida's program allows students to enroll in private schools at public expense if their public schools are graded F (the bottom rank on a letter grade scale) by the state of Florida for two years in a row. In 1999, two schools received their second F's and their students were given voucher eligibility, with 55 enrolling in private schools. Jay P. Greene analyzed data from the Florida Comprehensive Assessment Tests (FCAT) for two years, for public schools that received the various grades. In general, schools with lower grades in the first year showed larger gains in the second, with D and F schools showing especially large gains.[64] Greene also compared schools in the upper-scoring half of all schools receiving F's in the first year with schools in the lower-scoring half of all schools receiving D's in the first year. These two groups of schools had similar performance characteristics, but the D schools were not at risk of losing students even if they received an F in the second year. The lower-half D schools showed less gain than the upper-half F schools. The effect sizes Greene derived from this analysis he called the "voucher effect." The effect was small for reading (0.12), and larger for mathematics (0.31), and writing (0.41). The effect sizes of all schools compared to F schools are much larger, ranging from 0.80 to 2.23.[65]

Gregory Camilli and Katrina Bulkley of Rutgers University critiqued Greene's analysis,[66] arguing that much of the effect size was due to the sample that Greene used, the phenomenon of regression to the mean, and the level of aggregation.[67] Regardless of its accuracy, the Greene analysis does not address the question of whether standardized test scores indicate general improvements in achievement.

Privately Funded Vouchers

The previous examples of voucher programs have all been of programs where public funds sponsored children to go to private schools. There are also programs in which private individuals or organizations provide the funding.

Indianapolis. The oldest private voucher program is run by the Educational Choice Charitable Trust in Indianapolis. An evaluation by David Weinschrott and Sally Kilgore found that public school students showed a decline in reading, language arts and math test scores in Grades 6 and 8 while voucher schools did not.[68] However, they based their conclusions on a small number of voucher students enrolled in a smaller number of voucher schools. In addition, they did not control for demographic differences in students or the test scores of the students before they entered the voucher program, leaving their results inconclusive.

Milwaukee. One large voucher program, Parents Advancing Values in Education in Milwaukee, has been in existence since 1992, but only one evaluation attempted to examine the program's effect on achievement. It appeared to show that students attending private schools for their entire school careers scored higher than those who transferred in from public schools. No controls were in place to match the samples. This and other methodological problems prevent any firm conclusions.

New York, Dayton, and Washington, D.C. These three privately-funded programs are treated together because the evaluation teams have all included Paul Peterson and William Howell of Harvard, who have also written about them jointly.[69] The first-year evaluation of the New York City program included David Myers, a senior fellow at Mathematica Policy Research in Princeton. After the release of the first-year evaluation, Myers disavowed Peterson's characterization of the results.[70]

The researchers contend that these three studies are superior to most others because the scholarships are awarded by lottery, thus those offered a scholarship should not differ from those who are not. They do not investigate the possibility that those who actually use a scholarship might constitute a different group, or the likelihood that those continuing with the program will evolve into a non-comparable group. For example, in the Milwaukee program, those who left private schools had lower test scores than those who continued to participate.[71]

The New York evaluation by Peterson and Mathematica compared test scores of 750 students who used vouchers with the achievement of 960 students whose families sought vouchers but were unsuccessful. The first year evaluation in New York examined scores on the ITBS by grade.[72] Of the eight comparisons (four grades by two subjects—reading and mathematics), five were insignificant, and two were significant at the 0.10 level. Most social science researchers do not report 0.10 as indicating significance, using a more stringent 0.05 or 0.01 level. The remaining comparison, fourth-grade mathematics was significant at the 0.01 level. Combining all grades led to significance at the 0.05 level for mathematics and 0.10 for reading. Given the large sample sizes of 300 to 400 students per grade, the lack of significant findings seems significant itself—the larger the sample size the greater the likelihood of obtaining significant results.

When the evaluators examined the second year of the New York results, along with the first- and second-year results from Dayton and Washington, they categorized the data by ethnicity, not by grade.[73] Positive results only occurred for African American-students.[74] After one year, only mathematics had been significant and then only at the not-often-used 0.10 level. After two years, the mathematics gain was significant at the 0.05 level, the reading at the 0.10.

For other ethnic groups combined, the scores show a decline in both subjects for voucher students, but neither the reading nor mathematics decline attains statistical significance. The relatively weak and inconsistent findings and questions about how experimental and control groups were constituted contradict the authors' assertion that their outcomes are comparable to those found in Tennessee's Project STAR (Student Teacher Achievement Ratio) class-size reduction experiment.[75]

In considering possible explanations for their results, Peterson, Howell, Wolf and Campbell reject the contention that private schools have better facilities and smaller classes.[76]

San Antonio.   San Antonio has two privately funded voucher programs. The Children's Educational Opportunity Foundation (usually referred to as CEO America) funded both. One program, which began in 1992, provided scholarships for half of the tuition costs for private schools up to a maximum of $750, reflecting the foundation's philosophy that parents who contributed a share of the tuition would be more involved and push their children harder to succeed.

Researchers from the University of North Texas concluded that students choosing private schools had "marginal improvements in standardized reading scores and marginal declines in math,"[77] while students remaining in the public schools declined in both subjects in every year from third grade through ninth grade.

The research team found that the parents of voucher-using students were more involved in their children's education *before* the program began, but participation in the voucher program did not increase involvement. The voucher program had a 50% dropout rate with lack of money and/or lack of transportation being the two most frequently given reasons.[78] This outcome illustrates a continuing difficulty in comparing voucher students with public school peers: When a large proportion of the voucher families leave the program, then that program is likely losing its poorest families. Thus, even if the charter and public school students were comparable when the experiment began, they will likely differ because of this poverty-induced attrition.

A second study examining a private voucher program enrolling 847 students and paying up to 100% of private-school costs in the Edgewood School District, in San Antonio[79] concluded that "unlike the strong positive effects of the scholarship program on parent satisfaction [of parents whose children went to private schools with vouchers], its effects on education practices and student achievement in the Edgewood public schools were negligible at best."[80] The authors attribute Edgewood's lack of responsiveness to long-standing "machine politics" and the small financial losses thus far occasioned by the program. Edgewood students did gain on the Texas Assessment of Academic Skills tests, but Greene and Hall dismiss this as a voucher effect because comparable gains were made in demographically similar nearby districts that had no voucher programs. They do not address another possibility: that magnet schools Edgewood opened in 1998 represented an effective reform program before the voucher became available,[81] and that the school district might be unresponsive to other changes because of its commitment to that program.

Private and Public Schools

Discussions of voucher efficacy often involve discussions on public vs. private schools in general. Public school critics often contend that private schools produce higher achievement than do the publics. The difficulty with this assertion, though, is that publics and privates often differ on demographic characteristics that are known to affect achievement. In such a case, one can't determine if the private schools produce higher achievers or if they simply started with higher achievers.[82] In a different vein, Rothstein, Carnoy and Benveniste examined six common allegations about the superior accountability, rigor, discipline, efficiency at teacher selection and retention, academic achievement, and innovation of private schools and found that the type of school mattered much less than the area in which it was located. Affluent public schools resembled affluent private schools. Low-income public schools resembled low-income private schools. Affluent and low-income schools differed.[83]

Privatization

Privatization efforts in schooling in the United States take three forms. First there are private, non-profit schools such as those in the National Association of Independent Schools. Second there are private for-profit schools such as those represented in the National Independent Private Schools Association or private corporations such as Nobel Learning Communities, Inc., and Knowledge Universe. The third form, which is the principal subject of attention here, is through the management of public schools either through charters or through management contracts by firms often known as Educational Management Organizations, or EMOs.[84] The contracts might be for a limited range of services or for the entire operation of a school or schools.

A contract with Education Alternatives Inc. to manage schools in Baltimore was evaluated by the American Federation of Teachers and the University of Maryland Baltimore County (UMBC).[85] The UMBC study found that, contrary to earlier claims from EAI, test scores in the EAI schools had not risen since 1991–92, the year before the contract began. The evaluation also found that EAI teachers spent more time teaching in small groups and a great deal more time preparing students to take standardized tests. EAI, which reorganized and changed its name to TesseracT, now appears to be out of business.[86]

Evaluations of Edison Schools, Inc., which manages charter schools and contracts to manage some public schools, have been conducted by the American Federation of Teachers,[87] Western Michigan University,[88] and researchers at Columbia University.[89] The AFT concluded that Edison schools "mostly do as well as or poorer than comparable [public] schools; occasionally they do better."[90] The union suggested that the company selectively reported data and did not compile all data in one place. Miron and Applegate, in an intensive study of 10 older Edison schools, reached similar conclusions.[91] The Columbia University study looked at the academic climate and classroom culture of six schools, two each in California, Colorado and Michigan. In general, the study praised the academic climate of Edison schools but noted that most had trouble implementing Edison's design "because of its complexity."[92] The study included praise of Edison's operation of a charter elementary school in San Francisco,[93] but subsequent journalistic accounts have painted a more dire picture,[94] and on June 28, 2001, the San Francisco Board of Education voted to sever its ties to the school, which Edison continues to manage through a charter with the California State Board of Education.[95]

Boston-based Advantage Schools Inc. showed large gains on standardized test scores in its internally prepared annual report issued March 2001, but those gains were limited to grades K–2 and the Woodcock Reading Mastery Test. Scores at Grades 3 and higher on the SAT9 were much smaller. Unlike Education Alternatives or Edison, Advantage has never been evaluated by an external organization. Advantage has since been acquired by another EMO corporation, Mosaica.

Inferences and Conclusions

The various experiments in education, charter schools, vouchers, and takeover by private management companies have thus far failed to deliver what their advocates had hoped for. Charter schools have thus far proven difficult to evaluate in terms of improved educational achievement. Similarly, the results from voucher experiments have been contentious in some instances and ephemeral in others. Educational Management Organizations have issued reports claiming successes, but reviews by external organizations have failed to replicate the gains claimed.

Vouchers on a large scale appear to be for the moment at least without momentum. Two voucher referenda in Michigan and California in the 2000 election lost by wide margins. Congress dropped the voucher proposal in President Bush's education agenda.

In the charter realm, states appear to be moving to clarify and perhaps tighten accountability provisions. How this might affect charters' chances for charter renewal or revocation, though, is unclear. There as yet appears to be no consensus on how to evaluate charter school performance, nor how to interpret those evaluations, a state of affairs complicated by the fact that many who evaluate charter schools appear to be predisposed to their efficacy.[96]

The picture for EMOs is decidedly mixed. Of the three described in this paper, one is in bankruptcy and has sold many assets, one is having financial difficulties and losing contracts, and one has lost $197 million as of early 2001, but is still experiencing success in garnering new contracts.

SUMMARY AND RECOMMENDATIONS

None of the three proffered approaches to privatizing public education has yet uncovered or established any factors that can be systematically applied to increase children's achievement. Indeed, the data that have been reported so far do lead to three recommendations regarding voucher and charter school experiments in particular:

- No existing charter school or private school voucher program funded by public money should be expanded. The existing evidence fails to support such expansion.
- Policy makers seeking to implement or expand voucher or charter school experiments should first design and implement rigorous evaluation programs that comprehensively examine the impact of such programs both on the students who participate in them and on the larger school districts in which they are operating.
- School districts and state legislatures should institute monitoring systems to ensure that for-profit Education Management Organizations fulfill the obligations they undertake when they contract to manage local public schools, including conventional public schools as well as charter schools, and should rigorously enforce contract compliance.

REFERENCES

1. R. Budde, *Education by Charter: A Ten-Year Plan* (Andover, MA: The Regional Laboratory for Educational Improvement of the Northeast and Islands, 1998).
2. A. S. Shanker, "Convention Plots New Course–A Charter for Change." *New York Times*, 10 July 1998, sec. 4, p. 7.
3. J. Nathan, *Charter Schools: Creating Hope and Opportunity for American Education* (San Francisco: Jossey-Bass, 1996), xxviii.
4. C. E. Finn Jr., L. Bierlein, and B. V. Manno, *Charter Schools in Action: A First Look* (Indianapolis: Hudson Institute, 1996).
5. J. Henig, *Rethinking School Choice: Limits of the Market Metaphor* (Princeton: Princeton University Press, paperback edition, 1995), 234. The quoted passage did not appear in the original hardcover edition.
6. B. V. Manno, "Accountability: The Key to Charter Renewal," 1999, <http://edreform.com/pubs/accountabilityguide.htm>.
7. T. Patterson, "Arizona's Charter Schools: What Do We Know?" 2001, <www.goldwaterinstitute.org/perspectives/0104.htm>.
8. See Center for Education Reform "Charter School Laws: Scorecard and Ranking 2001," 2001, <http://www.edreform.com/charter_schools/laws/ranking_2001.htm>.
9. C. E. Finn Jr., B. V. Manno and G. Vanourek, "Accountability Through Transparency," *Education Week*, 26 April 2000, p. 42.
10. J. Horn and G. Miron, *An Evaluation of the Michigan Charter School Initiative: Performance, Accountability, and Impact* (Kalamazoo: The Evaluation Center, Western Michigan University, 2000).
11. D. Oplinger, "Charter School Trail Public Rivals on Proficiency Tests, Need to Improve." *Akron Beacon Journal* (28 February 2001).

Ohio Legislative Office of Education Oversight, *Community Schools in Ohio: Second Year Implementation Report, Volume I, Policy Issues* (Columbus: Author, 2001).

Ohio Legislative Office of Education Oversight, *Community Schools in Ohio: First Year Implementation Report* (Columbus: Author, 2000).

12. RPP International, *The Condition of Charter Schools: Fourth Year Report* (Washington, D.C.: United States Department of Education, 2000).

13. See, for instance:

K. J. Cooper, "For Texas Charter Schools, Shaky Grades," *Washington Post,* 15 October 2000, p. A10.

14. T. Henry, "Scores Go Up for Charters," *USA Today,* 28 March 2001.

15. G. Miron and C. Nelson, *Autonomy in Exchange for Accountability: An Initial Study of Pennsylvania Charter School* (Kalamazoo: The Evaluation Center, Western Michigan University, 2001).

16. L. Solmon, K. Paark, and D. Garcia, *Does Charter School Attendance Improve Test Scores? The Arizona Results* (Phoenix, AZ: The Center for Market-Based Education, The Goldwater Institute, 2001), <www.goldwaterinstitute.org>.

17. See:

Horn and Miron.

J. Horn and G. Miron, *Evaluation of the Michigan Public School Initiative: Final Report* (Kalamazoo: The Evaluation Center, Western Michigan University, 1999).

Public Sector Consultants/Maximus, *Michigan's Charter School Initiatives: From Theory to Practice* (1999).

D. Arsen, D. Plank, and G. Sykes, *School Choice Policies in Michigan: The Rules Matter* (East Lansing, MI: Michigan State University, 1999).

18. A. S. Wells, *Beyond the Rhetoric of Charter School Reform: A Study of Ten California School Districts* (Los Angeles: University of California at Los Angeles, 1998).

19. Miron and Nelson.

20. J. R. Henig et al., *Growing Pains: An Evaluation of Charter Schools in the District of Columbia, 1999–2000* (Washington, DC: The George Washington University, 2001).

21. Solmon, Paark, and Garcia.

22. G. V Glass, personal communication, June 2001.

D. Harris, personal communication, June 2001.

23. Solmon, Paark, and Garcia, 12–13.

24. W. J. Popham, "Why Standardized Tests Don't Measure Educational Quality," *Educational Leadership* (March 1999).

25. J. P. Greene, P. E. Peterson and J. Du, *The Effectiveness of School Choice in Milwaukee,* 1996, <http://data.fas.harvard.edu/pepg>.

26. P. E. Peterson, D. Myers and W. G. Howell, *An Evaluation of the New York Choice Scholarship Program: The First Year,* 1999, <http://data.fas.harvard.edu/pepg>.

W. G. Howell et al., "Test-Score Effects of School Vouchers in Dayton Ohio, New York City, and Washington, D. C.: Evidence from Randomized Field Trials," 2000, <http://data.fas.harvard.edu/pepg>.

27. SRI International, *Evaluation of Charter School Effectiveness, Part II* (Menlo Park, CA: Author, 1997).

28. Wells.

29. Izu et alia, 47.

30. Horn and Miron, *An Evaluation of the Michigan Charter.*

31. Public Sector Consultants/Maximus (1999).

32. Horn and Miron, *Evaluation of the Michigan Public School;* Horn and Miron, *An Evaluation of the Michigan Charter.*

33. Horn and Miron, *An Evaluation of the Michigan Charter.*

34. Ibid.

35. Ibid., vii.

36. E. Bettinger, *The Effect of Charter Schools on Charter Students and Public Schools* (New York: National Center for the Study of Privatization in Education, Teachers College, 1999), occasional paper no. 4, 3.

37. Ibid., 20.

38. R. W. Eberts and K. M. Hollenbeck, *An Examination of Student Achievement in Michigan Charter Schools* (Kalamazoo, MI: W. E. Upjohn Institute for Employment Research, 2001).

39. C. M. Hoxby, "School Choice and School Productivity: Could School Choice be a Tide that Lifts All Boats?" paper presented at the National Bureau of Economic Research, "The Economics of School Choice," Islamorada, Florida, February 2001.

40. Ibid., 36.

41. Ibid., 41.

42. Miron and Nelson.

43. Ibid.

44. Ibid.

45. Henig et al.

46. Ibid.

47. Ibid., 66.

48. Ibid.

49. See, for instance, Moe, 20: "Ideology aside, perhaps the most vexing problem [of voucher research] is that few researchers who carry out studies of school choice are sensitive to issues of institutional design or context. They proceed as though their case studies reveal something generic about choice or markets when, in fact—as the Milwaukee case graphically testifies—much of what they observe is due to the specific rules, restrictions, and control mechanisms that shape how choice and markets happen to operate in a particular setting."

50. P. E. Peterson and C. Noyes, "Under Extreme Duress: Choice Success," 1998, <http://data.fas.harvard.edu/pepg>.

51. Ibid.

52. J. F. Witte, T. D. Sterr and C. A. Thorn, *Fourth-Year Report: Milwaukee Choice Program* (Madison, WI: Department of Public Instruction, 1995).

53. Greene, Peterson, and Du.

54. C. E. Rouse, "Private School Vouchers and Student Achievement: An Evalu-
     ation of the Milwaukee Parental Choice Program," *The Quarterly Journal of
     Economics* (May 1998): 553–602.

55. C. E. Rouse, "School Reform in the 21st Century: A Look at the Effect of
     Class Size and School Vouchers on the Academic Achievement of Minority
     Students," working paper #440, Industrial Relations Section, Princeton Uni-
     versity, 2000, <www.irs.princeton.edu/pubs/working_papers.htm>.

56. J. P. Greene, P. E. Peterson, and W. G. Howell, "An Evaluation of the Cleve-
     land Scholarship Program," 1997, <Accessible at http://data.fas.harvard
     .edu/pepg>.

57. K. K. Metcalf, "Advocacy in the Guise of Science," *Education Week*, 23 Sep-
     tember 1998.

58. P. E. Peterson, J. P. Greene, and W. G. Howell, "An Evaluation of the Cleve-
     land Scholarship Program After Two Years," 1999, <http://data.fas.harvard
     .edu/pepg>.

59. M. Walsh, "Audit Criticizes Cleveland Voucher Program," *Education Week*, 14
     April 1998, 9.

     K. K. Metcalf et al., *A Comparative Evaluation of the Cleveland Scholarship and
     Tutoring Grant Program* (Bloomington: Indiana Center for Evaluation, Uni-
     versity of Indiana, 1998).

60. Peterson, Howell, and Greene.

61. P. E. Peterson, J. P. Greene, and W. G. Howell, "New Findings from the
     Cleveland Scholarship Program: A Reanalysis of the Data from the Indiana
     University School of Education Evaluation," 1998, <http://data.fas.harvard
     .edu/pepg>.

62. Metcalf.

63. P. E. Peterson, J. P. Greene, and W. G. Howell, "Voucher Research: Good
     Motives Aren't Sufficient," *Education Week*, 21 October 1998.

64. J. P. Greene, "An Evaluation of the Florida A-Plus Accountability and School
     Choice Program," 2001, <www.manhattan-institute.org/html/cr_aplus.htm>.

65. Ibid.

66. G. Camilli and K. Bulkley, "A Critique of 'An Evaluation of the Florida A-
     Plus Accountability and School Choice Program,'" 2001, <http://epaa
     .asu.edu/epaa/v9n7/>.

67. Regression to the mean refers to the fact that when one selects a group
     made up of low test scorers, they tend to score higher on a second adminis-
     tration of the test (high scorers tend to score lower the second time).
     Greene aggregated scores across grades which Camilli and Bulkley argue
     was inappropriate because the different grades showed very different
     effects, meaning that Greene aggregated "apples and oranges."

     See also:

     J. P. Greene, "A Reply to 'Critique of "An Evaluation of the Florida A-Plus
     Accountability Program"'," 2001, <http://www.manhattaninstitute.org>.

68. D. Weinschrott and S. Kilgore, *Educational Choice Charitable Trust: An Experi-
     ment in School Choice* (Washington, D. C.: Hudson Institute, 1996).

69. Howell, Wolf, Peterson, and Campbell.

     P. E. Peterson et al., "School Vouchers: Results from Randomized Experi-
     ments," paper presented at the Conference on School Choice, sponsored

by the National Bureau of Economic Research, Islamorada, Florida, February 2001.

70. K. Zernike, "New Doubt Is Cast on Study That Backs Voucher Efforts," *New York Times*, 15 September 2000, p. A21.

71. Witte et al.

72. Peterson, Myers, and Howell.

73. Howell, Wolf, Peterson, and Campbell.

74. Ibid., 32–33.

75. Ibid., 33.

See also:

J. D. Finn and C. N. Achilles, "Tennessee's Class Size Study: Findings, Implications, Misconceptions," *Educational Evaluation and Policy Analysis* (Summer 1999): 97–109.

J. D. Finn and C. N. Achilles, "Answers and Questions about Class Size," *American Educational Research Journal* (Winter 1990): 557–577.

76. Peterson, Howell, Wolf, and Campbell.

77. R. K. Godwin, F. R. Kemerer, and V. J. Martinez, *Final Report: San Antonio School Choice Research Project* (Denton, Texas: Center for the Study of School Reform, School of Education, University of North Texas, 1997), executive summary.

78. Ibid.

79. J. P. Greene and D. Hall, *The CEO Horizon Scholarship Program: A Case Study of School Vouchers in the Edgewood Independent School District, San Antonio, Texas* (Washington, DC: Mathematica Policy Research, Inc., 2001).

80. Ibid., 25.

81. J. Kronholz, "A Poor School District in Texas Is Learning to Cope in a Test Tube," *Wall Street Journal*, 11 September 1998, p. A1.

82. See, for instance:

A. S. Shanker and B. Rosenberg, "Do Private Schools Outperform Public Schools?" in *The Choice Controversy*, ed. Peter W Cookson (Newbury Park, CA: Corwin Press, 1992).

83. R. Rothstein, M. Carnoy, and L. Benveniste, *Can Public Schools Learn from Private Schools?* (Washington, DC: Economic Policy Institute, 1999).

84. For a comprehensive description of firms operating in this industry, see Molnar, Morales, and Vander Wyst, *Profiles of For-Profit Education Management Companies* (Milwaukee: Center for Education Research, Analysis, and Innovation, University of Wisconsin-Milwaukee, 2000).

85. L. C. Williams and L. Leak, *The UMBC Evaluation of the TesseracT Program in Baltimore City* (Baltimore, MD: Baltimore Center for Educational Research, University of Maryland Baltimore County, 1995).

86. H. Mattern, "TesseracT Nears $50 Million Deficit Mark," *Arizona Republic*, 23 May 2000, p. D1.

87. American Federation of Teachers, *Student Achievement in Edison Schools: Mixed Results in an Ongoing Enterprise* (Washington, DC: Author, 1998).

F. H. Nelson, *Trends in Achievement for Edison Schools, Inc. The Emerging Track Record* (Washington, DC: American Federation of Teachers, 2000).

88. G. Miron and B. Applegate, *An Evaluation of Student Achievement in Edison Schools Opened in 1995 and 1996* (Kalamazoo, MI : The Evaluation Center, Western Michigan University, 2000), <http://www.wmich.edu/evalctr>.

89. P. W. Cookson, K. Embree, and S. Fahey, *The Edison Partnership Schools: An Assessment of Academic Climate and Classroom Culture* (Washington, D. C.: Cookson, Embree and Fahey, 2000).

90. Nelson, 6.

91. Miron and Applegate.

92. Cookson *et al.*, 3.

93. Ibid.

94. See for instance:

T. Woodward, "Edison Exodus: Will a Teacher Revolt Spell an End to the School Privatization Experiment?" *San Francisco Bay Guardian*, 19 July 2000, 1.

E. Wyatt, "Challenges and the Possibility of Profits for Edison," *New York Times,* 1 January 2001.

E. Wyatt, "School Management Company Faces Ouster in San Francisco," *New York Times*, 28 March 2001.

95. J. Guthrie, "S. F. Schools Vote to End Edison Compact," *San Francisco Chronicle*, 29 June 2001.

96. K. Bulkley, "The Accountability Bind," paper presented at the annual convention of the American Educational Research Association, New Orleans, Louisiana, April 2000.

CONTRIBUTORS

Alex Molnar (Editor) is Professor of Education in the Division of Educational Leadership and Policy Studies at Arizona State University and director of the Education Policy Studies Laboratory. He is a member of the team evaluating Wisconsin's Student Achievement Guarantee in Education class-size reduction program. He is the editor or co-author of several books, including *Changing Problem Behavior in Schools* (Jossey-Bass, 1989) and has published widely on social and educational policy and practice. For the past several years he has studied and written about commercial activities in the schools and market-based school reforms such as private school vouchers, charter schools, and for-profit schools. His most recent books are *Giving Kids the Business: The Commercialization of America's Schools* (Westview/Harper Collins, 1996), *The Construction of Children's Character* (National Society for the Study of Education, 1997), and *Vouchers, Class Size Reduction, and Student Achievement: Considering the Evidence* (Bloomington, Ind.: Phi Delta Kappa, 2000).

W. Steven Barnett is Professor of Education Economics and Public Policy and Director of the National Institute for Early Education Research (NIEER) at Rutgers University. His work includes research on early education and child care policy, the educational opportunities and experiences of young children in low-income urban areas, the effects of preschool programs on children's learning and development, and benefit-cost analysis of preschool programs and their long-term effects. Recent publications include *Lives in the Balance* (High/Scope Press, 1996), a benefit-cost analysis of preschool education based on a 25-year study, and, with co-editor Sarane Spence Boocock, *Early Care and Education for Children in Poverty* (SUNY Press, 1998).

Gerald W. Bracey is an independent educational researcher and writer who specializes in assessment and policy analysis. He has held positions at Educational Testing Service, Indiana University, the Virginia Department of Education and Cherry Creek (Colo.) Schools. His book *The War Against America's Public Schools: Parents' Edition* (Allyn & Bacon) is scheduled for publication in September. He also has written *Put to the Test: An Educator's and Consumer's Guide to Standardized Tests* (Phi Delta Kappa Intl. Inc., revised edition due March, 2002) and *Setting the Record Straight: Responses to Misconceptions About Public Education in the United States,* (Assn. for Supervision & Curriculum Development, 1997)

Robert M. Carini is an analyst with the National Survey of Student Engagement at Indiana University Bloomington. His interests include educational policy and the intersection of education, family, and the workplace. He is co-author (with Lala Carr Steelman and Brian Powell) of "Do Teacher Unions Hinder Educational Performance? Lessons Learned from State SAT and ACT Scores," published in *Harvard Educational Review* (2000), and (with John C. Hayek, Patrick T. O'Day, and George D. Kuh) of "Triumph or Tragedy: Comparing Student Engagement Levels of Members of Greek-letter Organizations and Other Students," in *Journal of College Student Development* (Forthcoming).

Douglas B. Downey is Associate Professor of Sociology at The Ohio State University. His research, which has appeared in the *American Sociological Review, Social Forces, American Psychologist,* and other journals, addresses issues of stratification with an emphasis on education and the family. His article, "Sex of Parent and Youths' Well-Being in Single-Parent Households," published in the *Journal of Marriage and the Family* in 1998, received the Reuben Hill award for best family article combining both theory and research.

Jeremy D. Finn is Professor of Education at State University of New York at Buffalo. His research has focused on issues of educational equity, including studies of gender differences in educational attainment, students at risk and student resilience, and class size. He was external evaluator for Tennessee's Project STAR since its first year of operation (1985), and a consultant to the evaluation of California's class-size initiative. He has conducted numerous analyses of the STAR data and has authored a number of publications based on this work.

Gene V Glass is Professor of Education Policy Studies and of Psychology at the Arizona State University College of Education. His interests include evaluation methodology, psychotherapy and policy analysis, as well as the creation of new avenues for communications among researchers and the public. He edits two electronic journals, *Education Policy Analysis Archives* and *Education Review,* and is Executive Editor of the *International Journal of Education and the Arts.* Recent publications include (with Casey D. Cobb) "Ethnic Segregation in Arizona Charter Schools" (1999), in *Education Policy Analysis Archives.* A former president of the American Educational Research Association (1975), he was elected to membership in the National Academy of Education in 2001.

Craig Howley co-directs the ACCLAIM Research Initiative at Ohio University in Athens and is director of the ERIC Clearinghouse on Rural Education and Small Schools at AEL, Inc. He has studied rural education and published his findings widely. Together with two colleagues, he has also published the monograph *Out of Our Minds: Anti-intellectualism in American Schooling* (TC Press, 1995).

Haggai Kupermintz is Assistant Professor in the Research and Evaluation Methodology program at the University of Colorado, Boulder. His primary academic interests are educational measurement, social science methodology, and the structure and development of cognitive abilities. Recent publications include (with L. Corno, L. Cronbach, D. Lohman, E. Mandinach, A. Porteus, & J. Talbert) *Remaking the Concept of Aptitude: Extending the Legacy of R. E. Snow* (Lawrence Erlbaum Assoc., September 2001), and "The Effects of Vouchers on School Improvement: Another Look at the Florida Data," published in *Education Policy Analysis Archives* (2001).

Catherine A. Lugg is Assistant Professor of Education in the Graduate School of Education at Rutgers University, where she is also a Senior Research Associate at the Center for Policy Analysis and an Affiliate Member of the Center for Media Studies. Her research interests include educational history and policy, the influences of media on policy making, and social history. Her recent books include *For God & Country: Conservatism and American School Policy* (Peter Lang Publishing, 1996) and *Kitsch: From Education to Public Policy* (Garland Publishing, 1999).

Ulrich C. Reitzug is Professor of Education and chairs the Department of Educational Leadership and Cultural Foundations at the University of North Carolina at Greensboro. His research interests include democratic education, school renewal, school-based inquiry, and how principals might serve as instructional leaders in these areas. He is the author of several books including *Foundations of Democratic Education* (with Mary John O' Hair and James McLaughlin; Wadsworth Publishing Company, 2000) and many publications including: "A Case Study of Empowering Principal

Behavior" (*American Educational Research Journal,* 1994), "Images of Princi-
pal Instructional Leadership: From Super-vision to Collaborative Inquiry"
(*Journal of Curriculum and Supervision,* 1994), and "Miss Lincoln Doesn't
Teach Here" (*Educational Administration Quarterly,* 1992).

Barak Rosenshine is Professor Emeritus of educational psychology at the
University of Illinois College of Education at Urbana. He has been review-
ing research on classroom instruction and cognitive strategy instruction
since 1966 and has published widely on the subject. He is the author (with
C. Meister and S. Chapman) of "Teaching Students to Generate Questions:
A Review of the Intervention Studies," (*Review of Educational Research,* 1996)
and (with R. Stevens) of "Teaching Functions" in *Handbook of Research on
Teaching* (M. Wittrock, Ed., Macmillan, 1986).